Advanced English Grammar

Advanced English Grammar
A Linguistic Approach

Ilse Depraetere and
Chad Langford
Second Edition

BLOOMSBURY ACADEMIC
LONDON • NEW YORK • OXFORD • NEW DELHI • SYDNEY

BLOOMSBURY ACADEMIC
Bloomsbury Publishing Plc
50 Bedford Square, London, WC1B 3DP, UK
1385 Broadway, New York, NY 10018, USA
29 Earlsfort Terrace, Dublin 2, Ireland

BLOOMSBURY, BLOOMSBURY ACADEMIC and the Diana logo are
trademarks of Bloomsbury Publishing Plc

First edition published 2012
This second edition published 2020
Reprinted 2020 (twice), 2021 (twice), 2023

Copyright © Ilse Depraetere and Chad Langford, 2020

Ilse Depraetere and Chad Langford have asserted their right under the Copyright,
Designs and Patents Act, 1988, to be identified as Authors of this work.

For legal purposes the Acknowledgements on p. viii constitute an extension
of this copyright page.

Cover image: © Shutterstock

A catalogue record for this book is available from the British Library.

A catalog record for this book is available from the Library of Congress.

ISBN: HB: 978-1-3500-6989-3
         PB: 978-1-3500-6987-9
         ePDF: 978-1-3500-6991-6
         eBook: 978-1-3500-6990-9

Typeset by Integra Software Services Pvt. Ltd.
Printed and bound in Great Britain

A Companion Website for this book is available at:
www.bloomsbury.com/advanced-english-grammar- 9781350069879

To find out more about our authors and books visit www.bloomsbury.com
and sign up for our newsletters.

Contents

Introduction to Second Edition

Although the core of the first edition of this book remains in this second edition, especially in terms of approach and goals, readers familiar with our take on English grammar will recognize some changes. These essentially concern the fine-tuning of some of the descriptions and explanations on the basis of our experience teaching with the book, observations from readers – students and colleagues alike –, insights gained from research on various topics and the input from three reviewers on the first edition. We have also updated a number of examples. A few additional concepts have been included, exercises have been revised and a number of new exercises have been added. An important addition is an online glossary with an overview of the most important concepts introduced in the grammar. The glossary is available at www.bloomsbury.com/advanced-english-grammar-9781350069879. We are grateful to Joshua Albair for his invaluable help with the organization of the glossary and to Benoît Leclercq, who helped shape the entries relating to Chapter 1.

An additional set of exercises from the University of Lille's EGAD (*English Grammar at a Distance*) project, co-authored with Benoît Leclercq, is available at the following address: http://klip.univ-lille.fr/fiche/74-egad-entrainement-a-la-grammaire-anglaise-a-distance. EGAD includes exercises aimed at learners of various levels, from more remedial drills to more challenging exercises comparable to the ones in this book. Though not a companion compendium per se, EGAD is very much informed by the approach we take here and provides additional practice to learners from a wide variety of backgrounds.

We are very grateful to all the people who have written to us and who have shared their views on points addressed in the grammar, be they our current or former colleagues at the University of Lille or users of the book. We are grateful to the editorial board of Bloomsbury for their genuine encouragement as we updated the grammar. We would also like to thank the University of Lille for their support, which enabled the design of EGAD. Finally, we would like to thank our anonymous reviewers for the invaluable input they provided.

We hope that this new edition will continue to unravel in the minds of our readers the intricacies of English grammar and that it will spark in them the same sense of excitement we have for English and for language in general.

Ilse Depraetere (ilse.depraetere@univ-lille.fr)
Chad Langford (chad.langford@univ-lille.fr)
Villeneuve d'Ascq, December 2018

Introduction to First Edition and Acknowledgements

We came to the decision to write this book after our seventh year of teaching English grammar together at the University of Lille. Having used a number of course books, each of them very good in its own right, we had come to realize that none of them really corresponded to the way we wanted to approach grammar with our students. On the one hand, we wanted to step up our discussion of certain areas of grammar in ways that the more student-oriented manuals did not enable us to do optimally; on the other hand, the more linguistically oriented grammars were overwhelming in their completeness, leaving students with little idea as to what was and was not essential in their quest to learn English. What we needed was something in the middle, a compromise between our students' concrete needs and our desire to demonstrate to them that there is a logical system underlying the rules they were learning by rote memorization.

Our students study in different degree programmes, and not all of them specialize in linguistics. And yet we were convinced that an approach that made use of basic linguistic concepts could be beneficial to the description of the fundamentals of English grammar regardless of the specific study programme that students were enrolled in and would consequently have the effect of improving their spoken and written skills. We were driven by the belief that the teaching of grammar to non-native university language students can – and should – be made challenging and exciting by moving beyond an overview of seemingly unconnected rules and fairly repetitive, traditional exercises. Our experience using various experimental versions of this book in the classroom over the past few years has only strengthened this conviction.

We have done our utmost to make the link between theory and practice explicit. Our goal is usefulness rather than comprehensiveness: indeed, the aims of our book necessitated a selection in the topics to be addressed and a certain amount of simplification. The definitions of the concepts we introduce are accessible to students with no background in linguistics and are conceived in such a way as to benefit foreign language learning. We have also included a set of challenging exercises, many of which require students to back up their answers with some basic justification. A full key to all of these exercises as well as a set of additional exercises can be found at www.bloomsbury.com/ advanced-english-grammar-9781350069879. In short, we believe that any upper-intermediate or advanced learner of English can be counted among the target group of this grammar, be they enrolled in an English language programme, a programme in English linguistics or a teacher training programme. Native speakers looking for some insight to how their language functions may find the book useful, too, as will anyone interested in learning more about some of the ins and outs of how English grammar works.

A quick glance at the book will show that we make ample use of illustrative examples. This is not a corpus-based grammar, and examples are primarily our own; we do however occasionally use authentic examples (primarily from the British and American press), often simply to give some variation to the voice behind the examples, but also when we feel that an authentic example illustrated our point particularly well. In those instances where an example gleaned from the internet is no longer retrievable, we have simply indicated the source as 'www'.

We have been inspired – at times no doubt unconsciously – by the reference and pedagogical grammars we studied ourselves when we were students or that we have used with our students throughout the years. We have mentioned in the bibliography those grammars to which we are most indebted. Some of the insights in the aspect and tense chapter were inspired by Reichenbach (1947), Vendler (1967) and the theory of tense developed by Declerck (1991a). We have also included a list of references to articles and monographs which have directly or indirectly shaped our views on the issues we address.

Several colleagues have helped us to strike a proper balance between linguistic underpinnings and pedagogical aims; we are grateful to those colleagues-friends-experts who have commented on one or several chapters. Bas Aarts, Joost Buysschaert, Ruth Huart, Gunther Kaltenböck, Paul Larreya, Philip Miller, Kathleen O'Connor, Susan Reed, Raf Salkie and Christopher Williams all provided valuable feedback. Interaction with Renaat Declerck and Samuel N. Rosenberg over many years has been the source of stimulating discussion, the impact of which goes beyond what can be observed in this grammar. Their influence is nonetheless present here. We would also like to thank the colleagues teaching first- and second-year grammar at the University of Lille who tested chapters with their students and provided useful feedback on what to fine-tune or change. Any infelicities or inaccuracies are our sole responsibility.

We are also very grateful to Olivier Thierry for the exceptional patience he displayed in designing and redesigning our graphics.

It is our wish that readers of this grammar, as they work their way through it, will get a taste of the excitement we as authors and teachers experience when we talk about grammar and will perhaps even become enthusiastic grammar-lovers themselves. If they enjoy reading this book as much as we enjoyed writing it, we will have achieved at least part of our goal.

Ilse Depraetere (ilse.depraetere@univ-lille.fr) and

Chad Langford (chad.langford@univ-lille.fr)

Villeneuve d'Ascq, July 2011

One day while I was working on this project, an image all of a sudden came into my mind: an early childhood memory of my father sitting at the table in the living room, intently reading a set of A4s, slowly turning pages as he worked on what I now know was a communicative grammar of French *avant la lettre*, which would be used at the school he was teaching at. If linguistics is in the genes, then this is another reason why I'm pleased to have been born into the Depraetere family. I am grateful to my close family members for bearing with my preoccupation with this book for almost three years and for listening patiently to the issues I was thinking about in the various stages of the writing process. This book is dedicated, with so much love, to my staunchest supporters: Luc, Bram and Matilde.

Ilse Depraetere

Unlike Ilse, I was not born into a family of linguists, at least not in the strict sense. But my maternal grandparents spoke French before they spoke English, and my grandfather served in the First World War as an interpreter in France. My own life as a teacher of English in France involves going back and forth between these two languages every day. I would like to think that, in my own way, I have come to manage this tricky balance between two languages as my grandparents did before me. My regret is that I never had the opportunity to witness them do so together. I would thus like to dedicate this book to my grandmother, Eleanor Pilon, and to my grandfather, Viateur Pilon. I thought about them a lot while working on this book.

Chad Langford

List of Abbreviations and Symbols

Adj	Adjective
AdjP	Adjective Phrase
Adv	Adverb
AdvP	Adverb Phrase
aux	auxiliary
cf. x	Compare this (sentence, word, example etc.) to x
Conj	Conjunction
DO	Direct Object
E	Event time
IO	Indirect Object
NP	Noun Phrase
OC	Object Complement
Prep	Preposition
PC	Prepositional Complement
PO	Prepositional Object
PrepP	Prepositional Phrase
R	Reference time
S	Speech time
Sub	Subject
SC	Subject Complement
VP	Verb Phrase
*	ungrammatical sentence
?	questionable acceptability: many speakers of English will find this sentence less than grammatical
Ø	zero marker: signals the absence of an overt linguistic marker, such as a subordinating conjunction, a relative pronoun or an article
www	an example gleaned from the internet

1

Getting started: Forms and functions

1. Introduction

A book about grammar has to be quite explicit about the kind of book it is and how the word 'grammar' is being used. When people say '*a grammar*', they are often referring to an explanation of how a language works and what its possible constructions are. Traditionally, such an account takes the form of a book, and in this sense, the book you are reading right now is a grammar.

However, the word 'grammar' can also refer to what native or proficient speakers[1] of a language possess in their minds that enables them not only to use a language grammatically, but also to recognize when others are using it grammatically and when they aren't. This is often referred to as native-speaker

---

[1]Referring to 'speaker ~ writer' and 'hearer ~ reader' is cumbersome. For ease of reading, when we refer to 'speaker', it should be understood as referring either to speaker or to writer. 'Hearer' refers to hearer or reader. In this book, we will consistently use the pronoun 'she' to refer to speaker and 'he' to refer to hearer.

intuition. This definition of 'grammar' refers to the knowledge of possible constructions[2] in a particular language. Our goal in this book is to give you some insight into what speakers of English know about their language with an eye to helping you improve your own English. We do this by describing how speakers of English use the language while at the same time attempting to explain the system that underlies how they speak and write it.

Native speakers of any language occasionally have differing views on whether a particular sentence or structure is grammatical. Such differences in judgement are dependent upon a person's view as to what is meant by 'correct'. The terms **prescriptive** and **descriptive** are often used to define these different points of view. A grasp of these two terms is a basic step to understanding how we have conceived this particular book. A descriptive grammar takes stock of language use as it can be observed through different channels of communication (be they written or spoken) and genres (ranging from, for instance, informal conversation among friends to very formal contexts such as that of a political treaty). A prescriptive grammar is one that gives hard-and-fast rules about what is right (or **grammatical**) and what is wrong (or **ungrammatical**), often with advice about what not to say but with little explanation. In fact, what are considered mistakes are often examples of sociolinguistically marked variation – cases where people speak differently based on where they come from or their socio-economic background and level of education. As such, prescriptive grammar only addresses a very small part of how a language really works. Vast areas of language show little or no variation, or the variation is not sociolinguistically marked and therefore not the subject of prescriptivist debate. Four examples of commonly heard sentences that a prescriptive grammar would consider ungrammatical are given in (1):

(1) (a) I don't have no time to waste.
    (b) If he would have known, he wouldn't have said that.
    (c) You shouldn't have went there without me.
    (d) I don't know him good enough to have an opinion.

In (2), you'll find the 'repaired' sentences, all of which correspond to what a prescriptive grammar would consider grammatically correct in standard English:

(2) (a) I don't have any time to waste./I have no time to waste.
    (b) If he had known, he wouldn't have said that.
    (c) You shouldn't have gone there without me.
    (d) I don't know him well enough to have an opinion.

---

[2]'Construction' is used in a neutral way in this book and does not reflect any specific theoretical stance.

Prescriptivism seen from this angle seems like a helpful enough approach for someone learning English as a foreign language or seeking to improve their knowledge about how the language works. After all, you probably do not want to produce sentences that many speakers of English, even if they understand what you mean, will consider incorrect or indicative of a lack of education, which is the case for the sentences in (1).

There are problems inherent in a prescriptive grammar, however. For one thing, it can be quite arbitrary, meaning that the people establishing these rules often determine what is grammatically right or wrong without really backing up their claims. While we agree that the examples in (1) do not conform to the standard grammar of English used by educated speakers, other 'mistakes' which are targeted by prescriptivists are part and parcel of ordinary, educated English and are instances of variation that is unmarked. So, whereas a prescriptive approach might consider the (b) versions of (3) below to be more correct than the (a) versions, we do not consider variants of this kind to be incorrect:

(3) (a) My stepbrother is eight years older than me.
It sounds like you had a great time at the party.
Who do you think we should invite?
What do you attribute her success to?

(b) My stepbrother is eight years older than I.
It sounds as though (= as if) you had a great time at the party.
Whom do you think we should invite?
To what do you attribute her success?

Linguists are generally not interested in prescriptive grammar. Rather, they approach language as any scientist would investigate naturally occurring phenomena: by observing, taking note and ultimately trying to understand what's going on. Nowadays, most grammars of English written for non-native speakers are committed to describing rather than prescribing usage. The book you're reading now is a pedagogical grammar. We are first and foremost committed to describing English as it is actually used today, but we also recognize that language variation can be confusing for a learner. For that reason, a pedagogical grammar such as this one necessarily cleans things up somewhat and has at least a slight prescriptive slant to it. After all, advanced students of English have practical concerns as well. They have to show others (their teachers, namely) that they 'know the rules'. They have to take standardized exams demonstrating that they understand the core English spoken by educated native speakers regardless of where those speakers live. This core English is the variety we have set out to describe here, and our decisions concerning grammaticality and ungrammaticality are based on how native speakers actually use their language and at the same time on the idealized view they have on their language.[3] You might hear sentences such as those in (1a) to (1d), but they do not conform to the grammar of standard English, and we do not consider them grammatical either. Throughout this book, we use the convention of putting an asterisk (*) before an ungrammatical sentence:

(4) *I don't have no time to waste.

However, we consider the sentences in (3a) to be perfectly grammatical alternatives to the sentences in (3b). This is something that a purely prescriptive grammar might not do quite so willingly.

In this preliminary chapter, we introduce some basic terminology to describe language from the basic level of the word up to the level of the sentence. Linguistic terminology enables us to name types of words (or **parts of speech**), to describe the way these words combine to form larger units (units we'll call **constituents**) and to recognize the **functions** these constituents can have in the sentence. We will also see how a sentence can be made up of not only one, but two or more **clauses** (see Section 4 for a definition of clause). You are likely to be familiar with many of these terms. However, some concepts may be defined differently in different grammars, and so in order to avoid any terminological confusion, we will provide a brief overview of the concepts with examples for each of them. First, however, it is important to sketch out, in very broad strokes, the levels at which speakers of English can be said to know something about the language they speak. This will help us to be clear about what it means to take a linguistic perspective on the study of English grammar and what it is the different subfields of the science of linguistics address.

2. Syntax, semantics, pragmatics and grammar

For non-native speakers, understanding how English works and getting a grip on the (often unconscious) knowledge that enables speakers of English

---

[3]See, for example, Albert Valdman, 1988, *World Englishes*, 7 (2), 221–36. 'Classroom foreign language learning and language variation: the notion of pedagogical norms.' Among other things, Valdman argues that a pedagogical approach to grammar must take into account what native speakers consider correct or incorrect regardless of whether this is reflected in how they use the language themselves.

to speak and understand their language can at times seem a fairly daunting enterprise. It can be helpful to consider that this knowledge is of at least three different types.

- Native and proficient speakers have knowledge about words, not only what they mean, but also how they are pronounced and how they change in form. For instance, they know that we say *one child*, but *several children*, or that we say *this child*, but *these children*. We say *I am busy now* but *We are busy now* and *I was busy yesterday* but *We were busy yesterday*.

- They have knowledge of how words work together in units (constituents) that are smaller than sentences. They will all agree that we can say *some of my friends* and *some friends of mine*, but never *some of mine friends* or *some friends of my*. These same speakers also have knowledge of how to put a sentence together and how to interpret a sentence. For example, they know that *The cat chased the mouse* and *The mouse chased the cat* describe two different situations, even if they may not be well versed enough in grammatical terminology to explain why. They also know that *The cat was chased by the mouse* is a close paraphrase of the second sentence and not the first. And they know that *Chased the cat the mouse* is ungrammatical, meaning it does not conform to any of the possible structures of English.

- These same speakers, finally, know how to use **well-formed** or grammatical sentences appropriately in discourse. By discourse, we mean 'communication beyond the level of the sentence' and 'communication in context', be it in the written or spoken medium. Speakers know that in basically any discursive context, a question such as *What did you do last night?* can be used to request a specific piece of information, whereas the use of *You did* what *last night?!* [4] is highly constrained, and thus impossible in many contexts. We will address discourse more closely in Chapter 6.

Morphology refers to the different forms that words take. We use the word **syntax** to refer to the order of words in both constituents and clauses. This corresponds to the second type information we have referred to. **Semantics** refers to the meaning, both of words (**lexical semantics**) and sentences (**sentence semantics**). **Pragmatics**, finally, refers to the ways a communicative context contributes to meaning. This book is not an introduction to morphology, syntax, semantics and pragmatics. All are interesting but complex fields of inquiry with books of their own. However, we will sometimes refer to these subfields

---

[4]We will discuss the difference between *What did you do last night?* (with falling intonation) and *You did* what *last night?!* (with rising intonation) in Chapter 2. The fact that the two differ not only in their syntax (i.e. word order) but also in their intonation pattern is an interesting example of how pronunciation and grammar are inextricably linked.

of linguistics in a basic way when we consider it useful to illustrate our discussion. For a thumbnail description of these fields, you can consult the online glossary that accompanies this book.

In a sense, everything we discuss in this book will implicitly or explicitly make reference to one of the three levels above, and often more than one of them will be relevant to the subject at hand. In this chapter, we will mainly address the first and the second.

3. Forms and functions

3.1. Parts of speech

Sentences are made up of words. In principle, we could refer to these basic building blocks by indicating where in a sentence a word occurs. For instance, if we want to refer to *cat* in *My first cat was called Felix*, we might say 'the third word'. Or we could identify *wood carving* in *My brother's favourite hobby is wood carving* by referring to the 'sixth and seventh word'. It will be obvious that this is not a very efficient way of going about it. It is also counterintuitive: language functions in predictable, systematic, generalizable ways. And the fact that in *My first cat was called Felix*, we can replace the word *cat* with *dog, goldfish, monkey* or *parakeet* but not with *sings, handsome, quickly, behind* or *since* is no coincidence. Indeed, sentences are much more than simple strings of words.

Sentences in English are structured on the basis of a limited number of underlying principles. It is therefore much more efficient to use specific terms to refer to words in sentences that behave in the same way. For instance, **nouns** can be easily recognized because, unlike verbs, they can be preceded by words such as *the, these* or *every* (words we call **determiners**): *the grass, these birds, every student*. **Adjectives** can be identified relatively easily because they almost always either occur between a determiner and a noun (*the fluffy clouds*) or are used to characterize the Subject referent[5] after a verb like *be, look* or *seem* (*Those clouds are/look/seem fluffy*). When we use words like 'noun', 'determiner' and 'adjective', we are referring to what are traditionally called **parts of**

---

[5]It is important not to confuse the terms **Subject** and **Subject referent**. As will be pointed out in Section 3.3, the term 'Subject' refers to a function at the sentence level. A sentence can be broken down into two main functions, the Subject and the Predicate. 'Subject referent' refers to the extralinguistic entity corresponding to the linguistic expression. In *That young man over there is my brother*, the NP *that young man over there* functions as the grammatical Subject. The Subject referent is the actual man the speaker is talking about and pointing to.

speech. (Some use the term **word class** or **category** for part of speech.) The following are the parts of speech we will use in this book, followed in each case by a few examples[6]:

(5) Noun: wife, computer, happiness, Venus, him, mine
    Verb: (to) paint, (to) contemplate, (to) cost, (to) break
    Adjective: bright, solar, afraid, ill
    Adverb: surprisingly, diligently, today, afterwards
    Preposition: in, under, without, between
    Conjunction: and, or, if, since, but
    Determiner: the, a, this, many, every, three, his

Whereas some linguists consider the pronouns to be a separate word class, we consider pronouns (*he, she, they*) a subclass of the category 'noun' rather than a separate part of speech (see Section 3.2). We will use 'determiner' to refer to the part of speech that can precede the noun. As will be clear from the examples of determiners in (5), this category includes quite a number of sub-classes, including the definite article (*the book*), the indefinite article (*a book*), demonstrative determiners (*this/that book, these/those books*), quantifying determiners (*some/both/a few/many/a lot of books; every/each book*) and numbers (*seven books*). The possessive forms (as in *his book(s)*) preceding a noun are unique in that they have an antecedent with which they agree in person and number: *his* in *his book* refers, for example, to *John's* or *the boy's*. This is not the case for other determiners and, for that reason, some classify possessive determiners as pronouns. Since our discussion of these forms centres primarily on their determinative role, we categorize them with the class of determiners.

Although you probably have a basic understanding of the different parts of speech, we recommend you take a look at the online glossary, where an entry for each part of speech is provided. Here, we will highlight a few additional facts that seem particularly relevant from a learner's perspective.

3.1.1. Nouns and verbs

The shape a word has sometimes gives a clue to the part of speech it belongs to: words ending in *-ion* (such as *revolution, commission* or *explosion*) are invariably nouns, and words ending in *-ize/-ise* (such as *criticize*)[7] are very

---

[6]The traditional parts of speech also include **interjections**, which are relatively short units (*Wow! Damn! Oh my* etc.) expressing some sort of emotion.
[7]The verbal ending *-ize* can also be spelled *-ise* in many cases, most notably in British English. The spelling *-ize* is the norm in North America and is common in Britain as well.

often verbs. Compared to other languages, however, English has a large set of words (or **lexemes**[8]) that can function either as nouns or verbs. These are often extremely common, monosyllabic words:

(6) **Verbs**

They might *name* their baby Madeleine.
She wants to *drink* something.
You *work* far too much.

Nouns

They gave their baby the *name* Madeleine.
She wants a *drink*.
You take on far too much *work*.

Other words in this category include *blame, cause, fight, film, joke, rain, test, trust* and dozens of others. It also includes more recent creations such as *FedEx (something to someone)* and *Google (something)*.

An important subset of noun-verb lexemes includes words of more than one syllable (most often two), with a shift in stress according to the part of speech: as a verb, *conduct* is stressed on the second sylla-ble (conˈduct /kənˈdʌkt/), but as a noun it is stressed on the first syllable (ˈconduct /ˈkɒndʌkt/):

(7) Please *conˈduct* yourselves differently.
If you *inˈcrease* prices, you'll make a profit.
Please don't *inˈsult* other people.

Your *ˈconduct* was inappropriate.
The *ˈincrease* in price was a big surprise.
She took what I said as an *ˈinsult*.

Other words like this include *construct, contract, impact, intrigue, object, permit, rebel, record* and *subject*. For many such words, this alternation is stable. For others, there is some amount of geographical or individual variation: almost everyone will pronounce the verb *address* as /əˈdres/, but both /ˈædres/ and /əˈdres/ can be heard as a noun. Note that a large number of di- or multi-syllabic noun-verb pairs show no stress variation at all: ˈanswer, ˈbalance, ˈcomment, ˈcompromise, conˈtrol, deˈsign, ˈinfluence, ˈpromise, ˈques-tion and ˈstruggle, for example, are stressed the same way as nouns or verbs.

3.1.2. Compounds

English has a mechanism by which the juxtaposition of two nouns creates a new noun. It is convenient to refer to these two nouns as N1 and N2. The process of combining N1 and N2 is called **compounding**, and the resulting noun, such

---

[8]A discussion of what exactly a word is goes beyond the scope of this chapter. That said, 'lexeme' is a useful term as it enables us to recognize that although *eat, eats, eating, ate* and *eaten* are different **word forms**, they are all instances of the single lexeme *eat*.

as *boyfriend* or *bus stop*[9] is called a **compound**. In English, N1 is the semantic head of the combination and follows N2; N2 adds specifying or classifying
information to N1. In other words, a *boyfriend* is a kind of friend (not a kind of
boy), and a *bus stop* is a kind of stop (not a kind of bus). The order of N1 and N2
is not necessarily the same in other languages that use noun-noun compounds.

Other parts of speech can combine to form compounds as well, either within
parts of speech (*freeze-dry* (verb-verb), *bittersweet* (adjective-adjective)) or
across different parts of speech (*downsize* (adverb-verb), *greenhouse* (adjective-noun)). Given the last type, you might wonder how to distinguish between
an adjective-noun compound (which is a type of N) and an adjective + noun
that does not form a compound (it is a phrase (an NP) that consists of an adjective and a noun (see Section 3.2)). One difference concerns the stress pattern. In
a compound, the stress is on the adjective, as in (8a), whereas it is on the noun
when the adjective-noun combination is a phrase, as in (8b). There are also syntactic differences that distinguish compounds from phrases. The component
parts of a phrase can be individually modified or can be split up through the
insertion of modifiers; this is not possible with compounds (8c):

(8) (a) Tomatoes can be grown in a '*greenhouse*.
         There are lots of old '*brownstones* in that neighbourhood.
         My grandmother swears by '*cold cream*.
         '*Blackboards* have all but disappeared.

     (b) They live in a *green* '*house*.
         A footpath was made with *brown* '*stones*.
         Then add the *cold* '*cream* to the mixture and stir.
         They nailed *black* '*boards* across the window.

     (c) A footpath was made with black and brown stones. (*black* modifies *stones*)
         *There are lots of black and '*brownstones* in that neighbourhood.
         A footpath was made with dark brown stones. (*dark* modifies *brown*)
         *There are lots of very '*brownstones* in that neighbourhood.

It is important to add that the stress does not always fall on the first component of a compound. In some cases, the compound has a stress pattern that
is similar to that of a phrase. Consider the pair *paper factory* and *paper plate*,

---

[9]We will not treat in any detail the spelling of noun-noun compounds. They can be found written with a
space between N2 and N1 (*bus stop*) or without a space (*boyfriend*). There are no absolute rules, so you
should consult a dictionary if you are unsure. Note that noun-noun compounds written with a hyphen
are no longer very common, although a hyphen is often used with adjectival compounds: *good-looking,
fast-acting, slow-burning*.

both of which are compounds. In the former, the main accent falls on the stressed syllable of N2:

(9) paper factory (●••••)

This is different from what we find in the combination *paper plate*:

(10) paper plate (••●)

Here, the most salient syllable is the main accent we hear on *plate*, a stress pattern which is similar to that we get in phrases (as in (8b)). In other words, whereas in ′*paper factory*, the main stress is on N2 (= *paper*), in *paper* ′*plate* the main stress is on N1 (= *plate*). The presence of two possible accent patterns is something closely related to the meaning of the combination. We will refer to the stress pattern of ′*paper factory* as **left stress** (or **early stress**) and that of *paper* ′*plate* as **right stress** (or **late stress**).

Compounds with left stress generally refer to the function or the most salient trait of N1: a ′*paper factory* is a factory whose function is to produce paper. They often refer to (but are certainly not limited to) containers (′*coffee cup,* ′*shoe box,* ′*fish tank*), vehicles (′*freight train,* ′*ocean liner,* ′*battleship*) and places of commerce (′*bookshop,* ′*vegetable market, de*′*partment store*). Below you will find some other categories of left-stress compounds:

N2 -*ing* participle + N1, where the N2 typically refers to an activity: ′*skating rink,* ′*drinking game,* ′*driving licence*[10]

N2 + -*er* agentive N1, where N2 refers to the theme upon which the N1 agent acts: a ′*lorry driver, an* ′*English teacher, a* ′*house cleaner*

N2 + N1 ending in -*ion*, where N1 refers to an action and N2 refers to what is affected by that action: ′*air pollution,* ′*error correction, a* ′*job application*

With respect to meaning, a different set of categories can be recognized for compounds with right stress. In general, N2 is used to describe N1, as in *paper* ′*plate*. Some categories for this type are given below:

N2 refers to the material N1 is made out of: *leather* ′*shoes, silver* ′*spoon, stone* ′*wall*

---

[10]Note that there is a clear difference between the -*ing* participle functioning as a noun and the -*ing* participle functioning as an adjective. *Swimming pool* in (i) below is a compound (and, as such, is the head of the NP a *swimming pool*) whereas the head of the NP a *swimming dog* in (ii) is the noun *dog*. The accompanying difference in pronunciation is predictable:

(i) a ′*swimming pool* (a pool for swimming, where *swimming* has a nominal function)
(ii) a *swimming* ′*dog* (a dog that's swimming, where *swimming* has an adjectival function)

<u>N2 refers to a specific group of people</u>: *class 'clown, village 'idiot, team 'spirit*

<u>N2 situates N1 relative to something else</u>: *back 'room, top 'floor, bottom 'shelf*

<u>N2 refers to the temporal location of N1</u>: *autumn 'leaves, evening 'breeze, morning 'coffee*

<u>N2 refers to the spatial location of N1</u>: *bathroom 'floor, bedroom 'window, dining room 'table*

Compounding is a **productive process** in English, meaning that it enables speakers to create new combinations spontaneously when the need arises.

3.1.3. Adjectives and adverbs

Adverbs represent a highly heterogeneous word class, and observing a few examples is enough to make this clear. A basic class of adverbs are **adverbs of frequency**: *always, daily, hardly ever, never, often, monthly, rarely, sometimes, weekly.* We can also distinguish between **adverbs of degree**, which modify an adjective or an adverb and answer the question 'to what degree?'; **adverbs of manner**, which answer the question 'how?' or 'in what way?'; and **sentence adverbs**, which bear on the entire sentence, often expressing the point of view of the speaker. In all four cases, these adverbs often derive from adjectives by adding the suffix *-ly*:

> (11) He *rarely* socializes with his colleagues. (adverb of frequency (> Adj *rare*))
> Is it necessary to clean contact lenses *regularly*? (adverb of frequency (> Adj *regular*))
> That's an *extremely* simplistic version of what I saw. (adverb of degree (> Adj *extreme*))
> Stocks are performing *remarkably* well this quarter. (adverb of degree (> Adj *remarkable*))
> He *quietly* tiptoed into the sleeping baby's room. (adverb of manner (> Adj *quiet*))
> *Clearly* (= it was clear to me), he had been drinking. (sentence adverb (> Adj *clear*))

Many common adverbs such as *quite, very, almost* and *always* are not derived from adjectives and do not end in *-ly*. Conversely, a few words ending in *-ly* are not adverbs at all, but adjectives.[11] These include *elderly, cowardly, friendly, (un)likely, lovely, lonely, neighbourly*:

---

[11] There are also verbs (*apply, imply, supply*) and nouns (*assembly, jelly, rally*) that end in *-ly*. We address adverbs and adjectives here because their meaning and distribution can be a source of confusion.

(12) The judge said it would be hard to imagine a more *cowardly* act.
(*He acted cowardly. – He acted in a cowardly manner.)
His *friendly* answer to my letter put a smile on my face.
(*He friendly answered my letter. – He answered my letter in a friendly way.)

Words such as *early, far, fast* and *well*, and also *daily, nightly, weekly, monthly* and *yearly* can be adverbs or adjectives:

(13) He speaks Italian really *well*. (Adv)
Her brother is not *well*. He's seeing a specialist. (Adj)

You're driving too *fast*: please slow down. (Adv)
A defining characteristic of a sports car is that it is *fast*. (Adj)

When I was in hospital, he visited me *daily*. (Adv)
His *daily* visits to the hospital were appreciated. (Adj)

Some pairs of morphologically close adverbs such as *hard/hardly* and *late/lately* do not mean the same thing. Note that the first item in each pair is also used as an adjective:

(14) I've been working *hard* to update our website. (Adv = with a lot of effort)
We've *hardly* had the time to work on anything. (Adv = almost not at all)
It has been *hard* for me to work on this project. (Adj = difficult)

The plane from San Francisco arrived *late*. (Adv = with a delay)
I've been taking the plane a lot *lately*. (Adv = recently)
Late planes are the bane of busy executives. (Adj = delayed)

Finally, adjectives such as *slow, quick* and *easy* have derived adverbial forms (*slowly, quickly, easily*) but can often be found, at least informally, used as adverbs. Note, though, that many people consider this incorrect or sloppy:

(15) I hope to get a *quick* answer to my inquiry. (Adj)
Come *quick*! I need your help. (Adv – many prefer *quickly*, though *quick* is common)
The students all found the exam quite *easy*. (Adj)
This novel is not for anyone who scares *easy*. (Adv – many will prefer *easily* here)

The discussion above focuses on some formal aspects of adjectives and adverbs. The details of the different roles they play can be gleaned from the examples given so far: while adverbs qualify verbs (she spoke *softly*), adjectives (her *softly* spoken words) or other adverbs (she speaks *quite* softly), adjectives basically give more information about a noun (her *soft* voice). This additional, qualifying information can be mentioned in **attributive** position (her *soft* voice) or in **predicative** position (her voice is *soft*) (see Chapter 3, Section 4.1). As we will observe again at the end of this section, this point shows that understanding something about the **distributional properties** of parts of speech can be helpful to step up your proficiency in English.

3.1.4. Conjunctions

You probably recall that conjunctions in English are of two kinds: coordinating and subordinating. What these two subtypes have in common is that they link elements together. **Coordinating** conjunctions (or **coordinators**) usually serve to connect constituents of the same kind, be they phrases or clauses. One-word coordinators include *and, but, for, or* and *yet*:

(16) Fruits *and* vegetables are important to a balanced diet.
Each branch of the government is separate from – *yet* equal to – the other branches.
He has all the required education, *but* he hasn't got any experience.

In some contexts, coordinating conjunctions can also connect constituents of different kinds:

(17) 'We are really happy *and* in love,' Grammer said to reporters at the event. (www)[12]
The RCHT said it was disappointed *and* considering an appeal. (www)

Correlative coordinators work similarly, but have two parts, one before each joined constituent. These include *either ... or, neither ... nor, not only ... but also, both ... and* and *whether ... or*:

(18) She'll work *either* on Saturday *or* (on) Sunday, but not both.
The ideal candidate will be *both* dynamic *and* professional.
Whether he comes *or* doesn't come makes no difference to me.
In terms of images for the future, I was surprised nobody chose any of the photographs of a victorious President Obama, *either* alone *or* with his young family. (www)

Subordinating conjunctions (or **subordinators**), on the other hand, always introduce clauses and link them to another clause. *If, whether* and *that* are

---

[12]The links to the pages from which the examples were retrieved are provided in the list of sources of examples on pp. 340–343.

common subordinators. Others include *after, although, as much as, as long as, as soon as, because, before, in order that, lest, since, so that, than, though, unless, until, when, whenever, where, wherever* and *while*:

(19) *As soon as* he arrives, we'll pack up the car and get going.
We couldn't get in to the concert *because* we'd left the tickets at home.
Do you know *if* (or *whether*) he's coming to the family reunion?
We realize *that* this is not an easy situation for you.

Some subordinators, namely *before, after, since* and *until*, are also used as prepositions; *before* and *since* can be adverbs as well. Note that *afterwards*, rather than *after*, is the usual adverb meaning *later, subsequently*:

(20) Let's go out to eat	*before* the film.	(Prep)
	before the film starts.	(Conj)
	before.	(Adv)
I haven't seen my cousins	*since* 2005.	(Prep)
	since I was a child.	(Conj)
	(ever) *since*.	(Adv)
He thinks we should meet	*after* the meeting.	(Prep)
	after we've had the meeting.	(Conj)
	afterwards.	(Adv)

Parts of speech are the smallest building blocks in the sentence. Moving up to the next level in the syntactic hierarchy, we will now look at the ways in which words combine into phrases.

3.2. Phrases

Sentences do not just consist of a series of juxtaposed words that each belong to a particular part of speech. Intuitively, you know this already. If you were asked to analyse the sentence *When I was ten, my favourite teacher was Mrs Jenkins*, you would probably quite naturally intuit that the sentence is not so much made of ten words as it is of four chunks: [when I was ten], [my favourite teacher], [was] and [Mrs Jenkins]. Regarding that first chunk [when I was ten], you would probably agree that if you moved it from the beginning of the sentence to the end, the sentence would still be grammatical, and that you could even eliminate the first chunk from the sentence (though, crucially, not the other chunks) without doing any harm to its overall grammaticality.

Different parts of speech cluster together and form constituents, which have certain functions in the sentence. When words cluster around a noun, the constituent is called a **Noun Phrase** (NP), and when words cluster around an adjective, they make up an **Adjective Phrase** (AdjP). We can also identify **Adverb Phrases** (AdvP) and **Prepositional Phrases** (PrepP). For the moment, we will use the term **Verb Phrase** (VP) to refer to all the verbs that are used in a clause plus the constituents that follow it.

Another important concept is that of **head** or **headword**: the noun *teacher* is the head of the NP [my favourite *teacher*]. In exactly the same way, the head of a VP is a verb, the head of a PrepP is a preposition and so on. In this book, we will distinguish five types of phrases, which we illustrate below with some examples:

(21) NP   [*lemons*], [my *wife*], [the *computer* [I bought]], [such [great] *happiness*], [*Venus*]

VP   [*broke*], [is *painting* [the house]], [are *contemplating* [divorce]], [has *arrived*]

AdjP   [*ill*], [[terribly] *bright*], [*afraid* [of the dark]]

AdvP   [*frankly*], [[quite] *surprisingly*], [[extremely] *well*]

PrepP   [*in* [the winter]], [*under* [the covers]], [*without* [due warning]]

To help you to get a feel for these constituent phrases, we have in each case put the phrase in brackets ([]) and italicized the headword. To highlight that constituents can themselves be made up of other constituents, we have enclosed these 'constituents within constituents' in italicized brackets (*[]*). Note, finally, that NPs, VPs, AdjPs and AdvPs need not be made up of several words – an NP can be made up of the head N alone, the VP of the head V alone and so on. This means that *John loves radishes* and *My friend loves that film* will both be analysed as NP + VP, and the VP analysed as V + NP:

(22) [[NP]   [$_{VP}$ [V]   [NP]   ]   ]

[[$_{NP}$ John]   [$_{VP}$ [$_V$loves] [$_{NP}$radishes]   ]   ]

[[$_{NP}$ My friend] [$_{VP}$ [$_V$loves] [$_{NP}$that film]   ]   ]

In Section 3.1, we said that we consider **pronouns** a subclass of nouns. While informally we might define 'pro-nouns' as placeholders for nouns, a more accurate definition is that pronouns are on a par with NPs. This is clear from the fact that we can replace the NP constituents in [*My younger sister*] *loves* [*fresh radishes*] with pronouns, giving us [*She*] *loves* [*them*]; *she* and *them* fill the whole NP position. They are not on a par with *sister* and *radishes*.

Although it would be more accurate for that reason to use the label 'pro-NPs', we will keep to traditional label 'pronoun'.

It is important to understand that when we talk about a part of speech, we are referring to the **form** of the word in question; that is, we use a label that is associated with a set of **formal criteria**. For instance, a noun can be used in the plural (*boys, men*); it can be used in the genitive (*the boys', the men's*). In the same way, if we use labels to refer to types of phrases, we are again concerned with the form of constituents; that is, we use a label that is based on the part of speech of the headword.

3.3. Functions

The different kinds of phrases described in 3.2 perform certain **functions** in the sentence. The two most basic functions at sentence level are the **Subject** and the **Predicate**, which might somewhat informally be described along the following lines: in a sentence, we introduce someone or something and then say something about it. The functional label for the 'someone or something' is the **Subject**; we use the term **Predicate** to capture the function of 'what is said about the Subject'.[13] In other words, the Predicate is everything in a sentence except the Subject. In the examples that follow we have separated the Subject from the Predicate by a slash[14]:

(23) More than 200 people/lost their lives in an earthquake in Indonesia in 2018.
Prince Harry and Meghan Markle/got married on 19 May 2018.
The foreign secretary/announced that military forces might be withdrawn quickly.

Each of the constituents that make up the Predicate also performs a function. We will use the following labels to refer to the different functions:

(24) Direct Object (DO)
Indirect Object (IO)
Subject Complement (SC)
Object Complement (OC)

---

[13]In discourse analysis, the subject matter that is introduced by the Subject is often referred to as the **topic** of the clause. The information provided by the Predicate is said to be the **comment** (see Chapter 6, Section 1).

[14]This semantic characterization of the Subject is helpful, but it does not work all the time: in sentences such as *It could snow tomorrow* or *There are enough chairs*, we can hardly say the Subjects *it* and *there* are 'what the sentence is about'. Subject-auxiliary inversion (such as in an interrogative clause: see Chapter 2, Section 2.2.2) is a more helpful syntactic test that can identify the Subject. It can be applied to all clauses, including those with 'empty' Subjects like 'it' and 'there' in the examples cited: *Could it snow tomorrow? Are there enough chairs?*

Adjunct
Prepositional Object (PO)
Prepositional Complement (PC)

If we apply the functional labels to the first example in (23), we can say that *their lives* is the **Direct Object** and that *in an earthquake, in Indonesia* and *in 2018* are three Adjuncts. Below you will find some more examples that illustrate the other functions listed in (24):

(25) More than 200 people lost *their lives*. (DO)
Please give *her* your telephone number. (IO)
Please give your telephone number *to my mother*. (IO)
They are *English teachers/exhausted*. (SC)
She appeared *tired/out of sorts*. (SC)
His name was Benjamin, but they called him *Ben*. (OC)
They painted their house *red*. (OC)
I'll finish the work *tomorrow*. (Adjunct)
Henry started walking *when he was thirteen months old*. (Adjunct)
My grandmother gave me this bracelet *for my fifteenth birthday*. (Adjunct)
Sarah depends *on her husband* financially. (PO)
I ran *into an old school friend* when I was on a holiday in Scotland. (PO)
Put those books *on my desk*. (PC)

The labels **Subject Complement** and **Object Complement** are quite transparent and clearly indicative of the function they perform: that of 'complementing', that is, ascribing a property to the Subject and the Direct Object, respectively. Subject Complements occur after verbs like *be, become, appear* and *seem*: these are often called **linking verbs**.

A **Prepositional Object** is an object that is headed by a preposition. Prepositional Objects are found with prepositional verbs such as *look at, look for* and *look into*. These are fixed verb–preposition combinations that have acquired a specific lexical meaning. We will have more to say about prepositional verbs in Chapter 2 (Section 4.2.2.2).

The function of **Adjunct** is to capture the when, where and why of the situation referred to in the sentence. While this information may obviously be important from the point of view of *sentence semantics*, the constituents that perform the function of Adjunct can usually be left out without having an impact on the grammaticality of the sentence. From a *syntactic* point of view, they are optional:

(26) We listened to the radio [all night long]. (cf. We listened to the radio.)
He's [still] looking for his watch. (cf. He's looking for his watch.)

Put somewhat differently, Adjuncts provide information about the circumstances surrounding the event or state of affairs described by the verb, rather than about the participants in that event or state of affairs. However, constituents referring to the when, where and why are not always syntactically optional. Leaving them out may result in ungrammaticality, as in the examples in (27). For that reason, we do not call the italicized constituents in brackets Adjuncts, but rather refer to them as **Prepositional Complements**, a **complement** being an obligatory constituent:

(27) He has lived [*near the Thames*] [for a long time].
　　 *He has lived [for a long time]. (only possible if *live* means *be alive*)
　　 He has lived [*near the Thames*].
　　 John put the book [*on the table*].
　　 *John put the book.

Like any compulsory constituent, the Prepositional Complements in the examples in (27) cannot be left out – if they are, the sentences become ungrammatical. This issue will be taken up again in the next chapter, when we deal with the complementation of verbs (Chapter 2, Section 4).

While the function of Prepositional Object and Prepositional Complement is always performed by a PrepP, the examples in (28) show that there is no one-to-one relationship between a particular form (type of phrase) and a particular function. For instance, an NP can function as Subject, Direct Object, **Indirect Object**, Subject Complement and Object Complement. Take, for instance, the NP [the boy] and observe its functions in the following examples[15]:

(28) **Form = NP**   **Function**
　　 [The boy] was playing alone in his room.　　 Subject
　　 I know [the boy (who is playing in his room)].　 Direct Object
　　 I gave [the boy] a toy to play with.　　　　 Indirect Object
　　 John is [the boy (I was talking about)].　　 Subject Complement
　　 I consider John [the boy (for the job)].　　 Object Complement

Conversely, one particular function can be fulfilled by a variety of forms. For instance, an Adjunct can be an NP, a PrepP or an AdvP:

(29) **Function = Adjunct**   **Form**
　　 I enjoy reading the newspaper [every day].　 NP

---

[15]The NP [the boy] cannot function as an Adjunct, but other NPs can. In *I phone my mother [every day]*, the NP [every day] is an Adjunct.

She loves tending flowers [in the garden].   PrepP
They'll be taking the train [early tomorrow].   AdvP

As pointed out above, an exception to this generalization is that Prepositional Objects are always PrepPs:

(30) We listened [to the radio] all night long.
He's still looking [for his watch].

As will be clear from the examples in (27), Prepositional Complements are likewise most often PrepPs, with the exception of examples like *Put it [here]* and *Set it [there]*.

In this grammar, we concentrate on functions taken up by constituents in the sentence and will be less concerned with functions within a constituent. We will, however, distinguish between the **headword** or the **head** (the most important word in the phrase) and the other words in the phrase. This results in a distinction between a **prehead** (such as a determiner) and a **posthead** (such as a relative clause).

We will use the term **Object of a Preposition** to refer to the posthead in a PrepP, irrespective of whether the PrepP functions as, for instance, an Adjunct, a Prepositional Object, or an Indirect Object. In the examples in (31), the Object of the Preposition is in each case italicized:

(31) **PrepP (Prep + NP)**   **Function**
She's working [in [*the garden*]].   Adjunct
It all depends [on [*his answers*]].   Prepositional Object
I'm giving this book [to [*Tom*]].   Indirect Object
I put the box [under [*the table*]].   Prepositional Complement

It is important not to confuse Object of a Preposition and **Prepositional Object**. Prepositional Object is a function at the sentence level: it refers to a PrepP whose headword is part of a prepositional verb, as in the second example in (31), where the PrepP [on *his answers*] is a Prepositional Object, and the prepositional verb is *depend on (something)*. An Object of a Preposition is a posthead: it refers to an NP that follows a preposition and forms a constituent with that preposition, irrespective of the syntactic function of the PrepP. As opposed to all other phrases (NPs, VPs, AdjPs, AdvPs), a PrepP necessarily has a posthead:

(32) John is [afraid [of spiders]].
*John is [afraid [of]].

The above observations constitute the foundations of basic syntactic analysis.[16] An understanding of the fundamental difference between forms and functions is crucial to understanding linguistic descriptions of language facts. You will need the concepts introduced to step up your level of English since usage rules may apply to certain parts of speech or to constituents that perform particular functions in the sentence. To give just two examples, the function of SC can never be filled by an AdvP, which is why *The injured pole vaulter seems sadly* is not a grammatical sentence. In a similar way, an Adjunct can never be an AdjP, which explains why we say *He answered the question intelligently* rather than *He answered the question intelligent*. In other words, basic linguistic analysis can actually be quite helpful to learners since it can make patterns in language use more transparent.

4. The clause, the sentence and subordination

4.1. Declarative, interrogative, exclamative and imperative clauses

So far, we have been using the term **sentence** to refer to the strings of words that make up units of meaning and that, in writing, end with a full stop, an exclamation mark or a question mark. The term is useful enough when all we are referring to is a sentence consisting of a Subject and an accompanying Predicate with a finite verb. In linguistics we use the term **clause** to refer to sentences that minimally consist of a Subject and a Predicate. A sentence can consist of a single clause. However, clauses can combine in various ways to make more complex sentences. We will have more to say on this below. Limiting ourselves for the moment to single-clause sentences, we can distinguish between four basic, mutually exclusive clause types: declarative, interrogative, exclamative and imperative. Each clause type is associated with formal characteristics and a typical function. The word order in a **declarative clause** (or **declarative** (33a)) is Subject–verb–(Object), and its typical function is to provide information. In an **interrogative clause** (or **interrogative** (33b)) the

---

[16]It will be clear that slightly alternative approaches to syntactic analysis may well be taken in other grammars, and that slightly different terminology may be used or more fine-grained analyses proposed. The functions and labels introduced here have been inspired by the pedagogical aims of the book.

word order usually exhibits inversion, with an auxiliary preceding the Subject (auxiliary verb–Subject–(main verb)–(Object)); it is typically used to ask a question. An **exclamative clause** (or **exclamative** (33c)) begins with an NP, AdjP or AdvP constituent starting with *what* or *how* followed by Subject–verb word order as in a declarative. The typical function of an exclamative is to express emotion more emphatically than in a declarative. Finally, an **imperative clause** (or **imperative** (33d)) usually does not have an overt Subject and is typically used to issue a directive, that is, to tell or invite someone to do something:

(33) (a) Jane is (not) coming for dinner tonight.
　　 (b) Where do you live? Are you from around here?
　　 (c) What a talented student he is! How beautiful she looks!
　　 (d) Stop! Be careful. Come over whenever you'd like.

As we pointed out in our discussion of phrases, the form–function links mentioned are not in a one-to-one relationship. This is also the case here. For instance, an interrogative clause (a form) can be used not to ask a question (a function), but rather to express surprise, as in B's response to A in the following example:

(34) A: John is the best man for the job.
　　 B: *What are you talking about?* He knows nothing about the project!

Conversely, the function of asking a question may also be performed by a declarative clause, provided rising intonation is used:

(35) A: I have an alibi, officer. I was at the office all day.
　　 B: And after that, *you went directly home*?

Interrogative clauses will be discussed in more detail in Chapter 2 (Section 3).

The sentences in (33) above are all made up of a single clause. In some cases (for example, the imperative clause *Stop!* in (33d)), the clause is minimally made up of nothing more than a VP. At the other end of the spectrum are larger clauses made up of more than one clause. We will focus our discussion here on on the declarative clause. We need to recognize two basic distinctions that are relevant to declarative clauses. The first distinction is between **main clauses** and **subordinate clauses** (or **subclauses**). The second distinction is between **finite clauses** and **non-finite clauses**.

4.2. Main clauses and subclauses

Start by examining the following:

(36) She went to bed early.
We had dinner.
They'll send us the information.

The examples in (36) are single-clause sentences, made up of a Subject and the Predicate that goes with it. Since they are made of only one clause, the terms 'main clause' and 'subordinate clause' (or subclause) are not relevant to describe them.

In (37) below, the examples in (36) have been expanded with an additional clause, which we call a subclause. The subclause is **embedded** in what we will call the **main clause**. The main clauses in (37) are italicized, and the subclauses are underlined:

(37) *She went to bed early* <u>because she was tired</u>.
<u>As soon as they arrived</u>, *we had dinner.*
They'll send us the information <u>if we give them our address</u>.

As is the case for the phrasal constituents discussed in Section 3.3, subclauses have a function in the sentence as a whole. In (37), the subclauses function as Adjuncts, very similar to what we might see in an AdvP or a PrepP. Subclauses of this type are often referred to as **adverbial clauses**. Subclauses are not always Adjuncts, however; they can have a function that is syntactically obligatory in the sentence:

(38) (a) They said <u>that they'd be late</u>. (*They said.)
(b) I wonder <u>if they'll finish on time</u>. (*I wonder.)
(c) She explained <u>why she wanted to change jobs</u>. (*She explained.)
(d) <u>What he does for a living</u> is no business of yours. (*Is no business of yours.)
(e) She became <u>what she had always despised</u>. (*She became.)

The subclauses in (38a) and (38b), introduced by *that* and *if*, function as Direct Objects. The Direct Object subclause in (38c) is a *wh*-interrogative clause. The subclauses in (38d) and (38e) are *wh*-interrogative clauses as well, but with a different function: in (38d) the subclause functions as Subject, and in (38e) it functions as a Subject Complement. Compare (38) to (37), above: if we eliminate the subclauses in (37), what remains in each case is a grammatical main clause (see (36)). The subclauses in (38), however, constitute an obligatory part of the sentence as a whole (they are complements) – if we eliminate them, the sentence is incomplete. When analyzing clauses like those in (37) it is handy to have a concept to refer to the non-underlined part of the sentence, which is also a clause: we will use the term **embedding clause** to refer to that part of the sentence.

It can be helpful to be aware of two other kinds of subclause, which on the surface look similar to one another:

(39) (a) [The idea that/which she put forth at the meeting]$_{NP}$ is a good one.
(b) [The idea that/*which she might have to relocate]$_{NP}$ makes her anxious.

Both (39a) and (39b) contain subclauses. As the bracketing shows, these subclauses are part of NPs. The subclause in (39a) is a **relative clause**. Informally put, it can be said to answer the question 'which idea is a good one?'. In this case, *that* can be replaced by *which*. In (39b) the subclause is a *that*-clause; it is often referred to as an **appositive clause**. It does not serve to indicate *which* idea but, rather, states *what* the content of that idea is. Here, *that* cannot be replaced by *which*. Relative clauses – more common than the type of *that*-clause in (39b) – are discussed in Chapter 3, Section 4.2.

Note, finally, that sentences containing two or more clauses do not always enter into the hierarchical relationship of subordination. As seen above in our discussion of coordinating conjunctions (Section 3.1.4), **coordinated clauses** are linked by means of a coordinating conjunction:

(40) Give him a call *and* ask him if he'd like to come with us.
We could go straight to the cinema, *or* we could have a drink first.
I tried to convince them to stay, *but* they had other obligations.

As the examples of subclauses given so far have shown, they are often introduced by a subordinating conjunction (such as *because, if, why* etc.) or by a relative pronoun.

4.3. Finite versus non-finite clauses

The second distinction to be aware of is that between finite and non-finite clauses. A finite clause usually has an overt Subject, and the verb in the clause is marked for one of the tenses we discuss in Chapter 4 (41a) (this includes modal verbs (41b), which are marked for present or past tense (Chapter 5)). Imperative clauses (41c), which do not have to have an overt Subject, are also finite clauses, as are subjunctive clauses (41d) (Chapter 5, Section 7):

(41) (a) He's working tonight./He worked last night./He'll be working next week.
(b) He might be working./He can't work./He should work a little harder.

(c) Please work harder./Don't work so hard.
(d) (It is essential) that he work harder next term.

A finite clause can be a main clause (42a) or a subclause, underlined in (42b):

(42) (a) He's working tonight.
(b) She said (that) he's working tonight.

In a non-finite clause, the Subject is often not expressed and the verb is not marked for tense: the verb takes the form of a bare infinitive (43a), a *to*-infinitive (43b) or the -*ing* participle ((43c) – see footnote 2, Chapter 2) or a past participle (43d):

(43) (a) They saw him *leave* the premises.
(b) She wants us *to leave* now.
(c) I don't really enjoy *travelling* alone.
(d) *Given* the chance, I'd go back there again.

Whereas a finite clause can be a main clause or a subclause, non-finite clauses are necessarily subclauses. Seen from the opposite perspective, we can say that a subclause can be finite or non-finite, but that a main clause will always be finite.

5. Conclusion

The goal of this chapter was to refresh your knowledge of basic syntactic terminology. We have listed the major parts of speech, and we have shown how they combine into phrases that perform specific functions in the clause. The chapters that follow will give a structured overview of some of the crucial areas of English grammar, areas we believe are particularly challenging for the advanced language learner. It will become clear that the use of linguistic concepts is more than an intellectual exercise; it is genuinely beneficial to learning a foreign language. The linguistic concepts that have been and will be introduced will turn out to be relevant to generalizations about usage. In this way, we will lay bare some of the principles governing English usage and provide evidence that a language is more than a set of arbitrary, unrelated rules.

Exercises

Exercise 1. Comment on the grammaticality of the following sentences, taken from examples (1) and (3) on pages 2 and 3 of this chapter. What differentiates sentences (1) to (4) below from sentences (5) to (8)?

1. I don't have no time to waste.
2. If he would have known, he wouldn't have said that.
3. You shouldn't have went there without me.
4. I don't know him good enough to have an opinion.
5. My stepbrother is eight years older than me.
6. It sounds like you had a great time at the party.
7. Who do you think we should invite?
8. What do you attribute her success to?

Exercise 2. Look at the words below and identify the part of speech.

1. the   across   afraid   after   although   and   at
2. because   before   bird   book   must   during   theirs   write
3. enormous   fast   quickly   friendly   their   headache   Louise
4. house   if   man   many   from   record (stressed on 1st syllable)
5. or   London   sheep   since   work   record (stressed on 2nd syllable)
6. sing   cook   a   under   unless   wet   without

Exercise 3. Identify the phrases below, identifying in each case the head of the phrase. Then identify the function of each phrase.

1. [The boy] ate [an apple]. The boy [ate an apple].
2. She [gave her father a gift]. She gave [her father] [a gift]. She gave [a gift] [to her father].
3. My sister is afraid of [spiders]. My sister is afraid [of spiders]. My sister is [afraid of spiders].
4. I read the instructions [very carefully]. Your father is [very friendly].
5. He's been working [really hard]. The exam we took was [really hard].
6. It was [too late] for us to check in. We arrived [too late] to check in.
7. You'll find [the box] [under the bed]. [The box under the bed] belongs to me.
8. I asked [for a new computer]. They lived abroad [for many years].

Exercise 4. Identify the Subject in each of the following sentences and indicate what form the Subject takes.

1. This new English book is very interesting.
2. Without knocking, my sister walked right into my room.
3. Smoking cigarettes is strongly discouraged.
4. That he thinks I'm a fool is a little ironic.
5. To speak English perfectly requires lots of practice.
6. To facilitate matters, I will e-mail the info to you.
7. What she needs is a good, hot meal.
8. There were a lot of spelling mistakes in his essay.

9. There is time to work out this problem ourselves.
10. It's snowing outside.
11. Next to her is where I'd like to sit.

Exercise 5. Identify the Direct Objects and Indirect Objects in the following sentences and indicate what the form of each Object is.

1. I'm reading a really good book.
2. She lent her sister a really good book. She lent a really good book to her sister.
3. I bought my girlfriend a bouquet of roses. I bought a bouquet of roses for my girlfriend.
4. I explained the situation.
5. I explained the situation to my mother.
6. He did housework all day.
7. I suddenly realized that I'd forgotten my mother's birthday.
8. I've decided to go to India next summer.
9. I can't understand what you're saying. I don't know where it is.
10. Learning English grammar implies doing grammar exercises.
11. Can you make someone do something they don't want to do?

Exercise 6. Identify the following functions in the sentences below: Subject, Direct Object, Indirect Object, Adjunct, Prepositional Object, Subject Complement and Object Complement.

1. The package arrived yesterday morning.
2. Harry read a book. Sam read Harry a book. Sam read a book to Harry.
3. I baked a cake last night. I baked her a cake last night. I baked a cake for her last night.
4. Kevin asked us a very interesting question. I bet you ten quid I can beat you.
5. My father is a doctor. My father married a doctor.
6. I consider her the best candidate. They painted the house white.
7. She looked at me in total disbelief.
8. Marilyn bought a dress. Marilyn paid for the dress with a credit card.
9. You should look up that word in the dictionary. You should look that word up.

Exercise 7. Identify the function of *who(ever)* or *what*.

1. What are you looking at?
2. What do you want?
3. What's this?
4. What did you say you bought for her birthday?
5. What is the matter with you?
6. Who's your best friend?

7. Who did you sit next to?
8. Who's next?
9. Whoever did this must be slightly out of his mind.
10. Did you know there exists a book called *Who's Who?* It contains biographical information on prominent people.

Exercise 8. The following sentences are (structurally) ambiguous. The different meanings correspond to different constituent structures. Paraphrase the two meanings and explain, in syntactic terms, the origin of the ambiguity.

1. They prepared her chicken.
2. All young men and women should get a fair chance on the job market.
3. Jennifer is writing to her friends in London.
4. For some reason, he liked stalking students.
5. The idea of a black oak box appealed to all of us.
6. You have no idea how worried mothers sound.
7. He ran over the cat.
8. Jennifer scared the mouse in the house.
9. The general thinks he might have defeated soldiers.
10. I wonder if he knows how unfortunate people feel in such circumstances.

Exercise 9. Find the Direct Objects, Subject Complements and Object Complements in the following sentences and identify the forms they take.

1. Their house was painted bright yellow.
2. He lay motionless on the floor.
3. They found it an extraordinarily good proposal.
4. The menu sounds very tempting.
5. My neighbours have painted their house bright yellow.
6. His name is Jonathan, but all his friends call him Jo.
7. The soup tasted delicious.
8. He turned red in the face when I mentioned her name.
9. I feel good.
10. Sue seemed disappointed.

Exercise 10. Identify the Objects of Prepositions, Prepositional Objects, Prepositional Complements and Adjuncts in the following sentences.

1. Is something burning in the kitchen? – No, there's a cake in the oven.
2. Look at Maddie – she really takes after her mother, doesn't she?
3. Your keys are lying on the dining room table.
4. I didn't know you were so fond of baroque music.
5. Don't let me down. I'm really counting on you.

    6. She quietly slipped the letter into her back pocket.

    7. The destruction of Atlantis is a legend. Atlantis didn't really exist.

    8. They lived by the seaside for many years.

    9. He started making measurable progress from day one.

    10. There's no need to go to an exotic country to have a relaxing holiday.

    11. I've been looking for this first-edition book since last year.

    12. The picture was hanging from a rusty nail.

Exercise 11. Identify the Adverbs and the Prepositions in the sentences below.

    1. I haven't spoken to her since last Christmas.

    2. I'll join you later tonight.

    3. Besides Jennifer, I knew no one at the party.

    4. Why do you want to buy her a gift? Besides, you don't have any money.

    5. I haven't spoken to her since.

    6. I want a fast car, so that I can get to you really fast and not arrive late.

    7. She needs her daily portion of ham and cheese.

    8. Honestly, I can't remember who I sat next to.

    9. To say the least, she hardly made an effort to say a friendly word.

    10. I sat beside her during the Christmas dinner.

Exercise 12. Explain the statements below and illustrate them with examples of your own.

    1. The unmarked function of an interrogative sentence is to ask for information, but an interrogative sentence can also function as (a) a forceful statement, (b) an offer of service or (c) a suggestion.

    2. The unmarked function of an imperative sentence is to give an order, but an imperative sentence can also function as (a) a wish, (b) an exclamation or (c) an offer.

Exercise 13. Read the following sentences and identify the main clauses, the subclauses (or embedded clauses) and the embedding clauses.

Woman gives birth on hospital chair due to 'no staff'

A woman has given birth on a chair in a waiting room in an east London hospital amid claims there were no staff or beds available.

Frances Randall gave birth to her son while she was sitting on a chair with help from a stranger at Queen's Hospital in Romford.

The new mother said there had been no medical staff available and her son Freddie had fallen on the floor.

A hospital spokesman apologized but said no complaint had been received.

Miss Randall said she was disgusted that something like this should have happened in a new hospital.

'I was sitting on the chair sideways and I gave birth and that's when he fell on the floor,' she said.

'Luckily he fell on the floor because otherwise the cord would have been wrapped around his neck. I'm just disgusted, it's a brand new hospital and things like this shouldn't happen'.

Sue Lovell, head of midwifery at Queen's Hospital, said she was aware of the incident and added a new triage system was being put in place.

When labouring women arrive at Queen's Hospital they will be seen immediately by a midwife and moved straight to the most appropriate area – whether that be the labour ward or ante natal.

'This will eliminate the need for women to stay in waiting areas. I have not received a complaint from Miss Randall but would be more than happy to meet with her.' (www)

Exercise 14. These sentences, all of them authentic, contain features that some consider incorrect from a prescriptive point of view. Identify in each case what the 'problem' is and comment to what extent it can be considered a mistake.

1. (The main character in the novel) Grady is intoxicated by freedom (and much booze, and some marijuana as well), and she proves beyond all doubt that her parents were quite right to wonder if she were capable of handling this freedom. (www)
2. More than 100,000 people were stopped and searched by police under counter-terrorism powers last year but none of them were arrested for terrorism-related offences. (www)
3. I understand where you're coming from, but if I was you I wouldn't have the wedding ring you inherited from your grandma reset. (www)
4. 'It's fantastic, I'm really thrilled the way I played all week. To win a fifth time is obviously amazing, for the third time in a different place. Like I said before, it would be great to win in Houston, Shanghai and also now here in London.' (www)
5. We did not learn until after we'd ordered our main meals that they also have a pasta appetizer. If I had known I may have changed my selection and not ordered pasta as a main dish. (www)
6. 'They told me there was a mass on the pancreas and they thought it was cancer [...]. If it hadn't have been for the jaundice it wouldn't have been discovered [...] and within another couple of months I would have been dead.' (www)
7. The chief executive of Starbucks has revealed that the coffee shop giant is to more than double its opening of new stores globally over the next year. (www)
8. Tourist board organization Visit Scotland, which employs 1,000 staff, claims it has managed to do more with less people following an extensive restructure. (www)
9. (newspaper headline) Identity: A cop show that thankfully doesn't take itself too seriously. (www)

10. Stores look rather different than they used to: budget and own-brand ranges, once the faintly embarrassing end of product lines, are now found front and centre in displays. (www)
11. As for we Brits, while we are very good at hosting Wimbledon, we prefer to watch tennis, rather than play (we can't be bothered, in all honesty). (www)
12. She was thirteen years older than him and was a lady of some importance, married to Viscount Ranelagh. (www)
13. Efforts to sanitize classic literature have a long, undistinguished history. Everything from Chaucer's *Canterbury Tales* to Roald Dahl's *Charlie and the Chocolate Factory* have been challenged or have suffered at the hands of uptight editors. (www)
14. By the time Mozgawa moved to Los Angeles in 2008, she was a professional drummer, stepping in to tour with whomever might need her, but secretly wishing for a band of her own. (www)

2

The verb and its complements

1. Introduction

In the previous chapter we sketched out our approach to the study of grammar and gave a brief overview of some basic grammatical notions concerning the level of the word, the constituent, the clause and the sentence. We also reviewed the terminology we use to talk about these different levels and took a first look at the interface between form and function.

In this chapter we will zoom in on the verb phrase (VP) from different angles. We will first discuss the core element of any VP (i.e. the verb itself) and demonstrate the import of the distinction between lexical verbs and auxiliary verbs. This difference is primarily syntactic. We will then look more closely at lexical verbs, focusing on how a verb's basic meaning helps to determine how a sentence is built around it. Consider the following:

(1) (a) My mother has arrived.
   (b) Matthew has been reading <u>that book</u>.
   (c) Not everyone appreciates <u>my sense of humour</u>.
   (d) Matthew has been reading.
   (e) *Not everyone appreciates.

Some verbs require nothing more than the obligatory Subject to represent a situation, as in (1a). Other verbs can accept (1b) – or require (1c) – one or more constituents (underlined in these examples) in addition to the Subject. It is the verb itself that determines whether the absence of these latter constituents does (1d) or does not (1e) result in a grammatical sentence. The term **complementation** will be used to refer to the relationship between the verbs and the constituents other than the Subject that are grammatically obligatory in a given context.[1]

We will also see that if a verb takes one or more complements in addition to the Subject, the speaker can to a certain degree choose the order in which the information is presented. One way the speaker can do this is to opt for the passive voice (2) rather than the active voice (1):

(2) (a) That book has been read (by millions of people). (cf. 1b)
   (b) My sense of humour isn't appreciated (by everyone). (cf. 1c)

Our goal in this chapter is to make the syntactic behaviour of auxiliary verbs and the range of complementation patterns of lexical verbs as clear as possible. In our discussion of the passive, we attempt to create a balance between two perspectives: (i) the mechanics relating complementation patterns and passive clauses and (ii) the reasons underpinning the choice of a passive rather than active form. This is largely related to discourse (see Chapter 6), which implies that understanding how the passive works requires looking at its use within larger stretches of text.

---

[1]As we will see below, some transitive verbs always require a Direct Object (DO) complement. Many other transitive verbs are compatible with, but do not necessarily require, a DO. For that reason, when considering verbs out of context, it can also be said that a verb licenses (meaning 'is compatible with' or 'permits') complements rather than (obligatorily) requires complements. By saying that the verb *eat* licenses a DO, we account for the fact that both *Have you eaten anything?* and *Have you eaten yet?* are possible. When instantiated in a specific sentence – such as in *Have you eaten anything?* – we will say that the verb *eat* is complemented by a DO.

2. Lexical verbs versus auxiliary verbs

2.1 Introduction

There is a fundamental distinction in English between **lexical verbs** and **auxiliary verbs** (or **auxiliaries**).

Mastering the syntax of auxiliaries is crucial in English since it is at the core of a number of frequent constructions. As we will see in Chapter 4, the tense – aspect system makes wide use of them as well:

- the auxiliary *be* (in conjunction with the *-ing* participle (verb + -ING) of a verb[2]) is the marker for **progressive aspect** (3a)
- the auxiliary *have* (in conjunction with the past participle (verb + -EN) of a verb) is the marker for the **perfect tenses** (3b)
- the auxiliary *be* (in conjunction with the past participle) is also the usual marker for the **passive voice** (3c)

(3) (a) The birds *are* sing*ing*; it must be spring.
(b) Our guests *have arrived* – let's pop open the champagne!
(c) At the beginning of the term, students *are told* to buy the book.

Finally, English makes wide use of **modal auxiliaries** (see Chapter 5):

(4) That *must/can't/might/will* be him.

In the examples in (3), the sentences contain only one auxiliary. A sentence can include more than one auxiliary, however:

(5) He *may have* forgotten his appointment with the doctor. (modal auxiliary, perfect *have*)
He *has been* working a lot lately. (perfect *have*, progressive *be*)
Right now, Jason *is being* interviewed for a position as manager. (progressive *be*, passive *be*)
They *might be* coming along with us. (modal auxiliary, progressive *be*)
He *has been* taken to hospital more than once this semester. (perfect *have*, passive *be*)

If there is more than one auxiliary, the order in which they occur is invariable: modal auxiliary > perfect *have* > progressive *be* > passive *be*. A string of four auxiliaries, while grammatical, is unusual:

---

[2]See footnote 3 in Chapter 4. Instead of 'present participle' and 'gerund', we will use the generic, functionally neutral term *-ing* **participle** to refer to the *-ing* form that verbs take.

(6) A 13-year-old girl who died after falling from a block of flats *may have been being* bullied before her death, it has emerged. (modal auxiliary, perfect *have*, progressive *be*, passive *be*) (www)

What exactly is the distinction between lexical verbs and auxiliaries? One view is that lexical verbs have specific meaning referring to either actions (*eat, work, sleep, play*) or states (*love, consider, know, understand*) while auxiliaries (often called 'helping verbs' – the Latin word *auxiliaris* means 'helpful') constitute a small group of verbs used to convey grammatical meaning of secondary importance. This is an incomplete definition, however. The modal auxiliary *can* in *He can swim* does not convey less meaning than the lexical verb *know* in *He knows how to swim*: each sentence is a very close paraphrase of the other. Instead, we will rely on syntactic rather than semantic criteria to define these two categories of verbs. The generalization that will emerge is that auxiliaries have syntactic properties that lexical verbs do not share.

Lexical verbs form an **open class**, meaning that new members can be added to it infinitely. Think of verbs connected to social media, such as *unlike* or *defriend* – not long ago, these verbs did not exist. The set of auxiliary verbs in English is a **closed class** – it is not possible to add new verbs to it. This closed class includes the auxiliaries *be, have* and *do* (often referred to as the **primary auxiliaries**) as well as the nine central modal auxiliaries *can, could, will, would, shall, should, may, might* and *must*.[3] Syntactically speaking, *be* and the central modal verbs are always auxiliaries.[4] *Have* and *do*, however, can also be lexical verbs, in which case they no longer have the specific properties of auxiliaries. In *She has breakfast in bed on Saturdays* or *He does his homework every afternoon,* have and do do not function as auxiliaries but as lexical verbs, whereas in *She has just finished her breakfast* or *Does he understand the homework?*, they function as auxiliaries.

2.2 Syntactic characteristics of auxiliaries

As we said above, auxiliary verbs have certain properties that lexical verbs do not. Three of these – direct *not*-negation, Subject–auxiliary inversion and ellipsis – are particularly noteworthy. We will discuss each of them in this section.

---

[3]The semantics of modal verbs in English will be treated in Chapter 5. Alongside the central modal auxiliaries is the verb *ought to*, which shares the characteristics of the nine core modal auxiliaries with one exception: it is followed by *to*. *Need* is another modal auxiliary, but its uses are more highly constrained.
[4]Some grammars consider that *be* is not an auxiliary verb when it functions as a **copula** (or **copular verb,** or a **linking verb**), that is, when it is the only verb in the clause and is followed by a Subject Complement (*Jimmie is my brother, Jimmie is always good-humoured.*) Since *be* has all the formal characteristics of an auxiliary in such a context, we classify it as an auxiliary.

2.2.1 Direct not-negation

In English, negation at the level of the clause is achieved through the negative word *not*. If we want to say that {*John – be a doctor*} is not the case, we say *John is **not** a doctor*.[5] Only auxiliaries can be directly negated by *not*. We call this process **direct *not*-negation**:

(7) He *has* not (or *hasn't*) eaten a thing.
    She *does* not (or *doesn't*) eat meat.
    They *will* not (or *won't*) eat sweets.
    *He *eats* not meat.

As the examples in (7) show, most auxiliaries have a special negative form marked by -*n't*. We will call these forms **short negatives**. These are often used instead of the auxiliary followed by the full form *not*. Note that some adverbs with negative or near-negative meaning (e.g. *never, seldom* and *rarely*)[6] are used with lexical verbs as well as with auxiliaries and give a clause negative force:

(8) I will *never* let my children watch television after dinner.
    I *never* let my children watch television after dinner.

2.2.2 Subject-auxiliary inversion

The unmarked position in English for the Subject of a declarative clause is pre-verbal. However, in a number of cases, Subject and verb exchange positions in the sentence. This process requires the presence of an auxiliary; it is therefore called **Subject-auxiliary inversion (Subject-aux inversion)**:

(9)		She	*is*	still living at home.
		Is	she	still living at home?
	Where	*is*	she	living?
		They	*have*	never witnessed such behaviour.
	Never	*have*	they	witnessed such behaviour.
	If	I	*had*	known, I wouldn't have said anything.
		Had	I	known, I wouldn't have said anything.

---

[5]Negation in English – particularly the **scope of negation** (i.e. what part or parts of a sentence fall within the range of negation) – is a complex topic, and we hardly do it justice here. In passing, however, it is important to note that the presence of postverbal *not* does not invariably imply total clausal negation, as might mistakingly be inferred from the pair *John is a doctor / John is not a doctor*, above. *All the students did not pass the exam*, for instance, is ambiguous: it can mean either 'None of the students passed' (clausal negation) or 'Not all of the students passed, but some of them did' (partial negation) (cf. Chapter 3, Section 3; see also Chapter 5 (Section 3, Section 4.2), which treats scope of negation and modal verbs).
[6]Adverbs like *rarely, seldom* and *hardly* are said to be 'near-negative': while they are not straightforwardly negative, they do have a restrictive force (*not usually, not often*).

In English, only auxiliaries can invert with a Subject, which explains why the inverted forms of *be* and *have* in (9) above are grammatical, whereas in (10) below, inverted *lives* and *witnessed* and *knew* are ungrammatical; *live*, *witness* and *know* are lexical verbs:

(10) She *lives* at home.
    *Lives she at home?
    *Where *lives* she?

    They never *witnessed* such behaviour.
    *Never *witnessed* they such behaviour.

    If I *knew* what to say, I'd say something.
    *Knew I what to say, I'd say something.

If there is more than one auxiliary in the sentence, it is only the first that inverts with the Subject:

(11) *Will* they *be* waiting for us at the station?
    *Will be they waiting for us at the station?

The most common use of Subject-aux inversion is in interrogative clauses. The examples in (12) illustrate a few examples of non-interrogative inversion:

(12) **Preposed (near-)negative adverbs**
    Never *have* I been so insulted in my entire life.
    Only rarely *will* she agree to discuss such matters with us.
    No sooner *had* we slipped into bed than the doorbell rang.

    Counterfactual and hypothetical conditionals
    Had they known, they wouldn't have agreed to it.
    Were he to quit his job, he'd never find another one that pays as well.
    Should you need any assistance, please call our toll-free number.

    Exclamations[7]
    Wow, *can* she sing!
    Boy, *will* they be cross when they find out!
    My, *aren't* you a clever one!

---

[7]**Exclamation** is a functional label. We noted in Chapter 1 that the function of an exclamative clause (one that starts with a *wh*-word constituent and has no Subject-aux inversion: *What a talented student he is!*) is to express emotion, a function that could also be captured by the label 'exclamation'. The examples given show that sentence types other than the canonical exclamative can serve this purpose: in these examples, a clause that has an interrogative form is used not to ask a question but to exclaim the speaker's surprise or other emotion.

Affirmative and negative expressions of similarity
Peter can drive, and so *can* his sister.
Margaret won't do it, and neither *will* I.

2.2.3 Ellipsis

After an auxiliary, the rest of the VP can very often be left unexpressed:

(13) (a) *Can* you speak Russian? – Yes, I *can*.
(b) *Can* you speak Russian? – Yes, I *can* speak Russian.

The exchange in (13b) is not ungrammatical, but it is unlikely: communication is often more efficient if obvious information is left out. In some cases, ellipsis is obligatory:

(14) (a) Peter *can* drive, and so *can* his sister.
(b) *Peter *can* drive, and so *can* his sister drive.

Ellipsis is found in a number of extremely common structures which do not necessarily have direct correlates in other languages:

(15) **Short answers and short interrogatives**
(a) *Can* you speak Russian? – Yes, I *can*. *Can* you?
(b) *Is* she coming to the party? – No, she *isn't*. *Are* they?
(c) *Have* they decided yet? – Yes, they *have*. What about Sarah? *Has* she?
(d) *Was* your paper delivered this morning? – Yes, it *was*. *Wasn't* yours?
(e) *Does* she speak Russian? – Yes, she *does*. But *do* her children?
  (*Yes, she speaks. *But speak her children?)

In the above examples with short answers and interrogatives, (15a) has a modal auxiliary, (15b) has the auxiliary *be* used as a progressive aspect marker, (15c) has the auxiliary *have* used as a perfect tense marker and (15d) has the auxiliary *be* used as a passive marker. As is shown in (15e), ellipsis is not possible with a lexical verb such as *speak*. In contexts like these, a form of auxiliary *do* is required (see **do-insertion** in Section 2.3). A similar construction, which we will discuss below, is the tag. We refer to these as **interrogative tags:**[8]

(16) **Interrogative tags**
(a) But you *can* speak Russian, *can't* you?
(b) She*'s* coming to the party, *isn't* she?

---

[8]Interrogative tags are sometimes called **question tags** or **tag questions**. As explained in Chapter 1, the term *question* is a functional label while the term *interrogative* is a formal label. This explains why we prefer to use 'interrogative tag': it is indicative of a structural characteristic (with the auxiliary preceding the Subject) and does not specify the range of functions it can have.

(c) They *haven't* decided yet, *have* they?
(d) Your paper *was* delivered this morning, *wasn't* it?
(e) She *speaks* Russian, *doesn't* she?
   (*She speaks Russian, speaks she not?)

The above tags are all elliptical in the sense that everything following the auxiliary (including the lexical verb) is left unexpressed.

Ellipsis contributes greatly to overall **cohesion** in the context of wider written and spoken **discourse**. We address this in Chapter 6 (Section 2.1). For the time being, note that a variety of other, less easily categorized structures make use of ellipsis, as the examples in (17) show. Note too that, in an exchange, it is not necessarily the same auxiliary that is used in the follow-up:

(17) Why *don't* you ask Mary to help you? – Brilliant idea. I *will*.
I think you'*ll* love the film. If you *don't*, I'll be surprised.
Why *don't* you buy a new car? – I *would* if I *could*. But I *can't*, so I *won't*.

2.3 Syntactic restrictions on lexical verbs: *do*-insertion

It should now be clear that direct *not*-negation, inversion and ellipsis require an auxiliary. Given the mechanics of the verbal system of English, this is in many cases straightforward:

(18) She *is* coming tomorrow. (She *isn't* coming tomorrow. *Is* she coming tomorrow?)
They'*d* been working extremely hard, *hadn't* they? (They certainly *had*.)
Some problems *were* solved, but others *weren't*.

Sometimes, however, there is no auxiliary. In this case, English makes use of a device called **do-insertion**. This essentially involves adding *do/does* (present) or *did* (past) when the clause does not contain an auxiliary. This is precisely what occurs with non-progressive present and past tenses:

(19) Students today *don't* take as many exams as in my day.
*Students today take not as many exams as in my day.

How *did* he occupy himself when he wasn't at work?
*How occupied he himself when he wasn't at work?

Only rarely *do* I appreciate that sort of dark, morbid humour.
*Only rarely appreciate I that sort of dark, morbid humour.

My sister always says exactly what she thinks, and so *do* I.
*My sister always says exactly what she thinks, and so say I.

When *do* is used in the context of inversion, it is called **periphrastic *do***.

Do-insertion has so far been presented as a means of enabling the processes of negation, inversion and ellipsis to take place in the absence of an auxiliary. In fact, this characterization of *do*-insertion as a rescue device is incomplete; *do*-insertion can be used not only to satisfy a syntactic requirement, but also in affirmative declarative clauses, where it fulfils a variety of discursive functions. This use of *do* is often called **emphatic**:

(20) John certainly *does know* how to throw a party. I had a great time.

The inserted *do* here is different from the examples in (19) in that it is not syntactically required: *John certainly knows how to throw a party* is equally possible as the unmarked version of (20). Often, *do*-insertion in affirmative declarative clauses serves to point to a contrast rather than to emphasize something. When there is contrastive meaning, it is often used in conjunction with a negative element or a preceding or following expression of concession:

(21) [E]ven if the Google data does not imply that boyfriends are really twice as likely to avoid sex as girlfriends, it *does suggest* that boyfriends avoiding sex is more common than people let on. (www)

Significant parts of Mr Rose's evidence were heard in closed court, because of commercially sensitive matters. However, he *did admit* that Compaq had enjoyed a 'significantly lower price' for Windows compared with other PC makers [...]. (www)

The verb *do* is only an auxiliary when it is the result of *do*-insertion, be it as a syntactic requirement or to fulfil a function in the discourse. Otherwise, it is a lexical verb like any other: *do the washing up, do the dishes, do one's homework, do someone a favour, do the housework, do one's best, do business* and *do a course (in journalism, in fashion design)* are only a few expressions that make use of lexical *do*. Lexical *do* cannot invert or be directly negated. Nor is it used in elliptical contexts. In all three cases, *do*-insertion is required. In the following examples, auxiliary *do* is in italics and lexical *do* is underlined:

(22) In this country, young men *don't* do military service any more.
What *does* he do with himself in his free time?
Only rarely *do* I do the housework at the weekend.
My sister always does as she pleases, and so *do* I.
I would support the proliferation of CCTV cameras if they actually did what they were supposed to do [...]. They haven't. What they *do* do is manage to catch normally law-abiding people and prosecute them. (www)

2.4 *Have*: auxiliary or lexical verb?

Have is always an auxiliary when used as a tense marker in perfect tenses (*has he left?*, *they hadn't been working*); otherwise, *have* nearly always behaves as a lexical verb.[9] Like lexical *do*, lexical *have* is quite common. Some typical expressions with lexical *have* are given in (23). Here, *have* is often called a **light verb**. Other light verbs include *do, give, make* and *take*. Light verbs contribute very little content of their own. Their meaning is interpreted as a function of the NPs that follow them. Note, too, that the examples in (23) all refer to dynamic situations, which means they are compatible with *progressive aspect – I'm having breakfast; she's having a drink* (see Chapter 4, Section 2.2.3):

(23) *have* [=eat] breakfast (lunch, dinner, a snack, a bite to eat …)
    have a drink
    have a long walk (a quick run, a swim …)
    have [= give birth to] a baby
    have a look around
    have [= smoke] a cigarette
    have [= host] a party
    have a wonderful (really good, terrible) time

Since *have* in the examples in (23) is a lexical verb on a par with any other lexical verb, it cannot be directly negated with *not*, invert or be used in elliptical structures; rather, it relies on *do*-insertion:

(24) I *have* breakfast every morning, even if I'm not hungry.
    I *don't have* breakfast unless I'm particularly hungry.
    *I *haven't* breakfast unless I'm particularly hungry.

    He *had* a cigarette before going back to work.
    Did he *have* a cigarette before going back to work?
    **Had* he a cigarette before going back to work?

    She had a baby last month, *didn't* she? – Yes, she *did*.
    *She had a baby last month, *hadn't* she? – *Yes, she *had*.

---

[9]Although comparatively uncommon, *have* sometimes behaves as an auxiliary even when it is not a tense marker for the perfect tenses:
    Have you the time?
      (cf. *Do* you *have* the time? or *Have* you *got* the time?)
    She *hasn't* the slightest idea what happened.
      (cf. She *doesn't have* the slightest idea. or She *hasn't got* the slightest idea.)
Many consider this somewhat old-fashioned, and it is rare in North American English and among younger speakers. It is always possible to use lexical *have* or *have got* instead.

When lexical *have* expresses meaning associated with (for example) possession, physical description, family relationships or physical ailments or illnesses, the situations referred to are not dynamic, and progressive aspect is not possible (*I'm having a car*; *he's having long hair*). A specificity of these non-dynamic uses of lexical *have* is that it is also possible to use the verbal expression *have got*:

(25) *have* a car (a house, a new PC ...)
      have (the) time to do something
      have straight (long, brown, curly ...) hair
      have blue (grey, hazel, beautiful ...) eyes
      have a younger sister (an older brother, a stepfather ...)
      have a headache ((a) toothache, (the) flu, cancer, a cold ...)
      have a certain mystique (ring, charm, aura ...) to it
      have a lot of patience
      have a brilliant idea
      have a sour (bitter, sweet, funny, strange ...) taste
      have some cash (a credit card, a cigarette lighter, a fiver ...) on you

When *have got* is used, *have* is an auxiliary, which means that *do*-insertion is not required or possible.[10] Direct negation is possible; *have* can invert with the Subject and it can be used in elliptical constructions:

(26) She *has got* long black hair.

      She *hasn't got* long black hair.
      (*She doesn't have got long black hair.)
      (cf. She *doesn't have* long black hair.)

      Has she *got* long black hair?
      (*Does she have got long black hair?)
      (cf. *Does* she *have* long black hair?)

Have got has the same meaning as lexical *have*: we recognize no fundamental difference in meaning between *She has a headache* and *She's got a headache*. *Have got*, furthermore, is only used in the present. Any other form – the past tense, for instance – uses *have* and not *have got*:

(27) She *had* a headache. *She *had got* a headache.
      Did she *have* a headache? *Had* she *got* a headache?

---

[10]The modal verb *have to* (*You have to hand in your essay by Tuesday*) also alternates with *have got to* (*You have got to hand in your essay by Tuesday*).

Have + got can be the source of confusion, since *got* is also the past participle of the verb *get*. This means that *have/has* and *had* followed by *got* also correspond to the present perfect and past perfect tenses of the verb *get*:

> (28) He *has* (just) *got* a letter from the university he applied to and is too nervous to open it. (present perfect of *get*, with the meaning of 'receive')
> (cf. He *has (got)* a letter to show you – he's received a scholarship. (*have got* = the present of the verb 'have'))

> (29) Only two days before, he *had got* a nasty e-mail from his boss. (past perfect of *get*, with the meaning of 'receive')

When in doubt, a useful strategy is to reserve auxiliary *have* for perfect tenses (as in *He has arrived*) and to use lexical *have* in all other cases, even where (auxiliary) *have + got* is possible (as in the examples in (25) and (26)).

2.5 Contraction and weak forms

In spoken English, many auxiliaries have both a strong form and a weak form. The modal *can*, for instance, can be pronounced either /kæn/ (the strong form) or /kən/; *have* and *has* have both the strong forms /hæv/ and /hæz/ and (mainly when they are used as auxiliaries) the weak forms /əv/ and /əz/. The choice between a strong and weak form of an auxiliary is governed by both syntactic and semantic criteria. The example in (30a) shows that reduced forms do not occur when followed by a gap corresponding to ellipted VP, and (30b) shows that a strong form is required in an emphatic context:

> (30) (a) Can (/kæn/, /kən/) you swim? – I can (/kæn/, */kən/), but not very well.
> (b) You'd understand if you'd read the book. – But I have (/hæv/, */əv/) read it!

Furthermore, many auxiliaries – the primary auxiliaries, especially – have a contracted form. Contracted forms are essentially weak forms that have conventional, standard written forms. All present forms of *be* can be contracted (*I am → I'm; they are → they're*); the past forms *was* and *were*, however, do not have written contracted forms. Both the present and the past of *have* (*have/has, had*) have contracted forms (*you have → you've; she has → she's; they had → they'd*).[11] Neither the present nor the past forms of *do* have accepted contracted forms,

---

[11]When *have* is a lexical rather than an auxiliary verb, the contracted forms are less commonly used. When they are, it is usually in combination with the first-person Subject *I*: *I have a headache* is more frequent than *I've a headache*.

although weak forms are not uncommon in casual speech.[12] As for the modals, only *will* (and, to a lesser extent, *shall*) and *would* have written contracted forms: *we will* → *we'll; they would* → *they'd*. Note that *would* and auxiliary *had* both contract to *'d* and that *has* and *is* both contract to *'s*:

(31) She's studying French at university. (< she *is*)
She's already studied French for several years. (< she *has*)

(32) They'd come if they had the time. (< they *would*)
They'd come once before and so they knew their way round. (< they *had*)

When the auxiliaries *be* and *have* are negated, forms with either a short negative auxiliary (*he isn't; I haven't*) or contracted auxiliary (*he's not; I've not*) are possible. On the whole, the short negative auxiliaries are more common. In spoken English, short negative forms of modal auxiliaries followed by a contracted form of *have* are common. They can be found written as well as in casual or informal registers:

(33) I *wouldn't've* come if I'd known. (< I *would not have*)
They *shouldn't've* said that. (< they *should not have*)
She *won't've* finished before Monday. (< she *will not have*)

3. Interrogative clauses and tags

Having discussed the characteristics of lexical verbs and explored the mechanics of auxiliaries, we now turn to **interrogative clauses**. The presence or absence of inversion plays an important role in this clause type. An interrogative clause (or IC) is a form, the main function of which is to ask a question. We will see that there are two types of IC, and that each type of IC can be a main clause or a subclause. This distinction is important insofar as the presence or absence of inversion is largely determined by whether an IC is a main clause or a subclause.

Not all languages make use of a syntactically different form to ask a question. In some languages, a declarative clause gets the force of a question simply through rising intonation. Intonation is important for English interrogative clauses, too: *Are you hungry?* has a strong tendency for rising intonation whereas *What would*

---

[12]The contracted forms of *does* (*'s*) and *did* (*'d*) are not uncommon in spoken language, and their written forms can occasionally be found as well. They are only used (i) when they are inverted with the Subject and (ii) when they immediately follow a *wh*-expression (*where, what, who, how* etc.): *Where's he live? What's he do? Who'd he see? How'd he do it?* Many people will avoid using these forms in writing since they are not part of more standard written contractions. Awareness that such forms exist in colloquial speech is useful, however.

you like to eat? does not. But ICs in English additionally have a specific syntactic form which makes them different from declarative clauses: it is via an IC like *Is he Hungarian?* rather than the declarative *He's Hungarian?* that we ask a question.

3.1 Two major types of interrogative clauses

There are two basic IC types. The first type is often called a **yes-no interrogative clause**: *yes* or *no* is the only possible answer.[13] This clause type can also be referred to as a **total interrogative** (the scope of the interrogation is the entire clause rather than just one part of it) or a **closed interrogative** (the number of answers is limited to two):

(34) *Has she* accepted the position?   – Yes./Yes, she has.
     (cf. *She has* accepted the position.)
     Are you married?   – No./No, I'm not.
     (cf. *You are* married.)
     Do they understand the question?   – No./No, they don't.
     (cf. *They understand* the question.)
     Did you tell him about?   – Yes./Yes, I did.
     (cf. *You told* him about it.)

The defining feature of a yes-no IC is that the Subject and auxiliary are inverted. This is highlighted via italics in the examples in (34) (compare to the absence of inversion in the corresponding declarative clauses). In line with the general principles described in 2.2, *do*-insertion is required when there is no auxiliary to invert.

The examples in (34) are affirmative clauses, but yes-no ICs can be negative as well. They are noteworthy because they have a special kind of meaning. More specifically, a negative yes-no IC is often understood as a cue to an expectation on the part of the speaker:

(35) (a) *Are* you going to Greece this August?
     (b) *Is* the wine to your liking?

     (c) *Aren't* you going to Greece this August?
     (d) *Isn't* this wine superb?

In (35a) and (35b), the speaker does not show any expectation that 'yes' or 'no' will be the answer. The negative yes-no ICs in (35c) and (35d), however, suggest an assumption on the part of the speaker. In the case of (35c), the speaker

---

[13]Asked such a question, a speaker might also say 'Of course', 'I don't think so' or 'That's none of your business'. These are **responses**, but not answers. This is why it is possible to say that a yes-no interrogative clause allows only two possible answers.

perhaps remembers previously being told about a trip to Greece but she has come to wonder whether this trip will actually be taking place: she expects clarification on the part of the hearer. In (35d), the expectation is of a quite different kind. Here the speaker expects that the hearer will agree with her. The sentence serves the more social function of drawing the hearer further into the shared enjoyment of the wine.

Negative yes-no ICs are sometimes used to formulate a request. The negation has the effect here of making the request more pressing and reveals a speaker's hope or expectation that the answer will be 'yes'. They leave less room for a refusal and therefore serve as a strategy to put pressure on the hearer to go along with the speaker's request or suggestion:

> (36) *Won't* you come in for a drink?
> *Wouldn't* your parents like to stay with us for the weekend?

A negative yes-no IC can also convey frustration:

> (37) *Can't* you help me do the washing up for once?

The second type of IC is called an **information interrogative** or a ***wh*-interrogative**, so called because many interrogative elements in English begin with the letters *wh*. Here, *yes* or *no* is not a possible answer – the answer provides the information that the speaker is missing. For this reason, this type of interrogative can also be called a **partial interrogative** (the scope of the interrogation is limited to part of the clause) or an **open interrogative** (any number of answers are possible):

> (38) <u>Who</u> has he invited?   – His colleagues.
> (cf. He has invited <u>his colleagues</u>.)
> <u>Where</u> are you going?   – To the staffroom.
> (cf. You are going <u>to the staffroom</u>.)
> <u>When</u> does her train get in?   – This afternoon.
> (cf. Her train gets in <u>this afternoon</u>.)
> <u>Why</u> did they hire her?   – Because of her skills.
> (cf. They hired her <u>because of her skills</u>.)
> <u>How old</u> is your father-in-law?   – Seventy-two.
> (cf. My father-in-law is <u>seventy-two</u>.)
> <u>What</u> are you looking for?   – My mobile.
> (cf. You are looking for <u>your mobile</u>.)

There are four things to notice in the above examples: (i) information ICs, like yes-no ICs, are characterized by Subject-aux inversion (a notable exception being *wh*-Subject ICs, discussed below); (ii) *do*-insertion is used when needed; (iii) an IC clause is always introduced by a *wh*-expression; and (iv) the *wh*-expression occurs in initial position whereas the unmarked position of the corresponding constituent in a declarative is after the verb (unless that constituent functions as Subject). To get a feel for this, compare the underlined elements above in the ICs and declarative versions that follow them.

The difference in meaning between a yes-no IC and a *wh*-IC can thus be captured as follows: while in the examples in (34) the speaker wants to find out whether the relation between the Subject and the predicate ({*she – accept the position*}, {*you – be married*}, {*they – understand the question*} and {*you – tell him about it*}) is valid in the relevant time-sphere, her interest in the examples in (38) does not bear on the Subject-predicate relation as such. Rather, the speaker is looking for information about a subpart of the clause: the name or identity of someone (who?), the place (where?), the time (when?), the reason or purpose (why?) and so on.

There are nine basic interrogative **wh-words** used to form *wh*-ICs in English. Four of them (*where, when, why* and *how*) mainly function as Adjuncts; they can also function as Subject Complements (SC) in an IC. Crucially, though, they never function as Subject. The remaining five (*who, what, which, how many/how much* and *whose*) can – though do not always – function as Subjects. This distinction is important for the following reason: if the **wh-constituent** functions as the Subject of the IC, there is no inversion. Consequently, *do*-insertion is not necessary. The result is that the word order is identical to that of a declarative clause, with the Subject preceding the verb. In (39), all Subjects are underlined:

(39) <u>Which candidate</u> is leading in the polls?
        which candidate = Subject; no inversion
        cf. <u>The Green candidate</u> is leading in the polls.
    Which candidate *are* <u>they</u> backing?
        which candidate = DO; inversion

    <u>Who</u> met him in town last night?
        who = Subject; no inversion
        cf. <u>Matthew</u> met him in town last night.
    Who(m) *did* <u>he</u> see in town last night?
      who(m) = DO; inversion

    <u>What</u> is usually served for breakfast?
        what = Subject; no inversion
        cf. <u>Bread</u> is usually served for breakfast.
    What *do* <u>you</u> usually have for breakfast?
        what = DO; inversion

You may have noticed that all of our examples of ICs have thus far been main clauses. ICs can be subclauses as well, however. In this case, they usually function as the Direct Object (DO) of a main clause. The embedded ICs in the examples below are underlined:

(40) I wonder <u>which candidate they are backing</u>.
      Do you know <u>who he saw in town last night</u>?
      Tell me <u>what you usually have for breakfast</u>.[14]

What is noteworthy about the embedded *wh*-ICs above is that they are formed without inversion (and, accordingly, without *do*-insertion) in spite of the fact that the *wh*-constituents do not function as Subjects in the embedded IC. (They function as DO in the subclause.) Inversion, akin to what we find in a corresponding main clause IC, renders these ICs ungrammatical:

(41) *I wonder which candidate are they backing.
      (cf. Which candidate are they backing?)
      *Do you know who did he see in town last night?
      (cf. Who did he see in town last night?)
      *Tell me what do you usually have for breakfast.
      (cf. What do you usually have for breakfast?)

The examples in (42) also contain *wh*-ICs that are embedded in a main clause and that function as DO. Unlike in the examples in (41), however, the *wh*-constituents in (42) function as Subjects in the embedded IC. There is no inversion in the embedded *wh*-IC of this type either. However, there is little room for confusion here since the corresponding main clause interrogative does not have inversion either:

(42) I wonder <u>which candidate is leading in the polls</u>.
      (cf. Which candidate is leading in the polls?)
      Do you know <u>who met him in town last night</u>?
      (cf. Who met him in town last night?)
      Tell me <u>what is usually served for breakfast</u>.
      (cf. What is usually served for breakfast?)

When the embedded interrogative is a yes-no interrogative, it begins with the conjunction *if* or *whether* and is followed by the Subject and VP without inversion:

---

[14]In addition to the function of DO in (40) and (41) and Subject in (42), the *wh*-constituent in an IC which is a subclause can have other functions within the subclause. Compare the following to (38):
  Tell us <u>*how old* your father-in-law is</u>? (Subject Complement)
  Just tell me <u>*what* you are looking for</u>. (Object of a Preposition)
  Do you know <u>*when* her train gets in</u>? (Adjunct)
  I wonder <u>*why* they hired her</u>? (Adjunct)

(43) Please tell me if (whether) you will be able to come.
   *Please tell me will you be able to come.
   (cf. Will you be able to come?)

   I wonder if (whether) he likes his new position.
   *I wonder does he like his new position?
   (cf. Does he like his new position?)

   I don't know if (whether) they understood what I meant.
   *I don't know did they understand what I meant.
   (cf. Did they understand what I meant?)

Taking stock of all this, we can now describe the differences between the syntactic facts described concerning *wh*-ICs. We can observe that

- in main clauses, *wh*-expressions that do not function as Subject will always trigger inversion;
- *wh*-expressions that function as Subject do not trigger inversion;
- regardless of the function of the *wh*-expression, there is no Subject-aux inversion when the interrogative is embedded within a main clause – put in another way, ICs that are subclauses do not make use of inversion.

We mentioned above that there are nine basic interrogative *wh*-words used to form *wh*-interrogatives in English. Many of them are straightforward. Others require a few explanatory comments:

- We saw above that *what* can function as Subject (*What happened?*) or DO (*What did you see?*). It is also the form used to focus the interrogation on the entire VP: *What are you doing?* The function in a corresponding declarative clause is the entire predicate. As a determiner, *what* competes with *which* (see below).
- When *how* is an adverb of manner, it is used on its own. It means 'in what way?' or 'using what means?': *How do you spell your last name? How did you get here? How* can also be followed by an adjective or an adverb, in which case it means 'to what degree': *How tall is your father? How fast can he run?*[15]
- *Who* versus *whom* is a good example of a case where ordinary usage and prescriptive rules do not really match up. Traditionally, *who* is reserved for an interrogative Subject (*Who came? – Henry.*) or Subject Complement (SC) (*Who's Henry? – He's the one on the left.*) and *whom* for an interrogative DO (*Whom did he phone?*) or an Object of a Preposition (*With whom did she*

---

[15]In fact, when used as an adverb of manner and especially when used with *be*, *how* has meanings that go beyond the simple glosses we've given: *How are you? How is your father's health? How was the film?* obviously cannot be paraphrased by 'in what way', or 'using what means?'.

come? Whom did she come with?).[16] This distinction is largely ignored in modern English: there is a strong tendency to use *who* regardless of its function: *Who came?* (Subject), *Who did you invite?* (DO), *Who did she come with?* (Object of a Preposition). An important exception: when it immediately follows a preposition, *whom*, and not *who*, is usual.[17]

- Sometimes both *which* and *what* are possible with no fundamental difference in meaning: *Which cities/What cities have you been to in Italy?* However, when there is a pre-established, limited set of referents to choose from, *which* is usually used (and usually considered to be the more correct): *I'm hesitating between the blue tie and the red one. Which one should I buy?* (= 'which tie from this set of two ties?').

- *How many* and *how much* are used to ask about the quantity (number or amount) of the noun that follows. Only the status of the following noun as countable or non-countable conditions the choice between the two: *How many tables are there? How much furniture is there?* (We discuss the countable/uncountable dichotomy in greater detail in Chapter 3.)

- The *wh*-word *whose* is the interrogative possessive determiner or pronoun that corresponds to the possessive determiners (*my, your, his, her, its, our, their*) and possessive pronouns (*mine, yours, his, hers, ours, theirs*). Other languages do not necessarily have a direct equivalent to *whose*. (If you speak a language other than English, ask yourself how you would say *Whose watch is this?* in that language.)

In Table 2.1, we illustrate the different types of ICs we have discussed. The overview brings out the similarities and differences among the different types: +/– Subject-aux inversion and, depending on the form of the verb used, +/– *do*-insertion.

As seen in Section 2.3, *do*-insertion can be used for discursive rather than syntactic reasons. Given an appropriate context, *do*-insertion is not uncommon in cases where the above generalizations might lead you to believe it is not used. You can compare the following examples to those in (39) above:

(44) So who did shoot the doorman? Mystery surrounds [...] shooting after acquittals (www)
Just what does happen after the drama of election night? We asked three novice MPs to let us in on the behind the scenes intrigue as they start one of the hardest jobs in the country. (www)

---

[16]Note that in *Whom did she come with?* the Object of the Preposition *whom* has been moved from the PrepP *with whom* (cf. She came *with John*).

[17]Even the rule prescribing the use of *whom* after a preposition is not quite accurate. Short, non-clausal questions especially seem to violate this rule quite easily in colloquial spoken English: *I went to the movies this morning. – Oh really? With who?* (or even *Who with?*).

Table 2.1 Interrogative clauses

Interrogative main clauses		
yes/no interrogative	_wh-interrogative (non-Subject wh-constituent)_	_wh-interrogative (wh-constituent = Subject)_
Did you see anyone last night? Are you seeing anyone tonight?	Who did you see last night? Who are you seeing tonight?	Who saw you last night? Who is seeing you tonight?
Interrogative subclauses (embedded clauses)		
yes/no interrogative	_wh-interrogative (non-Subject wh-constituent)_	_wh-interrogative (wh-constituent = Subject)_
I wonder if (whether) he saw anyone last night.	I wonder who he saw last night.	I wonder who saw him last night.
Do you know if (whether) he is seeing anyone tonight?	Do you know who he is seeing tonight?	Do you know who is seeing him tonight?

3.2 Echo questions

Thus far, we have implicitly shown that, like any other phrase, a _wh_-constituent always has a function within the sentence such as Subject, SC, DO or Adjunct:

(45) [Who]'s coming to the party?   Subject
[What]'s the occasion?   SC
[Who(m)] did you invite?   DO
[What time] will they be getting here? Adjunct

We have highlighted that the _wh_-constituent must be put in clause-initial position in a _wh_-IC. Bearing in mind the discussion in Chapter 1, it will be clear that the usual place for the constituents functioning as SCs, DOs and Adjuncts in a declarative clause is elsewhere in the clause:

(46) The occasion is [my sister's wedding anniversary/what].   SC
You invited [your parents-in-law/who(m)].   DO
They will be getting here [at around 8 pm/what time]?[18]   Adjunct

There is one case – which we have already alluded to several times – where a _wh_-constituent is found not fronted but in the position it would ordinarily occupy were it not a _wh_-constituent. This is commonly called an **echo question**:

---

[18]Note that, while the interrogative PrepP [_at what time_] is possible (and, given the answer 'at around 8 pm', is expected) to inquire about the time, the _wh_-constituent most ordinarily used in English is the NP [_what time_]. This is also true when the interrogative is embedded, as in _Do you know what time he's coming?_

(47) Last night, we had moose for dinner. – You had *what*?! (cf. What did you have?) (*what* is a DO)

He called me at 3 this morning. – He called you *when*?! (cf. When did he call you?) (*when* is an Adjunct)

They called me stupid. – They called you *what*?! (cf. What did they call you?) (*what* is an OC)

She gave *her little girl* a cigarette. – She gave *who* a cigarette?! (cf. Who did she give it to?) (*who* is an IO)

The above sentences are in fact declarative clauses with a *wh*-constituent *in situ*, meaning it is found in its default position and not at the beginning of the clause as in an IC. Declarative clauses with the *wh*-constituent *in situ* are commonly used in two circumstances: (i) to request the speaker to repeat – or 'echo' – the information because it was simply not understood the first time round; or (ii) to express surprise. Echo questions have rising intonation.

A declarative clause without a *wh*-constituent can also function as a (yes-no) echo question. Intonation – and, nearly always, the absence of Subject-aux inversion – signals an echo question as such. A yes-no echo question is really only used to express surprise:

(48) I'm going to Alaska for a month. – You're going to Alaska? Amazing!

This concludes our discussion of interrogative clauses. We will now move on to a related structure relying on auxiliaries and Subject-aux inversion called the tag.

3.3 Tags

Interrogative tags (as in *You're John's brother,* <u>aren't you</u>?) provide an interesting case study of the interaction between syntax and intonation. An interrogative tag is a short, elliptical IC immediately following an affirmative or negative declarative clause. The tag uses the same auxiliary as in that clause, with obligatory *do*-insertion if the main clause does not have an auxiliary. The Subject is always a personal pronoun or *there*; full NPs are not found in interrogative tags. In the most common type of interrogative tag, we observe a phenomenon called **reverse polarity** – if the clause is affirmative, the tag is negative and if the clause is negative, the tag is affirmative. This principle is illustrated in the following examples:

(49) **Affirmative main clause – negative tag**
She's already started school, hasn't she?
Megan's already started school, hasn't she?

Megan's already started school, *hasn't Megan?
She's already started school, *hasn't Megan?

Negative main clause – affirmative tag
Megan has*n't* already started school, has she?

Predictably, *do*-support is required for non-progressive present and past tenses:

(50) They arrived last night, didn't they?
You eat meat, don't you?

As we already noted in (31) and (32), contracted auxiliaries can represent different full forms. The examples in (51) show that *'s* can be the contracted form of *is* or *has*:

(51) Phil's work*ing* late tonight, isn't he/*hasn't he?
Phil's work*ed* weekends before, though, hasn't he/*isn't he?

The auxiliaries are especially easy to confuse in the case of *'d < had/would* when the verb in the main clause has an irregular past participle identical to the verb base, such as *come, cost, let, put* or *hit*:

(52) You'd *put* your name on the waiting list, hadn't you?
You'd *put* your name on the waiting list (if there were one), wouldn't you?
It'd *cost* less than the previous year, hadn't it?
It'd *cost* less if production were local, wouldn't it?

A number of negative elements other than *not* result in a negative clause; accordingly, an affirmative tag is necessary. These include not only *never, neither, nobody* and *nothing* but also near-negative items (see Section 2.2.1) such as *scarcely, barely, hardly, hardly ever, rarely* and *seldom*.

(53) They'll never be taken seriously, will they? (*won't they?)
We can hardly blame him, can we? (*can't we?)
Nobody's perfect, are they? (*aren't they?)

Finally, there are a couple of unpredictable tags, including tags following imperatives or *let*'s:

(54) But I'm still allowed to enrol, *aren't* I? (*amn't I?)
Close the window, *will* you/*won't* you/*can* you?
Let's continue our visit of the grounds, *shall* we?

The intonation of interrogative tags is also an aspect that requires special attention – an interrogative tag has either a rising or a falling intonation, and the choice communicates different kinds of meaning with respect to the clause preceding it. The general function of an interrogative tag is to elicit some sort of reaction from the hearer with respect to information contained in the preceding clause. Take a look at the following four examples:

(55) (a) Is Marie-Hélène Belgian⇑?
    (b) Marie-Hélène is Belgian⇓.
    (c) Marie-Hélène is Belgian, isn't she⇑?
    (d) Marie-Hélène is Belgian, isn't she⇓?

In (55a), we have a straightforward yes-no IC: the speaker is not likely to be surprised by an answer of 'yes' or 'no', since she has no expectations. The intonation is rising. In (55b), the speaker states what she knows or claims to know. Via this declarative clause, she asserts that the predicative relationship {*Marie-Hélène – be Belgian*} holds. The intonation is falling. In both (55c) and (55d), we find an intersection between what we have in (55a) and (55b): the speaker both establishes a predicative relationship and questions the validity of that predication. When she uses (55c) (rising intonation), she is more or less certain that what she is saying is true, and yet there remains a doubt. In (55d) (falling intonation), the speaker is not so much asking for confirmation as she is establishing some common ground for what is to come next in the exchange. In essence, then, (55c) is akin to (55a) whereas (55d) is akin to (55b). The corresponding intonation patterns only confirm this.

In certain contexts, the difference between rising and falling intonation is particularly clear. When on a warm summer day a speaker says *It's a beautiful day, isn't it*⇓?, falling intonation is more likely than rising: the speaker has no doubt concerning the weather and simply wants the hearer to agree with her. No answer per se is expected. Indeed, the speaker's aim may simply be to draw the hearer into the conversation. Conversely, if she says *You haven't seen my glasses, have you*⇑?, rising intonation is likely – she considers it possible that the hearer knows where her glasses are and formulates a question in a way that is somewhat less direct than *Do you know where my glasses are?* She does expect an answer, though.

The reverse polarity tag described above is by and large the most common. But 'affirmative–affirmative' tags, without reverse polarity, are sometimes used as well. This is called **constant polarity**. They usually serve to convey some sort of emotion and consequently have a strong affective charge to them not found in the canonical tags above. The emotion expressed can range from interest to surprise to irony, or even indignation. Given the communicative effects, it is somewhat unexpected that these tags have rising intonation:

(56) You're a famous actor, *are you*⇗? Then why have I never heard of you?
So, he's filed for divorce, *has he*⇗? Fine. He'll be hearing from my lawyer
soon enough.

In the first part of this chapter, we discussed the distinction between lexical verbs and auxiliaries in detail and showed how their syntactic behaviour is different. This has an effect on negative sentences, interrogative clauses (including tags) and ellipsis. In the next section, we leave the syntax of auxiliaries behind and zoom in on lexical verbs to show how they sometimes call for the addition of constituents other than the Subject in order to be used grammatically. We refer to this requirement by means of the label **complementation**.

4. Complementation of lexical verbs

Our choice of the term **complementation** highlights the following observation: depending on their lexical content, verbs may require certain elements (or **complements**) to be expressed in order for their meaning to be complete. In other words, they cannot be used in a grammatical way unless they are used with (or **complemented by**) constituents other than the Subject. Other verbs disallow complements of any kind.

All sentences have a Subject,[19] but there is some variety concerning the constituents that can or must be used when building a sentence around a lexical verb. A verb's core meaning itself already reveals to a certain extent how many participants it requires in addition to the obligatory Subject. Inherent in the verb *send*, for instance, is the notion that someone is sending something to someone. *Smile*, on the other hand, does not evoke any another necessary participant besides the Subject referent. Complements are very regularly NPs, but our discussion will progressively reveal that PrepPs and clauses can complement verbs as well.

Lexical verbs can be **intransitive, transitive** or **ditransitive**. We will describe each type in the section that follows.

4.1 Intransitive, transitive and ditransitive verbs

The sentences in (57) contain lexical verbs which require nothing more than a Subject. Such verbs are said to be **intransitive**:

---

[19]Imperative clauses do not have an overt Subject. Even though it is not overtly expressed, one might argue that it is implicitly present. (*Come here! (You come here!)*)

(57) We must be *leaving*.
I really have to *go*.

This does mean that intransitive verbs cannot be followed by other constituents in the sentence; *from inside his cradle, after many years of illness* and *because of the heat* in (58), however, are not complements – they are Adjuncts:

(58) Henry *smiled* from inside his cradle.
The old man *died* after many years of illness.
The young man *fainted* because of the heat.

The intransitive verbs *leave, go, smile, die* and *faint* cannot take a DO or an IO.[20] Other such verbs include *appear, arrive, collapse, come, cough, cry, deteriorate, disappear, emerge, fall, happen, laugh, lie, occur, recede, remain, rise, sleep, sneeze, stay, swim* and *vanish*. We will see that intransitive verbs cannot be used in the passive voice.

The verbs in (59), conversely, require a DO:

(59) I *like* detective novels from the 1930s. (cf. *I *like*.)
She *wants* a second opinion. (cf. *She *wants*.)
They *need* our help and support. (cf. *They *need*.)

Verbs such as *like, want* and *need* are **transitive**: as shown above, without a DO the sentences are ungrammatical. The same can be said for verbs such as *admire, carry, catch, face, love, hate* and *throw*.

Finally, the examples in (60) require both a DO and an IO; the verbs *hand* and *give* are said to be **ditransitive**:

(60) Sarah *handed* Brian the parcel./She *handed* the parcel to Brian.
(cf. *Sarah *handed* Brian./*Sarah *handed* the parcel./*Sarah *handed* to Brian.)

We'll *give* them the leftover food./We'll *give* the leftover food to them.
(cf. *We'll *give* them./*We'll *give* the leftover food./*We'll *give* to them.)

Verbs that are always ditransitive form a very small class in English. Other examples include *land* (*The hit song landed her a record deal*) and *award* (*The*

---

[20]We are interested here in establishing the basic patterns of transitivity. We will not address more peripheral cases where an ordinarily intransitive verb such as *die* or *smile* can occur with a cognate Direct Object (i.e. with a DO of the same word family as the verb): *He died a tragic death. She smiled her radiant smile.* Neither will we address what is sometimes called the resultative construction, as in *I smiled my way into their good graces.* While it is important to be aware of these possibilities, mastering the basic patterns of complementation outlined in this section is a good starting point.

judge awarded them compensation). Most transitive and ditransitive verbs can be used in the passive voice.[21]

In reality, lexical verbs do not always fall into tidy categories. It is very often the case that a verb can have different complementation patterns. For example, many transitive verbs can be used without a DO complement. In this case, we can say that a (normally) transitive verb is being **used intransitively**:

> (61) I'd like to eat something before we set out.
> Don't talk while you're eating. It's rude.
>
> I'm reading a book about the Renaissance.
> She was quietly reading in her room.
>
> He writes murder mysteries.
> He writes with passion and conviction.

Conversely, a great many transitive verbs can optionally take an additional complement, in which case they are being **used ditransitively**:

> (62) Sarah *bought* a book.
> Sarah *bought* Brian a book.
>
> It *costs* a lot to travel first class.
> It *will cost* us a lot to travel first class.
>
> Don't forget to *feed* your cat. (Here, *your cat* is a DO)
> Never *feed* your cat chocolate. (Here, *your cat* is an IO)

In our discussion of the passive voice in Section 5, we will briefly address a category of verbs that can be used in what is called the **middle voice**, illustrated in (63). Verbs like *open* and *shake*, which allow for the middle voice, are special in that they combine features of transitivity and intransitivity. The overview below shows in what ways:

> (63) (a) I opened the door. (the door = DO) (active voice)
> (b) The door was opened by a man dressed in black. (passive voice)
> (c) The door opened. (the door = Subject) (middle voice)

---

[21]There are a few exceptions to this generalization. The verb *lack*, for example, obligatorily takes a DO but cannot be used in the passive: *They lack the necessary skills*, but not **The necessary skills are lacked by them*. The stative uses of *have* (see Section 2.4) require a DO as well, but no passive sentence is possible: *She has straight hair*, but not **Straight hair is had by her*.

(a) The wind shook the roof. (the roof = DO) (active voice)
(b) The roof was shaken by a sudden gust of wind. (passive voice)
(c) The roof shook in the wind. (the roof = Subject) (middle voice)

Active voice: active verb   DO   DO = theme
Passive voice: passive verb   no DO   Subject = theme
Middle voice: active verb   no DO   Subject = theme

As shown in the (c) examples above, the middle voice shares features with the active and the passive voice. We will return to the middle voice in Section 5.3.

Awareness of the different patterns illustrated above is an important first step in understanding how complementation works. Mastering the form or forms a complement takes is another matter. You may intuitively feel that a verb like *send* requires a DO and an IO and yet not know whether the constituent functioning as IO takes the form of an NP or a PrepP. And if the IO is realized as a PrepP, there is the additional question of whether the PrepP is headed by *to* or *for*. The examples in (64) show that, when they function as IOs, NPs can sometimes alternate with PrepPs (headed by *to* or *for*):

(64) They'll offer *the best person* the job.
     They'll offer the job *to the best person*.
     He'll prepare *us* a nice, hot meal.
     He'll prepare a nice, hot meal *for us*.

This alternation is not always possible, however:

(65) The teacher didn't explain the diagram *to them*.
     *The teacher didn't explain *them* the diagram.
     Do you think you can describe the process *to us* again?
     *Do you think you can describe *us* the process again?

We observe a similar situation with DO complements. Although DOs are quite regularly NPs, transitive verbs can also be complemented by a non-finite clause (a *to*-infinitive clause or an -*ing* clause) or a finite clause (a *that*-clause):

(66) I chose *to look the other way*. (cf. I chose a vegetarian dish.)
     They enjoy *spending time with their children*. (cf. They enjoy rock concerts.)
     She said *(that) she'd do it later*. (cf. She said something unusual.)

However, the forms these clausal DOs take are usually not interchangeable:

(67) *I chose *looking the other way*.
     *They enjoy *to spend time with their children*.
     *She said *to do it later*./*She said *doing it later*.

Finally, in those cases when a verb can combine with more than one type of clausal DO, there is often a difference in meaning between the different structures (as in (68)); in other cases there is no real difference (as in (69)):

(68) She remembered *switching* off all the lights in the house. (She recollected the event.)
She remembered *to switch* off all the lights in the house. (She didn't forget to do it.)

(69) He began *switching* all the lights in the house off.
He began *to switch* all the lights in the house off.

Apart from again bringing to the fore the interplay between function and form (the idea that specific functions – here, DOs or IOs – can be realized as different forms), the examples in this section show that there are constraints on the forms that can be used to express a particular function. These constraints depend on the verbs themselves, and competing structures can, but do not always, convey different meanings. The next section will therefore address the following issues:

– What forms can function as verbal complements?
– What functions do they have in the clause?
– If a verb can be complemented by more than one form, are the forms interchangeable or are there constraints on their use?

4.2 Form of complements

In this section, we will look at three different forms complements can take (namely, NPs, PrepPs and clauses) and the specific syntactic functions they have in the clause.

4.2.1 NP

The following examples include DO and IO complements, all of them realized here as NPs. The DOs are italicized and the IOs are underlined. We hold that an IO (nearly) always occurs with a DO, which is why there are no examples provided with only an IO:[22]

---

[22]This is a simplification of sorts. A few verbs, such as *tell* and *pay* can have a single complement (*Tell him now. Pay her later.*) Compare this to cases where these verbs are used ditransitively (*Tell him the truth. Pay her the difference.*), and you will see that it is not clear what the function is of *him* or *her* when they are used without a second complement. If such single complements are analysed as IOs, these would in fact be cases where an IO is possible without a DO.

(70) I don't really like *your new hairstyle*.
  If her car is broken down, she can borrow *mine*.
  Could someone please answer *the door*?
  It's risky to trust *people you've never met before*.

  The university cannot refuse <u>people</u> *admission*.
  I bought <u>everyone</u> *a drink* to celebrate.
  The carollers sang <u>us</u> *two or three traditional tunes*.
  Can you actually teach <u>children</u> *good manners*?

These examples also illustrate how common it is for Subjects, DOs and IOs to be realized as NPs.

We saw in Chapter 1 that it is important not to confuse a DO with a Subject Complement (SC) or an Object Complement (OC). The relevance of the distinction will become clear in our discussion of the passive in Section 5. NPs functioning as SCs occur after a linking verb (most commonly *be* or a change-of-state verb (most commonly *become*)). An SC ascribes a property to the Subject[23]:

(71) Her father is a world-renowned physicist.
  (cf. He married a world-renowned physicist. (*a world-renowned physicist* is a DO))

  Someday she'll become a famous opera singer.
  (cf. She'll meet a famous opera singer. (*a famous opera singer* is a DO))

An OC ascribes a property to the DO. The relationship between the DO and the OC can be made explicit by linking the DO with the OC through *be:*

(72) They called *him* a liar. (DO = him, OC = a liar: He is a liar.)
  We found *it* a good solution. (DO = it, OC = a good solution: It is a good solution.)

4.2.2 PrepP
4.2.2.1 NP/PrepP alternation

An IO can also be realized as a PrepP. PrepPs functioning as IOs are headed by *to* (73) or *for* (74). The IO realized as a PrepP often alternates with an IO realized as an NP. When the IO is a PrepP, it regularly follows the DO NP. When the IO and DO are both NPs, however, the IO must precede the DO:

(73) The magician handed *a black hat* <u>to his assistant</u>.
  The magician handed <u>his assistant</u> *a black hat*.
  *The magician handed *a black hat* <u>his assistant</u>.

---

[23]We are interested here in SCs that are realized as NPs since they are often confused with NPs functioning as DOs. Recall however that a SC is not necessarily an NP (cf. Chapter 1):
  Those blueberry pancakes you're making smell [divine]. (SC is an AdjP)
  They've grown [weary of her constant complaining]. (SC is an AdjP)

My father gave *some orchids* <u>to my mother</u>.
My father gave <u>my mother</u> *some orchids*.
*My father gave *some orchids* <u>my mother</u>.

(74) Can you book *a room* <u>for me</u> in that hotel?
Can you book <u>me</u> *a room* in that hotel?
*Can you book *a room* <u>me</u> in that hotel?

If you get to the theatre first, save *two seats* <u>for us</u>.
If you get to the theatre first, save <u>us</u> *two seats*.
*If you get to the theatre first, save *two seats* <u>us</u>.

Other verbs like those in (73) include *award, lend, offer, owe, pass, show, teach, tell* and *throw*. Verbs like those in (74) include *build, buy, catch, choose, cook, fetch, find, get, make, order* and *pour*.

The IO realized as a PrepP occasionally precedes the NP functioning as DO when the DO is particularly long or when its position after the DO could lead to a structurally ambiguous sentence:

(75) (a) My colleague announced <u>to the entire staff</u> *the confidential details of a private message my boss had sent*.
(b) My colleague announced *the confidential details of a private message my boss had sent* <u>to the entire staff</u>.

The sentence in (75b) can convey the idea that the boss sent the private message to the entire staff. This is not the case in (75a).

In some cases, the IO can be realized only as a PrepP (usually with *to*) – the alternation with an NP is impossible:

(76) She announced *her pregnancy* <u>to the entire staff</u>.
*She announced <u>the entire staff</u> *her pregnancy*.

I'm going to introduce *my boyfriend* <u>to my parents</u> this Christmas.
*I'm going to introduce <u>my parents</u> *my boyfriend* this Christmas.

Other verbs like those in (76) include *acknowledge, address, admit, affirm, confess, declare, dedicate, deliver, demonstrate, describe, devote, explain, mention, point out, propose, prove, remark, reply, report, reveal, say, signal, state* and *suggest*.

It may at first sight seem difficult to determine when to choose a *to*-PrepP or a *for*-PrepP when the PrepP functions as an IO. In fact, this can often be captured in semantic terms. IOs realized as *to*-PrepPs usually have the role of **recipient** (i.e. the receiver in a transfer of ownership or possession) whereas IOs realized as *for*-PrepPs are usually understood as having the role of **beneficiary** (i.e. one for whose benefit something is done). The difference between the notion of recipient and that of beneficiary is easier to grasp if you look at concrete examples:

(77) (a) Her assistant will send <u>their partners</u> *the new plans.*
Her assistant will send *the new plans* <u>to their partners.</u>
(b) The company built <u>them</u> *a very sleek website.*
The company built *a very sleek website* <u>for them.</u>

The situation in (77a) involves a transfer of the plans from the Subject (*her assistant*) to the partners. In (77b), the company has created something for the benefit of the client: we do not see a transfer as in (77a).

With some verbs, an IO can be either a recipient or a beneficiary, and the use of *to* or *for* in these cases is predictable:

(78) Could you please write <u>me</u> *a letter* as soon as you arrive? (= recipient)
(> write *a letter* <u>to me</u>)

You're not my GP, but could you write <u>me</u> *a prescription* anyway? (= beneficiary)
(> write *a prescription* <u>for me</u>)

Other verbs like those in (78) include *bring, leave, pay, play, read, sell, send, sing* and *take.* Note that when the IO takes the form of an NP, it is very often understood as being a recipient and not a beneficiary:

(79) I'll tell my assistant to send *the package* to you. (= recipient)
I'll tell my assistant to send *the package* for you. (= beneficiary)
I'll tell my assistant to send you *the package.* (= to send it to you, rather than for you)

Finally, there are cases where the IO can only be realized as an NP and not as a PrepP. This small class of verbs includes *bet, bill, cost, fine, forgive* and *spare*:

(80) He bet <u>her</u> *five dollars* that he could beat her at chess.
(cf. He bet five dollars *to her/*for her.)
This trip is costing <u>us</u> *an awful lot of money.*
(cf. This trip is costing an awful lot of money *to us/*for us.)

The specificity of these verbs is that the IO is neither a recipient nor a beneficiary. In a sense, it is the negative correlate of transfer (*He gave her five dollars*), in that the Subject causes the IO *not* to have the DO.

Table 2.2 sums up the different forms the IO can take. It is followed by a list of common verbs that illustrate the different categories.

Table 2.2 Possible forms of the Indirect Object[24]

Indirect Object	NP	*for*-PrepP	*to*-PrepP
(73)	+	−	+
(74)	+	+	−
(76)	−	−	+
(78)	+	+	+
(80)	+	−	−

See (73): *award, lend, offer, owe, pass, show, teach, tell* and *throw*
See (74): *build, buy, catch, choose, cook, fetch, find, get, make, order* and *pour*
See (76): *acknowledge, admit, affirm, confess, declare, dedicate, deliver, demonstrate, describe, devote, explain, mention, point out, propose, prove, remark, reply, report, reveal, say, signal, state* and *suggest*
See (78): *bring, leave, pay, play, read, sell, send, sing* and *take*
See (80): *bet, bill, cost, fine, forgive, spare*

4.2.2.2 Particle verbs and prepositional verbs

We have seen above that PrepPs can function as IOs. This is clearly distinct from cases where PrepPs function as Adjuncts, in which case they are not selected by the verb and are syntactically optional. They are therefore not considered complements:

(81) He gave a book [to his sister].   PrepP is an IO
      (cf. He gave his sister a book.)

He accompanied his sister [to the station].   PrepP is an Adjunct
      (cf. He accompanied his sister.)

He bought a book [for his sister].   PrepP is an IO
      (cf. He bought his sister a book.)

He bought a book [for his beach holiday].   PrepP is an Adjunct
      (cf. He bought a book.)

If a verb is followed by a PrepP headed by *to* or *for*, the PrepP does not necessarily perform the function of IO or Adjunct. The PrepP in the following sets of examples complements the verb (i.e. it is not an Adjunct), but not in the same way as an IO. The function it fulfils is that of **Prepositional Object**. Prepositional Objects can be headed by a wide variety of prepositions in addition to *to* and *for*:

---

[24]When an IO can be realized as both a PrepP and an NP, the complementation pattern with two NPs (IO and DO) is the more neutral one. We are much more likely to say *Hand me that book* than *Hand that book to me*, especially if there is no other person the hearer might hand the book to.

(82) This string of pearls belonged [*to* my mother].
He was looking [*for* his keys].
They've already dealt [*with* the problem].
You can always rely [*on* me].
She never laughs [*at* my jokes].
He suffers [*from* anxiety].

Verbs of this kind are called **prepositional verbs**, and the complement they take is called a Prepositional Object. As explained in Chapter 1 (Section 3.3), the bracketed constituents in (82) are Prepositional Objects because the head of the PrepP is part of the prepositional verbs *belong to, look for, deal with, rely on, laugh at* and *suffer from*.

Not every combination of a verb and a functional word that looks like a preposition is a prepositional verb. Consider the following sentences:

(83) He was thinking *over* the plan.
He was thinking *about* the plan.

At first sight, the sentences in (83) seem to have the same basic structure. However, one important difference between the two is that the word *over* in the first sentence can also occur after the constituent [*the plan*]. This is not the case for *about*:

(84) He was thinking the plan *over*.
*He was thinking the plan *about*.

Furthermore, when we replace the constituent *the plan* with the pronoun *it*, we find another difference concerning word order: the pronoun must precede *over*, whereas it must follow *about*:

(85) He was thinking it *over*. (*He was thinking *over* it.)
He was thinking *about* it. (*He was thinking it *about*.)

These differences naturally lead us to the conclusion that the sentences in (83), although they look the same on the surface, are structurally different. The difference can be captured as follows: *think over* is not a prepositional verb but a **particle verb**. *Think about* is a prepositional verb like those shown in (82). Particle verbs can be transitive or intransitive. When they are intransitive, the particle is not followed by a constituent. (*Cheer up!; The president has stepped down.*) When they are transitive, they require a DO, usually realized as an NP. (*He handed in the key.*) The structure of a sentence with a transitive particle verb is shown below:

(86) [Subject] [$_{VP}$ [V + particle] [$_{NP}$ Direct Object]]

In other words, the particle is an integral part of the verb, and the two-word transitive verb is used with a DO. As is the case for any transitive verb (e.g. *consider*), it is generally impossible to insert an Adjunct between the verb and its DO: within the VP, a verb and its DO form a tight unit, and an Adjunct cannot 'get inside':

(87) He was [considering the plan] carefully.
　　*He was [considering carefully the plan].
　　　　(the verb *consider* cannot be separated from its DO *the plan*)

　　He was [thinking *over* the plan] carefully.
　　*He was [thinking *over* carefully the plan].
　　　　(the verb *think over* cannot be separated from its DO *the plan*)

The syntactic structure of a sentence with a prepositional verb like *think about* is as follows:

(88) [Subject] [$_{VP}$ [V] [$_{PrepP}$ Prepositional Object]]

In other words, the preposition goes with the following NP, with which it forms a PrepP that functions as Prepositional Object:

(89) [Subject] [$_{VP}$ [V] [$_{PrepP}$ P [NP]]]

This explains why (84), repeated below, is ungrammatical: the verb is complemented by a Prepositional Object; the preposition in the PrepP cannot be separated from the NP:

(90) *He was thinking the plan about.

For the same reason, it is not possible to insert an Adjunct between the preposition and the NP with which it forms a PrepP (compare with the example with a particle verb in (87)):

(91) *He was thinking about carefully the plan.

The difference in the structural make-up of particle verbs and prepositional verbs also explains why Adjuncts can be inserted between the verb and the Prepositional Object, but not between the verb and the particle.

(92) He was thinking carefully [$_{PrepP}$ about the plan]
　　*He was thinking carefully over the plan

Some further syntactic manipulations confirm the structural differences between sentences with prepositional verbs and sentences with particle verbs.

For example, one way to give particular focus to an Object is to move it from its normal position to a position earlier in the sentence:

(93) He was developing [a plan]. > It was [a plan] (that) he was developing.

This type of sentence, called a **cleft sentence** (see Chapter 5, Section 1), serves to highlight a specific constituent: by moving it away from its canonical position (here, a DO complement), the speaker puts this piece of information in the foreground. Whereas this manipulation is possible with a prepositional verb, as in (94a), a similar attempt with a particle verb yields the impossible sentence in (94b). This is because the PrepP *about the plan* is a constituent, whereas *over the plan* is not:

(94) (a) It was [about the plan] that he was thinking.
     (b) *It was over the plan that he was thinking.

Another example of the difference comes to the fore in pairs of sentences such as in (95). In (95a), a second Prepositional Object is coordinated with the first: the sentence is fine. But in (95b) the attempt to coordinate is not possible since *over our plan* is not a constituent:

(95) (a) Was he thinking about our plan or about theirs?
     (b) *Was he thinking over our plan or over theirs?

As seen in Chapter 1 (Section 3.1.3), a coordinating conjunction such as *or* brings together constituents of equal status.[25] Coordinating *over theirs* with *over our plan* would again imply that *over our plan* is a constituent.

The following examples illustrate the different possible word orders we find:

(96) <u>Transitive particle verbs</u>   <u>Intransitive prepositional verbs</u>

(a) They've called *off* [$_{NP}$ the meeting].   She's looking [$_{PP}$ *for* her lost keys].
    They've called the meeting *off*.   *She's looking her lost keys *for*.
    They've called it *off*.   *She's looking them *for*.
    *They've called *off* it.   She's looking *for* them.

(b) She checked *out* [$_{NP}$ this library book].   I'm listening [$_{PP}$ *to* the radio].
    She checked this library book *out*.   *I'm listening the radio *to*.
    She checked it *out*.   *I'm listening it *to*.
    *She checked *out* it.   I'm listening *to* it.

---

[25] As observed in Chapter 1, coordination without constituents of equal status is also possible.

(c) You must fill *in* [_{NP} your colleagues].   You can depend [_{PP} *on* your friends].
You must fill your colleagues *in*.   *You can depend your friends *on*.
You must fill them *in*.   *You can depend them *on*.
*You must fill *in* them.   You can depend *on* them.

The particle verbs mentioned so far are transitive, but there are many examples of intransitive particle verbs: *break down, stand up, take off* and *wake up* are but a few representative examples:

(97) What time did you *wake up* this morning?
Our car has *broken down*. Can you call a mechanic?
When the president walked into the room, everyone *stood up*.
The plane was initially supposed *to take off* at 8 o'clock.

In a similar way, while the examples of prepositional verbs in (82) above are intransitive (the verb is complemented by a PrepP functioning as Prepositional Object), prepositional verbs can take a DO as well, in which case they are transitive. The DOs in (98) are underlined:

(98) (a) She says she's tired, but I think we can *talk* <u>her</u> *into* coming.
(b) This book *reminds* <u>me</u> *of* a story I heard when I was a kid.
(d) I'd like to *thank* <u>you</u> *for* everything you've done.

Take example (98a): the verb *talk someone into something* is transitive – it takes a DO in the form of an NP. *Into* is a preposition, and the PrepP [into coming] functions as Prepositional Object.

We also find examples of particle verbs that combine the use of a particle and a PrepP complement; we call such verbs **prepositional particle verbs**:

(99) I've always *looked up to* my great-aunt Camilla.

In (99), *up* is a particle, *to* is a preposition and the PrepP *to my great-aunt Camilla* functions as a Prepositional Object. *Look up to* is an intransitive prepositional particle verb.

The verb in (100), *take someone up on something*, looks quite similar: here, *up* is a particle, *on* is a preposition and the PrepP *on her offer* functions as Prepositional Object. Unlike in the case of transitive particle verbs, with transitive prepositional particle verbs, the particle nearly always follows the DO, hence the questionable acceptability of (100b):

(100) (a) You ought to *take* your sister *up on* her offer.
(b) ?You ought to *take up* your sister *on* her offer.

The different types of particle verbs discussed in the preceding description are exemplified in Table 2.3 (T1–T6). Remember that in the case of T2, the particle can precede or follow the DO.[26]

Once you get the gist of these six basic configurations, it is easier to understand that many verbs can quite easily fit into more than one configuration:

(101) I smoke far too much. I really need to *cut down*. (T1)
         My doctor says I need to *cut down on* smoking. (T5)

         You're driving too fast – *slow down*! (T1)
         The new software is actually *slowing* the whole network *down*. (T2)
         (cf. The new software is actually *slowing down* the whole network.)

         The bus pulled to a stop, and I *got off*. (T1)
         As I was *getting off* the bus, I realized I'd forgotten my bag. (T3)
         (cf. *As I was *getting* the bus *off*, I realized I'd forgotten my bag.)

Table 2.3 Survey of prepositional verbs, particle verbs and prepositional particle verbs

	Verb	DO	Part.	Prep.	Object of Prep.
T1: Particle verb (intrans.)	*speed*	Ø	*up*	Ø	Ø
T2: Particle verb (trans.)	*write*	*sth.*	*down*	Ø	Ø
T3: Prepositional verb (intrans.)	*look*	Ø	Ø	*for*	*sth./s.o.*
T4: Prepositional verb (trans.)	*read*	*sth.*	Ø	*into*	*sth.*
T5: Prep. particle verb (intrans.)	*cut*	Ø	*down*	*on*	*sth.*
T6: Prep. particle verb (trans.)	*put*	*s.o.*	*up*	*to*	*sth.*

T1 I couldn't *speed up* because there was no traction.
T2 Don't forget to *write* his telephone number *down*.
     Don't forget to *write down* his telephone number.
T3 They've been *looking for* a new house since February.
T4 Did he really mean that? Maybe you're *reading* too much *into* it.
T5 We should all *cut down on* polyunsaturated fats.
T6 This must be a joke – who *put you up to* this?

---

[26]The position of a particle before or after a DO NP can be shown to be sensitive to the status of the information in the discursive context. As we will see in our discussion of the passive (see Section 5.4.3), old information tends to be mentioned first, whereas new information features in final position. A pronoun by definition refers to what has been previously mentioned, but NPs can represent old information too. Though less absolute than with pronouns, a DO realized as an NP that represents old information is often more likely to precede the particle, as in (i). When the NP introduces new information into the discourse, as in (ii), it tends to follow the particle:
    (i) I didn't know who originated the phrase, so I *looked the quotation up*.
    (ii) Please remember to *switch off your mobile phones* before the performance.

While it is important to be aware of the distinct formal behaviour of particle verbs, prepositional verbs and prepositional particle verbs, the main challenge is that of familiarizing yourself with the meaning of these verbs, which is often not predictable. For instance, it is hard to infer the meaning of *run into someone* (meet unexpectedly) or *give in* (agree after having resisted) from the meaning of its component parts.

So far, our focus has been on phrasal constituents (NPs and PrepPs) that can perform the function of DO, IO and Prepositional Object. You may remember from Chapter 1 that clauses can perform certain syntactic functions as well.

4.2.3 Clauses

Clausal complements may take the form of a finite **that-clause**,[27] which, depending on the verb, is sometimes preceded by an IO. Note that the *that* in the *that*-clause is sometimes not realized:

> (102) He said (that) it was OK. (He said something./*He said.)
> He told her (that) it was OK. (*He told that it was ok./*He told.)
> She believed (that) he was coming. (She believed it./*She believed.[28])

The examples in (103) show that the non-finite form may be an infinitive clause, with or without *to*. We refer to these two possibilities as **to-infinitives** (or **to-infinitive clauses**), with the infinitive marker *to*, and **bare infinitives**, (or **bare infinitive clauses**), without the infinitive marker *to*. The non-finite form can also be an **-ing clause**. These are sometimes preceded and/or followed by an NP:

> (103) DO
> (a) I really like *to read books/reading books*.
> (b) He avoided *talking to her*.
> (c) I resent *Tom('s) accusing me of that*.
> (d) I watched *Eve bake a cake/Eve baking a cake*.
> (e) The professor had *her students read the first chapter*.
> (f) The professor made *her students read the first chapter*.
> (g) We've decided *to cancel next week's meeting*.

---

[27] As discussed in Chapter 1 (Section 4.3), a finite verb phrase is a VP that is marked for tense: in *John is working hard*, the VP [*is working hard*] has a present tense inflection. It is a finite VP. In *Peter wants John to work harder*, the VP [*to work harder*] has *John* as a Subject, but there is no temporal marker. In other words, the VP is not marked for tense and is thus non-finite.

[28] Note that *believe* is sometimes used intransitively to mean 'have (religious) faith', 'be a believer': *She had doubts for years, but now she believes*.

In (103c) to (103f), the NP preceding the non-finite form is part of the DO. This becomes clear when we consider that the answer to the question *What do I resent?* in (103c) is not *Tom* or *accusing me*, but rather *Tom('s) accusing me*.

In (104), on the other hand, the verbs take an IO complement and a DO complement in the form of a finite or non-finite clause:

(104) IO + DO
   (a) The manager advised everyone *not to mention the problem*.
   (b) They allowed Tom *to visit the premises*.
   (c) I told her *(that) her application had been accepted*.

The NP preceding the non-finite complement usually functions as Subject of that complement. The NP following the non-finite verb functions as its DO. (*What did Eve bake? A cake* (cf. 103d).)

Table 2.4. below gives an overview of non-finite complementation patterns organized in terms of the form of their complements.[29]

Generally speaking, the complementation pattern associated with a given verb is invariable. Knowing a verb consequently implies mastering the complementation pattern associated with it. However, some verbs are compatible with more than one complementation pattern. The most common alternation is between a *to*-infinitive clause and an *-ing* clause. Sometimes, there is no fundamental difference in meaning associated with the alternation. In other cases, the difference in meaning is quite substantial. The following section will

Table 2.4 Survey of non-finite complements

-ing clause	Infinitive (*to*-infinitive or bare infinitive)
I. Verb + *ing*-form (+ NP) (cf. Section 5.5.1.3)	**III. Verb +** *to*-infinitive (+ NP) (cf. 5.5.1.4)
(a) Verbs of cognition (e.g. *consider, imagine, remember*) He considered buying a small flat in London.	(a) Verbs like *start, begin, continue, appear, seem, tend, come* He started to kick the car.
(b) Verbs of affective stance (i.e. liking and hating) (e.g. *enjoy, resent*) He resented leaving her alone.	(b) Verbs like *agree, aim, attempt, try, hope, refuse, struggle*[30] She agreed to sell the house.
(c) Some other verbs like *avoid, delay, deny, describe* He avoided meeting her.	

[29]Certain verbs feature in more than one class. This follows from an observation made in Section 4.1, namely that one verb may be compatible with a number of complementation patterns.
[30]The two separate classes reflect meaning distinctions that can be observed in the passive (cf. Section 5.5.1.4).

-ing clause	Infinitive (*to*-infinitive or bare infinitive)
II. Verb + NP + *ing*-form (cf. 5.5.1.5)	**IV. Verb + NP + *to*-infinitive** (cf. 5.5.1.6 and 5.5.3.2)
(a) Verbs of cognition (e.g. *anticipate, forget, imagine, recall, remember*) I anticipated Jim saying this.	(a) Verbs like *can't bear, hate, love, need, prefer, want, wish* I want him to play that tune.
(b) Verbs of affective stance (e.g. *anticipate, appreciate, dislike, dread, hate, like, (not) mind, regret*) I resented Tom('s) winning the prize.[31]	(b) Verbs like *expect, feel, mean, report* I expected him to help me. The teacher reported Jim to be absent.
(c) Verbs like *bring, catch, find, keep, send, show*[32] I kept the guests waiting in the lounge for a while.	(c) Verbs like *allow, advise, ask, instruct, mean, order, persuade, require, teach, tell, understand, warn*[33] The police warned everyone to stay inside. I persuaded her to try again.
(d) Verbs of the senses I saw Eve walking across the street.	
	V. Verb + NP + bare infinitive (cf. 5.5.1.7) (a) Verbs of the senses I saw Eve walk across the street.
	(b) Causative verbs The professor had her students read the first chapter. The professor made her students read the first chapter.

shed some light on some common verbs that show both complementation patterns.

Start, begin, continue, cease, propose, bother, can't bear

These verbs can generally be followed by a *to*-infinitive clause or by an *-ing* clause. The difference between the two forms is relatively small, and many speakers use both complementation patterns indifferently.[34] An *-ing* clause is

---

[31] An NP preceding an infinitive clause is never in the genitive (cf. Chapter 4), but an NP preceding an *-ing* clause can be:

They appreciated our/Louise's saying such a thing.

They appreciated us/Louise saying such a thing.

[32] Biber *et al.* (1999) offer a corpus-based survey of the semantic classes that are compatible with each of the clausal complementation patterns listed here (*-ing* clauses: 740–746, *that*-clauses: 661–667 and infinitive clauses: 694–705).

[33] The NP that follows the verbs listed under (a) and (b) is part of the DO (cf. 5.5.1.6), while the NP that follows the verbs listed under (c) functions as IOs (cf. 5.5.3.2.).

[34] Some maintain a distinction between, for example, *start to do* and *start doing*. For them, the *to*-infinitive clause highlights the beginning of a situation whereas the *-ing* clause stresses the duration of the situation:

When she heard the news, she started crying. (= and she kept on crying)

When she heard the news, she started to cry, but then got a hold of herself.

These shades of meaning are not necessarily perceived by all speakers of English.

often avoided if the main verb has progressive aspect, which itself is marked by an *-ing* form in conjunction with the progressive marker *be*:

(105) I *began* working/to work here as soon as I finished university.
Some people *continue* working/to work after retirement.
He loathes her. In fact, he *can't bear* being/to be in the same room with her.
?She's *starting* working next week. (cf. She's starting to work next week.)

Verbs of permission: *allow, authorize, permit, advise, encourage, forbid*

These verbs combine with either an *-ing* clause or an NP followed by a *to*-infinitive. The pattern with the *-ing* clause implies that there is an implicit, general Subject, whereas the construction with the NP renders the Subject of the verbal *to*-complement explicit:

(106) We do not *allow* smoking on campus.
I don't *allow* my children to smoke at all.

The travel agency strongly *encourages* booking flights well in advance.
He *encouraged* me to book my room as soon as possible.

In a number of cases, a verb can be followed either by an *-ing* clause or by a *to*-infinitive, but with a significant difference in meaning.

Stop and *go on*

Stop can be followed by an *-ing* clause or by a *to*-infinitive clause. The *to*-infinitive is a subclause of purpose (stop in order to do something). The *-ing* clause refers to an activity which ceases to occur (discontinue doing something):

(107) He *stopped* to drink. (= so that he could drink)
He *stopped* drinking. (= he no longer drinks)

Go on followed by an *-ing* clause means 'continue (with the same activity)'; *go on* followed by a *to*-infinitive means 'move on to the next activity':

(108) She just *went on* explaining the topic of her thesis, although no one was listening.
After a brief introduction, she *went on* to explain the details of her analysis.

Remember, forget, regret

With *remember, forget* and *regret*, the difference between a *to*-infinitive clause and an *-ing* clause is temporal. With *remember*, the *-ing* clause refers to a situation that is anterior to the situation referred to by the verb in the main clause; the *to*-infinitive clause refers to a situation that is posterior to that referred to by the main verb:

(109) I *remember* sending her a birthday card.
(My sending the card happened before my remembering it now.)

I *remembered* to send her a birthday card.
(I remembered to send a card and subsequently sent it.)

The same can be said for *forget*, although a *that*-clause is more common than an -*ing* clause:

(110) I often *forget* buying certain clothes and am surprised when I find them in my closet.
(= I often forget that I've bought certain clothes …)
(First I buy the clothes, then I forget that I've bought them.)
I often *forget* to buy soap and shampoo when I go shopping.

In the case of *forget* + *to*-infinitive above, one might even consider that 'not buying soap and shampoo' is actually simultaneous with 'forgetting'. *Regret*, finally, is similar to *remember* and *forget* when followed by an -*ing* clause (i.e. the situation in the -*ing* clause is anterior to the situation in main clause), but when followed by a *to*-clause, the relation between the two situations is clearly one of immediate sequence:

(111) I *regret* insulting you in front of all those people.
(First, I insulted you, and now I regret it.)
I *regret* to tell you that your application has been rejected.
(My regret and the expression of my regret are almost simultaneous.)

Try

Try followed by an -*ing* clause means 'experiment, check to see what happens'; the message it conveys is 'it might be a good idea to do this'. When followed by a *to*-infinitive clause, *try* means 'attempt or endeavour to achieve something':

(112) Why don't you *try* sending her an e-mail? She usually responds right away.
(= see what happens – sending an e-mail might work)
I'll *try* to send the package by the end of the day, but I can't promise anything. (= I'll make an effort to do it)

In colloquial English, *try and* + verb is common as well, but it is fairly restricted in its use. It is used only in the infinitive form (including, for example the future with *will*) and the imperative: *I'll try and send the package; Please try and send the package* (but not **I tried and sent the package*).

Mean

When the meaning of the verb *mean* is 'have as a consequence', it is followed by an *-ing* clause; in this case, it can also be followed by an NP. When *mean* means 'intend', it is followed by a *to*-infinitive clause, and an NP complement is not possible:

> (113) I'll do anything necessary to succeed, even if it *means* working long hours. (I'll do anything necessary to succeed, even if it *means* a lot of work.)
> I *meant* to ring you up last night, but I just didn't have the time. (NP complement not possible.)

Verbs of perception: *feel, hear, notice, observe, perceive, see, watch*

Verbs of perception can also be followed by two types of clausal complement:

> (114) (a) I *saw* Eve cross/crossing the street.
> (b) I *heard* the dog bark/barking.

When the *-ing* clause is used, the action referred to is ongoing at the time of perception (I saw Eve while she was walking across the street; I heard the dog while it was (repeatedly) barking). The meaning associated with a bare infinitive is particularly clear when there is reference to what we will call an Accomplishment in Chapter 4. An Accomplishment is a dynamic situation with a clear beginning and end. In the case of (114a), for instance, the use of the bare infinitive implies that I observed the complete situation of Eve walking across the street: she was on one side of the street, she crossed the street and reached the other side. This is less the case with the *-ing* clause, where Eve's reaching the opposite side of the street, though possible, is not conveyed by the linguistic form used. In the case of (114b) (a dynamic situation without duration – we will call this an Achievement (see Chapter 4)), the bare infinitive implies that I heard the dog bark once; using an *-ing* clause form implies it did so repeatedly. The generalization that emerges here is that the *-ing* clause has the meaning associated with progressive aspect in a finite clause whereas the bare infinitive is associated with non-progressive aspect in a finite clause (see Chapter 4):

> (115) I *saw* Eve cross the street. (cf. Eve crossed the street.)
> I *saw* Eve crossing the street. (cf. Eve was crossing the street.)
>
> Did you *hear* the dog bark? (cf. Did the dog bark?)
> Did you *hear* the dog barking? (cf. Was the dog barking?)

Verbs of preference: *like, love, hate, prefer*

With these verbs, an *-ing* clause is most commonly used. A *to*-infinitive clause can be used as well:

(116) I *like* dancing. It's my favourite pastime.
I *prefer* working in the morning.

I *like* to dance. I go dancing every Saturday night.
I *prefer* to work in the morning.

Although some grammarians maintain a nuance in meaning between the two patterns, many speakers do not perceive any important distinction. When in doubt, use an *-ing* clause. What is important to remember is that with *would like* or *would prefer*, both of which refer to a specific, future situation, a *to*-infinitive clause is the only one possible:

(117) I'd *like* to go to the theatre next week. Can we still get tickets?
I'd *prefer* to work tomorrow morning rather than tomorrow afternoon.

4.2.4 Conclusion

We have chosen to approach complementation patterns in terms of forms and functions.[35] Table 2.5 below summarizes the basic patterns we have identified and brings out, once again, the form-function interface. This overview is not comprehensive – the discussion in this section has already shown that other complementation patterns do exist. Advanced learner's dictionaries provide helpful information on the different complementation patterns a verb can have.

Verbal complementation has other ramifications on how sentences and clauses are organized. For instance, these patterns will determine whether it is possible or not to build a passive sentence as well as the form that passive sentence will have. In other words, complementation is important not just because additions to the verb (of a specific form) are necessary to build acceptable sentences, but also because it influences the order in which the information can be presented in a sentence. It is this issue that we will address in the next section.

---

[35]We approach complementation patterns in terms of the different forms that may be required by the verb (NP, PrepP, clause) while at the same time providing a more detailed functional analysis of complements, making explicit the different functions fulfilled by the forms. Others do not necessarily use functional labels such as Prepositional Object, Subject Complement or Object Complement and prefer to highlight only the obligatory nature of the additions to the verb through the use of the term *complement*. In this case, complements are subcategorized by referring to the forms (a PrepP complement, an NP complement, a clausal complement).

Table 2.5 Transitive and ditransitive verbs: formal realization of DOs and IOs

Transitive verbs		
DO realized as	NP	He's read <u>that book</u>.
	that-clause	He said <u>(that) he'd read that book</u>.
	(NP +) *-ing* clause	He enjoys <u>reading books</u>.
		I noticed <u>him reading a book</u>.
	(NP +) *to*-infinitive clause	I want <u>(him) to read that book</u>.
	NP + *bare* infinitive clause	She made <u>him read that book.</u>
	bare infinitive clause	He helped <u>write the letter</u>.
Ditransitive verbs		
IO realized as NP combines with DO realized as	NP	She gave him <u>a book</u>.
	that-clause	She told him <u>that she'd read the book</u>.
IO realized as PrepP combines with DO realized as	NP	She gave <u>a book</u> to him.
	that-clause	She mentioned to him <u>that she had read the book</u>.

5. The passive

5.1 Introduction

Our discussion of complementation has highlighted the fact that a sentence is made up of a set of constituents that cluster around a verb. There is a certain amount of choice when it comes to how these constituents are arranged. Let us take as our point of departure the sentences in (118), where the Adjuncts *last week, for her birthday* and *not surprisingly* show a certain degree of mobility within the structure of the sentence. The nuances associated with these different positions have little effect on the overall content of the message:

(118) (a) [Last week], Parliament passed legislation legalizing online gambling.
Parliament [last week] passed legislation legalizing online gambling.
Parliament passed legislation [last week] legalizing online gambling.
Parliament passed legislation legalizing online gambling [last week].

(b) [For her birthday], we sent the manager a bunch of roses.
We sent the manager a bunch of roses [for her birthday].

(c) [Not surprisingly], someone addressed a letter of complaint to the manager.
Someone addressed a letter of complaint to the manager, [not surprisingly].
(*Someone addressed the manager a letter of complaint, [not surprisingly]. (cf. (76))

However, Adjuncts are not the only constituents that can be found in different positions:

(119) (a) Last week, [legislation legalizing online gambling] was passed.
    [Legislation legalizing online gambling] was passed [by Parliament] last week.
    [Legislation legalizing online gambling] was passed last week [by Parliament].
    [Legislation legalizing online gambling] was passed last week.

(b) [The manager] was sent [a bunch of roses] for her birthday.
    For her birthday, [the manager] was sent [a lovely bunch of red tulips].
    For her birthday, [a bunch of roses] was sent [to the manager].
    [A bunch of roses] was sent [to the manager] for her birthday.

(c) Not surprisingly, [a letter of complaint] was addressed [to the manager].
    [A letter of complaint] was addressed [to the manager], not surprisingly.
    *Not surprisingly, [the manager] was addressed [a letter of complaint]. (cf. (76))

The difference between the sentences in (118) and (119) goes beyond the mobility of the Adjuncts. It reflects the difference between what is called the **active voice** (sentences in (118)) and the **passive voice** (sentences in (119)), an alternation which is considerably determined by the complementation patterns outlined in Section 4 above. The most basic illustration of how complementation comes into play concerns transitivity: whereas any verb can be used in an active clause, it is mainly verbs taking Objects that are possible in a passive clause. This explains why the Subjects in the sets of sentences in (118) correspond to Objects in (119): Objects only occur with transitive or ditransitive verbs.

5.2 The form of the passive

Forming the passive is straightforward enough. Whereas the active voice is signalled by the absence of any specific markers, the passive voice is signalled by **passive markers** used with the verb. In English, the passive markers are the auxiliary *be*, used in the form required by the context of the utterance (this concerns primarily tense and aspect), combined with the past participle of the verb.[36] The passive can combine with modal verbs (addressed in Chapter 5) as well:

---

[36]In theory, the passive voice is compatible with all tenses and aspects. In practice, it is rare with the future and past future when the progressive is used (?*A decision will be (would be) being made*) and with all the perfect tenses when they have progressive aspect (?*A decision has been (had been/will have been/ would have been) being made*). These combinations feel cumbersome and are often hard to process.

(120)	A decision	is	made	at the beginning of the year.
	A decision	is being	made	at the moment.
	A decision	was	made	some time ago.
	A decision	was being	made	when we walked in.
	A decision	will be	made	in the near future.
	A decision	has (just) been	made.	
	A decision	had (already) been	made	when I was hired.
	A decision	can't be	made	until the problem is solved.
	A decision	must be	made	sometime soon.
	A decision	might have been	made	in our absence.

Instead of *be*, the lexical verb *get* is sometimes used to form the passive as well. It is never obligatory. It is sometimes said to be more common with verbs with an unpleasant connotation (*get robbed, get killed, get attacked, get broken*), but this is not always the case.

(121) The dog got (= was) run over by a bus.
They eventually got (= were) fired soon after the scandal went public.
Were it not for your recommendation, I would not have got (= have been) promoted.

Get tends to have a slightly more informal feel than *be*. Furthermore, it cannot usually be used in contexts where duration is implied:

(122) The book was written by an international specialist.
*The book got written by an international specialist.

Bear in mind that the use of *get*, though common with certain verbs such as *run over* in (121), is never obligatory.

5.3 The passive and semantic roles

The passive is often presented as the result of a kind of conversion mechanism that derives a passive sentence from an underlying active sentence. This can be a helpful approach since the mapping between an active sentence and its passive counterpart has some intuitive appeal. The generalization that passive NP Subjects correspond to active NP Objects is especially easy to see when the passive and active sentences are presented together:

(123) A fire destroyed [the old theatre] in August of last year.
> [The old theatre] was destroyed (by a fire) in August of last year.

The supervisor gave ([everyone]) [an explanation] on day one.
> [Everyone] was given [an explanation] (by the supervisor) on day one.
> [An explanation] was given (to [everyone]) (by the supervisor) on day one.

Several members suggested [the new proposal] [to the committee].
(*Several members suggested [the committee] [the new proposal]. (cf. (76))
> [The new proposal] was suggested [to the committee] (by several members).
*[The committee] was suggested [the new proposal] (by several members). (cf. (76))

This transformational account of passive sentences is incomplete, however. For one thing, it implies that once the original Object has taken the place of the Subject, something must be done with the original Subject. The examples in (119) above show that the original Subject can occur in a *by*-phrase. In many cases, though, passive sentences are used without a *by*-phrase. This is particularly the case when the doer of the sentence is unimportant, or obvious, or even unknown:

(124) The old theatre was destroyed in August of last year.
My sister was given a stern talking to after the incident.
She was/got mugged while walking home.
The new proposal was suggested to the committee.

It also obscures the fact that verbs such as *fine, hospitalize, make redundant (lay off)* or *put down (an animal)* seem to occur more regularly in the passive voice than in the active or that verbs like *repute* or *rumour* have no active counterpart at all:

(125) I've been fined several hundred dollars for disturbing the neighbours.
She'll have to be hospitalized for at least two weeks following the surgery.
The company is rumoured to be launching the computer next year.
(*They rumoured the company to be launching the computer.)

It is also commonly thought that although the motivation for and effect of choosing a passive or an active are different, the basic meaning of an active-passive pair is the same. Even this is not always the case:

(126) (a) Cows produce milk for human consumption.
(b) Milk for human consumption is produced by cows.

For many people, the passive and active sentences in this pair do not have the same meaning: the passive sentence in (126b) seems to imply that all milk for human consumption is produced by cows. The implication is absent in the active sentence in (126a).

Given these facts, emancipating the passive voice from the active voice and viewing it simply as an alternative way of organizing information goes a long way to explaining how the passive is used. This view involves looking at the different **semantic roles** the different participants in a sentence can have and the way they are organized around the verb.

We have already mentioned in Section 4.1 that IOs can be either recipients (*I gave <u>him</u> a book*) or beneficiaries (*I made <u>her</u> a cake*) and that this is reflected in the form the IO takes when it is a PrepP: *I gave a book <u>to him</u>, I made a cake <u>for her</u>.* When we refer to a constituent as being a recipient or a beneficiary, we are referring to the semantic role it has in the clause rather than its grammatical function. Informally put, semantic roles say something about how Subjects and Objects participate in a situation based on the verb. The following examples illustrate some of the semantic roles of Subject NPs:

(127) (a) The children built a treehouse.
      (b) The children could hear the birds.

Although the constituent [*the children*] in both sentences functions as Subject, the semantic role it has in the sentence is not the same. In (127a), *the children* are the doers or the instigators of building: we call this role **agent** – agents are doers or instigators. It is clear in (127b), however, that *the children* are not actively doing anything but rather are experiencing something. We call this role **experiencer**. Finally, the DOs *the birds* and *the tree house* in these sentences have in common the fact that they undergo the activity or experience denoted by the verb. We call this role **theme**. There is a great deal more to semantic roles than this, and linguists do not agree on the number or precise characterization of what differentiates one semantic role from another. Still, this bare-bones sketch can be helpful in understanding the passive as a form in its own right. The organization of different NPs to the left and right of transitive or ditransitive verbs is motivated by the order in which the speaker chooses to mention the participants, and the passive or active form of the verbs falls out from this: when the Subject chosen is an agent or experiencer, the verb is in the active voice, whereas when the Subject chosen is a theme, a recipient or a beneficiary, the verb is in the passive voice.

Before we address the function of the passive, we would like to draw attention to a type of verb that was briefly mentioned in Section 4.1; the examples are repeated below:

(128) (a) I opened the door. (the door = DO (active))
     (b) The door was opened by a man dressed in black. (passive)
     (c) The door opened. (the door = Subject (middle))

(129) (a) The wind shook the roof. (the roof = DO (active))
     (b) The roof was shaken by a sudden gust of wind. (passive)
     (c) The roof shook in the wind. (the roof = Subject (middle))

(130) (a) The government increased taxes. (taxes = DO (active))
     (b) Taxes were increased by the government. (passive)
     (c) Taxes increased. (taxes = Subject (middle))

The examples in (a) illustrate the canonical case in which the theme features in DO position in an active sentence. The passive voice (examples in (b)) makes it possible to mention the theme in Subject position, in which case the Agent is added in a *by*-PrepP at the end of the clause. In the examples in (c), the theme likewise features in Subject position but the sentence is active; the agent cannot be expressed. Put differently, we could say that the verb here is at the intersection of intransitivity and transitivity: from a formal perspective, it is like an intransitive verb in that it does not take a complement; from a semantic perspective, it is like a transitive verb because the theme is expressed (be it not in the form of a DO). The term **middle voice** is sometimes used and captures this idea.

5.4 The passive in discourse

5.4.1 Agent as Subject as unmarked choice

The unmarked (or, in more technical terms, canonical) order of constituents in a transitive or ditransitive clause in English is semantically organized as follows:

(131) The police$_{(agent)}$ arrested the escaped convict$_{(theme)}$ two days later.[37]

The people in charge$_{(agent)}$ renovated the museum$_{(theme)}$ in 2005.

Thousands of people$_{(experiencer)}$ have seen this film$_{(theme)}$.

Someone$_{(agent)}$ gave him$_{(recipient)}$ this book$_{(theme)}$ when he was 5.

My parents$_{(agent)}$ bought me$_{(beneficiary)}$ a bike$_{(theme)}$ for Christmas.

However, as we have already explained in Section 5.3, the speaker in certain cases may be interested not in what an agent does or an experiencer experiences,

---

[37]Note that the Adjuncts (underlined in (131)) do not have thematic roles, at least not at the same level as Subjects and complements.

but rather in the referents associated with the theme, recipient or beneficiary. This choice is reflected in the order in which the constituents are mentioned:

(132) The escaped convict$_{(theme)}$ was arrested   two days later.
The museum$_{(theme)}$ was renovated in 2005.
This film$_{(theme)}$ has been seen by thousands of people$_{(experiencer)}$.
He$_{(recipient)}$ was given this book$_{(theme)}$ when he was 5.
This book$_{(theme)}$ was given to him$_{(recipient)}$ when he was 5.
I$_{(beneficiary)}$ was bought a bike$_{(theme)}$ for Christmas.[38]

The passive makes it possible to put not the agent or experiencer but rather the theme, recipient or beneficiary in initial position.

5.4.2 Maintaining topic continuity when the topic is not an agent

Another factor that has an impact on the order of the constituents in a clause becomes clear when we consider the wider context of the discourse. Consider the following example:

(133) (a) *The College of William and Mary* is a public university located in Williamsburg, Virginia, United States. *It* is the second-oldest institution of higher education in the United States and is one of the original eight Public Ivies. *It* is also considered a Southern Ivy. *The college* was founded in 1693 by a Royal Charter issued by King William III and Queen Mary II, joint sovereigns of England, Scotland and Ireland. (www)

(b) *The College of William and Mary* is a public university located in Williamsburg, Virginia, United States. *It* is the second-oldest institution of higher education in the United States and is one of the original eight Public Ivies. People consider *it* a Southern Ivy. *A Royal Charter issued by King William III and Queen Mary II*, joint sovereigns of England, Scotland and Ireland founded *the college* in 1693.

It is not a coincidence that the text flows more naturally in (133a). This is because the topic of the story – the College of William and Mary – appears each time in Subject position regardless of its semantic role. We call this principle **topic continuity**. If there is no topic continuity (133b), the text becomes harder to process.

---

[38]In reality, beneficiary Subjects are much rarer than agent, experiencer, theme or recipient Subjects, and not all speakers agree on whether they are well-formed or not. That said, any corpus search confirms that beneficiary Subjects are used in certain circumstances.

5.4.3. Old, given, shared information before new information

It is a general characteristic of English that old information, or information that is shared by speaker and hearer in a given context, is mentioned in Subject position. New information features at the end of the clause. The speaker can also give extra prominence to the agent by mentioning it in final position. Consider the following examples:

> (134) (a) A book on modern art is coming out next spring. It was written by eminent art critic Bill Graham.
> (b) A book on modern art is coming out next spring. ?Eminent art critic Bill Graham wrote it.
> (c) A mathematician has written a new book about modern art.
> (d) A new book about modern art has been written by a mathematician.

The second sentence in (134a) puts the old information first and the new information after it. The pronoun *it* here is characteristic of information that is necessarily shared by speaker and hearer: the referent of *it* constitutes 'old information' because it has already been introduced into the discourse in the sentence immediately preceding it. It is the passive that enables us to place the new information last: as it is an Agent, its normal position would be that of Subject. (134b), compared to (134a), is odd, precisely because in the second sentence, the new information comes first and the old last. In (134c), all the information is new. We might imagine this sentence at the beginning of a newspaper article treating both the book and its author. The relatively neutral way of organizing the information corresponds to the usual, canonical ordering of semantic roles we discussed in Section 5.4.1 above. In (134d), as in (134c), all the information is new as well; here, though, the passive allows us to give the agent extra prominence, something we might want to do if we consider, for instance, that a mathematician writing a book about art is unusual.

5.4.4. Leaving the agent unexpressed

We mentioned before that the agent or experiencer need not be mentioned at all. This characteristic constitutes yet another reason why a passive rather than an active sentence may be used: the speaker may simply not know who or what the agent or experiencer is or may decide not to mention the agent or experiencer explicitly in the clause, either because it is not important or because she chooses to conceal it. The following examples illustrate this fourth context of use of the passive:

(135) The cuts being introduced will result in job losses.

I've been robbed./My bike has been stolen.

Having detected certain irregularities in the company's internal accounts, Vestas Eólica has found out that fraud has been committed against the company. (www)

A British teenager (who was) found dead on a beach in India was murdered, a second post-mortem examination has suggested. The partially clothed body of (the victim) was found in the resort of Anjuna in Goa on 18 February. (www)

The following example shows that the reasons mentioned determining the choice in favour of a passive are not mutually exclusive and can work together: here we can see how both topic continuity and prominence to the agent by mentioning it in final position in a *by*-phrase are achieved through the use of the passive:

(136) eBay Inc. is an American Internet company that manages ebay.com, an online auction and shopping website where people and businesses buy and sell goods and services worldwide. [...] The online auction website was founded in San Jose, California on September 3, 1995 by computer programmer Pierre Omidyar. (www)

We have dealt with the use of the passive in some detail. Like the choice of aspect and the choice of tense (see Chapter 4), the passive has a particular discursive effect. However, unlike the use of the progressive and the tenses, the passive is only very rarely a compulsory form. Although there are contexts in which the use of the passive is far more appropriate than the use of the active, the choice of one or the other form will not actually result in an ungrammatical sentence. The discourse is much more fluent in the example in (133a) than in (133b), for instance, but taken individually, the sentences are grammatically acceptable all the same.

It should be clear now that a speaker opts for a passive construction for semantic reasons and that the use of a passive sentence is better viewed as a communicative strategy than as the result of a mechanical conversion or transformation of an active sentence.

5.5 Complementation and the passive

Having outlined some of the basic complementation patterns in English and given an account of how the passive is used, we will now show how complementation and the passive interact. The link between the two is not trivial: the form of a passive sentence and the constituents that can appear in Subject position are determined entirely by the complements a verb takes. While we argued against an approach to the passive exclusively in terms of an active-to-passive conversion process, the relationship between pairs of active and passive sentences can be useful once the primacy of the passive as an independent form is understood. The following verbal complementation patterns, each of which was discussed in Section 4, will be considered in light of this.

Transitive verbs

V + NP

V + *that*-clause

V + *-ing* clause + NP

V + *to*-infinitive + NP

V + NP + *-ing* clause

V + NP + *to*-infinitive

V + NP + bare infinitive

V+ Prepositional Object

Verbs with two Objects

V + DO + OC

V + IO + DO

5.5.1 The active sentence contains a DO

5.5.1.1 The DO is an NP

A DO realized as an NP in an active sentence corresponds to the Subject in the passive sentence:

(137) Someone has forced the lock on my front door.
   The lock on my front door has been forced.

5.5.1.2 The DO is a *that*-clause

When the DO in an active sentence is a *that*-clause, we can in theory find the DO in Subject position:

(138) They reported that the tsunami had reached the coast.
   That the tsunami had reached the coast was reported.

The passive sentence in (138), however, is difficult to process and is not an optimal way of communicating the information so as to highlight the event rather than the reporting of it. In this case, a process called **extraposition** (see Chapter 6, Section 1) takes place: the Subject is moved to end position and empty *it* becomes its placeholder in initial position. The label **impersonal passive** is sometimes used to refer to this type of sentence. An alternative construction which is often used raises the Subject in the *that*-clause to Subject position in the passive clause. This is referred to as **Subject raising**:

(139) It was reported that the tsunami had reached the coast. (impersonal passive)
      The tsunami was reported to have reached the coast. (Subject raising)

Subject raising is possible with verbs of saying and verbs of cognition, such as *acknowledge, assume, believe, claim, consider, declare, expect, feel, find, know, report, say, see, suppose, think* and *understand*. Here are some more examples that illustrate both solutions:

(140) They acknowledged (that) he was a loyal friend.
      It was acknowledged (that) he was a loyal friend.
      He was acknowledged to be a loyal friend.

      They claimed (that) the factories had caused extensive water pollution.
      It was claimed (that) the factories had caused extensive water pollution.
      The factories were claimed to have caused extensive water pollution.

Verbs in the active voice may also be complemented by a non-finite clause, that is, an infinitive clause or an -*ing* clause.[39]

5.5.1.3 The DO is an -*ing* clause with an NP

In sentence (141a), the clausal complement *carrying my daughter* – which is itself a DO (*What do I not like? Carrying my daughter*) – contains its own internal DO (*Who do I carry? My daughter*). This internal DO can be found in Subject position in a passive sentence, but the change from active to passive (141b) coincides with a change in meaning. Passive auxiliary *be* is added to the -*ing* clause and not to the main verb:

(141) (a) I don't like carrying my daughter. She's too heavy.
      (b) My daughter doesn't like being carried. She's quite independent.

The example in (142) below is similar, but in this case the Object internal to the clausal DO is an IO:

(142) They denied telling him that prisoners had been tortured.
      He denied being told that prisoners had been tortured.

---

[39]The classes of verbs that are discussed in Sections 5.5.1.3 to 5.5.1.7. correspond to those listed in Table 2.4.

Other verbs with this type of alternations include verbs of cognition (e.g. *consider, imagine, remember*), verbs of affective stance (e.g. *enjoy, resent*) and a few others (e.g. *avoid, delay, deny, describe*).

5.5.1.4 The DO is a *to*-infinitive with an NP

In our survey of non-finite complements in Table 2.4, we distinguished two subclasses under verb + *to*-infinitive + NP (category III). The subclasses reflect a structural and semantic difference that especially comes to the fore in the passive. With the verbs *begin, continue, start, appear, seem, tend* and *come*, the clausal complement does not function as a DO. *Appear, seem* and *tend* enable the speaker to be noncommittal; the others zoom in on a stage of the process referred to by a lexical verb. Simplifying somewhat, all of these verbs give further information about how the lexical verb that follows should be looked at. The DO NP in the infinitival complement in the active is in Subject position in the passive. Passive auxiliary *be* is added to the infinitive clause and not to the main verb:

(143) My senior colleagues have started to resent me.
I have started to be resented by my senior colleagues.

The examining board seems to have misunderstood my request.
My request seems to have been misunderstood (by the examining board).

Extroverts tend to overshadow introverts in the classroom.
Introverts tend to be overshadowed in the classroom (by extroverts).

As the examples show, the passive and the active sentences have basically the same meaning.

The verbs *agree, aim, attempt, try, hope, refuse* and *struggle* differ from the previous set in that the *to*-infinitive + NP is the DO of the main verbs. Here, the meaning of the corresponding passive sentence is considerably different:

(144) The army refused to induct the soldier.
The soldier refused to be inducted.

They hope to recruit several of the applicants.
Several of the applicants hope to be recruited.

When the non-finite clause (be it an -*ing* clause (5.5.1.5) or an infinitive clause (5.5.1.6)) is preceded by an NP, two types of pattern emerge: either (i) the NP can be used in Subject position with no fundamental difference in meaning or (ii) the passive voice cannot be used at all.

5.5.1.5 The DO is an NP followed by an -*ing* clause

With the verbs of the senses like *see, hear* and *notice* and verbs like *bring, catch, find, keep, send* and *show*, it is the NP that precedes the -*ing* clause that is found in Subject position in the passive. Apart from the usual shift in topic associated with a passive construction, the active sentences and the passive sentences are synonymous:

(145) The neighbours heard the children sneaking back home after midnight.
       The children were heard sneaking back home after midnight.

       Has the dentist ever kept you waiting at his office?
       Have you ever been kept waiting at the dentist's office?

Not any verb that takes an NP + -*ing* clause complement can be used in the passive voice. Verbs of affective stance (e.g. *anticipate, appreciate, dislike, dread, hate, like, (not) mind, regret*) and verbs of cognition (e.g. *forget, imagine, recall, remember*), for instance, are not compatible with a passive sentence in which the NP is found in Subject position:

(146) I really appreciate you helping me through this very difficult time.
       *You are really appreciated helping me through this very difficult time.

       She just barely remembers her older brother leaving for college.
       *Her older brother is just barely remembered leaving for college.

5.5.1.6 The DO is an NP followed by a *to*-infinitive clause

Verbs such as *can't bear, hate, love, need, prefer, want* and *wish*, which are complemented by a DO realized as an NP + *to*-infinitive in the active, cannot be used in a passive sentence:

(147) I prefer others to take the lead and show me what to do.
       *Others are preferred to take the lead and show me what to do.

       They need the organization to support them financially.
       *The organization is needed to support them financially.

With a number of verbs such as *expect, feel, mean* and *report*, the NP preceding the *to*-infinitive can become Subject:

(148) They felt her to be too absent-minded.
       She was felt to be too absent-minded.

       My friend expected me to give her some money.
       I was expected to give my friend some money.

At first sight, the examples that follow look similar to the examples in (147) and (148): the main verb is followed by an NP + *to*-infinitive. However, in the examples in (149), the NP functions as IO. Therefore, these examples will be discussed in Section 5.5.3, which focuses on verbs that take two complements, including ditransitive verbs like *teach* and *instruct*:

(149) My first piano teacher taught me to appreciate the harpsichord.
I was taught to appreciate the harpsichord by my first piano teacher.

Someone must have instructed her to refuse entry to anyone under 18.
She must have been instructed to refuse entry to anyone under 18.

5.5.1.7 The DO is an NP followed by a bare infinitive clause

Verbs of the senses may be followed by an *-ing* clause or a bare infinitive clause in an active sentence. We discussed the difference in meaning between the two types of complementation in Section 4.2.3. The same difference in meaning can also be observed in the passive constructions with this kind of verb:

(150) Some have heard him telling people that he's resigning.
He has been heard telling people that he's resigning.

Witnesses saw the suspect run in the opposite direction.
The suspect was seen to run in the opposite direction.

Note that while the bare infinitive is used in the active sentence, the passive sentence requires a *to*-infinitive.

Like verbs of the senses, verbs with **causative meaning** like *make* and *have* (verbs that communicate that someone wants someone else to do something) are complemented by an NP followed by a bare infinitive. *Get* can also have causative meaning, but it takes an NP followed by a *to*-infinitive complement:

(151) The teacher made the pupils recite the rule every day.
The pupils were made to recite the rule every day.

She had her assistant prepare the slides for the presentation.
She had the slides for the presentation prepared by her assistant.

We finally got him to admit that he'd been wrong.
(no passive possible; see below)

While the causative meaning of the three verbs is similar, passive sentences give rise to different constructions. With *make*, it is the NP preceding the infinitive clause that corresponds to the Subject in the passive; it is followed by passive auxiliary *be* + the past participle of *make* + a *to*-infinitive:

(152) The evil stepmother made Cinderella scrub the floor until it was spotless.
Cinderella was made to scrub the floor until it was spotless.

The students made the administration accept their proposal.
The administration were made to accept the students' proposal.

In a sentence with causative *have*, the passive is realized in the infinitive clause following *have*. The NP that is DO in the active infinitive clause functions as Subject in the passive. Passive auxiliary *be* is not added; the only verb form is the past participle of the lexical verb in the infinitive clause. The NP that is Subject in the active infinitive clause, if mentioned at all, is found in a *by*-PrepP:

(153) The director had her secretary retype the entire report.
The director had the entire report retyped (by her secretary).

Can't you have someone water the plants while you're away?
Can't you have the plants watered while you're away?

In other words, in passive sentences with causative *make*, it is the person targeted by the instruction (the beneficiary) that features in Subject position; in passive sentences with causative *have*, it is the theme that occurs in Subject position.

Causative *get* is not usually used in the passive at all:

(154) They got him to admit that he had stolen tins of coffee from the staffroom.
*He was got to admit that he had stolen tins of coffee from the staffroom.

5.5.2 The active sentence contains a Prepositional Object

Apart from taking a DO as a complement, a verb may also require a Prepositional Object. If the verb is complemented by a Prepositional Object (i.e. when we are dealing with a prepositional verb), the NP functioning as Object of the Preposition within the PrepP can occasionally be the Subject of the passive sentence, but this is not always the case:

(155) Grandparents often look after their grandchildren when both parents work.
Grandchildren are often looked after by their grandparents when both parents work.

Do you really think I take after my mother more than my father?
*Do you really think my mother is taken after by me more than my father?

It is not possible to make hard-and-fast generalizations that explain which prepositional verbs allow the NP to be moved and which ones do not.

The relevance of the distinction between a particle and a preposition is now particularly clear as particle verbs, unlike prepositional verbs, can be used in a passive construction. As pointed out on p. 63, a transitive particle verb is a multi-word verb that requires a DO. The DO of a transitive particle verb can always be the Subject of a passive sentence:

(156) I've dropped the children off at school. Someone will need to pick them up later.
The children have been dropped off at school. They'll need to be picked up later.

Has a colleague ever asked you out on a date? How did he bring the subject up?
Have you ever been asked out on a date by a colleague? How was the subject brought up?

Finally note that a PrepP following the verb is not necessarily required by the verb. Put differently, it is not necessarily a complement – it may also function as an Adjunct. It is generally not possible for an NP that is Object of a Preposition to (be moved out of the PrepP and) become the Subject of a passive sentence when the PrepP is an Adjunct:

(157) Hardly anyone came to their impromptu housewarming party.
*Their impromptu housewarming party was come to by hardly anyone.

There are a few exceptions to this, however. In such cases, the Object of a Preposition is felt as having been somehow affected:

(158) The receptionist didn't believe me when I said my bed had been slept in.
That old pool of theirs hasn't been swum in for years.
After the accident, the car looked like it had been sat on by an elephant.

5.5.3 The active sentence contains two objects
If the verb is complemented by two objects, the possibility to use either Object in Subject position in a passive sentence depends on their function and their form.

5.5.3.1 DO + OC
If the verb is followed by a DO and an OC, it is the DO that becomes Subject and the OC becomes SC:

(159) American voters elected Roosevelt President of the United States in 1932.
Roosevelt was elected President of the United States in 1932.

They considered the results promising enough to warrant further trials.
The results were considered promising enough to warrant further trials.

Verbs like *appoint, call, consider, believe* and *name* also belong to this category.

5.5.3.2 IO + DO

The verb may also be followed by an IO and a DO, in which case the following correspondences can be observed between the active voice and the passive voice:

1. If the DO is a *that*-clause or a *to*-infinitive clause, only the active IO (NP) can be the Subject in a passive sentence:

> (160) Someone should tell them (that) they're making a terrible mistake.
> They should be told (that) they're making a terrible mistake.
> *That they're making a terrible mistake should be told to them.

> (161) Someone asked us to keep our voices down during the recital.
> We were asked to keep our voices down during the recital.
> *To keep our voices down during the recital was asked of us.

Verbs such as *assure, convince, remind* and *warn* are found with a *that*-clause; verbs such as *advise, allow, ask, instruct, mean, order, persuade, require, teach, tell* and *understand* are found with a *to*-infinitive clause (see category IV (c) in Table 2.4).[40]

2. If the DO is an NP and the IO is always realized as a *to*-PrepP, only the active DO can be the Subject in a passive clause:

> (162) The researchers should explain the results to the subjects of the study.
> *The subjects of the study should be explained the results.
> The results should be explained to the subject of the study.

> (163) The composer dedicated the concerto to the victims of the disaster.
> *The victims of the disaster were dedicated the concerto.
> The concerto was dedicated to the victims of the disaster.

3. If the DO is an NP and the IO can take the form of a PrepP or an NP, both the active DO NP and the IO NP can be the Subject in a passive sentence. If the active DO is Subject in the passive, the form of the IO is obligatorily a *to*-PrepP:

---

[40]It may be useful to point out once more that not any 'NP + clausal complement' can be analysed as an IO (realized as an NP) followed by a (clausal) DO. In some cases (cf. Section 5.5.1.6), the NP is part of the constituent functioning as DO.

(164) The management promised a 5 per cent pay rise to senior staff.
(cf. The management promised senior staff a 5 per cent rise.)

Senior staff were promised a 5 per cent pay rise.
A 5 per cent pay rise was promised to senior staff.

(165) I've read my children this book of fairy tales hundreds of times.
(cf. I've read this book of fairy tales to my children hundreds of times.)

This book of fairy tales has been read to my children hundreds of times.
My children have been read this book of fairy tales hundreds of times.

In Section 5, we have studied passive constructions. It is especially important to realize that this structure is used for a variety of reasons that we explained in Section 5.4. In Section 5.2, we looked at the formal characteristics of a passive clause. We showed what kind of constituents can occur in Subject position and compared active and passive constructions with a variety of complementation patterns in Section 5.5. Although we view the passive voice as more than a mere conversion of the active voice, it is helpful to have an insight into the formal characteristics and mechanics of the passive: knowledge of the strictly formal correspondence between active and passive may well be what ultimately helps you to get the sentence right.

6. Conclusion

Our goal in Chapter 2 was ambitious, and we covered a lot of ground. Going into a certain amount of detail about the verb and the VP is justified, however, given that any sentence can very informally be conceived as having at its crux a verb. Auxiliaries, we saw, have syntactic properties inextricably linked to functions as basic as formulating a question. Omnipresent, they also play a crucial role in the tense and aspect system we will explore in Chapter 4. Constituents cluster around lexical verbs in much the same way as we saw, in Chapter 1, different parts of speech cluster around the head of a phrasal constituent. Indeed, in much the same way as determiners and adjectives cluster around the head of an NP, constituents functioning as Subjects, DOs and IOs cluster around a lexical verb. In the next chapter, we will momentarily leave the verb aside and take a look at the noun and the noun phrase (or NP), focusing on the characteristics of nouns themselves, the internal organization of the NP and, of course, the way NPs participate in building a meaningful, grammatical sentence. The notion of reference –

that is, the link between a linguistic entity (e.g. an NP) and what it refers to in the real world – will be another topic we will examine in some detail.

Exercises

Exercise 1. Complete the sentences with the correct form of *have* or *do*. Determine whether the forms are auxiliary verbs or lexical verbs. Negative forms may be required.

1. You've written an interesting essay, but I _____ think it could be shorter.
2. He offered to sell me his computer, but I _____ already bought one.
3. What _____ you think we should _____ to solve the problem?
4. Unfortunately, I _____ see the exhibition. I _____ buy the catalogue, however.
5. You'll definitely recognize her. She _____ a very angular face and short black hair.
6. By the time we got there, the concert _____ started.
7. They _____ a Volkswagen now. I think they _____ always _____ Volkswagens.
8. We _____ a look around before deciding whether to stay there.
9. Too bad she doesn't like strawberries. – But she _____ like strawberries!
10. I'm sure he's not a doctor, but I _____ know what he actually _____ _____ for a living. _____ you know what he _____?

Exercise 2. First, identify in which sentences below *have/has* is an auxiliary. Then determine for the remaining sentences when *have got/has got* is also possible. Finally, give the negative and interrogative forms for each sentence with *have/has* and *have got/has got*. Use the information provided in brackets for the interrogative clauses when necessary.

1. I often have a drink after work. (you)
2. He has his father's eyes.
3. I have read Ian McEwan's latest book. (you)
4. William has a twin brother.
5. They always have a good time at parties.
6. I have an idea where she could be hiding. (you)
7. They have finally reached a mutual agreement.
8. He hardly goes out any more – he has children now.
9. They have a summer house by the seaside.
10. My parents usually have a Christmas party. (your parents)

Exercise 3. Rewrite the sentences, moving the italicized elements to the beginning of the sentence and making any other necessary changes.

1. She did *not once* ask me about what was going on in my life.
2. She mentions her husband's vital role in the project *at no point*.

3. We will *not* know the answer *until late in the day*.
4. There will *never* be another actress like Elizabeth Taylor.
5. He had *barely* arrived when she said it was time to leave again.
6. I *only occasionally* felt lonely during my year abroad.
7. The new fad had *no sooner* caught on than it disappeared.
8. You will *seldom* experience such genuine hospitality.
9. You do *not often* see an actor accept criticism humbly.
10. I did *not* mean *in any way* to offend you with that comment.
11. I have *not at any time* transferred money into that account.
12. You will *not* find a restaurant of this quality *anywhere else*.

Exercise 4. (i) Transform each of the following declarative clauses into a yes-no interrogative clause. Use *you* when it is provided in brackets. (ii) Transform each of the declarative clauses into a *wh*-interrogative clause, using a *wh*-constituent that corresponds to the italicized segment. If two segments are italicized, provide two separate *wh*-interrogatives. Pay particular attention to the subordinator *that* in the interrogatives corresponding to the even-numbered sentences.

1. We have enrolled *150* students for the summer session.
2. The director claims <u>that</u> *150* students have enrolled for *the summer session*.
3. She scribbled down the message with a red crayon *because she didn't have a pen*.
4. I suppose <u>that</u> *she* scribbled down the message with *a red crayon*. (you)
5. *The orchid* show will be taking place *in the northeast pavilion*.
6. I think <u>that</u> *the orchid show* will be taking place in *the northeast* pavilion. (you)
7. We're taking care of *Paul's* children *tomorrow night*.
8. You said <u>that</u> *something funny* happened to *Paul's children*.
9. You should have your teeth cleaned *every six months*.
10. Most dentists say <u>that</u> *children* should *have their teeth cleaned* regularly.
11. He saw *several teenagers* walking away from the scene of the crime.
12. He claimed <u>that</u> *several* teenagers were walking away from the scene of the crime.
13. *Several things* need to be accomplished by next Wednesday.
14. She said <u>that</u> *these things* need to be accomplished by *next Wednesday*.
15. *The train for Geneva* is scheduled to leave *at 8:23* from platform 8.
16. They said <u>that</u> *the train for Geneva* would be leaving late *because of fog*.

Exercise 5. Study the charts below. Then complete the sentences in three different ways.

The same situation applies: (+)

Affirmative context

		So aux Subject	or	Subject aux, *too*.
		(+)		(+)
He likes fish.	→	So does she.	or	She does, too.

Negative context

		Neither aux Subject	or	Subject neg-aux *either*.
		(+)		(+)
She can't sing.	→	Neither can they.	or	They can't either.

<u>**The same situation does not apply: (–)**</u>

Affirmative context

		(–)
He will succeed.	→	but I won't.

Negative context

		(–)
They haven't finished.	→	but I have.

1. I was a rebellious teenager, and/but …
   (+) my brother   (–) my best friend   (+) most of my friends
2. I get up at 7 o'clock every day, and/but …
   (–) my boyfriend   (+) my wife   (–) my children
3. I can't run very fast, and/but …
   (–) Julia   (+) my mother   (–) they
4. I never work on Sundays, and/but …
   (–) my brother   (+) my best friend   (–) some people
5. When I was a kid, I loved Brussels sprouts, and/but …
   (+) my boyfriend   (–) my wife   (+) my sister
6. I've never met anyone famous, and/but …
   (+) my girlfriend   (–) a couple of my friends   (+) Stephen
7. When I was in high school, I didn't like French, and/but …
   (+) Julia   (–) almost everyone else   (+) my classmates

Exercise 6. Complete the following dialogue using the correct auxiliary to form interrogative tags (with or without reverse polarity) or short questions/ short answers.

He: I'm in no mood to prepare dinner. Let's go out instead, _____ we?

She: Fine with me. It's been a long week for both of us, _____ it?

He: Indeed it _____. We can go to that Chinese place round the corner. Wait a minute – you like Chinese, _____ you?

She: Yes, I _____, though perhaps not as much as you _____. I think we should ask Rebecca to join us.

He: _____ you? She won't want to come along. She's just started that new job.

She: Oh, so she got the job, _____ she? I wasn't aware of that.

He: There were ten other candidates. She was a shoo-in, though.

She: _____ she? I suppose so. I've always thought she was a bit of a slacker.

He: _____ you really? Interesting, I didn't know that.

Exercise 7. Add interrogative tags to the following sentences.

1. You'd rather go to a Japanese restaurant.
2. You went to last year's job fair.
3. People seldom say what they really think.
4. He hates swimming in that dirty lake.
5. They rarely eat out.
6. But I'm an experienced teacher.
7. Let's take a break and have some lunch.
8. There's a shorter way to get there from here.
9. Everyone has 'the perfect solution'.
10. Everybody's got 'the perfect solution'.
11. They've never even tried oysters.
12. Give me a hand moving these chairs.
13. That's John sitting over there.
14. She'd better start working.

Exercise 8. Add interrogative tags to the following sentences and determine whether the intonation is more likely to be rising (⇑) or falling (⇓). Try in each case to explain why.

1. You didn't laugh once during the movie. You didn't think it was funny, _____?
2. Let's ask Monica to come along, _____? I haven't seen her in such a long time.
3. You don't know what time the play starts, _____? I thought I'd written it down.
4. You really don't like the new physics teacher, _____? It was pretty obvious.
5. I've offended you, _____? Sorry, I didn't mean it.
6. This chocolate cake is just divine, _____?
7. Hey, keep it down in there, _____? Some of us are trying to sleep!
8. Where's Katie? She's not late again, _____?

Exercise 9. Provide a negative short answer to the questions below. Then complete the answer by using two different structures to express causality: (i) *have someone do something* and (ii) *have something done (by someone)*. Use the cues in brackets to complete your answer.

ex: Did you do it yourself? (someone else)
No, I didn't. I had someone else do it.
No, I didn't. I had it done (by someone else).

1. Will you repair the carburettor yourself? (the mechanic)
2. Did she make that cocktail dress herself? (her mother)
3. Does he renovate the rooms himself? (interior designer)
4. Are you going to plant those trees yourself? (the gardener)
5. Do they always develop the photographs themselves? (a professional)

6. Will you prepare the presentation yourself? (my assistant)
7. Did you frame that picture yourself? (a local artist)

Exercise 10. Decide which of the following verbs are intransitive, transitive and ditransitive. Use simple NPs to construct sentences illustrating the different possibilities. Which verbs usually require a Prepositional Complement? Use a dictionary if necessary.

hesitate	cook	sleep	afford	put	love
take place	fetch	last	greet	hand	obey

Exercise 11. Identify the Indirect Objects realized as PrepPs in the following sentences. Determine in which cases they can be also realized as NPs and rewrite the sentence accordingly. Finally, provide all possible passive sentences for each sentence.

1. The foreman will demonstrate the procedure to the new employees.
2. The woman had left $10,000 to her favourite nephew.
3. Only rarely do they read bedtime stories to the children.
4. The astronaut described the feeling of weightlessness to the journalists.
5. Someone ought to write a nasty letter to the editor.
6. Patriotic citizens will often send letters to soldiers fighting overseas.
7. Parents should never entrust their children to just anyone.
8. The teacher brought frosted cupcakes to his students.
9. The captain of the team introduced all the players to us.
10. I repeated the instructions to my assistant very slowly.

Exercise 12. Identify the Indirect Objects realized as NPs in the following sentences. Determine whether *to* or *for* is used when the Indirect Object is realized as a PrepP and rewrite the sentence accordingly. Finally, provide all possible passive sentences for each sentence.

1. I hope the travel agent can find us a quiet hotel by the seaside.
2. We thought it'd be easier to prepare everyone a simple picnic lunch.
3. They left the babysitter specific instructions on the dining room table.
4. That shop will lend us the costumes for two weeks.
5. The realtors are offering potential buyers £500 off their monthly mortgage.
6. If you show a dog a bone and then hide it, he'll look for it until he finds it.
7. You should bake the twins a cake yourself rather than buy one.
8. My father bought me this dress when I was only 17.
9. The dean has promised all incoming freshmen a new laptop computer.
10. The buyer will pay the vendor the full price within thirty days.

Exercise 13. Analyse the following sentences, identifying particles and prepositions that function with particle, prepositional and prepositional particle verbs. Determine whether the verbs are transitive or intransitive and, if transitive, identify the Direct Object. Identify which sentences can be used in the passive.

1. Sorry to cut in, but I really must object to what's being said.
2. Don't mind me, I'm just going about my business.
3. Why don't you just drop by on the way home?
4. It's his passion for painting that got him through that difficult period.
5. We have run up against some unforeseen problems.
6. I really must brush up on my Japanese before my trip to Tokyo.
7. Personally, I think you've let him off too easily.
8. He takes after his mother in more ways than one.
9. I'm sure she put her brother up to this.
10. I can't make anything of this chicken scratch.
11. The police will have to look into the disturbances.
12. You can run the machine off four AA batteries.

Exercise 14. Analyse the following sentences, identifying particles and prepositions that function with particle, prepositional and prepositional particle verbs. Determine whether the verbs are transitive or intransitive and, if transitive, identify the Direct Object. Identify which sentences can be used in the passive.

1. The car's acting up again. I think we need to have it tuned up.
2. His plane didn't take off until almost 10 pm.
3. I like it when my boyfriend takes me out for a romantic meal.
4. Someone should fill the others in on what's been going on.
5. Would someone please let me in on the big secret?
6. You'll never be able to talk them into participating in your scheme.
7. His laidback personality has not rubbed off on his children.
8. Hasn't anyone filled you in? They've put off the meeting again.
9. I must take the matter up with my husband.
10. You're crazy if you think she's going to fall for that old trick.
11. They laid off seventy-five employees in only two months.
12. I think I'm coming down with a bad cold.

Exercise 15. Complete the sentences using the correct form (*-ing* or *to*-infinitive) of the verb in brackets. More than one answer may be possible.

1. His friends quit (invite) him out when they realized he never accepted their invitations.
2. If you decide (sign) the lease, show it to someone else first.

3. My grandfather started (work) when he was only fourteen years old.
4. I'd like (remind) everyone (keep) the last weekend of June open for the company picnic.
5. You must come with us. I refuse (take) 'no' for an answer!
6. Have they discussed (close) down the plant, or is that just a rumour?
7. Would you mind (save) us a couple of seats? We have to finish (write) up this report.
8. They don't expect (finish) before this afternoon.

Exercise 16. Complete the sentences using the correct form (*-ing* or *to*-infinitive) of one of the following verbs. More than one answer may be possible.

understand	convince	stay	get	love
quit	have	be able	leave	play
prepare	meet	read	work	regret

1. I fail _____ why anyone would want to climb Mount Everest.
2. Once I've finished _____ dinner, I can help you with your homework.
3. They appreciate _____ to spend time with their grandchildren.
4. By the time I'd begun _____ the second chapter, I knew how the story would end.
5. They intend _____ with us for only a few days. At least that's what they say.
6. They want _____ their jobs and move to a commune in the mountains.
7. SWF seeks SWM for romance. Enjoys outdoor activities and _____ sports.
8. If you continue _____ such long hours, you'll end up _____ it.
9. I don't see how they manage _____ anything done with so many children in the house.
10. I would avoid _____ during rush hour if I were you.
11. You say I've met your parents, but I don't recall _____ them at all.
12. She hopes _____ the entire staff that an open office plan is best.
13. Do you promise _____ this woman till death do you part?
14. He freely admits _____ a real weakness for cakes and sweets.

Exercise 17. Complete the sentences using the correct form (*-ing* or *to*-infinitive) of the verb in brackets. More than one answer may be possible.

1. (a) The driver of a truck who stopped (assist) at an accident scene died early this morning.
   (b) The government stopped (consider) military action.
2. (a) He founded an organization to help veterans of the war, many of whom went on (fight) elsewhere.
   (b) The attendees went on (talk) even after they'd been asked to lower their voices and pay attention.

3. (a) If all staff remembered (turn off) equipment at night, the University could save around 10 per cent of its carbon emissions.

   (b) I remembered that we were having chicken because I distinctly remembered (turn on) the hot water in the sink to defrost it. The thing is, I couldn't remember (turn) the hot water off. The moral: don't forget (turn) off the tap! (www, adapted)

4. (a) The doctor explained what I should do to protect myself from unplanned pregnancy if I forget (take) my birth control pill.

   (b) I'll never forget (see) my new-born son for the very first time.

5. (a) The Rector regrets (announce) the death of Professor John Baker, Emeritus Professor of the University.

   (b) Clark said the Prime Minister regretted (announce) reforms of MPs' expenses without consulting the party first.

6. (a) I've tried (give up) smoking many times, but have always failed.

   (b) If you want to lose weight, why don't you try (give up) up junk food?

7. (a) I meant (attend) the funeral to show respect to the family, but I could not get off work.

   (b) For her, a spiritual experience necessarily meant (attend) a traditional religious service.

8. (a) I like (talk) to people about their lives, even if I don't know them well.

   (b) She would like (talk) to us about some interesting new ideas she has for our firm.

Exercise 18. Integrate the information in brackets into the first clause, using either an -*ing* clause or a bare infinitive clause. In some cases, either form is acceptable (with or without a difference in meaning). If more than one form is possible, paraphrase the difference in meaning, if any, associated with each form.

1. (a) I watched the children (play a game of hide and seek).

   (b) I watched the students (demonstrate against the higher fees).

2. (a) The parents are now listening to their children (play a Bach sonata).

   (b) The proud parents heard their daughter (play a Bach sonata).

3. (a) I felt a bee (crawl over my skin).

   (b) They felt the tension (rise).

4. (a) They saw the water level (rise to over 2 metres).

   (b) I watched my sister (win the race).

5. (a) The teacher noticed one of her students (cheat at the exam).

   (b) We noticed the head of department (be told off by one of his colleagues).

6. (a) I could hear car after car (whirr down the county road).

   (b) I suddenly heard the vase (shatter into a million pieces).

Exercise 19. Read the following two excerpts below. In what way(s) do they differ in form and what is the difference in effect that is achieved? Pay particular attention to the italicized forms.

(a) The Rosetta Stone is a fragment of an Ancient Egyptian stone slab, or stele, with an engraved text that provided the key to the modern understanding of Egyptian hieroglyphs. *The original stele* is thought to have been displayed within a temple. *It* was probably moved during the early Christian or medieval period and eventually used as building material in the construction of a fort in the town of Rosetta (now Rashid) in the Nile Delta. *It* was discovered there in 1799 by a soldier of the French expedition to Egypt. (adapted from www)

(b) The Rosetta Stone is a fragment of an Ancient Egyptian stone slab, or stele, with an engraved text that provided the key to the modern understanding of Egyptian hieroglyphs. *People today* think that *people in the past* displayed the original stele within a temple. *Unidentified people* probably moved it during the early Christian or medieval period and eventually used it as building material in the construction of a fort in the town of Rosetta (now Rashid) in the Nile Delta. *A soldier of the French expedition to Egypt* discovered it there in 1799.

Exercise 20. Identify and comment upon the passive forms in the following text. Give an active form for all passives with an identifiable agent.

Walter Mbotela recounts the tales of how his grandfather was captured as a slave by Arab traders and shipped away from his birthplace in Nyasaland with great emotion.

Mr Mbotela senior, along with other slaves, were driven away from their villages and loaded into ships destined for Zanzibar, East Africa's main slave market until 1873. These captives were however lucky, as after they were purchased and in transit to work in plantations, their ship was intercepted by the British Royal Navy, which was patrolling the Indian Ocean slave routes to enforce the UK ban on the slave trade, adopted in 1807. For close to 70 years after abolition, the trade continued to flourish on the East African coast. 'The boat my grandfather and other slaves were sailing on was brought to Mombasa, instead of being taken to other freed slaves settlements in India', Mr Mbotela, a 93-year-old retired journalist recalls. Other lucky slaves, aboard cargo ships that were intercepted by the British Navy, found themselves relocated to a freed slave settlement, christened Frere Town. This area in the port city of Mombasa was named after the Sir Bartle Frere, who abolished the Zanzibar slave trade. (www)

Exercise 21. Identify the passive and active forms in this text and comment upon them.

In a language or dialect, a **phoneme** is the smallest segmental unit of sound employed to form meaningful contrasts between utterances. A phoneme is thus a group of slightly different sounds which are all perceived to have the same function by speakers of the language or dialect in question. An example of a phoneme is the /k/ sound in the words *kit* and *skill*. (In transcription, phonemes are placed between slashes, as here.) Although most native speakers don't notice this, in most dialects the k sounds in each of these words are actually pronounced differently: they are different speech sounds, or phones (which, in transcription, are placed in square brackets). In our example, the /k/ in *kit* is aspirated, [kʰ], while the /k/ in *skill* is not, [k]. The reason why these different sounds are nonetheless considered to belong to the same phoneme in English is that if an English speaker used one instead of the other, the meaning of the word would not change: using [kʰ] in *skill* might sound odd, but the word would still be recognized. By contrast, some other phonemes could be substituted (creating a minimal pair) which would cause a change in meaning: producing words like *still* (substituting /t/), *spill* (substituting /p/) and *swill* (substituting /w/). These other sounds (/t/,/p/and /w/) are, in English, different phonemes. In some languages, however, [kʰ] and [k] are different phonemes, and are perceived as such by the speakers of those languages. (adapted from Wikipedia)

Exercise 22. Identify the passive and active forms in this text and comment upon them.

Origami is the art of paper folding, which is often associated with Japanese culture. In modern usage, the word 'origami' is used as an inclusive term for all folding practices, regardless of their culture of origin. The goal is to transform a flat square sheet of paper into a finished sculpture through folding and sculpting techniques. Modern origami practitioners generally discourage the use of cuts, glue or markings on the paper. Origami folders often use the Japanese word *kirigami* to refer to designs which use cuts, although cutting is more characteristic of Chinese papercrafts. The small number of basic origami folds can be combined in a variety of ways to make intricate designs. The best-known origami model is the Japanese paper crane. In general, these designs begin with a square sheet of paper whose sides may be of different colors, prints or patterns. Traditional Japanese origami, which has been practised since the Edo period (1603–1867), has often been less strict about these conventions, sometimes cutting the paper or using nonsquare shapes to start with. The principles of origami are also used in stents, packaging and other engineering applications. (adapted from Wikipedia)

Exercise 23. Consider the different active and passive sentences that can be created from the cues in the following chart. Choose a logical verb tense and add any Adjuncts to flesh out the context.

	Agent	Verb	Theme	Recipient	Beneficiary
1.	my children	cook	a fine meal		I/me
2.	the doctors	examine	the burn victims		
3.	elderly people	not use	the metro		
4.	they	tear down	the old buildings		
5.	they	give	strict instructions	all of us	
6.	they	tell	the whole truth	everyone	
7.	the parents	buy	a new car		the girl
8.	the police	question	the pedestrians		

Exercise 24. Identify the passive forms in the following passages and explain why they are being used.

1. Yogurt is simply milk that has been soured by various strains of *Lactobacillus*. The most common strains found in active cultures are *L. bulgaricus* and *L. acidophilus*. Yogurt was originally made with ewe's milk and, if you happen to have a nursing ewe around, you are welcome to repeat the original recipe. I haven't. Cow's milk is too easy to come by. Yogurt was originally discovered in Central Asia by the nomadic tribes there. (www)

2. 'The next two years are going to be incredibly difficult, and budget cuts will have to be made,' said board member Ronald Bunce. (www)

3. If life were discovered on another planet, what would the consequences be for us?

4. Having detected certain irregularities in the company's internal accounts, Vestas Eólica has found out that fraud has been committed against the company. (www)

5. Zidane appeared to react to something that was said and was dismissed for his violent charge into his opponent. 'He told me Materazzi said something very serious to him but he wouldn't tell me what,' agent Alain Migliaccio told BBC Five Live Sport. Sources in France say it is believed Materazzi insulted Zidane's family. (www)

6. It has been argued that most interdisciplinary research at least in the past 150 years has been carried out in applied contexts. (www)

Exercise 25. Consider the complementation patterns in the following sentences and give a related sentence in the passive if possible. If there is more than one possibility, give all of them and indicate whether the meaning of the active and passive sentence is basically the same or different. Some sentences may have no corresponding passive.

1. Someone must have seen the women leaving together.
2. The commission will have to have someone translate the document.
3. We all know the suspect has been found guilty of this crime before.
4. You mentioned nothing about this to me when we first spoke.
5. Most parents appear to appreciate the new language teacher.
6. Something is holding up traffic, so I'm afraid I'll be late.
7. Scientists have observed the birds migrating further south than usual.
8. I can still remember taking John to the hospital when he broke his arm.
9. The board made him assistant district manager after only six months.
10. They'll give most of us a generous bonus just before Christmas.
11. They might cancel the concert due to poor ticket sales.
12. I think they actually meant us to hear everything they were saying.
13. No one had brought that delicate matter up in a long time.
14. That young ruffian continued to taunt her every day after school.
15. You shouldn't expect anyone to accept such poor working conditions.

16. The head of the orphanage made the poor children sleep on the cold floor.
17. The prison warden caught the prisoner trying to escape from her cell.
18. I often got my older sister to do my homework for me.
19. Someone needs to fill this application form out and sign it.
20. She wants her gardener to plant more rose bushes this year.

Exercise 26. Consider the complementation patterns in the following sentences and give a related sentence in the passive if possible. If there is more than one possibility, give all of them and indicate whether the meaning of the active and passive sentence is basically the same or different. Some sentences may have no corresponding passive.

1. They will name him interim coordinator until they find someone permanent.
2. They expected that the president would nominate someone from the opposition.
3. No one has lived in that property for at least eight or nine years.
4. I really enjoy reading to my children before they go to sleep.
5. We have seen these methods work with children as young as 5.
6. They have reminded the pupils that the bus will wait for no one.
7. A progressive school is trying to hire my younger sister.
8. She won't buy a cot that another baby has already slept in.
9. They agreed to promote him without a significant increase in salary.
10. Most children can't imagine their parents meeting and falling in love.
11. I'm sorry, but we can't put off this meeting any longer.
12. Someone has completely reorganized next month's schedule.
13. Will they propose another option to those people who do not qualify?
14. I really hate you saying such nasty things about me behind my back.
15. You should pay the volunteers a small amount of money to cover expenses.
16. The boss is having an intern transcribe the minutes from today's meeting.
17. Have you told them to sit in the first two rows?
18. Who got you to do such an unpleasant task?
19. You shouldn't make your secretary do any work over the weekend.
20. The master taught his followers to meditate three times a day.

3

The noun and the noun phrase

Chapter Outline

1. The structure of the noun phrase

Our goal in this chapter is to examine that part of speech referred to as the **noun** and the phrasal constituent the **noun phrase** (NP). We will examine some important properties of the noun itself, especially the notion of countability. We will also discuss the question of nominal reference, that is, how the choice of a determiner in the NP is indicative of the (assumed) shared knowledge between speaker and hearer.

An NP is made up minimally of a noun head (e.g. [*Grass*] *is green*), but the noun head in the NP is often further expanded with other elements. These include not only prehead determiners (such as articles) and prehead modifiers (such as adjectives), but also posthead modifiers (such as PrepPs or relative clauses). Consequently, this chapter provides a more unified account of areas of grammar you may previously have considered unrelated.

The noun is usually easily identifiable since nouns often refer to concrete entities we perceive in our everyday existence. Furthermore, the NP, like the VP, is a fundamental building block in the clause. Every clause has a Subject (see footnote 19, Chapter 2), and the function of Subject is quite regularly fulfilled by an NP.[1] We show this in (1a) and (1b), where the bracketed NPs function as Subject and where the head nouns are underlined. NPs can have a variety of other functions as well: Direct Object (1c, 1d and 1e), Indirect Object (1f), Subject Complement (1g) and Object Complement (1h). They can also function as Adjuncts (1i). Finally, the posthead of a prepositional head in a PrepP is almost always an NP[2] (1j) and (1k):

(1) (a) [The book *you're reading*] has been banned in several countries.

   (b) [The books *piled on the table*] need to be taken back to the library today.

   (c) I don't appreciate [the notion *that children should be seen and not heard*].

   (d) She gave a few motivated students [a little homework] over the break.

   (e) When I announced [my decision *to resign*], he did not react well.

   (f) She gave [a few motivated students] a little homework for over the break.

   (g) My aunt is [a woman *with strong principles*].

   (h) I consider my sister [a likeable enough person].

   (i) [That day], I had an appointment with my shrink.

   (j) Her parents always spend their holidays [with [their neighbours]].

   (k) I've carefully studied the applications [of [those candidates *being considered*]].

These example sentences also illustrate some of the ways the head noun of an NP can be preceded or followed by other elements to build an NP. For example, an NP head may be preceded by the following preheads:

   – the definite article *the* (in (1a), (b) and (c)) or the indefinite article *a(n)* (in (1g) and (h))
   – a determiner which is not an article
      a quantifier (*a little* in (1d), *a few* in (f))
      a demonstrative determiner (*that* in (1i), *those* in (k))
      a possessive determiner (*my* in (1e), *their* in (j))
   – an adjective (*motivated* in (1f), *likeable* in (h)).

---

[1]This does not mean that NPs are the only possible constituents that can function as the Subject of a sentence (see Chapter 1):
   [In the bathtub] is not a very comfortable place to sleep. (a PrepP as Subject)
   [That she said I had cheated her] is inexcusable. (a clause as Subject)
[2]Although Objects of Prepositions are very regularly NPs, prepositions can be complemented by other types of phrase as well:
   He'll be working [until [after midnight]]. (the Object of the Preposition is a PrepP)
   They haven't been living here [for [very long]]. (the Object of the Preposition is an AdvP)

And the noun head may be followed by the following postheads:

- a relative clause, italicized in (1a)
- a non-finite clause, italicized in (1b), (e) and (k)
- an appositive clause, italicized in (1c)
- a PrepP, italicized in (1g).

The same pattern we have noticed before is yet again emerging: the function of providing modifying information can be fulfilled by different forms. Much of this chapter will serve to demonstrate the effects preheads and postheads have when combined with a head noun. As the most important element in the NP is the head noun, it is this element that we will examine first before looking at how the definite and indefinite articles are used to establish reference.

2. The noun

2.1 Types of nouns

Nouns can be classified on the basis of a number of criteria. A noun may denote something **concrete** (such as *rain, table* or *factory*) or something **abstract** (such as *happiness, bravery* or *trust*). Abstract nouns tend to be uncountable in English (?*happinesses*, ?*braveries*, ?*trusts*).[3] Another distinction concerns the difference between **common nouns** (such as *dog, cat* or *woman*) and **proper nouns** (such as *Rover, Fluffy* or *Rebecca*). As we will see below, this distinction can sometimes be relevant when it comes to the use of the article since proper nouns do not usually combine with *a(n), the* and other determiners, unless they are used as common nouns (see Section 3.1.1).

The distinction between **animate nouns** (such as *girl* or *shopkeeper*) and **inanimate nouns** (such as *coffee table* or *television set*) determines the choice of Subject or Object pronoun in the third person. The singular pronoun *it* functions as a Subject or an Object and corresponds to an inanimate NP. The pronouns *he* and *she* (Subject) (compare to *him* and *her* (Object)) correspond

---

[3]The sentences below are probably not counterexamples to this, if we interpret *happinesses* as 'moments of happiness' and *braveries* as 'acts of bravery'.

    Life is full of small, unexpected happinesses.

    Minor braveries can sometimes become major revolutions.

Many abstract nouns, furthermore, are perfectly countable in all contexts: *ideas, memories, beliefs, thoughts* etc.

to NPs with an animate (human[4]) head noun. No such distinction occurs in the plural: the pronoun corresponding to both *the men* (animate) and *the books* (inanimate) is *they* (Subject)/*them* (Object). The animate ~ inanimate distinction is important to speakers of languages where nouns obligatorily fall into different grammatical genders: referring to *a chair* as *she* or *a knife* as *he* is not uncommon for such speakers. It will be shown in our discussion of relative clauses in Section 4.2 that the animate ~ inanimate distinction is also important when it comes to the choice of relative pronoun.

One final distinction we will discuss in greater detail below (Section 5.2) concerns **individuating nouns** and **collective nouns**. We use the term collective noun in a specific sense to refer to a noun that can optionally combine with a plural verb even when the form of the noun is singular: *My family is* (or *are*) *coming for the holidays*.[5] Such nouns are notionally plural. The much larger class of individuating nouns can only combine with a plural verb when the head noun of an NP is marked for plural.

The above distinctions are all secondary to a major distinction that is crucial for the choice and use of determiners in English as well as for Subject-verb agreement: the distinction between **countable** and **uncountable nouns**.

2.2 Countable and uncountable nouns

2.2.1 A definition of (un)countability

The countable ~ uncountable distinction is primarily a grammatical one. This means that it must be understood as a property of nouns themselves (a linguistic form) rather than as a property of their referents (in the 'real' world). For the purposes of this grammar, a countable noun is a noun that can occur in both the singular and the plural. Nouns that do not fit into this basic singular ~ plural dichotomy are uncountable. In fact, the very notion of singular versus plural is irrelevant to uncountable nouns; uncountable nouns trigger singular verb agreement by default:

(2) (a) That tree *is* at least 100 years old. ←→ Those trees *are* at least 100 years old.
   (b) The bark of that tree *is* highly toxic. (cf. *the barks *are*)

---

[4]The pronouns used to refer to animals vary: when the sex of the animal is known, *he/she* and *him/her* are common, especially with dogs, horses, cows etc. The pronoun *it* will be used with animals whose sex is unknown or unimportant (ants, squirrels, hummingbirds etc.).

[5]Some use the term **collective noun** to refer to nouns representing specific groups of entities, often animals (a *gaggle* of geese, a *school* of fish, a *herd* of cattle). This is a lexical question rather than a grammatical one, and we will not address it here.

The noun *tree* in (2a) can occur in the singular and the plural; it is a countable noun. The noun *bark* in (2b) only occurs in the singular and with singular verb agreement; it is an uncountable noun.

Another way of characterizing this distinction makes use of semantic rather than formal criteria: while the referent of an uncountable noun is 'the same all the way through', the referent of a countable noun is not. Any subpart of *milk* remains *milk*, and any subpart of *bark* is still *bark*. The technical term used to refer to this property is 'homogeneity': an uncountable noun is said to be homogeneous. The same cannot be said of a countable noun: a subpart of a countable noun cannot be referred to by the same countable noun. A subpart of *a tree* is no longer *a tree*. Countable nouns are said to be heterogeneous rather than homogeneous.

2.2.2 (Un)countability and determiners

The examples in (1) on p. 106 show that (un)countability is a basic property of the noun that limits the way it can combine with determiners. In (1d) and (1f), for example, the form of the determiner preceding the head noun is determined solely by whether the head noun is grammatically countable or uncountable: the head noun *homework* (1d) can combine with the quantifier *a little* (but not with *a few*) because it is uncountable, whereas the head noun *students* (1f), which is countable and plural, can combine with the quantifier *a few* (but not with *a little*). The quantifiers *a few* and *a little* both mean 'a small quantity (number or amount) of'. It is the status of the head noun as (plural) countable or uncountable that determines which we use. The same can be said for the pair *many ~ much*, which means 'a large quantity (number or amount) of': *not much homework*, but *not many students*. When constructing an NP, the choice between *a few* and *a little* or between *many* and *much* is not at all the same kind of choice we make when we choose to use the passive voice rather than the active voice. The latter choice reflects the perspective that a speaker wants to give to her message. The former choice is triggered by a formal feature encoded in the noun.[6]

The indefinite article *a* can only combine with a singular countable noun. The definite article *the* is insensitive to the countable ~ uncountable distinction

---

[6]This is not to say that a speaker cannot sometimes force a typically countable noun to have an uncountable reading:

    The dirty locker room smelled of *teenage boy*.

    There was *tomato* on his shirt.

We will come back to this idea in Chapter 4. We point out that verbs typically associated with one situation type can be used to refer to other situation types depending on the perspective the speaker is adopting in a given instance: see the examples in (9), (26) and (27) in Chapter 4.

and can combine with both types of head noun: *the student(s)*, but also *the homework*. Countables in the plural and uncountables often function together when it comes to the use of quantifiers: *lots of* and *some*, for instance, can only combine with a plural countable noun or an uncountable: we cannot say **lots of pencil* or **some pencil*.[7] In a similar way, both plural countable nouns and uncountable nouns can occur without any determiner at all to indicate, for example, 'an unspecified quantity (number or amount) of': *Students are complaining*, or *Homework is never fun*. This is not possible for a singular countable noun (e.g. **Student is complaining*).

For the demonstrative determiners, the form is conditioned by whether the head noun is countable singular (or uncountable) or countable plural: *this* (or *that*) *student*, *this* (or *that*) *homework*, but *these* (or *those*) *students*.

This leads to the following formal combinations illustrated with NPs with *student* and *homework* as the head nouns:

(3) **student (countable)**	**homework (uncountable)**
a student	*a homework
five students	*five homeworks/*five homework
(not) many students	*(not) many homework
(a) few students	*(a) few homework
fewer students	*fewer homework
a (large) number of students	*a (large) number of homework
these/those students	*these/*those homework
*(not) much students	(not) much homework
*(a) little students	(a) little homework
*less students	less homework
*a great deal of students	a great deal of homework
the students	the homework
some students	some homework
a lot of (lots of) students	a lot of (lots of) homework
more students	more homework
my (his, their) students	my (her, our) homework
Ø students (cf. *Ø student)	Ø homework
this/that student	this/that homework

---

[7] If we say *He wrote the letter using some pencil he'd found*, the determiner *some* does not indicate quantity. Here, *some* has a different meaning, comparable to the article *a*.

2.2.3 Linguistic (un)countability versus perceptual (un)-countability

In the vast majority of cases, the way nouns are grammatically encoded falls out from what we can directly perceive in the natural world: referents referred to by countable nouns can actually be counted whereas referents referred to by uncountable nouns cannot. The noun *tree* is grammatically countable (*one tree, two trees, trees*), and the referent in the real world is observably countable as well. The *bark* of the tree is not observably countable, and the grammar of English encodes this as well: NPs such as **one bark*, **two barks* and **barks* do not occur. Remember though that countability is in essence a grammatical property of a noun and not a property of a noun's referent. This implies that in some cases countability is idiosyncratic and unpredictable. More specifically, certain nouns in English are uncountable where intuition might suggest the contrary. Quantitatively, this concerns relatively few nouns, but many of the nouns it does affect are extremely common. For example, there is nothing inherently uncountable about furniture as we perceive it with our senses: that is, we can count chairs and tables. And yet the noun *furniture* in English is encoded as uncountable in the mind of speakers of English, who refer to *furniture* rather than **furnitures* or **a furniture*. Below are some more examples of nouns which, though uncountable in English, are often not encoded as uncountable in other languages and are thus commonly misused:

(4) They've bought a house, but they haven't bought any *furniture* yet.
    (*furnitures, *a furniture, *several furnitures)
  I haven't got the *information* you're looking for.
    (*informations, *an information, *those informations)
  She needs some *advice* about what to do next.
    (*advices, *an advice, *three advices)
  How much *luggage* will you be checking?
    (*luggages, *a luggage, *how many luggages)

Other common uncountable nouns include *clothing, dust, equipment, evidence, independence, information, knowledge, news, progress, research, smoke, software, traffic, waste* and *weather*.

In contexts where it is necessary to refer to a single unit, or several units, of an uncountable noun, English makes use of a **unitizer** (often called a **unit noun**) followed by the preposition *of* and an uncountable noun. The unitizer, which is itself countable, is often the noun *piece*:

(5) *a furniture, *three furnitures
        a *piece* of furniture, three *pieces* of furniture
     *an information, *several informations
        a *piece* of information, several *pieces* of information
     *an advice, *many advices
        a *piece* of advice, many *pieces* of advice

Certain uncountable nouns combine with more specific unitizers which have a collocational link (often in terms of shape or form) with the uncountable noun. These are not predictable and must be learned individually:

(6) *a soap, *three soaps
        a *bar* of soap, three *bars* of soap
     *a bread, *several breads
        a *loaf* of bread, several *loaves* of bread
     *a grass, *many grasses
        a *blade* of grass, a few *blades* of grass

If there is no reference to a single unit or a specific number but rather to some unspecified quantity, the use of a unitizer is often unnatural. In (7), the exact number of pieces of information or the precise amount of soap is not an important part of what is being communicated, and therefore no unitizer is necessary:

(7) If you need any information, ask John. (rather than *pieces of information*)
     I think we're out of soap. (rather than *bars of soap*)

Uncountable nouns can also be used after countable head nouns referring to recipients or terms of measurement. There is no particular collocational link as is the case for many unitizers, and no restriction on the head noun other than what common sense allows. They can in certain cases be followed by plural countable nouns. In other words, the containers and measurements used in the NPs below are not unitizers but have a function similar to that of unitizers since they enable an otherwise uncountable noun to be quantified:

(8) a glass of beer (orange juice, milk …) (cf. a glass of ice cubes)
     three bottles of champagne (white wine, whisky …)
     a few tubes of glue (paint, toothpaste …)

     two pounds of meat (butter, sugar …) (cf. two pounds of tomatoes)
     several gallons of ice cream (petrol, cooking oil …)
     a couple of yards of twine (fabric, yarn …)

2.2.4 Nouns that are both countable and uncountable
2.2.4.1 Countable and uncountable with different meaning

Some nouns appear to be both countable and uncountable. As the following examples show, the referent with uncountable and countable use is not the same:

(9) This bag is made of *paper*. (uncountable)
I have to write a 50-page *paper* (= assignment) for school. (countable)
Which *papers* do they sell at that newsagent's? (countable)

Most window panes are made of *glass*. (uncountable)
Wine is best served in *glasses*.[8] (countable)

I'm a vegetarian. I don't eat *chicken*. (uncountable)
They raise *chickens* on their farm. (countable)

He's finding *grammar* much more interesting than he'd thought before. (uncountable)
He owns at least five or six reference *grammars*. (countable)

Nouns such as *paper* or *chicken* can be seen a single lexical item that can be both countable and uncountable (with, as the examples show, a difference in meaning). Conversely, one might consider that in each case there are two separate lexical items, each of which is predictable with respect to countability. In fact, for a number of similarly related pairs of countable ~ uncountable words, the lexicon has two completely different words: *a cow/a bull* (both countable), but *beef* (uncountable); *a steady job* (countable), but *steady work* (uncountable); *intermittent showers* (countable), but *intermittent rain* (uncountable).

The difference in meaning between the countable and uncountable uses of nouns like those in (9) above cannot be accounted for with any single rule relating the two. Sometimes, however, the interplay between a single noun with both a countable and uncountable use is completely predictable and generalizable. Take the following example:

(10) Naan is *a bread* made from white flour which is lightly leavened by a natural yeast starter developed from airborne yeasts. (www)

In (10), we are referring not to the object that comes out of the oven when bread is baked (to do this, we could use the unitizer *loaf: a loaf of bread*) but rather to a type of bread. Indeed, *a bread* in (10) can be replaced by 'a type

---

[8]We could also mention *glasses*, referring to 'lenses set in a frame one wears to see better'. *Glasses* in this sense, however, is always plural and belongs to the same category of nouns as *trousers and scissors*: see Section 2.2.6.2.

of (sort of, kind of …) bread'. Seen this way, *a bread* is not an exception to anything we have said about countability. What is being counted are different kinds of bread (rye, wheat, whole grain …) and not the referents. Below are a few similar examples:

(11) Gorgonzola is *a very pungent cheese*. (= a kind of cheese that is very pungent)
I'm looking for *a mineral water* with low sodium content. (= a kind, or brand, of mineral water)
Forbidden rice is *a rice* that is black when raw and dark purple when cooked. (= a kind of rice) (www)

We find a similar phenomenon concerning liquids such as *coffee, beer* and *tea*, all of which are observably uncountable. The nouns which are used to refer to such liquids – but also to powders (*laundry detergent, baking soda, talcum, flour, sugar, ground coffee, dust, sand, snow, ash*) and other such non-discrete substances (*rubber, plastic, gold, silver, grease*) – tend to be grammatically as well as observably uncountable:

(12) He doesn't drink *much coffee* now that he's retired.
There's *a little beer* left in that bottle – care to finish it off?
The Irish actually drink *more tea* than the English.

And yet nothing stops us from referring to *a tea, a few* beers or *a couple of coffees*. In such cases, the referent is not the substance itself but a serving (or servings) of it.

2.2.4.2 Countable and uncountable with similar meaning

There are also cases where what is clearly a single lexical item can be used as both a countable and an uncountable without a fundamental difference in meaning:

(13) There has been far *too much rumour* and speculation surrounding this case.
During the trial, *a number of rumours* were circulated in the press.

It was only after *serious discussion* that they were able to settle their grievances.
We've had *several serious discussions* but have yet to come to an agreement.

The bank refuses to give him a loan: he has *too much debt/too many debts* already.
For vegetarians, there is *very little choice/are only a few choices* on the menu.

When such nouns do not make reference to anything individuated or segmented, they can quite regularly be used uncountably. These are very often abstract nouns. Some concrete nouns have this potential as well: while *church*, *bed* and *train* are unambiguous countable nouns, they are used uncountably in *at church*, *in bed* and *by train*. Here, the nouns refer to a function rather than to an individuated, countable entity.

2.2.5 Countable nouns and plurality

In the vast majority of cases, plurality in English is overtly marked on countable nouns, usually by the plural marker *-(e)s*. English in this respect is highly regular: *a computer > several computers, that magazine > those magazines* and so on. The pronunciation /ɪz/, reflected in the spelling as *-es*, results in a plural that has an additional syllable compared to the singular form: *dress, rose, church* and *judge* have one syllable, but *dresses, roses, churches* and *judges* have two.[9] The plural of nouns, however, is not always formed by adding the plural marker *-(e)s*. Many nouns ending in *-f* have plurals in *-ves*: *calf > calves, half > halves, knife > knives, shelf > shelves, thief > thieves, wife > wives*. Others are regular: *belief > beliefs, chief > chiefs, roof > roofs*.

A small number of commonly used nouns in English have completely unpredictable, irregular plural forms: *child > children, foot > feet, goose > geese, man > men, mouse > mice, tooth > teeth* and *woman* (/ˈwʊmən/) *> women* (/ˈwɪmɪn/), for example. A number of nouns borrowed from Latin or Greek take a plural ending different from *-(e)s*, like *-i* or *-a* (*stimulus > stimuli, criterion > criteria*).[10]

Some nouns, although they can have singular or plural reference, do not change form in the plural. These include the nouns *series, species, means, crossroads* and *barracks*[11] and also a certain number of nouns referring to

---

[9]Some countable nouns ending in *-o* take *-es* rather than *-s* in the plural: *hero > heroes*. Others simply take *-s: piano > pianos*. In some cases, finally, both spellings can be found and are considered correct: *volcano > volcano(e)s*. Contrary to the *-es* ending in *churches*, however, the ending in this case has nothing to do with pronunciation: there is no additional syllable in *heroes*. Consult a dictionary if you are not sure how to spell the plural of words in *-o*.

[10]As for *phenomenon* and *criterion* (plural *phenomena* and *criteria*), native speakers themselves sometimes hesitate, and using the plural form with a singular verb is common. Using a singular verb with *data* and *media* (singular *datum* and *medium*) is common enough to suggest that both might be considered 'correct', although prescriptivists maintain that only a plural verb is acceptable.

[11]Words like *crossroads* end in an *-s* in both the singular and plural form: *this crossroads* (one intersection), *these crossroads* (more than one intersection). In terms of the determiners they combine with and verbal agreement, they behave like ordinary countable nouns. This is not the case for nouns such as *valuables, scissors* and *phonetics* discussed in Section 2.2.6.

fish and other animals: *one salmon > several salmon; that sheep > those sheep.* Other nouns like this include *pike, trout, bison, deer* and *moose.* The word *fish* itself is usually invariable, unless the meaning is 'species of fish':

> (14) *That sheep* belongs to a farmer a few miles down the road.
> There is *a dangerous crossroads* (*a dangerous crossroad) in this part of town.
> The BBC are producing *a new television series* (*a new television serie).
>
> *Those sheep* (*those sheeps) belong to a farmer a few miles down the road.
> There are *some dangerous crossroads* in this part of town.
> The BBC are currently producing *several new television series.*
>
> A large proportion of European freshwater *fish* belong to the carp family, Cyprinidae, and related *fishes* are found in Asia, Africa and North America. (www)

2.2.6 Apparent exceptions to the basic tenets of countability
2.2.6.1 Nouns of the type *assets* or *dregs*

There is a restricted set of nouns in English that only occur in the plural; when a singular form exists, it is usually a countable noun that does not have the same meaning:

> (15) When questioned, the CEO was reluctant to reveal her *assets* (*her asset).
> (cf. A network of professional contacts is *a big asset* in today's job market.)
> Going through *customs* (*a custom) at most airports is easier than it used to be.
> (cf. I find this local *custom*/these local *customs* fascinating.)

Nouns like this include *(good/bad) manners, minutes (of a meeting), regards* and *resources.* Some nouns, such as *dregs, earnings, outskirts, remains, savings* and *valuables,* occur only in the plural:

> (16) He refers to those less fortunate than us as 'the *dregs* of society'. (*the dreg)
> If you have any *valuables*, the receptionist will put them in the hotel safe.
> (*any valuable)
> He squandered away his wife's *savings* on speculative investments. (*his wife's saving)

Nouns that have a different meaning in the plural (such as *customs*) as well as those used only in the plural (such as *valuables*) are more or less likely to accept quantification. The same quantifiers we find with plural countable nouns can, to a greater or lesser extent, occasionally be found with such nouns. Here, however, there are no clear-cut rules, and there is a certain amount of unpredictable variation in what can be considered grammatical:

(17) Bring as *few valuables* as possible with you.
Many natural resources have been depleted this past century.
?The city doesn't have *many outskirts*.
**His many remains* were cast into the ocean.
(cf. *His few remains* were later identified thanks to DNA testing.)

2.2.6.2 Nouns of the type *trousers* or *scissors*

English has a class of nouns referring either to items of clothing (*trousers, shorts, jeans, cords* etc.) or to tools (*scissors, tweezers, binoculars, sheers* etc.) consisting of two equal, usually conjoined parts that form a single unit. Because the referent has two parts, these nouns are conceptualized as plurals. These nouns always end in plural *-s* and always take a verb in the plural (when the NP features in Subject position), even when there is reference to one item[12]:

(18) Woollen trousers are what you need to go hiking in the mountains.
*A woollen trousers/*A woollen trouser is what you need to go hiking in the mountains.
Those shorts you're wearing are worn-out; you'd better get rid of them.
*This shorts/This short you are wearing is worn-out; you'd better get rid of it.

The determiners *the, these, those, some* and the zero article Ø (see Section 3.1.1) are used regardless of whether reference is being made to one item or more than one, meaning that the following sentences can have plural reference or singular reference:

(19) *The/These/Those trousers* are worn-out. I need to replace *them*. (can refer to one pair or two or more pairs)
I bought *(some) new trousers. They*'re very trendy, aren't *they*? (can refer to one pair or two or more pairs)

Out of context, it is impossible to say whether the italicized NPs in (19) refer to one article of clothing or more. If you want to make it clear that there is reference to one, the unitizer *pair* ('a pair of', 'two pairs of') is used:

(20) I need (some) new trousers. (singular or plural reference)
I need a new pair of trousers. (singular reference)
I need two new pairs of trousers. (plural reference)

---

[12]Note that the forms *a trouser* or *this short* are commonly used (in advertising, for example) when what is being referred to is a specific type or model of the clothing in question (compare to (18) and (19), above):

It doesn't matter what body shape you are, there is *a trouser* for everyone. (www)
This women's short is made of cotton. It's lightweight, comfortable, and fits just right. (www)

2.2.6.3 Nouns of the type *mathematics*

Nouns in *-ics* (*mathematics, acoustics, aesthetics, athletics, economics*), like nouns of the *trousers* type and most of the items discussed in Section 2.2.6.1, cannot be used without *-s*. When nouns like these are not modified, they denote a subject, a science or a branch of study and take a singular verb. When they are pre-modified or post-modified, they denote some practical application or manifestation of the Subject referent, in which case they combine with a plural verb:

(21) Mathematics was (*were) his least favourite subject at school. (the subject in general)
Your mathematics are (*is) not very accurate. (a personal application of the theory)

Acoustics is (*are) the branch of physics that deals with the properties of sound.
The acoustics in the new symphony hall are (*is) expected to be brilliant.

Nouns like these also include *ethics, gymnastics, linguistics, metaphysics, phonetics, physics, politics* and *statistics*.

Usually, nouns can be classified as either countable or uncountable. The nouns illustrated in (4) above are invariably uncountable in standard English, and the same can be said for any number of nouns which are always countable. Awareness of the countable ~ uncountable distinction in English is key when we use these nouns in NPs and choose from the range of available determiners to establish reference and express quantity. Having said this, the notion of countability is at times immaterial: the special cases discussed in the previous sections show that it may be difficult to pin down the status of certain nouns with respect to countability. These nouns nonetheless have specific requirements in terms of the determiners they combine with.

Now that we have discussed the notion of (un)countability in detail, it is time to look at another component of the NP: determiners. We will first focus on the meaning of two of the most common determiners, the definite article and the indefinite article. In Section 3.2, we will address the meaning and formal behaviour of quantifiers.

3. Determiners

Determiners enable us to take a noun from our mental dictionary and assign reference to it. By 'assign reference', we simply mean that we create a link between an NP and the object (or place, or person, or notion) it refers to in the real (or, in more technical terms, **extralinguistic**) world. If you ask *Where is **the** frying pan?*, you consider that the person you are addressing will know which frying pan you are talking about. In fact, the hearer may or may not know what you are referring to: the choice of the determiner *the* reflects what information the speaker *thinks* she shares with the hearer.

Determiners in English are preheads: for instance, the determiners *all, the* and *other* in (22) always come before the head noun *books*. As is clear from (23), however, these three determiners can all be used within a single noun phrase, although the order in which they are used is invariable:

(22) *All* books borrowed from the library must be returned two weeks later.
The books you borrow should be returned in good condition.
Other books can be found on the third floor.

(23) *All the other* books you're looking for are in the children's section.
*The other all books you're looking for are in the children's section.
*Other all the books you're looking for are in the children's section.

The articles (*a* and *the*), the possessives (*his, my, our*) and the demonstratives (*this/these, that/those*) are **central determiners**: they cannot be used together, which explains why NPs such as **the my books* or **his those books* are impossible. Central determiners also include *some, any, no, either, neither, each* and determinative genitives (see Section 3.4.2).

3.1 The article

3.1.1 Definite article versus indefinite article

English has two articles, the **definite article** *the* and the **indefinite article** *a(n)*. The form *an* is used before nouns beginning with a vowel sound: *an apple, an FBI agent, an honour, an NP* but *a European country, a US citizen, a houseboat, a one-woman show*. Note that it is the pronunciation and not the spelling of the noun that conditions the use of *a* versus *an*. English also makes use of what some call a **zero article** (represented by Ø), that is, the absence of any determiner, as in the following examples:

(24) Ø Milk is white.
Ø Apples are red.

The term 'zero article' is controversial: some object to it because it implies the abstract presence of something that cannot be heard or seen. It is nonetheless a useful term for us since it highlights the important fact that the absence of an article carries as much meaning as the presence of a definite or indefinite article. NPs without an article or other determiner are only possible with uncountable nouns (Ø *milk*) or plural count nouns (Ø *apples*): **Ø Apple is red* is ungrammatical in English because *apple* is a singular countable noun.

Articles – indeed, determiners in general – are only used with common nouns. This makes sense: proper nouns are self-sufficient and require no further determination.[13] While the examples in (25) appear to be exceptions to this, they are in fact not:

> (25) *The Louises* in my class are all very shy.
> *A Zach Wilson* stopped by to see you this morning.
> The museum has recently acquired *two Picassos*.

When used as such, what look like proper nouns are in fact common nouns in disguise, as the following paraphrases should make clear:

> (26) The *girls* in my class named Louise are all very shy.
> A *man* by the name of Zach Wilson stopped by to see you.
> The museum has recently acquired two *paintings* (*works, sculptures, portraits* …) by Picasso.

3.1.2 Generic, non-generic specific, non-generic non-specific NPs

Our discussion of NPs with common noun heads that combine with articles takes as its point of departure the following breakdown:

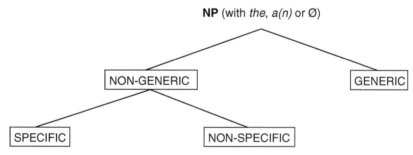

Figure 3.1 Non-generic versus generic and specific versus non-specific NPs.

NP reference is of two basic kinds: **non-generic** and **generic** (Figure 3.1). NPs with non-generic reference as in (27a) refer to an item or group of items

---

[13] An exception would be certain geographical names requiring a definite article: *the Alps, the Pyrenees, the Rockies, the Hebrides, the Caribbean, the Netherlands, the United States* etc.

from the whole class of like items whereas NPs with generic reference as in (27b) refer to the entire class:

(27) (a) *The computer* is still on. Could you turn it off before you leave?
My grandmother has bought *a computer*. Now she's got to learn to use it.
There are Ø *computers* and printers in the computing lab.
(b) *The computer* is an important tool in our day-to-day life.
A computer is an electronic device for storing different kinds of data.
Ø *Computers* are electronic devices for storing different kinds of data.

Non-generic reference can be further divided into **specific** or **non-specific**. In (28a), the speaker refers to a specific lion or garden, whereas in (28b), she refers to a potential instantiation of a lion or garden (in other words, non-specific):

(28) (a) I once saw *a lion* at the zoo. It was a female.
We've bought a house. *The garden* is big enough for the children to play in.
(b) What would you do if you came face to face with *a lion* in the jungle?
If we buy a house, I want *the garden* to be big enough for the children to play in.

These examples show that the articles *a(n)* and *the* as well as Ø do not, on their own, encode an NP as non-generic or generic, or specific or non-specific. The context of the sentence contributes considerably to the interpretation. We will start by discussing non-generic reference with *a(n), the* and Ø. We will then present generic reference.

3.1.3 Non-generic definite NPs: definite reference

Lists of when we use the definite article and indefinite article obscure the fact that the choice stems from one basic tenet: each time a speaker uses an NP for non-generic reference, she judges whether or not the referent is unambiguously identifiable by the hearer. For instance, when the speaker constructs an NP with the head noun *book*, she has to decide whether the hearer is going to know which book she is talking about. The choice of the definite determiner *the* means that the speaker considers that the hearer can identify the referent. In any context where the speaker can assume that the hearer can identify what is being pointed to by the definite article, *the* is appropriate. The most obvious case is when the referent is physically present at the time of the utterance, as in *Could you pass the salt, please?* Another fairly obvious case is where the referent is not present but has previously been mentioned and is thus part of the discourse. This is often found in narration:

(29) There was once *a princess* who lived with *an old woman* in *an enormous castle*. *The castle* was located so far from civilization that *the princess* had never met another living soul in her entire life. And it was *the old woman's* intention that this must never change.

The speaker, however, can also fairly assume in many cases that the hearer can make a logical deduction in order to identify the referent even when it is not physically present or has not been previously mentioned:

(30) I've just finished reading a fantastic detective novel. *The author* is American, but she lives in England.

In (30), the speaker deems it unnecessary to make explicit the fact that the book has an author: she assumes the hearer can infer this. Definite reference can also be established within an NP through the addition of pre- or post-modifying information. In this case, the post-modifiers and pre-modifiers help the speaker to establish reference:

(31) (a) The man *who's walking into the room right now* is Sarah's husband. (NP with a relative clause)
  (b) The lady *in the red hat* is my mother-in-law.
   (NP with a post-modifying PrepP)
  (c) The *only* person *I would never give money to* is my sister.
   (NP with pre-modifier *only* and a relative clause)
  (d) The *best* player will be awarded a medal.
   (NP with an adjective in the superlative form)

Sometimes the existence of an NP's referent can be assumed given the contextual or general knowledge that the speaker assumes she and the hearer share: when a speaker says *I'll meet you in front of the fountain*, she considers that the hearer can identify which fountain, because there is only one fountain in front of which it would be possible or logical to meet. Indeed, in certain cases, there is only one possible referent (or set of referents) regardless of the knowledge the speaker shares with any single hearer: *the sun, the moon, the sky, the stars*.

Definite NPs can have a determiner other than the definite article: possessives and demonstratives, for instance, always have definite reference. This makes sense if you consider that a paraphrase of *my car* is 'the car that belongs to me' and not 'a car that belongs to me' and that *those men* means 'the men "over there"' and not '(some) men "over there"'. In the same way, the genitive marks definite reference. *My sister's boyfriend* can be paraphrased (albeit awkwardly) as '*the* boyfriend of my sister': it is the post-modifying PrepP (see (31b)) that helps the hearer identify the referent.

3.1.4 Non-generic indefinite NPs: specific or non-specific reference

Use of the indefinite article *a(n)* (or, if the head noun is plural or uncountable, the zero article Ø) establishes indefiniteness: the speaker considers that the NP is not unambiguously identifiable by the hearer. Existential sentences with *there is* or *there are* are clear examples of what this means:

(32) There's *a woman* on the phone who'd like to talk to you. (cf. *The woman* I told you about is on the phone and wants to talk to you.)
The judge asked whether there were Ø *stains* on the suspect's shirt. (cf. In the end, *the stains* on the suspect's shirt were not blood stains after all.)

The main function of *there is/there are* is to introduce a new referent into the context. Since a definite NP presumes the hearer can identify the referent (this implies that the hearer is already aware of its existence), it will not ordinarily be used with the existential structure *there is/there are*:

(33) *There's *the woman* on the phone who'd like to talk to you.
*The judge asked whether there were *the stains* on the suspect's shirt.

Similarly, the function of Subject Complement is filled by an indefinite NP when it serves to classify the Subject referent by saying that it is 'one of a category'. When the Subject is plural, the Subject referents are 'several of a category':

(34) My sister-in-law later became a heart surgeon.
Their children were Ø medical students at the time.
This (= this object) is a stone arrowhead.
These (= these objects) are Ø wild begonias.

A final defining characteristic of indefinite NPs with *a(n)* or Ø is that they can be specific or non-specific:

(35) (a) I've got a new computer. (= an actual computer; I can point to it, specific)
(b) I want/I need a new computer. (= an item belonging to the class 'computer', non-specific)

(36) (a) She's going to marry a millionaire. His name is Walter McGillan, and he's in oil. (specific)
(b) I'm sure she'll marry a millionaire one day. She just has to meet the right one. (non-specific)

In actual discourse, the fact that an indefinite NP can be specific or non-specific hardly ever poses any breakdown in communication between speaker and hearer: in (35) above, the verbs themselves (*have got* versus *want/need*) unequivocally bring about the interpretation, and in (36), the immediately surrounding co-text makes it clear whether the NP is specific or non-specific.

To sum up, the use of definite and indefinite NPs with non-generic reference is inextricably linked to the general knowledge shared by speaker and hearer as well as the context in which the interaction takes place.

3.1.5 Generic NPs

It is also possible for the speaker to refer not to one or more individual members of the set but to all members of the set. This kind of reference is called generic reference. In (37), we reproduce the same examples as in (27b). Generic reference makes it clear that the NPs with the head *computer* serve to represent all computers. Rather than referring to any object or objects in the actual world, a generic NP refers to the common denominator or defining features shared by all members of the set.

> (37) *The computer* is an important tool in our day-to-day life.
> *A computer* is an electronic device for storing different kinds of data.
> Ø *Computers* are electronic devices for storing different kinds of data.

An important difference between generic and non-generic reference is that the choice of the article in the former case in no way depends on shared knowledge between speaker and hearer or on the immediate context of the utterance in the way the interpretation of non-generic NPs do. Hard-and-fast rules are not easy to formulate for generic reference, but a few general tenets show that the choices available (*the, a,* Ø) cannot be used interchangeably.

3.1.5.1 Generic NPs with Ø (+ countable plural OR uncountable): Ø *computers*, Ø *petroleum*

The most common way to establish generic reference in English is with no article at all (Ø) with either an uncountable noun or a countable noun in the plural. In fact, it is the only way an uncountable head noun can have generic reference: *Advice is cheap* (the NP *the advice* is necessarily non-generic: *The advice (you gave me) was very helpful.*) Generic NPs with Ø are the best choice for generic reference if you have a doubt since they are never incorrect:

> (38) *Computers* have changed the way we communicate with one another.
> *Petroleum* is primarily used as fuel oil, such as petrol and diesel fuel.

The fact that Ø + uncountable/countable plural head noun has generic reference in (38) does not mean the NPs with Ø necessarily have generic reference:

(39) *Computers* and printers are available in the library for student use twenty-four hours a day.
Petroleum was added to the solution and caused a chemical reaction.

In (39), neither *computers* nor *petroleum* refers to the entire class of computers or petroleum.

For countable nouns, there are two other ways to express generic reference: *the* and *a* with a singular countable noun head.[14] They are less commonly used than Ø in this way.

3.1.5.2 Generic NPs with *the* (+ countable singular): *the computer*

Consider the following example:

(40) *The computer* has changed the way we communicate with one another. (cf. *Computers* have changed the way we communicate with one another.)

In (especially) written English, a generic NP with *the* is often used to introduce the topic of a more lengthy discussion to follow and is often found in explanatory, encyclopedia-type prose. Generic NPs of this type tend to fall into one of three categories. They refer to (i) species of animals and plants or (ii) subparts of a larger whole, such as body organs or parts of a machine. Finally, they quite commonly refer to (iii) inanimate objects presented as human inventions with a traceable history:

(41) *The sea turtle* is now officially on the list of endangered species. (i)
In Turkey, *the tulip* is considered the embodiment of perfection and beauty. (i)
The heart pumps blood to each and every cell of the human body. (ii)
The automotive radiator is an engine-cooling device in a motor vehicle or aircraft. (ii)
The laser has revolutionized the treatment of many diseases. (= the invention of) (iii)
The wheel has changed how human beings work today. (= the invention of) (iii)

---

[14] A third possibility – *the* + plural countable noun, such as *the Italians* – might also be considered generic. A similar generic use occurs with uninflected de-adjectival nouns (nouns derived from adjectives) that refer to human beings: *the rich, the poor, the old, the young*. Although they do not take a plural -*s*, these NPs always combine with a plural verb. Generic reference to all inhabitants of a country also takes the form of an uninflected de-adjectival noun with certain adjectives ending in /ʃ/, /tʃ / or /iːz/: *the Welsh, the French, the Japanese*. Again, a plural verb is used in these cases.

Generic NPs with *the* cannot usually have generic reference with inanimate head nouns like *book* or *bottle*, which have been part of humankind for so long that they are usually not conceived as inventions in the same way as the computer and the laser are. Nor are they considered subparts of a larger whole:

(42) ?*The bottle* can be made of plastic or glass. (generally not possible with a generic reading)
?*The book* has changed the way people get information. (generally not possible with a generic reading)

The following sentence sounds much more natural because human invention of the object and subsequent human intervention is brought to the fore; this is not the case for the example in (42):

(43) The bottle has developed over millennia of use, with some of the earliest examples appearing in China, Rome and Crete. (www)

In the same way, if a subcategory is created, for example, 'the printed book', this brings back to the fore the idea of a human invention and the NP can thus be used generically:

(44) The printed book has changed the way people get information.

Finally, a sentence with a generic NP with *the* is usually interpreted as focusing on the entire class rather than all the individual members of the class; for that reason, it is particularly compatible with definitions.

3.1.5.3 Generic NPs with *a(n)* (+ countable singular): *a computer*

When an NP with *a(n)* is used to make generic reference, the sentence is true not only for the entire class but for any individual member of the class as well. Compare the following two sentences:

(45) (a) **A computer* has changed the way we communicate nowadays. (cf. *the computer*)
(b) *A computer* is useful for organizing music, digital photographs and documents.[15]

The sentence in (45a) is unlikely to be used in any meaningful way in English when the NP is indefinite (i.e. *a computer*): it is not true that any single example of a computer has changed the way we communicate. Rather, it is the set of

---

[15]Note that in the related sentence *A computer would be useful for organizing music, digital photographs and documents*, the Subject NP is non-generic, non-specific.

all computers that has had this effect. (Indeed, we can also say 'Ø Computers have changed … '). Sentence (45b), however, is fine: it is as though the speaker is saying 'for any example you can find of a computer, this is true'.

We have seen how the definite and indefinite articles, as well as Ø, can be used to express non-generic and generic reference. Of the nominal preheads, the articles are indeed the most basic. Another common kind of prehead is the quantifier, and this is what we address in the following section.

3.2 Quantifiers

3.2.1 Overview

Definite and indefinite articles enable us to make reference to the existence of something, but they are not equipped to provide any information on the quantity of the head noun in the NP, be it in terms of number (for countables in the plural) or amount (for uncountables). For this we need another type of determiner called a **quantifier**.[16] Quantifiers are always preheads in English. Of course the most basic kind of quantifier is a number, used (necessarily) with a countable noun: *two gloves, eighty-eight piano keys*.

At one end of the spectrum are quantifiers such as *all, both, each* and *every*; they refer to the entire set (for countables) or entire amount (for uncountables) of whatever noun they form an NP with. *All* is the only quantifier that can combine with a (plural) countable or an uncountable; the others can only combine with a countable:

(46) *All people* are created equal./*All the people* I invited to the reception came. (countable)
All luggage must be checked./The airline lost *all the luggage* he checked. (uncountable)

Both teachers gave their students a list of books to read. (countable, plural)
The teacher gave *each student* a list of books to read. (countable, singular)
The teacher gave *every student* a list of books to read. (countable, singular)

At the opposite end of the spectrum, *no* (or *not … any*) refers to an empty set or zero amount. Like *all*, *no/not … any* is insensitive to countability:

---

[16]Many, though not all, quantifiers can also function as pronouns. In this section, we are primarily interested in their use as determiners:

Many people agreed to participate. (determiner) (cf. Many refused. (pronoun))
Some people are bilingual. (determiner) (cf. Some aren't. (pronoun))

Some use the term **indefinite pronoun** or **indefinite determiner** to refer to quantifiers. This terminology can be useful in the sense that it differentiates between pronouns and determiners. But while the majority of quantifiers have indefinite meaning, some of them do not (*both, all, each*).

(47) They'll make *no* (= they won't make *any*) *exceptions* for us. (countable)
      She found *no* (= she didn't find *any*) *information* on the website. (uncountable)

Clearly, though, we can use quantifiers to refer to numbers and amounts between these two extremes. To give you an idea of the wide variety of quantifiers in English, take a look at the NPs in (48) and (49), where the head nouns are preceded by quantifiers, in italics. The quantifiers in (48) have a more positive orientation whereas those in (49) have a more negative orientation. From (a) to (e) in (48), we very schematically move from smaller to larger quantities.[17] The respective examples (a) to (e) in (49), although not strictly speaking exact opposites of their correlates in (48), do in a sense contradict what we find in (48):

(48) (a) *some* trees, *some* wine, *a few* errors, *a little* help, *a couple of* questions, *several* people
      (b) *quite a few* errors, *quite a little* time
      (c) *a lot of* recordings, *a lot of* music, *(a great) many* films, *a (great) deal of* research, *a (good) number of* comments, *much* discussion, *plenty of* films
      (d) *almost all* errors, *almost all* help, *most* teenagers
      (e) *all* trains

(49) (a) *no* trees/*(not) any* trees, *no* wine/*(not) any* wine
      (b) *few* errors, *little* time
      (c) *just/only a few* errors, *just/only a little* help
      (d) *not a lot of* recordings, *not a lot of* music, *not many* films, *not much* research
      (e) *hardly/scarcely any* errors, *hardly/scarcely any* help
      (f) *not all* trains, *most* trains + *not* (e.g. most trains do not …)

Let us now take a closer look at a few important details concerning some of these quantifiers.

3.2.2 A lot of (lots of), many, much, (a) few, (a) little
3.2.2.1 *A lot of (lots of)* and *many ~ much*

The quantifiers *a lot of/lots of* mean 'a (relatively) large quantity of'.[18] They can be used with both (plural) countable and uncountable nouns; some speakers

---

[17]Note that quantifiers that refer to all items in a set (like *both, all, each, every*) are sometimes called **universal** quantifiers while those that refer to some items of a set (*some, any, a few*) are called **existential** quantifiers.

[18]As is the case for quantification in general, the notion of relativity is important: most people will consider four spoonfuls of sugar 'a lot of sugar' if it's being put in a cup of coffee whereas the same amount may be considered 'not much sugar' if it's in a recipe for chocolate cake.

feel that *lots of* is more informal than *a lot of. Many* is used only with (plural) countables, and *much* only with uncountables.

In ordinary English, *many ~ much* is most commonly used in what are called non-assertive contexts (see Section 3.2.3.3), that is, clauses that are either negative or interrogative. If the sentence is assertive, that is, affirmative (non-negative) and declarative (non-interrogative), *a lot of, lots of* is more likely:

(50) I've got *a lot of* homework this weekend.
She's had *lots of* trouble understanding the symbolism in the novel.
My parents eat *lots of* grains and vegetables although they are not vegetarians.
You *don't* have *much* patience with him.
Are there *many* bank holidays in your country?

In more formal registers, however, *many ~ much* can be used in assertive contexts as well:

(51) *Many* decisions have yet to be made by the upper echelons.
There has been *much* discussion about whether the new motorway is really necessary.

In reality, the distribution described is far more obviously the case for *much* than for *many*. While there is nothing particularly formal about *many* in the first sentence below, the second will be felt to be unidiomatic by most native speakers, who will nearly always prefer *a lot of* (*lots of*):

(52) I've got *many* (or, more usual, *a lot of*) bags. Could someone help me carry them?
?I've got *much* luggage. Could someone help me carry it, please?
(cf. I've got *a lot of* (*lots of*) luggage. Could someone help me carry it, please?)

3.2.2.2 *Too many ~ too much, how many ~ how much, so many ~ so much, (not) enough*

Quantifiers indicating a relatively large quantity can be further qualified by *too, so* and *how. Too many* and *too much* mean 'more than wanted, more than needed, more than allowed, more than should be the case'. The characterization we mentioned above concerning level of formality does not apply to *too many* and *too much*, which are used in all registers. *Too many* is used with plural countables, and *too much* with uncountables. The opposite meaning is expressed with *not enough*, used with plural countables and uncountables alike. Affirmative *enough* (plural countable and uncountable) is situated right in the middle of the quantification continuum described:

> (53) *Too many* questions have gone unanswered by the current administration.
> I've got *too much* time on my hands. I don't know what to do with myself.
> She wanted to make an omelette, but there weren't *enough* eggs or *enough* milk.
> There's *enough* food for the weekend, but we should go to the market before Monday.

We saw the interrogative quantifiers *how many* and *how much* in Chapter 1. Again, both of these are used in all registers. *How many* is used with plural countables, and *how much* with uncountables:

> (54) *How many* times will we have to meet with the board of directors?
> *How much* time can we spend negotiating the contract?

The adverb *so* in *so many ~ so much* simply adds the idea 'to such an extent that' or sometimes simply 'to an extreme degree':

> (55) He has *so many* grandchildren (that) he sometimes forgets their names.
> (= the number of grandchildren is large to such an extent that he forgets their names)
> My parents have *so much* time on their hands since they've retired. (= the amount of time they have on their hands is extremely large)

3.2.2.3 (A) little ~ (a) few, how little ~ how few, so little ~ so few

The exact quantities referred to by *little* and *a little* and *few* or *a few* may be the same. The choice reflects the speaker's stance with respect to that quantity: is it more positively oriented (closer to 'there is/are some' – the glass is half full), or more negatively oriented (closer to 'there is/are none' – the glass is half empty)? Examples illustrate this best. Take the following pairs of sentences:

> (56) He has *few* friends to go out with at weekends. I feel kind of sorry for him.
> (= He doesn't have many friends to go out with. This is sad.)
> Sorry, but I really have *little* time to spare. Can we discuss this next time?
> (= I don't have much time to spare. I can't help you now.)

> (57) He's only lived here for a month, but he's already got *a few friends* to go out with.
> (= He has friends to go out with in spite of being a newcomer. I'm impressed.)
> Actually, I have *a little time* to spare. Shall we grab a quick coffee?
> (= I have some time. Not much, but some, enough.)

In the sentences in (56), we are close to the idea of zero quantification – *no time* or *no friends* – which is not at all the case in (57), which highlights that, though limited, the quantity of time or number of friends has a more positive feel about it. Again, the actual amount of time (say, fifteen minutes) or number of friends (three or four) is compatible with both sentences in each pair: it is a matter of how the speaker intends to convey her message. Note moreover that *little time* and *few friends* are both rather formal in register. In more ordinary English, *not much* (instead of *little*) and *not many* (instead of *few*) are far more common. Conversely, there is nothing at all formal-sounding about *a little* and *a few*.

Finally, *few* and *little* can combine with *so*, *too* and *how*:

(58) My sister is always losing her temper. She has *so little* patience.
(= the amount of patience she has is extremely limited)
There were *too few* candidates for the position, so we had to advertise the opening again.
I'm surprised at *how little* sleep I can actually get by on.

3.2.3 Some *and* any
3.2.3.1 *Some* /səm/ versus *some* /sʌm/

We have already mentioned strong and weak forms with respect to certain auxiliaries (see Chapter 2, Section 2.5). Another such case of pronunciation and grammar closely interacting involves the quantifier *some*: using this quantifier correctly means, in part, knowing how to pronounce it.

One form of *some* is regularly pronounced /səm/ or even /sm/ – it is unstressed in the NP and very regularly alternates with Ø. Like Ø, it combines with plural countable nouns and uncountable nouns:

(59) You're going to Turkey? I have Ø friends (or *some* /səm/ friends) there.
She's hungry? Tell her there are *some* /səm/ apples (or Ø apples) in the kitchen.

*The schoolgirl gave her teacher Ø flower.
*The schoolgirl gave her teacher *some* /səm/ *flower*.

Whether it combines with a plural or an uncountable, the basic meaning of *some* /səm/ is 'an unspecified, imprecise quantity of'. It is not to be confused with *some* pronounced /sʌm/. The meaning of *some* (/sʌm/), which is always stressed, often means 'a certain amount or number of, *but not all*'. In other words, this use of *some* often establishes a contrast. *Some* /səm/ does not have this 'but not all' as part of its core meaning:

(60) /səm/ rather than */sʌm/ (= the quantity is imprecise)
There are *some* books on the French Revolution in our school library.
I'm looking for *some* furniture for my new flat.

(61) /sʌm/ rather than */səm/ (= but not all)

Some books in our school library would never have been found on the shelves fifty years ago.

Regardless of what the salesperson says, some furniture can be difficult to assemble yourself.

3.2.3.2 *Some* /səm/ versus Ø

We mentioned above that *some* /səm/ often alternates with Ø with little difference in meaning (see (59), above). There are, however, a couple of fundamental differences between the two. First, only Ø (and never *some* /səm/) can be used for generic reference:

(62) I love Ø dark chocolate, but I don't care for Ø white chocolate.

*I love some /səm/ dark chocolate, but I don't care for some /səm/ white chocolate.

(cf. I like some /sʌm/ dark chocolate, but only if it's of the highest quality.)

Second, the use of *some* /səm/, although it is used to quantify vaguely, is not usually used for quantities that are unlimited: it somehow implies limitedness. On the other hand, when there is no logical expectation as to the amount or number of something, Ø is often preferred:

(63) The victims of the tsunami are in truly dire straits: they need Ø food, Ø clean water and Ø shelter. (= the idea of quantity is not relevant – what is important is *what* they need)

There's some food and some water in the kitchen. Help yourself to whatever you'd like. (= the amount is unspecified, but clearly limited)

3.2.3.3 *Some* /səm/ versus *any*

You have probably learned that, whereas we use *some* in affirmative contexts, it is 'replaced' by *any* in non-assertive contexts (i.e. negatives and interrogatives). You probably also recall that, in some interrogative clauses functioning as offers, *some* is used rather than *any*. This rule of thumb actually does account for quite a bit of data and shouldn't be dismissed too quickly:

(64) I have some fresh pasta (*any fresh pasta), if you'd like to stay and eat with me.

Do you have any fresh pasta this week? (*some fresh pasta* is also possible)

Sorry, I don't have any fresh pasta (*some fresh pasta) this week.

Would you like some pasta for dinner? (*any* pasta is unlikely)

However, it does not account for the following example:

(65) Didn't I give you *some* money earlier this week?

The sentence is non-assertive from a formal point of view (it is both nega-tive and interrogative, in fact). And yet *some money* rather than *any money* will be used by a mother addressing her son when he asks for more pocket money. The reason is simple: while the sentence in (65) is interrogative in form, it has the force of an affirmative declarative sentence. The message communicated is an assertion: *I'm sure I gave you some money earlier this week.* Examples like this show that it is best to redefine our definition of non-assertive utterances as negative or interrogative *in meaning*. Here, the interrogative has the value of a confident statement. When we replace *some money* by *any money*, the meaning of the interrogative changes: the speaker genuinely believes that she may not have given money to the hearer.

3.2.3.4 *Some* /sʌm/ versus *any*

Some /sʌm/ can also alternate with *any*. The meaning is clear when you recall that some /sʌm/ implies 'but not all':

(66) (a) He didn't invite *any* colleagues. (= not a single colleague was invited)
    (b) He didn't invite *some* colleagues. (= some colleagues were not invited; others were)
    (c) I don't like *any* of his novels. (= not even one of them)
    (d) I don't like *some* of his novels. (= other ones, however, I do like)

The examples in (66) make it clear that the presence of *not* does not auto-matically result in the use of *any*. The paraphrases below show that *not* does not necessarily have scope over the whole sentence; *any* is only used if it does:

(67) (a) There isn't one single colleague that he did invite.
    (b) There are some colleagues that he didn't invite.
    (c) There isn't a single novel that I like.
    (d) There are some novels that I don't like.

Saying that *not* has scope over only a part of a clause means that the negation does not encompass the whole clause but only certain elements of it. Applied to the examples in (67) it means that in (b) and in (d) *not* only bears on *invite* and *like*. The issue of scope of negation will be taken up again in the discussion of modals in Chapter 5 (Section 4.2).

3.2.4 Either, neither,[19] each, every, all *and* both

This final set of quantifiers (with the possible exception of *either*) refer to all members from a set. *Both, each* and *every* are central determiners; *all* comes before a central determiner such as *the* and can also be used as the only (central) determiner:

> (68) *Both* books/*all* (the) books on that shelf deal with genericity.
> *Neither* book considers the issue of genericity.
> *Each/every* book has a section on genericity.

In each of the examples in (68), all members of the set of books are referred to: when *both* and *neither* are used, there is reference to two items. When *each* is used, there may be reference to two or more items; *every* implies reference to more than two. In the case of *all*, the number is not specified, but there is reference to more than two. Note that each of these determiners, with the exception of *every*, can also be used as a pronoun:

> (69) *Both/all* deal with genericity.
> *Neither* considers the issue of genericity.
> *Each/*every* has a section on genericity.

Neither is the opposite of *both*: whereas *both* means 'one as well as the other', *neither* means 'not one and not the other':

> (70) Which book will you buy? I'll take *both* (books). *Neither* (book). I don't want *either* book/*either* of them.

Even though *neither* is synonymous with *not either*, when used without *not, either* means 'one or the other':

> (71) Should I read this grammar or that one? – *Either* will do. ('You can choose one from the set.')
> My thesis is being directed by two professors. If *either* of them is not satisfied, I will have to revise my analysis. (For it to be necessary to revise my analysis, it's enough for one of them not to be satisfied.)

---

[19]In this chapter, we are referring to *either* and *neither* as determiners or pronouns; they are also used – with similar meaning – as adverbs (i) and as correlative conjunctions (ii) (see Chapter 1, Section 3.1.3):
>   (i) He doesn't live here anymore, and *neither* does she.
>   They don't live here any longer and I don't *either*.
>   (ii) I'd like to visit *either* Greece *or* Turkey next spring.
>   *Neither* James *nor* Jennifer came to the meeting.

Occasionally, *either* can mean *both*, but only in combination with nouns such as *side, end, extreme*:

(72) There were trees on *either* side of the road. (= on both sides)
Toilets can be found at *either* end of the building. (= at both ends)
Politicians from *either* extreme of the political spectrum are opposed to it. (= from both extremes)

There is more to be said about quantification than we have addressed in this section. From a practical point of view, though, the survey given here lists the points that deserve the learner's attention. We will now continue the discussion and turn to two more types of definite determiner.

3.3 Demonstrative determiners: *this* (*these*) and *that* (*those*)

This and *that* combine with a singular countable noun or an uncountable noun. *These* and *those* require the head to be a countable noun in the plural. *This* and *these* are often called **proximal demonstratives**: proximal means 'near the centre of', the centre in this case being the speaker. When used in this way, demonstratives are sometimes called **deictic markers**: the hearer needs to know where the speaker is in order to determine their meaning. The speaker functions as the so-called **deictic centre**.

This and *these* are used to refer to items that are physically or temporally close to the speaker, whereas *that* and *those* (called **distal demonstratives**, away from the centre) indicate that the speaker is physically or temporally distant from the referent of the noun head:

(73) *This* table (the one the speaker is standing next to) would be too big, but *that* one (pointing to another one across the room) will fit just fine.
These glasses (the ones the speaker is holding) should be stored with *those* over there.

She's too busy to see us *this* weekend.
Remember helping me move house? *That* weekend was without a doubt the worst of my entire life.
These days, we e-mail more and hardly ever write letters.
When our grandparents were younger, things were different. In *those* days, they often wrote several letters a week.

Bear in mind that 'distance' from the speaker can be a projection into the past or the future and does not necessarily locate the sentence in the past. As shown in (74), an Adjunct with *that* can also refer to a situation in the future. What is important about moving away from the centre is the movement away from the present time-sphere:

> (74) **Present time-sphere:** Thank you for your application. At *this* point, we still need to receive three letters of recommendation before the application is complete.
>
> **Past time-sphere:** Thank you for your application, which we received two weeks ago. At *that* point, we had not yet updated our website. Please check as the information has changed somewhat.
>
> **Post-present time-sphere**[20]**:** If your application is accepted, we will notify you within two weeks' time. At *that* point, you will need to confirm in writing that you will be attending the course.

There are three other important generalizations concerning demonstratives that are helpful to grasp from a usage point of view:

1. Occasionally, the interplay between the proximal and distal sets of demonstratives is purely sequential, in which case proximal usually precedes distal:

> (75) (pointing, at a bakery) I'd like two of *these* and two of *those*, please.

In (75), the distance between the speaker and the two kinds of pastry may very well be the same.

2. At a more abstract level, what remains to be said is somehow felt to be closer to the speaker than what has already been said. *This* announces what is to come whereas *that* refers back to what has been said. In cases like these, *this* is said to have **cataphoric reference**:

> (76) Listen to *this* (*that): they're raising the price of stamps again, effective from 1 September.
> All cooks should have *these* (*those) fresh herbs available at all times: parsley, sage, rosemary and thyme.

While *this/these* can be used cataphorically (referring ahead) or **anaphorically** (referring back – this is called **anaphoric reference**), *that/those* can only be used anaphorically:

> (77) I hear there might be a meeting this afternoon. If *this/that* is so, I'd like to be there.

---

[20]We will have more to say about the present, past and post-present time-spheres in Chapter 4.

3. It is often stated that *that* and *those* can also be used to establish emotional distance between the speaker and a referent that she views negatively or with disapproval:

> (78) Have you ever met Margaret Wakefield? She works in accounting. – Margaret Wakefield? I absolutely despise *that* dreadful woman!

> (79) Get *those* filthy shoes of yours off my brand new carpet!

What is often not made clear is that there is a strict hierarchy concerning the possible interpretation of *that* and *those*, placing spatial distance higher than affective distance: if a spatial interpretation of the demonstrative is available, it will always win out over an affective interpretation. Imagine a driver at the wheel of his car expressing exasperation when the car won't start and saying:

> (80) ?Damn! I am so sick and tired of *that* car!

When the hearer attempts to assign a referent in the real world to the NP *that car*, there may be a number of potential cars; the one car the NP cannot refer to, however, is the car the speakers are sitting in – precisely the referent the speaker is attempting to refer to disparagingly. This is because if a spatial interpretation is available, it will necessarily be understood first. For that reason, only *this car* is possible in (80).

Some of the examples above show that singular *this* and *that* can be used as pronouns. In other words, they can be used alone as a nominal head. When used alone, however, they are not usually placeholders for NPs. Sometimes, they can represent an actual referent the speaker and hearer can immediately identify in the context:

> (81) Why don't you take *this* with you? (speaker holding out an umbrella)
> And don't look at *that*, please. (speaker pointing to a confidential document)

In this case, extralinguistic referents of *this* and *that* are retrievable thanks to the surrounding context. In other cases, *this* and *that* can have a much more general kind of reference. In the following examples, *this* and *that* represent the situation the speaker is referring to rather than to any specific extralinguistic entity:

> (82) My picture has been posted on a website without my permission. Can someone explain how *this* can be legal?
> Let's drive until we're tired, then find a local hotel for tonight. – *That's* an excellent idea.

In other words, the examples that illustrate the pronominal use of *this* and *that* show that they do not act as anaphoric placeholders for a previously mentioned NP, which is a function that third-person pronouns like *he, she* and *it* can usually have. To refer back to an NP in the preceding discourse, *this one* or *that one* is used; here, *this* and *that* are determiners, and the pronoun *one* is a placeholder for a noun:

(83) I'm not sure which of these two shirts I should buy. *This one* fits me better (= this *shirt*), but *that one* is on sale (= that *shirt*).
I'm not sure which of these two shirts I should buy. ?*This* fits me better, but ?*that* is on sale.

Conversely, plural *these* and *those* can be used as pronouns to refer back to something, thus avoiding repetition. Note that although *these ones* and *those ones* are sometimes heard, many people consider this use incorrect:

(84) I'm not sure which gloves I should buy. I like the colour of *these* better (= *these gloves*), but *those* look warmer (= *those gloves*).

With an intervening adjective, using *these* and *those* with the pronoun *ones* is standard usage:

(85) I'm not sure which gloves I should buy. I like the colour of *these green ones* better, but *those woollen ones* look warmer.

The final determiner in the list of markers that establish definiteness is the possessive determiner. Like the demonstrative determiner, and any other marker that establishes definiteness, the use of a possessive determiner is indicative of the fact that the speaker assumes that the hearer can identify the referent of the NP.

3.4 Possessive determiners and the genitive

3.4.1 The possessive determiner and the possessive pronoun
The following examples all contain a possessive determiner:

(86) my grammar, your car, her birthday, his job, its tail, our duty, their fault

Note that the term 'possessive' is an umbrella term covering much more than straightforward ownership. This notion will also come to bear in our discussion of genitives in Section 3.4.2:

(87) my new computer   (possession, ownership)
his sister, her boss, their best friends   (various human relationships)
his beautiful eyes, her jet-black hair   (physical traits)

her uncontrollable temper   (behaviour)
your doctoral thesis   (creation of something)

As we pointed out in Chapter 1 (Section 3.1), these possessives often have an antecedent in the form of an NP and are therefore sometimes considered pronouns. We have opted to concentrate on their determining function and call them determiners. Recall that English *his* and *her* refer to the gender of the possessor and are not determined by any feature of the head noun.

(88) My father is part Asian: his (*her) mother was born in Vietnam.
My mother is part Kenyan: her (*his) father was raised in Nairobi.

Unlike the demonstratives, possessives also have a pronominal form distinct from the determiner form:

(89) my house, your house, her other house, our house by the lake, their house. Whose house is this? It's *mine/yours/hers/ours/theirs*.[21]

In one case, the possessive determiner and pronoun have the same form, *his*:

(90) *His house* is the last bungalow on the left.
Whose house is that? It's *his*.

Do not confuse the possessive determiner *its*, associated with an inanimate NP, with *it's*, which is the third-person pronoun *it* followed by the contracted form of the third person of the verb *be*:

(91) *It's* my birthday today. My parents gave me a new car. *It's* simply wonderful with *its* glossy exterior and high-tech stereo system. I just love it!

In the possessive determiner *its* and in the possessive pronouns, -*s* is not separated from the determiner/pronoun by an apostrophe. The morpheme -*'s* can express possession, but only in combination with lexical items, not with pronouns. The determiner *one's* is the only exception to this:

(92) One never knows when one's relatives are going to show up unannounced.

We will now turn to another determiner that is associated with possessive case[22]: the genitive.

---

[21]The possessive pronoun *its* does not exist: *Which dog does this toy belong to? – *I think it is its*. The rather formal possessive determiner *one's* has no corresponding pronoun either.
[22]**Case** is a label that refers to the specific form a word may take as a result of being used in a specific function. For instance, the personal pronoun *I* in Subject position becomes *me* in Object position.

3.4.2 The genitive: meaning and form

The **genitive** is a form relating two NPs:

(93) **N$_2$** [$_{NP}$ my grandmother]
N$_1$ [$_{NP}$ the garden]

           > [$_{NP}$ [my grandmother's]   [garden]]
           = [$_{NP}$ [her]   [garden]]

Its written form is spelled -'s ('apostrophe s') or -s' ('s apostrophe') when the noun ends in plural -s[23]:

(94) my parents' wedding anniversary
the neighbours' new car

The genitive is usually added to definite NPs with animate reference, including NPs that refer to animals, or names of institutions that bear some relationship to human activity[24]:

(95) [$_{NP}$ *the vice president's* speech]
[$_{NP}$ *the giraffe's* incredibly long neck]
[$_{NP}$ *the university's* most prestigious alumni]

When mating, the male lion bites [$_{NP}$ *the female lion's* mane], which is another evolutionary trigger for sexual activity. (www)

Barack Obama has accepted [$_{NP}$ *the Democratic Party's* historic nomination to run for president of the US] in front of a crowd of some 75,000 people. (www)

As [$_{NP}$ *Boston's* 30-year battle over desegregation] continues, a federal judge ruled that [*the city's* school assignment plan] did not discriminate against white students. (*New York Times*, 25 April 2003)

The above examples all have a definite NP, but indefinite NPs in the genitive are equally possible.

(96) *A cat's* eye is very similar to *a human's* eye. ('the eye of a cat')
This must be *a child's* book because it has been drawn in with crayons. (= a book belonging to a child)
The suspect admitted that he'd been stealing *men's* wallets for many years. (= wallets belonging to men)

---

[23]Note that -'s or a simple ' (apostrophe without 's') is added to names ending in –s: *James'(s) book, Dickens'(s) life and times.*
[24]Grammatical tradition states that the genitive is possible only with 'higher animals' and not with insects, for example. The restriction seems extreme: examples such as *the bee's wings* or *an ant's brain* are common.

The genitive is closely related to the possessive in that it is traditionally defined as the marker that indicates possession or possessive case. However, like the possessive determiners and pronouns, it does not always mark possession in the strict sense of the word[25]:

(97) [$_{NP}$ *the woman's* arrest] (*the* arrest *of the woman*/*the woman has an arrest*)

[$_{NP}$ *those young girls'* behaviour] (*the* behaviour *of those young girls*/*those young girls have behaviour*)

Though dealers at [$_{NP}$ *this year's* European Fine Art Fair] came prepared for the worst, they were able to see a vast selection of what the market has to offer. (*New York Times*, 18 March 2003)

In English, *of*-phrases that paraphrase genitive case are sometimes possible alongside the genitive:

(98) The secretary of state gave no details, but a senior US official said that Syria had shut down [$_{NP}$ *the offices of three organizations*]/[$_{NP}$ *three organizations' offices*]. (*New York Times*, 4 May 2003)

West Yorkshire Police said that no further details concerning [$_{NP}$ *the woman's arrest*] were expected to be released until lunchtime today. (www)

Police have not yet confirmed [$_{NP}$ *the arrest of the woman*], [...] but [...] police say they found [...] explosives buried in [$_{NP}$ *the garden of a house of [her] father-in-law*]. (www) (*her father-in-law's house's garden)

As a result, besides its youth, [$_{NP}$ *London's population*] in this period was also characterised by its diversity. (www)

Because of the conflicting definitions of London and Greater London, [$_{NP}$ *the population of London*] varies accordingly. (adapted from www)

Often, however, NPs with post-modifying *of*-PrepPs of this type are ungrammatical: *the book of my friend*, although perfectly clear, is not correct in Standard English. Two basic rules of thumb are useful in teasing apart N_2's N_1 and N_1 of N_2:

1. If the N_2 is human or animate, use the genitive rather than *of*: *our friends' house, the horse's head. Of* is possible when the N_2 is a complex NP: *the son of my mother's colleague* (although *my mother's colleague's son* can be used as well).

---

[25]We will see below and in Section 3.4.3 that genitives can also have the function of establishing reference to a subclass (classifying genitive) or that of measuring time (genitive of measure).

2. *Of* is usually not possible if the relationship between N_1 and N_2 can be paraphrased with the verb *have*: 'John *has* a nephew', so English uses *John's nephew* rather than **the nephew of John*. Conversely, *the arrest of the woman* (along with *the woman's arrest*) is fine, since the paraphrase '*the woman *has* an arrest*' is impossible.

The italicized words in the paraphrases added to the examples in (97) make it clear that the genitive NP constitutes the determiner to the NP.

As the genitive functions as a determiner (and usually establishes definite reference), we use the term **determinative genitive**.[26] The difference with the other definite determiners mentioned so far (the definite article and the demonstrative and possessive determiners) is that in the case of the genitive, the determiner takes the form of a genitive NP.

The following examples appear to go against the characterization of the genitive as a determiner:

(99) [$_{NP}$ The *men's and women's* basketball tournaments] will go ahead as scheduled, but Major League Baseball has canceled the scheduled opening of its season in Japan. (*New York Times*, 19 March 2003) (the basketball tournaments *for men and women*)

[$_{NP}$ a *boys'* school] (a school *for boys*)

The examples in (99) would appear to contain two central determiners (a genitive NP and an article), which we know is impossible. The type of genitive illustrated in (99) functions not as a determiner but as a modifier and is called a **classifying genitive**. Table 3.1 shows the number of ways in which a determinative genitive differs from a classifying genitive:

Table 3.1 Formal characteristics of the determinative genitive and the classifying genitive

Classifying genitive	Determinative genitive
The classifying genitive forms a unit with the noun head;	The determinative genitive does not form a unit with the noun head;
the genitive and the noun head cannot be separated by an adjective:	the constraint on the insertion of an adjective does not apply:
*a children's new museum (a new [children's museum])	the children's new playroom
*goat's creamy cheese (creamy [goat's cheese])	that goat's shaggy beard

[26]Occasionally, an NP with a determinative genitive can have indefinite specific reference: *The suspect has been stealing men's wallets* (= wallets belonging to specific men).

Classifying genitive	Determinative genitive
The determiner preceding a classifying genitive determines the NP as a whole:	The determiner preceding a determinative genitive bears on the genitive:
that [new [children's museum]]	[[the children]'s] new playroom
this [creamy [goat's cheese]]	[[that goat]'s] shaggy beard

Applying these observations to the examples in (99), the genitive *men's and women's* and *boys'* function more like a modifier to the noun head than as a determiner to the head noun. As is clear from the paraphrases, they establish reference to a subclass of tournaments or schools.

3.4.3 The genitive of measure

Another common use of the genitive is in expressions that indicate a measure:

(100) a mile's walk, in a month or two's time, a week's holiday, nine months' experience, three hours' delay, two days' permission, one minute's silence, three hours' journey

The paraphrase for examples like *a mile's walk* is obviously not 'a walk that belongs to a mile' but rather 'a walk of a mile' or 'a walk the distance of which equals one mile'. With what is called the **genitive of measure**, the head of the NP is always an uncountable noun and the NP in the genitive is indefinite. In other words, the indefinite article (such as *a(n)*, or Ø) determines the noun in the genitive, and not the head noun:

(101) [nine months]' experience, [two days]' permission, [a mile]'s walk, in [a month or two]'s time, [a week]'s holiday

If the head is a countable noun, the genitive of measure cannot be used: **a [two hours]' presentation*. The reason it is not possible to combine a genitive of measure with a determiner falls out naturally from that fact that it is not possible to use two markers that fulfil the role of central determiner:

(102) **a [one mile]'s walk, *a [one week]'s holiday, *a [nine months]' internship*

When the head noun is countable, the genitive has to be replaced by a complex prehead modifier. Observe that the noun is in the singular although the numeral can be a number higher than one:

(103) a two-month period   **a two months' period*
      a nine-month internship   **a nine months' internship*
      a two-hour presentation   **a two hours' presentation*

If the head noun can be used both countably and uncountably, both constructions are possible:

(104) a three-hour delay   three hours' delay
       a one-week holiday   a week's holiday
       a three-hour journey   three hours' journey
       a three-hour drive   three hours' drive
       a one-mile walk   a mile's walk
       a two-day leave   two days' leave
       Compare
       *a two-day permission   two days' permission

Table 3.2 summarizes the generalizations made above. It should be added that certain nouns like *drive* (*a two-hour drive/two hours' drive*), *walk* (*a one-mile walk/a mile's walk*) and *journey* (*a three-day journey/three days' journey*) do not have an uncountable use outside this specific construction.

Table 3.2 The genitive of measure

Noun in genitive + head	Complex prehead modifier + head	Head noun
She'll be back in [two weeks'] time.	*She'll be back in [a [two-week] time].	only uncountable
She'll be back in [a week's] time.	*She'll be back in [a [one-week] time].	
*I've just seen a [two hours'] documentary.	I've just seen a [two-hour] documentary.	only countable
*I've just seen [an hour's] documentary.	I've just seen a [one-hour] documentary.	
The plane had [three hours'] delay.	The plane had a [three-hour] delay.	countable or uncountable
The plane had [an hour's] delay.	The plane had a [one-hour] delay.	

It should now be clear that countability interacts with other grammatical features; the usefulness of understanding countability goes beyond basic article use.

3.4.4 The independent genitive

The head word in an NP with a genitive can be left unexpressed. This is called an **independent genitive**:

(105) (a) It would serve not only *the country's interests* but also *the president's* to
           retain Alan Greenspan as chairman of the Federal Reserve Board. (*New
           York Times*, 23 March 2003)
       (b) the butcher's, the baker's, the dentist's, the doctor's
       (c) at *the O'Briens'*, next to *my nephew's*, kitty-corner from *her boyfriend's*,
           at *our parents'*

Each of the sets of examples in (105) illustrates a different use. In (105a) the head-word is ellipted to avoid repetition of the same word: the paraphrase *the country's interests but also those of the president* is also possible, but less common and more formal. The examples in (105b) illustrate the use of the independent genitive of common nouns denoting professions when they refer to their place of business. In (105c), finally, the headword of a genitive of a proper name or a name of a relationship can be left out when it denotes where the referent lives.

3.4.5 The double genitive

A common genitive construction in English is the **double genitive**, so called because it contains two markers for possession: *'s* (or a possessive pronoun) and an *of*-phrase:

(106) (three) colleagues of my father's, a student of mine, a book of Noah's, no fault of hers
In an article in *New York Times* about Mr. Puff, *two friends of his* said they were surprised that Mr. Puff, who had worked as a home-repair contractor and run a small limousine company, had built such a large enterprise. (*New York Times*, 14 January 2010)

In the examples in (106), **partitive** meaning is expressed. That is, one or more items are picked out from a set. This construction is subject to a number of constraints:

(a) the noun in the genitive must be definite
(b) the noun in the genitive must have an animate referent
(c) the NP as a whole must be indefinite.

The examples with partitive genitives below are ungrammatical. In each case we have indicated which constraint has been violated:

(107) *a cocker spaniel of a neighbour's (cf. (a))
*a leg of the coffee table's (cf. (b))
*the friend of my father's (cf. (c))

Note that a double genitive in a definite NP is possible if the determiner is a demonstrative or if the head is modified by a relative clause. The examples that follow illustrate these contexts of use and show that the double genitive is not restricted to partitive constructions:

(108) Those friends of yours are some of the funniest people I've ever met.
That nasty daughter of his has been suspended from school again.
The only books of hers I've not read are the ones that are out of print.

As is clear from the first two examples in (108), using a demonstrative determiner often gives the double genitive a more emotive reading.

4. Modifiers

As pointed out in the introduction, an NP may include additional pre-modifying and post-modifying information which can be expressed in different forms:

(109) his *second* wife
that friend of yours *who went back to university*
the woman *in the miniskirt*
the office *opposite*
the people *living across the street*
the news *that they're moving to Ireland*
the ruins *left behind*

In the examples in (109), the modifying information is not syntactically obligatory: leaving it out does not result in an ungrammatical NP.

Many of the forms that give modifying information about the head noun are relatively unproblematic. NP-internal adjectives in English are nearly always placed before the head noun (following any determiners), for instance: *red roses, the bright sun* and so on.[27] Accordingly, we will not devote much space to adjectives within the NP. Conversely, modifying information that takes the form of a relative clause can bring up some usage issues. We will focus on this in Section 4.2.

4.1 Adjectives

Regardless of its function in the clause, the head noun of an NP can be modified by one or more adjective phrases (AdjPs):

(110) *beautiful* girls, that *fascinating* book, a *French white* wine

An AdjP can consist of its head alone or be more complex; a complex AdjP within the NP is most often preceded by an AdvP:

(111) an *incredibly shocking* revelation, a lot of *really probing* questions

---

[27]Some adjectives in *-ible* or *-able* can in certain contexts follow the noun in the NP: *the only option possible, the best seats available.* Adjectives used to form NPs with pronouns such as *something, everything, anything, nothing, somebody (someone), everybody (everyone), anybody (anyone)* and *anywhere* obligatorily follow the head: *something interesting, nothing special* and so on.

When adjectives are found within the NP, as in the examples above, their function is **attributive**. This is not the only syntactic position for AdjPs in English: they can also be outside the NP, in which case they are related to an NP through the verb *be* or another linking verb (*seem, look* etc.). Here we say that the function is **predicative** (i.e. 'part of the predicate'):

> (112) Is that beautiful girl your daughter?/That girl is beautiful.
> The tired workers returned home./Those workers looked tired.

Most adjectives in English are like those in (112): they can be used both attributively or predicatively. Other adjectives are restricted to either one function or the other: we can say *the baby is asleep* (predicative), but not **the asleep baby* (attributive); conversely, we can say *my former roommate* (attributive), but not **my roommate is former* (predicative). In (113), we give some examples of adjectives that are ordinarily used only attributively or only predicatively:

> (113) **attributive, but not predicative:** former/latter, present/past/future, late (= dead), major, sole, utter, daily (weekly, monthly, yearly), chief, main, principal, sheer
> **predicative, but not attributive:** asleep, alive, ill (many adjectives beginning with the letter 'a' are part of this group (*afloat, afraid, aglow, alone, asleep*))

If more than one adjective is used attributively, the order in which the adjectives occur is not free. The closer an adjective is to the noun head, the more objective the property is that it refers to. Take, for example, the NP *a big blue car*: a referent can only be judged as 'big' within its own class – *a big car* is still much smaller than *a small house*. The colour 'blue', though, usually qualifies in the same way regardless of the noun it modifies: *a blue car, a blue house, a blue sky*. The hierarchy in (114) and the illustrative examples below it illustrate this generalization. It is rare to find more than three attributive adjectives in English, and our examples reflect this:

> (114) opinion > size > age > shape > colour > origin > material + head noun
> Did you see [that crazy old French woman] on the metro this morning?
> (opinion > age > origin)
>
> They all sat waiting around [a huge round wooden table].
> (size > shape > material)
>
> [The oblong red Italian tomatoes you bought] are not ideal for this recipe.
> (shape > colour > origin)

AdjPs can be restrictive or non-restrictive:

> (115) (a) Class lectures will be supplemented with weekly articles from scholarly journals. This *compulsory reading* must be done before the lesson without exception.

(b) Much of what you need to glean from this course comes from reading. The *optional reading* can be done at your leisure, but the *compulsory reading* must be done before each lesson.

In (115a), *compulsory* gives us more information about the nature of the reading without contrasting it with anything else – we can suppress the adjective without fundamentally changing the meaning or grammaticality of the sentence. In (115b), though, *compulsory* and *optional* contrast two types of reading – suppressing the adjectives results in a nonsensical sentence. In other words, in this example the AdjPs allow us to establish two subcategories of reading, compulsory and optional.

While adjectives narrow down the reference of the NP, they are not the only modifiers that serve this purpose. We will now deal with a type of modifier that follows the noun head: the relative clause.

4.2 Relative clauses

4.2.1 Restrictive relative clauses versus non-restrictive relative clauses

A **relative clause** (RC) is a post-modifying clausal adjective that is (usually) part of an NP. Like prehead adjectives, RCs provide additional information about the head noun. This additional information may merely describe, but it may also restrict, narrowing down the referent of the NP in the sense that the addition of the modifier restricts the number of potential referents in the real world. The function of the AdjP pre-modifiers in the (a) examples and the RC post-modifiers in the (b) examples is the same:

(116) (a) **Adjectival pre-modifier:** The ballroom was positively teaming with [$_{NP}$ *stunningly beautiful* women]. (Here, the AdjP is non-restrictive: all the women in the ballroom were stunningly beautiful.)

(b) **Clausal post-modifier:** The ballroom was positively teaming with [$_{NP}$women, *all of whom were stunningly beautiful*]. (The RC is non-restrictive, on a par with the non-restrictive AdjP in (a).)

(117) (a) **Adjectival pre-modifier:** Snob that he is, he will only be seen in the company of [$_{NP}$ *stunningly beautiful* women]. (Here, the AdjP is restrictive: the referent is narrowed down – he is only seen in the company of some women, namely, stunningly beautiful women.)

(b) **Clausal post-modifier:** Snob that he is, he prefers the company of [$_{NP}$ women who are stunningly beautiful]. (The RC is restrictive, on a par with the restrictive AdjP in (a).)

The function of a restrictive AdjP or RC is different from that of a non-restrictive AdjP or RC. However, whereas restrictive and non-restrictive AdjPs in the NP have no formal distinction (and therefore pose little problem for the advanced learner), the formal features of restrictive RCs are different from those of non-restrictive RCs. For that reason we will concentrate on each kind of RC individually.

4.2.2 Relative pronouns and antecedents in restrictive relative clauses

A **restrictive RC** (or RRC) is also sometimes referred to as a **defining RC** or **limiting RC**. Take a look at the following examples:

(118) (a) [The <u>books</u> *(which) he reads*] are not appropriate for a boy his age.
    (b) [<u>Children</u> *who read such books*] will often have nightmares.
    (c) [The <u>books</u> *(that) he's looking for*] are out of print.

The bracketed NP Subjects in these sentences each have a head noun (under-lined). Each Subject NP also has a post-modifying RC (italicized). Like an AdjP, the RC tells us something more about the head noun. These particular RCs are restrictive in the sense that they tell us 'which books' or 'which children'. This information is not incidental: we are not interested in 'books in general' or in 'children in general', but rather a subclass of books (the ones he reads and those that he's looking for) and a subclass of children (the ones who read such books).

An RC in English is often signalled by a **relative pronoun**. In (118), the rel-ative pronouns are *which, who* and *that*. The relative pronoun in an RC always has an identifiable **antecedent**. For now, we will define an antecedent as the item a relative pronoun 'refers back to'. We will also see that relative clauses do not always have to have an overt relative pronoun. This explains why *which* and *that* in (118) above (but not *who*) are in parentheses.

The general idea of what an RC is should be clear regardless of your language because the RC is a universal linguistic device: all languages can have (at least) an NP Subject with a modifying RC as in (118). The mechanics of RCs and the func-tional distribution of the NPs they are found in, however, differ from one language to another. Keeping this in mind might help you to understand why some RCs seem relatively straightforward whereas others seem more problematic:

(119) **NPs containing an RC**   **Function of the NP**

[_{NP} The book *(which/that) I lent you*] was a gift from   Subject
my mother.

Did you like [_{NP} the book *(which/that) I lent you*]?   Direct Object

I lent [$_{NP}$ the student *who sits next to me*] my grammar   Indirect Object
book.

[$_{NP}$ The moment *(that) I met him*], I knew we'd become   Adjunct
friends.

I looked [for [$_{NP}$ the books *(which/that) she had lost*]].   Object of a Prep

The examples above indicate which items can function as relative pronouns: *which, who, that* or the zero relative pronoun. Two factors determine the choice of pronoun in restrictive RCs: the function of the relative pronoun in the RC and the nature of the antecedent.

It is helpful to show how the function of the relative pronoun can be identified and how it influences the choice of relative pronoun. Let's go back to the first two examples we cited at the beginning of this section:

(120) (a) [The books *(which) he reads*] are not appropriate for a boy his age.
      (b) [Children *who read such books*] will often have nightmares.

The antecedent and the relative pronoun are co-referential: we might even say that the antecedent actually features in the relative clause as well, but in the guise of a relative pronoun rather than in its full-fledged form. This becomes clear if we manipulate the RC and replace the relative pronoun by the antecedent, provided we revert to the canonical word order in a clause (in an RC, the relative pronoun always stands at the beginning of the clause, irrespective of the function it has):

(121) (a) ... which he reads – He reads books.
      (b) ... who read such books – Children read such books.

This kind of manipulation is useful when it comes to determining the function of the relative pronoun. It shows that in (120a), the relative pronoun 'which' functions as a DO: *What does he read? He reads books.* In (120b), the relative pronoun 'who' functions as a Subject: *Who reads such books? Children read such books.*[28] In other words, while we have so far talked about the function of the relative pronoun in the clause as one of the factors determining the choice of pronoun, we might just as well say that it is the function of the antecedent since the former is a kind of placeholder for the latter. If we replace the pronoun by the antecedent in (118c), we get the following result:

---

[28]It is important to note here that the NPs in square brackets in (120a) and (120b) are both Subjects of the main clause. However, in (120a), the relative pronoun (*which*) is Direct Object in the relative clause whereas in (120b), the relative pronoun (*who*) is Subject in the relative clause. It is the function of the relative pronoun in the relative clause that determines the choice of pronoun.

(122) He is looking [$_{\text{PrepP}}$ **for** *the books*].

Here, the antecedent is part of a PrepP that functions as a Prepositional Object. In order to construct an RC, two options are available: the preposition of the PrepP can either remain in its normal position after the verb (123a) or it can be found before the relative pronoun (123b). In the latter case, the relative pronoun is always *which* (rather than *that*), unless the antecedent is human (*The person for whom you're looking is not here*):

(123) (a) [The books *(which/that) he was looking* **for**] greatly impressed him.
    (b) [The books **for** *which he was looking*] greatly impressed him.

Preposition stranding as exemplified in (123a) is more common in the ordinary register than the more formal-sounding solution in (123b).

Recognizing the function of the relative pronoun is vital in English for the following reason: relative pronouns functioning as a DO or as an Object of a Preposition are grammatically optional. In other words, the following remain perfectly grammatical without an overt relative pronoun:

(124) [The books *which he reads*] are not really appropriate for a boy his age.
    [The books Ø *he reads*] are not really appropriate for a boy his age.
    [The books *which he's looking* **for**] are out of print.
    [The books Ø *he's looking* **for**] are out of print.

This is not the case, however, when the function of the relative pronoun is Subject. Omitting a relative pronoun in such cases results in an ungrammatical sentence:

(125) (a) [Children *who read such books*] will often have nightmares.
    (b) *[Children Ø *read such books*] will often have nightmares.

As mentioned above, the nature of the antecedent also plays a role. More specifically, the status of the head noun determines the choice of relative pronoun. The antecedent of an inanimate head noun is incompatible with the relative pronoun *who*, whereas the antecedent of an animate head noun is incompatible with the relative pronoun *which*:

(126) (a) *[The books *who he reads*] are not appropriate for a boy his age.
    (b) *[Children *which read such books*] will often have nightmares.
    (c) *[The books *who he's looking* **for**] are out of print.

Note that both *who* and *which* in restrictive RCs can be replaced by *that*:

(127) (a) [The books (*that*) *he reads*] are not appropriate for a boy his age.
(b) [Children *that read such books*] will often have nightmares.
(c) [The books (*that*) *he's looking **for***] are out of print.

One final issue that we need to explain is the range of factors that determine the choice between *who* and *whom*. We discussed the question of *who* versus *whom* when we addressed interrogative structures in Chapter 2. We discovered that interrogative *whom*, although always prescriptively correct when functioning as an Object, is very often replaced by *who* in ordinary use. We also saw that *whom* is nonetheless generally preferred when it directly follows a preposition. The same characterization can be maintained for the relative pronoun *who(m)*: functioning as an Object, *whom* is always correct, but most often replaced by *who*; following a preposition, however, *whom* is nearly always preferable in careful English:

(128) (a) [The people *whom* we invited] all came to the party.
[People with *whom* we have things in common] often become friends.
(b) [The people *who* we invited] all came to the party.
[People *who* we have things in common with] often become friends.
(c) [The people *that* we invited] all came to the party.
[People *that* we have things in common with] often become friends.
(d) [The people Ø we invited] all came to the party.
[The people Ø we have things in common with] often become friends.

The sentences in (128a) are perfectly grammatical, albeit particularly formal-sounding. The equivalent sentences in (128b) are far more usual. The equivalent sentences in (128c) serve as a reminder that the relative pronoun *who(m)* (like *which*) is often replaced by *that*. And the equivalent sentences in (128d), finally, show that we can have an RC with no overt relative pronoun when the antecedent functions as an Object.

Table 3.3 Survey of relative pronouns used in restrictive relative clauses (see examples in (129))

	Subject	Direct Object	Object of a Preposition (with or without stranded preposition)
Animate antecedent	who, that (a)	that, who, whom, Ø (c)	who(m)/that/Ø … prep prep whom … (e)
Inanimate antecedent	which, that (b)	that, which, Ø (d)	which/that/Ø … prep prep which … (f)

Table 3.3 and the set of examples in (129) show how the choice of relative pronoun is determined:

(129) (a) People *who (that) have read this book* generally agree that it's a masterpiece.
(b) She has just published a series of books *which (that) both frighten and delight young children*.
(c) The two professors *Ø I liked the most (that/who/whom I liked the most)* have both retired.
(d) The vegetables *Ø you can grow (that/which you can grow) in a small city garden* are limited.
(e) The woman *Ø he's sitting behind (who(m)/that he's sitting behind)* seems to have fallen asleep. (the woman *behind whom he's sitting* is rather formal)
(f) I think the pen *Ø you're writing with (which/that you're writing with)* is mine. (the pen *with which you're writing* is rather formal)

4.2.3 Relative pronouns and antecedents in non-restrictive relative clauses

We have so far focused on RCs whose function is similar to that of restrictive adjectives: they all restrict the reference of the head word. As explained in Section 4.2.1, **non-restrictive relative clauses** (NRRCs) give useful additional information about the antecedent, but the information does not serve to narrow down the possible referents of the NP.

As in the case of restrictive RCs, the choice of pronoun in non-restrictive RCs is determined by two factors: the nature of the antecedent and the function of the relative pronoun in the RC. An overview is given in Table 3.4 of the pronouns that can be used and an example is given for each of the different possibilities:

Table 3.4 Survey of relative pronouns in non-restrictive relative clauses (see examples in (130))

	Subject	Direct Object	Object of a Preposition (with or without stranded preposition)
Animate antecedent	who (a)	who/whom (c)	who(m) … prep prep whom … (e)
Inanimate antecedent	which (b)	which (d)	which … prep prep which … (f)

(130) (a) Her son, *who is now studying at university*, has always been quite bright.
  (b) The article she's written, *which is of publishable quality*, is about relative pronouns.
  (c) This is my friend Matilde, *who(m) I'm sure you've already met*.
  (d) This book, *which I bought only yesterday*, has already proved quite useful.
  (e) Next to my grandmother is my cousin David, *who(m) I am quite fond of*. (*of whom I am quite fond* is much more formal)
  (f) This silver spoon, *which I'm quite fond of*, was given to me by my grand-mother. (*of which I am quite fond* is much more formal)

As is clear from the examples just given, NRRCs are formally marked by the use of commas: there is a comma after the antecedent and, if the relative is followed by the rest of the clause, one after the NRRC. This rule is often not strictly applied by native speakers writing English, even in fairly edited prose; however, omitting it is considered incorrect by many. Note that the relative pronoun *that* is not used in NRRCs:

(131) *The article she's written, that is of publishable quality, is about relative pronouns.

Another way in which NRRCs differ from RRCs is that they can have what is called a sentential antecedent. In this case the relative pronoun used is *which*, and its antecedent is a complete clause (132a) or a predicate (132b). NRRCs of this type are commonly referred to as **sentential NRRCs**:

(132) (a) My grandmother gave her credit card number to a stranger on the phone, *which* has happened before.
  (b) My grandmother gave her credit card number to a stranger on the phone, *which* she has done before.

4.2.4 The relative determiner *whose*

All of the relative words discussed above are pronouns: they are placehold-ers for an NP. English also has the possessive **relative determiner** *whose*. The antecedent is regularly animate (compare to the relative pronoun *who*)[29]:

(133) I once met a man *whose* fingernails were five inches long.

Whose can also be used with an inanimate antecedent when that antecedent – an organization, a country or a city, for instance – is notionally made up of animate human beings:

---

[29]As in the case of the possessive determiner, there is something 'pronoun-like' about *whose*: even though it is followed by a noun head (*the man whose car got stolen*), it is at the same time on a par with an NP (*the man's*).

(134) Firms *whose* employees are happy tend to have a low rate of absenteeism.
Amsterdam is a city *whose* immigrant population is booming.

Even when the antecedent has straightforward inanimate reference, *whose* is often found:

(135) The product we want to present is IKEA PS BÖLSÖ, a little table *whose* legs are made of plastic PET recyclable material. They look like bottles of water and can be filled. (www)
It's hard to see what is democratic about a British foreign policy *whose* very fundamentals [...] are consistently opposed by voters. (www)
Diamonds *whose* price is measured in gold (headline in the *Guardian*, 29 October 2004)

If you are afraid of misusing relative *whose* with an inanimate antecedent, there is usually another way to get the message across:

(136) The product we want to present is IKEA PS BÖLSÖ. The legs of this little table are made of plastic PET recyclable material.
It's hard to see what is democratic about this kind of British foreign policy. The very fundamentals of it [...] are consistently opposed by voters.

4.2.5 RCs with partitive meaning

In Section 3.4.5, we observed that a double genitive is sometimes used with partitive meaning (i.e. to refer to one, several or all members of a set or to refer to a subpart or all of an amount). RCs can be used in such contexts, as illustrated by the examples in (137). The structure is used with many of the quantifiers we have seen (*all, both, each, many/much, little/few, neither/either, none*) but also numbers (*one, two, three ... the first, the second, the third*) and superlatives (*the longest, the most interesting*):

(137) I've read two novels by Dickens, *neither of which I particularly enjoyed*.
The young teachers, *many of whom had never taught before*, were nervous the first day.
My boss asked me to summarize the information, *very little of which I understand*.
My grandmother had two sons, *the first of whom died in infancy*.
Prokofiev composed nine piano sonatas, *the most challenging of which is the sixth*.

Having discussed the internal structure of the NP – its determiner, pre-modifiers and post-modifiers – we will look at how it interacts with the rest of the clause.

5. Subject-verb agreement

5.1 Subject-verb agreement in English: basic principles

To close this chapter on the NP, we will address a topic that very nicely brings the NP and the VP together: Subject-verb agreement.

Verbal agreement refers to the phenomenon in which the Subject of a sentence determines the form of the verb. With only one exception (*be*), verbal agreement in English is limited to the third person of the present tense, the distinction being between third-person singular (*He eats too much*) and third-person plural (*They eat too much*). The principle whereby the number of the verb is determined by the number of the head of the Subject NP is called **formal agreement**.

While the principle of formal agreement is rather straightforward to apply, it may be useful to highlight number agreement with certain types of Subject NPs. For instance, non-NP Subjects are always treated as singular:

> (138) That he refuses to get in touch with her *is* ridiculous. clausal Subject
> On the floor *isn't* a very comfortable place to sit.   PrepP Subject

Similarly, NPs that refer to amounts or measurements are usually treated as singular:

> (139) For someone who doesn't have much money, *fifty dollars is* quite a lot.
> *Five miles was* too far to walk, so we took a taxi instead.

As observed in Section 2.2.5, the heads of certain NPs are invariable, meaning their form does not change (*this sheep/these sheep; one television series/two television series*). When the reference is plural, a plural verb has to be used. We also pointed out that some nouns look singular but are in fact plural: these include some irregular plurals such as *data* (singular *datum*), *phenomena* (singular *phenomenon*) and *criteria* (singular *criterion*). These are forms that give pause even to speakers of English, who will often say *the media is* and *the media has* instead of the more prescriptively correct *the media are* and *the media have*.

When singular NPs are conjoined by *and*, they usually call for a plural verb (see 5.3.4, below):

> (140) My sister and (my) brother *are* both heart surgeons. (not **is*).

Note that in this case we will say that there is **referential agreement**: even though the form of component NPs of the Subject is singular, the fact that there is reference to two individuals results in the use of a plural verb.

Compared to languages where verbal agreement affects not only singular and plural but person as well (e.g. languages where *I eat* versus *you eat* have different verb forms), this is all relatively straightforward. There are a few cases of verbal agreement with NP Subjects, however, that merit further discussion.

5.2 Agreement with collective nouns/NPs

Certain NPs in English have a head noun that we referred to above as a collective noun. A collective noun is one that can have plural reference in its singular form. Such nouns characteristically refer to entities made up of several members: *family, government, team* ... The very definition of these head nouns necessarily includes the notion 'a group of people'. In English, then, the verbs of such collective NP Subjects can show either formal agreement (agreement with the singular form of an NP) or notional, referential agreement (agreement with the plural notion referred to by that NP). Other such nouns include *committee, company, enemy, group, public, crowd, press* and *audience* (141). Names of businesses or organizations (e.g. *the BBC, Barclays* (142) and (143)) and names of countries when the meaning is that country's team ((144) to (145)) also belong to the category of collective nouns. A learners' dictionary will tell you whether or not a given noun can be used as a collective noun:

(141) The committee *are* (or *is*) meeting later this afternoon.
His family *is* (or *are*) coming to spend the holidays with him.
The enemy *was* (or *were*) approaching – they had to act fast.
The public *were* (or *was*) misled on the candidate's previous voting record.

(142) Contrary to previous rumour-fuelled posts [...], the BBC *have reported* that a takeover bid by US-based Elevation Partners has been accepted by the UK publisher. (*Guardian*, 22 May 2005)

(143) The BBC *has reported* that the warmest year recorded globally was 1998. (www)

(144) France *are unbeaten* in their last eight finals games, although they have drawn half of those matches. (*Guardian*, 16 June 2010)

(145) France *is unbeaten* and England and Ireland have one loss after the third week end of play in the Six Nations rugby tournament. (*New York Times*, 28 February 2002)

A few details concerning collective nouns and the NPs they head: first of all, notional (= plural) agreement with singular collective NPs is characteristic of British English only – North American speakers will nearly always opt for formal (= singular) agreement. Second, for those speakers who do show such variation, both forms of agreement can be found and are considered correct. Rare exceptions might be the nouns *staff* and *crew*, which, in British English, nearly always have notional, plural agreement:

> (146) The staff *have* been assigned to their new duties.

Finally, notional agreement also brings about other kinds of plural agreement (with determiners, for example):

> (147) The audience *were* standing on *their* feet, clapping *their* hands wildly.

When in doubt as to how to treat collective NPs, the safest bet is to use a singular verb.

5.3 Agreement with complex NPs

There are other cases in English where one finds a kind of tension between the competing forces of formal agreement and notional agreement common in all varieties of English. In this section, we will focus on complex NPs.

5.3.1 Agreement with the head of the NP

When the constituent that functions as Subject of the sentence contains several NPs, it is the head of the NP that determines whether the verb is singular or plural:

> (148) [The noise of screaming children] *drives* me mad.
> [The situation currently experienced by so many people] *is expected* to change soon.

5.3.2 A number of, the number of, majority *and* per cent

A complex NP with *a number of* is used with plural countable nouns and is close in meaning to *many, a lot of*. When it functions as Subject, this kind of NP predictably takes a plural verb. In an NP with *the number of* (+ plural NP), however, *the number* is the Subject and it takes a singular verb:

> (149) *A number of* students *have* complained about the new policy.
> *The number of* students *has* risen sharply since the implementation of the policy.
> *A growing number of* scientists and public health officials *say* that exposure to vast amounts of concentrated animal waste can be linked to a variety of health problems. (*New York Times*, 13 May 2003)

With complex NPs with *majority of* or *per cent of*, which are followed only by uncountables or plurals, agreement is determined by the second noun in the NP:

(150) The majority of the *information* on their website *is* correct.
A majority of *voters are* not satisfied with the present government's stance.
A whopping 90 per cent of the *milk* we drink *comes* from cows.
More than 70 per cent of *teachers* in the school district *are* unionized.

If the number of the verb is determined by the noun that is closest to the verb, as in the preceding examples, we say that the principle of **proximal agreement** applies.

5.3.3 Either, neither *and* none

NP Subjects headed by the pronouns *either, neither* or *none* and followed by a PrepP in *of* with a plural NP – for example, [*either* [*of my parents*]], [*neither* [*of them*]], [*none* [*of the writers*]] – can take a singular verb (formal agreement) or a plural verb (proximal agreement):

(151) Neither of my parents *is coming/are coming* to my graduation ceremony.
None of the writers *has* ever *won/have* ever *won* the prestigious award.

The fact that two options are available stems from the fact that the pronouns *either, neither* and *none* are grammatically singular whereas the Objects in the PrepPs, which are proximally closer to the verb, are plural. In formal English, a singular verb is held by many to be the more correct. In ordinary discourse (written and spoken), however, both are found, and the plural is extremely common.

5.3.4 Conjoined NPs

We pointed out in Section 5.1 that two singular NPs conjoined by *and* usually take a plural verb. This is predictable, as the conjoined NPs can be replaced by the (plural) pronoun *they*. Sometimes, however, conjoined NPs represent a single concept, easily replaced by the (singular) pronoun *it*. In this case a singular verb is common, though not necessarily required:

(152) Fruit and vegetables *are* good for you. *They* contain vitamins and minerals.
but
Bacon and eggs *is* the only thing he'll have for breakfast. *It's* his favourite.

6. Conclusion

In this chapter, we have gone into some detail about how the noun and the NP function in English. We have looked at some of the basic facts concerning countability of nouns and how different determiners can combine with them. We have seen how these determiners serve to establish different kinds of reference, how pre-modifiers (in the form of AdjPs) and post-modifiers (in the form of relative clauses) can be used to expand the NP, and how the NP determines verbal agreement in ways that are sometimes formal (*The committee is meeting*) and sometimes semantic (*The committee are meeting*).

In the following chapter, our main goal will be to describe a complete tense system for the verb and the VP, at first sight a topic completely unrelated to the NP. And yet the various components that make up the grammar of English are not so compartmentalized as one might think. Take a look at the following sentence:

(153) Much like a human mother with her baby, *a mother lion* protects her cub at any cost.

Nothing prevents us from transposing this sentence (which you will now recognize contains a generic NP) into the past – imagine, for instance, that we want to make a similar generalization about prehistoric mother dinosaurs:

(154) It is quite likely that *the mother dinosaur* protected her young as *mother lions* do today.

A question that arises is why the sentences in (153) and (154) are impossible with *be* + V-*ing* (a feature we will call progressive aspect in the next chapter):

(155) *A mother lion *is protecting* her cub at any cost.
 *The mother dinosaur *was protecting* her young as mother lions *are doing* today.

This restriction has nothing to do with lions or dinosaurs. Rather, the core meaning of progressive aspect is generally incompatible with a generic Subject. In other words, the aspect a verb allows in a given sentence can be closely linked with reference. It is the forms a verb can take, in terms of aspect and tense, that form the backbone of the following chapter.

Exercises

Exercise 1. Identify the NPs in the following sentences, put brackets around them and identify the noun head. Is the noun head countable or uncountable? If it is countable, is it singular or plural? Is the head noun individuating or collective? Is it common or proper? Identify any preheads or postheads in the NP. Identify the function each NP has within the sentence (Subject, Direct Object, Indirect Object etc. – see Chapter 1).

1. I don't have any time to waste. My research keeps me extremely busy.
2. His refusal to delegate is going to get him into trouble at work.
3. That night, the children had prepared a wonderful surprise for their parents.
4. Manchester United are but a shadow of their former selves, some people say.
5. The phonetics class I'm taking meets every other Monday.
6. All students preparing the international business degree must study abroad for one semester.
7. Music is an international language that everyone speaks with a different accent.
8. The dead leaves strewn on the cobblestone streets announced the arrival of autumn.
9. The committee claim to have no knowledge of the situation.
10. The new recruit is a man with a mission. Nothing will stop him.
11. Why don't you cut that string with a knife instead of with those scissors?
12. My sister-in-law can't stand the idea that some people might not like her.
13. The CEO has just made my colleague district manager.
14. Have you ever sent your mother fresh flowers for her birthday?
15. Do you prefer fiction or non-fiction? – Frankly, I'd rather read poetry.

Exercise 2. Choose the pair of nouns that can be used in the sentences below, changing the form of the noun if necessary and making any other changes in the sentence that are necessary.

Example: thunderstorm/rain
The number of _____ this month has far exceeded the norm for the month of July.
> The number of thunderstorms this month has far exceeded …
> The amount of rain this month has far exceeded …

advice/suggestion	change/coin	equipment/machine
	evidence/indication	furniture/chair
homework/assignment	housework/chore	information/detail
	jewellery/necklace	luggage/suitcase
progress/improvement	software/application	underwear/T-shirt
	weather/condition	

1. The number of _____ you can check depends on the airline you choose.
2. According to the report, there are _____ that unemployment is on the decrease.
3. I've had this _____ for too long. It's time to throw it out and buy some new clothes.
4. Do you have _____ for our first-year university students in English?
5. All the _____ about the package tour will be sent to you three weeks in advance.
6. The _____ is such that a picnic in the park is ill-advised today.
7. There was a bunch of _____ lying on his desk, but most of it was foreign.
8. Most of the _____ on this computer need to be replaced by more recent versions.
9. Our biology teacher doesn't give us much _____, but when she does, it's too hard.
10. The _____ in the old factory were in a state of neglect and disrepair.
11. I have witnessed a certain number of _____ in the way we work here.
12. There was so little _____ in his office that half of us had to sit on the floor.
13. Many of the antique _____ being sold at the fair were overpriced.
14. Doing the _____ is something no one at our house likes to do.

Exercise 3. Look at the words in italics. Determine which words can be used as they are and eliminate the choices that are not possible.

1. You're going to the supermarket? Don't forget to buy *rice/strawberry/egg/garlic*.
2. And why not pick up some *cereals/carrots/breads/cheese* as well?
3. He hasn't got much *furniture/tables/chairs/space* in his flat, has he?
4. I need some *help/advice/information/documentation*. Can you be of any assistance?
5. You have a few *choice/alternatives/leeway/possibility*. Think hard before you decide.

Exercise 4. The following exercise should first be done orally, then written. Many of the NPs in the following sentences are singular. Make them plural when logically possible and make any other necessary changes in the sentence. In which of these sentences does this change affect the verb form, and in which cases does it not? Explain.

1. Each unexplained phenomenon you cited can be easily explained.
2. The piano had been tuned before the concert.
3. That church was built in the eighteenth century.
4. A child who likes school tends to succeed.
5. The woman he's talking to is a colleague of mine.
6. My foot really hurt after the hike.
7. A goose flying south may be a sign that winter is on its way.
8. That judge has never heard such an explanation in her career.
9. The crisis the visiting alumnus was talking about seems to be an exaggeration.
10. A fish swims in water and a sheep walks on land, but they are both animals.
11. That man gave me lots of useful information and advice about buying used furniture.

12. Peter informed the school nurse that he'd found a louse in his daughter's hair.

Exercise 5. The following exercise should first be done orally, then written. Many of the NPs in the following sentences are plural. Make them singular when logically possible and make any other necessary changes in the sentence. In which of these sentences does this change affect the verb form, and in which cases does it not? Explain.

1. Those series have been far more successful than I thought they would be.
2. The tomatoes I bought looked good but had little taste.
3. My big toes touch the tips of the shoes.
4. Those men are doctors. They studied medicine at university.
5. My chipped teeth will be repaired once I can afford it.
6. Having mice in the house is a real nuisance. They can carry diseases as well.
7. The islands' volcanoes haven't erupted for over twenty years.
8. These criteria are not useful when writing up such reports.
9. These kitchen knives are too dangerous for young people.
10. The so-called heroes were in their early twenties; they had very few belongings.
11. The scientists claim they have never come across such fascinating species.
12. All the horror films I saw with my friends gave me the jitters.

Exercise 6. Start by matching the NPs in 1–6 with the descriptions of the NPs in a–f.

1. a basket of cherries
2. a bowl of oatmeal
3. a grain of rice
4. a stick of butter
5. an item of news
6. a slab of meat

a. This is a unitizer followed by an uncountable noun. The unitizer represents the shape or form of the uncountable noun. This enables us to refer to the item as a whole.
b. This is a unitizer followed by an uncountable noun. The unitizer refers to the sub-part of a larger whole, or even a portion.
c. This is a noun followed by a countable noun in the plural. The first noun is a container of some sort.
d. This is a unitizer followed by an uncountable noun. The combination refers to a specific instance of the uncountable noun.

    e. This is a unitizer followed by an uncountable noun. The unitizer represents the smallest possible undivided part of the uncountable noun.

    f. This is a noun followed by an uncountable noun. The first noun is a container of some sort.

Now find the natural collocations between the set of nouns in I and the set in II, forming similar NPs with an indefinite article *a*. Countable nouns in set II will need to be used in the plural, and each noun in I and II should be used only once. Which NPs correspond to which descriptions in a–f above?

(I)					
bag	bar	book		clap	kernel
	clove	flash		glass	item
chunk	bucket		loaf	lump	
	roll	shelf		stalk	tube	wedge

(II)					
clothing	water	asparagus		book	ice
	bread	coin		corn	garlic
lightning	marble	cheese		soap	
	stamp	thunder		toothpaste	sugar	wine

Example: item (noun from I)
              clothing (noun (uncountable) from II)
              > an item of clothing, which can be compared to 5, above

Exercise 7. Identify the plural NPs in the following sentences. Determine in each case whether the head noun is always plural or whether it can also occur in the singular with a different meaning. If a non-plural form is possible, indicate whether it is countable or uncountable.

1. Has anyone seen my tweezers? I can't find them anywhere.
2. A fortnight's holiday abroad can cost close to a month's wages.
3. The programme's ratings have fallen drastically since last season.
4. The whereabouts of the suspected criminal are not yet known.
5. There's more to being polite than simply having good table manners.
6. Please be sure not to leave any personal belongings on the bus.
7. It takes a true man of letters to write a weekly literary column.
8. There are a number of crossroads between here and the school. Some don't have traffic lights.
9. I got through customs more quickly than usual.
10. When we were younger, we all got new clothes before the start of the school year.
11. Great pains have been taken to restore the painting to its original splendour.
12. Leftovers have an undeserved bad reputation: some things just taste better the next day.

13. He thinks his charm and good looks alone will get him a promotion.
14. Damages were awarded to three claimants in the case.
15. The city itself is crowded, but the outskirts have a quaint, old-world charm.
16. The grounds, though once beautiful, had not been tended to in years.
17. If your yearly earnings exceed a certain amount, your benefits will be suspended.
18. Can coffee grounds be disposed of in the sink, or will this stop up the pipes?
19. Take the stairs on the left and turn right on the third floor: my flat's on the left.
20. Many thanks to all those who have agreed to help with this year's fundraiser.

Exercise 8. Describe the features the nouns in the following list share and those they do not share. Discuss plural inflection, determiners they are used with and verbal agreement: *trousers, dregs, acoustics, resources, moose, headquarters, media.*

Exercise 9. Read the following newspaper article, and complete the blanks with *a(n), the* or Ø.

Look around you. On _____ train platform, at _____ bus stop, in _____ car pool lane: these days someone there is probably faking it, maintaining _____ job routine without having _____ job to go to.

_____ Wall Street type in _____ suspenders, with his bulging briefcase; _____ woman in pearls, thumbing her smartphone; _____ builder in his work boots and tool belt – they could all be headed for _____ same coffee shop, or bar, for _____ day.

'I have _____ new client, _____ accountant, who's commuting in every day – to his Starbucks,' said Robert C. Chope, _____ professor of counseling at San Francisco State University and president of _____ employment division of _____ American Counseling Association. 'He gets dressed up, meets with _____ colleagues, networks; I have encouraged him to keep his routine.'

_____ fine art of keeping up _____ appearances may seem shallow and deceitful, _____ very embodiment of denial. But many psychologists beg to differ.

To _____ extent that it sustains _____ good habits and reflects _____ personal pride, they say, this kind of play-acting can be _____ extremely effective social strategy, especially in _____ uncertain times.

'If showing pride in these kinds of situations was always maladaptive, then why would _____ people do it so often?' said David DeSteno, _____ psychologist at Northeastern University in Boston. 'But they do, of course, and we are finding that pride is centrally important not just for surviving _____ physical danger but for thriving in _____ difficult social circumstances, in ways that are not at all obvious.' (*New York Times*, 7 April 2009, adapted)

Exercise 10. Look at the nouns in brackets and decide which form or forms – *a*, *the* or Ø – are best suited to express generic reference in the following sentences. Nouns should be made plural if necessary. Be able to justify your choices.

1. (friend) should be there for you through thick and through thin.
2. Many ancient peoples held that the leaves and bark of (willow tree) had medicinal properties.
3. (book), more than anything else, might be said to contribute most to the evolution of ideas from one generation to the next.
4. Nowadays, (fuel pump) {is, are} most often electric. It supplies petrol to the engine.
5. (smartphone) may best be described as the combination of a handheld computer and a mobile phone.
6. Before (telephone), people used to send telegrams to convey important information quickly.
7. Nearly 75 per cent of all elemental mass is constituted by (hydrogen).
8. His thesis deals with how (fairy tale) can serve to show us how to navigate through life's ups and downs.
9. (blue whale) {has, have} a heart the size of a small two-door car.
10. (father) should be able to talk openly and frankly about the simple facts of life.
11. (appendix), also called vermiform appendix, {is, are} located between the small and large intestine.
12. (corn syrup) {is, are} commonly used in prepared foods to prevent sugar from crystallizing.
13. (blue whale) {is, are} the largest mammal in the world.
14. Though primarily associated with Asia, (rice) can be grown virtually anywhere.

Exercise 11. Complete with *some*, *any* or Ø. If more than one is possible, give all answers. Indicate whether or not there is a change in meaning.

1. Yogurt is made from _____ milk.
2. I don't eat _____ vegetables.
3. Don't _____ of her close friends live near by?
4. _____ doctors claim that doing puzzles is good for the mind.
5. I'm sorry, I'm a little confused. In fact, I don't have _____ idea what you're talking about.
6. I hardly have _____ time to study now that I've taken on a job – I hope I'll manage to pass my exams.
7. She's planning on inviting _____ friends over for dinner next week, but she doesn't really like to cook.
8. And that's the end of today's lesson. Does anyone have _____ questions?
9. _____ student caught cheating during the exam will immediately be sent to the principal's office.

10. I'm leaving next week for Tunisia ... I can't wait! – But don't you have _____ important work to finish before? The boss won't be happy if you don't get it done before you leave.
11. _____ books are not suitable for young children. That's why parents should always verify that the books their children are reading are appropriate for their age group.
12. They've never had _____ problems with the law, as far as I know. They're fine, upstanding citizens.
13. There are seldom _____ people in this restaurant in the evening. They must do most of their business at lunchtime.
14. I hope to have _____ free time this summer to travel. I haven't been on holiday in ages.
15. Would you mind buying _____ apples when you go to the market? I'd like to bake a tart this afternoon.

Exercise 12. Complete the following sentences with *some* or Ø. If both are possible, give both answers. Indicate whether or not there is a change in meaning.

1. _____ students at this university live quite close to campus.
2. Should young children drink _____ milk? Specialists are far from agreeing on what's best.
3. _____ people agree with the mayor's proposal; others are opposed to it.
4. He's decided to spend the summer holidays with _____ friends of his.
5. _____ 350 factory workers are expected to be laid off by the end of the year.
6. _____ cats are generally more independent than _____ dogs.
7. Could you take a look at _____ figures I've come up with for next year's budget?

Exercise 13. Complete the following sentences with *few, a few, little, a little, much* or *many*.

1. _____ is known about the silver-spotted skipper, a rare butterfly found only in the south of England. Its origins remain shrouded in mystery.
2. In spite of what I've been told, this website does not provide _____ practical information.
3. Students often have _____ basic questions even if they've understood the lesson.
4. He never drinks spirits or beer, but he does drink _____ wine now and then.
5. Even her _____ remaining friends have become increasingly intolerant of her irresponsible behaviour.
6. There are too _____ staff in this department. We're going to have to cut back.
7. _____ has changed in the banking industry since the recent financial crisis. This is unfortunate.
8. Although _____ has been written on the subject, this new book takes a brand new look at early black and white photography.

9. Don't worry, I can finish the project. All I need is _____ time.
10. _____ days ago, I saw a really good film about Marie Antoinette.
11. _____ things are as heart-warming as a child's laughter. In fact, there's probably nothing that cheers me up more.
12. The government's reaction has been minimal. The newspapers have given the public _____ information on the events, and the radio even less.

Exercise 14. Complete the following sentences with *much, many,* or *a lot of/ lots of,* and then choose the correct form of the noun that follows. Your choice should reflect ordinary spoken English, and not formal, academic English.

1. This cereal is called 'Fruit and Fibre', but honestly, I can't see _____ [fruit/fruits] in it at all besides a few raisins.
2. She claims she has _____ [friend/friends], but I don't think she's being honest. She often has nothing to do at weekends.
3. I hear you're doing a report on American politics. Have you been able to find _____ [information/informations] on the internet?
4. I haven't seen _____ [film/films] this past year. Nothing has really interested me, and besides, I'd rather spend my time reading.
5. Now that I'm on holiday, I've got _____ [time/times] on my hands. I'll probably spend most of it sleeping!
6. Fortunately, I haven't got _____ [luggage/luggages]. I'm not even going to check it.
7. Did you see that crowd at the concert? I'd never seen so _____ [people/peoples/person/persons] in one place before in my entire life.
8. There is seldom _____ [work/works] to be found in that area of the country. Unless you've already found a job, I wouldn't move there if I were you.
9. *Gone with the Wind*? No thanks, I've seen that film so _____ [time/times] that I don't care if I ever see it again!
10. I haven't got _____ [film/films] left and I'd still like to take a couple of pictures. Can I borrow your camera?

Exercise 15. *Either, neither, both, all, every, each*: choose the correct quantifier(s) and add –s to the noun that follows if necessary. There may be more than one possible answer.

1. There were people watching on (both/either/every/each) side of the street.
2. I cannot make up my mind. I like (both/either/neither/every) ring: I'm not sure whether to choose the silver one or the white gold one.
3. There was a journalist in (both/either/neither/every/each) corner of the tennis court.
4. I treated myself to the all-you-can-eat buffet. I tasted (both/either/neither/every/each) dish mentioned on the day's special.

5. (Both/Either/Neither/Every/Each) book appeal to me. If you don't mind, I'd rather borrow something else.

Exercise 16. Insert any necessary apostrophes before or after 's' and indicate how they are being used. There may be more than one possible solution. When this is the case, explain why.

1. Womens and childrens clothes can be found on the second floor. Boys shoes are on the fifth.
2. I'd like to get my hands on an old dentists chair. Joannes got one, and I want one like hers.
3. Are these yours? – No, they must be Carls. Or maybe his wifes. Or his daughters.
4. Peoples opinions have changed since last years elections.
5. One never knows who ones friends are. She certainly doesn't know who hers are, does she?
6. Have you ever heard of St Sebastians? – Yes, I have; its my cousins daughters school.
7. Working in labour relations involves listening closely to workers complaints.
8. My colleagues husbands company has announced massive lay-offs.
9. The students demand is on everyones mind at the university these days.
10. The partys being held at the Smiths. Everyones supposed to bring something to drink.
11. Please remind the mens team to put everything back in its proper place.
12. The old houses doors and windows will be replaced in two years time.

Exercise 17. Rewrite the following sentences using a double genitive when possible. When a double genitive is not possible, explain why.

1. The book's final chapters were long and monotonous.
2. *Les Quatre Cent Coups* is one of my all-time favourite films.
3. One of Iris Murdoch's novels is being turned into a musical.
4. That nephew – I'm talking about your nephew – is clever for his age.
5. A colleague's spouse has just been hired by our competitor.
6. Women's blood pressure tends to rise during pregnancy.
7. This idea – the one Julie has – might actually solve our problem.
8. I'd like to introduce you to my good friend, Clarissa Van Arden.
9. I'd like to introduce you to my mother, Clarissa Van Arden.
10. One of the car's rear tyres had gone flat.

Exercise 18. Rewrite the following sentences using an independent genitive when possible. When an independent genitive is not possible, explain why.

1. I spent half an hour in the professor's office trying to get my mark changed.
2. I waited nearly an hour at the doctor's office before I was seen.
3. Shall we meet at my girlfriend's flat or somewhere else? – Let's meet in front of her flat.
4. Have you any idea whose book this is? – Yes, it's Elisabeth's book.
5. What is that lying on the kitchen table? – It's Elisabeth's book.
6. His attitude is the sort of thing that inspires and motivates those around him.
7. His attitude is the kind of positive attitude we need in times like these.
8. I can't e-mail you this weekend; I'll be at my parents' house, and their internet is down.
9. Jane Austen's novels are still widely read, as are Emily Brontë's novels.
10. Reducing your intake of refined sugar is good for your health, and your family's health, too.

Exercise 19. Rewrite the sentences using a genitive of measure, if possible. Is there an alternative construction? Why or why not?

1. We went on a trip. It lasted four days.
2. The second-year students have to do an internship. It lasts for five months.
3. The injured worker was given leave. It lasted for two months.
4. Candidates should have work experience. It should have lasted for at least two years.
5. He was absent for a period. It lasted for three weeks.
6. Will the children keep quiet during the drive to the sea? It will take two hours.
7. I've signed up for an online course. It will go on for eight weeks.
8. Hesitation is a sign of nervousness. This is especially true when it lasts several minutes.

Exercise 20. Determine whether the order of modifiers in the modified NPs below is appropriate, and rearrange the order if necessary. Sometimes there is more than one NP to consider.

1. The orchestra, made up of dozens of Canadian young talented teenagers, will be performing at 8 o'clock tonight.
2. If you use those small rectangular cardboard boxes to pack the books, they'll be easier to carry.
3. That blue Italian collection miniature plate might actually be worth something.
4. Formerly a magnificent railway Victorian old station, the building will soon be an upscale vegetarian restaurant.

5. An oblong bevelled wall mirror hung majestically against the aging yellow wallpaper.
6. He's just a lazy old chemistry teacher who's never updated his lecture notes.
7. I'd buy that antique china pale-blue teapot if it weren't so expensive.
8. The costume included a plastic ugly little nose with an elastic to slip behind your head.

Exercise 21. Turn the two clauses into one sentence using a relative clause. Begin your sentence with the italicized NP. What happens to the determiner? Why is this the case?

1. You were telling me about *a book*. It's going to be turned into a film.
2. I'm applying for *a job*. It will require me to travel at least once a month.
3. *A book* is lying on the table. It needs to be taken back to the library.
4. I slept in *a room*. It was in the attic of a charming nineteenth-century inn.
5. She gave me a *box of chocolates*. It was in the shape of a big heart.
6. *A woman* lives next door to me. She is a widow.
7. They come from *a town*. It is in the middle of nowhere.
8. You're making fun of *a man's* photograph. He is my father.

Exercise 22. Determine whether the following sentences include a restrictive or a non-restrictive relative clause. Supply the missing relative pronoun, indicate when a zero relative pronoun is possible and punctuate the sentences accordingly. If both a restrictive and non restrictive reading seem possible, choose the most plausible.

1. I'm pleased to introduce you to Regina O'Shea _____ will be taking Chris's old position.
2. He has no desire to travel to a foreign country _____ I find shocking.
3. What I'm looking for is a desk _____ is at once stylish and practical.
4. The bed _____ you're sleeping in is actually two hundred years old.
5. My only daughter _____ I've always been so proud of just defended her doctoral thesis.
6. I think you ought to ask Cecil _____ experience far exceeds my own.
7. Unfortunately, the books _____ she wrote earlier in her career are all out of print.
8. His second film _____ is arguably one of his best was panned by the critics when it came out.
9. I think the man _____ he's yelling at is the one who backed into his car.
10. Most people _____ have travelled to Ireland recommend hiring a car.
11. The CEO finally revealed the hacker's identity _____ he had kept secret for security reasons.
12. He's teaching a course on Victorian literature _____ he doesn't know the first thing about.

13. Besides Sylvia, I don't think you know any of the people _____ I've invited to the party.
14. Anyone _____ parents live far away feels lonely from time to time.
15. I just ran into my old friend John _____ I hadn't seen in nearly ten years.
16. I told her to see a doctor _____ is always the best thing to do if you've got a fever.

Exercise 23. For all sentences in exercise 22 above, identify the function of the relative pronoun (including zero) as well as the function of the NP in which the relative clause is embedded. If the antecedent is not an NP, explain precisely what it is.

Exercise 24. Incorporate the second sentence into the first, using 'some/(n)either/etc. of which' or 'some/(n)either/etc. of whom'. Maintain the word order of the first sentence.

1. The five delegates had no choice but to use English. The delegates didn't speak the same language.
2. The campus housing contract is signed by hundreds of students. Few of the students have actually read it.
3. Art is replete with images of rabbits and eggs. Rabbits and eggs are symbols of fertility.
4. All the staff are getting close to retirement. Several of the staff have worked here since the company's inception.
5. He gave me a set of 24 keys. The keys could not open the door of the vault.
6. The students are looking forward to the trip. Many have never travelled abroad before.
7. North America is home to many species of snakes. The most common species is the garter snake.
8. The author grew up in what used to be a thriving market square. Little of the market remains today.
9. The department has two laptop computers. You can use one or the other if need be.
10. Several women were the inspiration for characters in Williamson's early novels. The most influential woman was his own mother.
11. Excavators recently discovered three mummies. Two of the mummies are thought to be over 4000 years old.
12. The committee is made up of twelve members. Each member is in charge of something.
13. Both candidates are as confident as ever. The candidates have never been elected for public office.

14. Annual precipitation rarely exceeds 3000 mm. Much of the precipitation falls as snow in the mountainous regions.

Exercise 25. In each of the following sentences, two choices are given. Choose the correct answer or answers. There may be cases where neither choice is possible. Justify your answers.

1. Neither of the solutions you suggest *meet/meets* with the director's approval.
2. The majority of my books *deal with/is* about ancient Asian civilization.
3. The number of people interested *haven't gone up/are* constantly *changing*.
4. *Fifty dollars/Fifty miles* are really too much. He's being unreasonable.
5. A number of workers *are complaining/has been complaining* about the new policy.
6. Accounting, payroll, human resources … everything *close/shut down* at 5 pm.
7. Each student *is responsible for/has to prepare* a twenty-minute presentation.
8. The government *is working out/are working out* the details of the amendment.
9. Nearly 90 per cent of all lost luggage *are/is* ultimately returned to the passenger.
10. *A good advice/Good advice* is what I need right now.
11. The entire audience *were clapping/was clapping* their hands.
12. Neither of my parents *is/are* happy with my decision.
13. Once the jury *are/is* chosen, the trial will begin.
14. I studied lots of things at university, but economics *were/was* by far my favourite subject.
15. Overall, her CV looks good. What concerns me *is/are* the previous positions she's held.
16. Do you think the answers are correct? – Frankly, I don't think any of them *is/are* right.
17. After an entire week of intensive training, the whole team *is/are* feeling invigorated.
18. All of the machinery *are/is* in perfect working order, having been replaced only 6 months ago.

Exercise 26. Comment on the following sentences, all of which contain agreement errors with respect to standard English. Indicate in each case what you think the source of the error is. The examples are from the 21 September 2010 posting of Philip B. Corbett's *New York Times* blog cataloguing errors spotted by attentive readers. (topics.blogs.nytimes.com)

1. The relocation of underground utilities, including water pipes, gas lines, fuel tanks and electrical wires, are to blame for at least six months of delays.
2. A huge part of the population – from robust newborns to the frail elderly, and many others in between – are deficient in this essential nutrient.
3. He had dissolved his own practice because the service nature of the profession and the slow pace of the work was profoundly irritating to him.

4. The size of the individual stitches vary considerably.
5. Uecker is one of a small group of baseball broadcasters whose endurance with one or more teams make them greater symbols for those franchises than most players.
6. Ms. Kelch is one of those people who always makes small talk with cabdrivers, but on this day, after all that had happened, she was invested enough to take on a riskier conversation.

4

Aspect and tense

Chapter Outline

1. Introduction

In Chapter 2, we looked at how one builds well-formed finite clauses around transitive, ditransitive and intransitive verbs based on the different complements the verbs require or can accept. However, we did not address how a speaker communicates to the hearer at what point in time the information in the clause holds. In other words, we have said little thus far about how a speaker **locates a situation** in time.

In order to establish the temporal location of a situation referred to in a clause, English mainly uses tenses: the difference in meaning between *John is at work* and *John was at work* is that in the former case, John is at work at the moment we utter the sentence (at the **moment of speech (S)**) while in the latter case, John's presence at work is located in the past (before the moment of speech). *Is* is a present tense and it (usually) locates situations in what we will call the **present time-sphere**; *was* is a past tense and it (usually) locates situations in what we will call the **past time-sphere**.

There is no consensus on the number of tenses there are in English. The reason for this is that linguists do not necessarily apply the same criteria to determine exactly what a tense is. One common criterion used to define tense in English is **inflection** (the change in the form of a word, typically the ending: *talk > he talks/he talked*). If we base our definition of tense on inflection, there are only two tenses in English, the present (*he talks*) and the past (*he talked*). We will define tense differently in our approach. The criterion we use is based not on inflection but on meaning: a tense locates a situation in time. In some cases, a tense also gives information about the temporal relation between situations: it tells the hearer whether a situation happens before (or is **anterior** to) or after (or is **posterior** to) another.

In this chapter, we will outline a temporal system for English that includes eight distinct tenses. We will also lay bare the ways the system as a whole sticks together. In the overview in (1), V represents the **verb base**[1] (see Chapter 1 and the Appendix):

(1) present tense   *talk*   (V (+ -*s* in the third-person singular))

   past tense   *talked*   (V + -ED)

   present perfect tense   *have/has talked*   (*have* + V + -EN)

   past perfect tense   *had talked*   (*have* + -ED (= *had*) + V + -EN)

   future tense   *will talk*   (*will* + V)

   future perfect tense   *will have talked*   (*will* + *have* + V + -EN)

   past future tense   *would talk*   (*will* + -ED (= *would*) + V)

   past future perfect tense   *would have talked*   (*will* + -ED (= *would*) + *have* + V + -EN)

The above examples show how each tense is built by adding to the verb base (V) what we will call **tense markers**. In some cases (e.g. the past tense), the tense marker is an ending appended to the verb base: *he talked*. The abstract marker -ED corresponds to the -*ed* spelling for the past tense of regular verbs (*talk* + -ED = *talked*) but also to the irregular past tense forms found in the Appendix (*fall* + -ED = *fell*). In other cases (e.g. the future tense), the tense marker is an independent lexical form: *he will talk*. Some tenses, finally, are formed by a combination of tense markers: in *he had talked*, the past perfect tense is formed using the lexical verb *talk* plus the marker -EN (a form that is called the **past participle**: talk + -EN = *talked*) with the tense marker *have*, to which the tense marker -ED has been added (*have* + -ED = *had*). Note that like

---

[1] The **verb base** is the most basic form of the verb without any grammatical markings. In addition to being the form found in a dictionary, it is also the form used for the (non-progressive) present tense (except for the third-person singular form: *he works*), the imperative and the subjunctive. It also corresponds to the infinitive of the verb. **Bare infinitive** (as in *I must go now*) is the label we use to refer to the infinitive without *to*. When the infinitive is marked by the infinitive marker *to* (as in *I want to go now*), we use the label *to*-**infinitive**.

-ED, -EN is an abstract marker that can, but does not always, correspond to the spelling -*en: fall* + -EN = *fallen, ring* + -EN = *rung*. Note too that, with regular verbs, the addition of the markers -ED and -EN results in forms that have the same shape: *talked* corresponds to both the past tense form (-ED) and the past participle (-EN) of the regular verb *talk*.

There are other verb forms apart from the above tenses that can be used to locate situations in time (namely, *be going to* and *be to*), and they will be dealt with in this chapter as well.

Tenses locate situations in the past, present and future with respect to the moment of speech, that is, the time the clause is uttered. When more than one form can be used to refer to a particular time-sphere, each of the alternative forms highlights a particular vision of the situation or time-sphere. For instance, in order to locate a situation in the future (we call this the **post-present time-sphere**), at least five different forms can be used. In the description of the tenses that follows, we will indicate in each case what specific temporal information the form chosen communicates.

Temporal Adjuncts in the form of NPs (*yesterday, last week, tomorrow afternoon*), AdvPs (*right now, just, previously*), PrepPs (*in summer, on the occasion of his 50th birthday*) and clauses (*when I was a student, before they arrived, once she gets here*) also provide information about the temporal location of situations. We will give due attention to temporal Adjuncts that can (or cannot) combine with different tenses and to the impact these Adjuncts have on the choice of one tense over another. This is particularly important in keeping distinct the past tense and present perfect tense.

Before we examine the meanings of each tense, however, we need to introduce another grammatical feature whose meaning is different from that provided by the tense markers but, like the tense markers, is added to the verb base. This feature is called **aspect**. Apart from informing the hearer that the situation is located in the past, the present or the future, the speaker chooses either to represent a situation in its entirety or to refer only to the 'middle of the situation', opting to keep the beginning and the end of the situation out of focus. This choice is **linguistically expressed** in English. This means that the information conveyed is not simply inferred from the context but, rather, expressed grammatically through the use of **linguistic markers**. In order to focus on the middle of the situation, the speaker will use what is called **progressive aspect**,[2]

---

[2]Some grammars refer to progressive forms whereas others refer to **continuous** forms. This is purely a terminological question: there is no difference between the two. We have chosen to use the term *progressive*.

which is built by adding **aspect markers** to the verb base. The aspect markers in English are a form of the verb *be* and the ending -ING appended to the verb base. We will call the form resulting from V + -ING the *-ing* **participle**.[3] Take the following examples as a starting point of this discussion:

(2) (a) Jim scratched his knee.
(b) Jim was scratching his knee.

The situation – what the person who utters either of these sentences is reporting – may well be exactly the same. The sentences, however, are aspectually different. In (2a), the speaker uses a non-progressive form to represent the action as a single, complete event. One might say that she gives a bird's eye view of the situation in which the Subject referent (Jim) did something (scratch his knee), and that this perspective necessarily implies a view of the situation in its entirety. In (2b), the speaker gives a view from the inside using a progressive form. She indicates that the activity of Jim scratching his knee is ongoing at a past moment in time. This vantage point necessarily implies viewing only a slice of the situation. The representation in Figure 4.1 might help to bring out the difference:

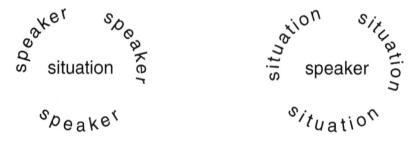

Figure 4.1 Perspectives associated with non-progressive and progressive aspect.

We will discuss aspect in greater detail in Section 2, where we provide more examples to show that aspect refers to the point of view one takes when presenting a situation in a clause. It must be borne in mind from the onset that aspect is concerned with an issue that is very different from tense, but that both are linguistically expressed by adding markers to the verb base. For the time being, consider that any finite verb phrase[4] in English will necessarily give us two kinds of information – information on tense and information on aspect:

---

[3]You may be familiar with the terms **gerund** (V-*ing* functioning as a noun, as in *Smoking is prohibited*) and **present participle** (V-*ing* functioning, as here, as a verb (often in conjunction with the auxiliary *be*: *he's smoking*) or as an adjective, as in *a smoking gun*). We will use the term *-ing* **participle** in both cases.
[4]See Chapter 1 (Section 4.3) for the definition of finite clause and non-finite clause.

the speaker always encodes tense and aspect on the verbs she chooses to use in a sentence, placing the action in one of the time-spheres and choosing to take a view either from the outside (representing the situation as a single, unanalysable whole) or from the inside (representing the situation as ongoing).

The combination of tense and aspect results in the following set of forms:

(3) **present** non-progressive   **present** progressive
  past non-progressive   **past** progressive
  present perfect non-progressive **present perfect** progressive
  past perfect non-progressive **past perfect** progressive
  future non-progressive   **future** progressive
  future perfect non-progressive **future perfect** progressive
  past future non-progressive **past future** progressive
  past future perfect non-progressive **past future perfect** progressive

Aspect and tense necessarily function together. However, a clear presentation requires us first to concentrate on each of these features one at a time. We will first home in on progressive aspect and explain in more detail how it works.

2. Aspect and situation types

Lexical verbs have meaning independent of their use in a given sentence. Consider the basic dictionary meaning of verb like *eat*. We will see in this section that mastering the linguistic mechanism of aspect requires us to be interested not only in the meaning of individual verbs, but in the meaning of the entire VP a verb is used in. We might not intuitively think there is much difference between the VP *eat* (used intransitively, as in *John's eating now*) and the VP *eat a biscuit* (used transitively, as in *John's eating a biscuit*), but the way progressive aspect interacts with these two VPs is quite different. Keeping that in mind, we will now discuss a linguistic concept which will prove very useful in our discussion of aspect and tense: that of **situation types**.

2.1 Situation types

Imagine a situation in which five people are observing Jennifer, who is making a drawing using brightly coloured pencils. If we ask each of these people to describe that situation, the following are all potential descriptions they might give:

(4) (a) Jennifer is drawing a tree.
  (b) Jennifer is drawing.
  (c) Jennifer is working hard.

(d) Jennifer likes bright colours.
(e) Jennifer has dropped a pencil.

None of the above sentences are in conflict with the others. We might simply say that each person witnessing the same situation is reporting a different facet of that situation. Accordingly, the linguistic resources each one uses to represent the situation will be different. For what is to follow, it is important to notice that the sentences in (4) make use of different verbs (*draw, work, like, drop*), different verb tenses with different aspects (*is drawing, likes bright colours, has dropped*) and finally that the VPs sometimes do and sometimes do not have an NP functioning as Direct Object (DO) (*is drawing, is drawing a tree*).

In (4a), the situation as it is represented in the sentence is that of drawing a tree, a situation which includes at least the possibility of a finished product. In (4b), the situation is perceived and presented as simply one of drawing – there is no mention of a finished product. In (4c) the speaker makes a judgement concerning not the process of Jennifer drawing, but her assiduousness in doing so (using the verb *work*), while in (4d), the speaker makes an inference based on Jennifer's choice of colours (using the verb *like*). In (4e), finally, the speaker has chosen to focus on yet another facet of the situation, namely the fact that at some unspecified point Jennifer dropped one of her pencils.

When we take a closer look at the sentences, we observe that the nature of the VP used is not the same. What we are interested in is how all these expressions of the same extralinguistic reality (Jennifer with her coloured pencils) are different and in what ways they are similar. In other words, what are the differences and similarities between the non-finite expressions *draw a tree, draw, work hard, like bright colours* and *drop a pencil*? One important difference is that they do not instantiate the same situation type. We will now take a look at how three parameters – duration, dynamicity and inherent endpoint – can help us to describe these situation types and to understand how aspect interacts with them.

The first four non-finite expressions (*draw a tree, draw, work hard*, and *like bright colours*) refer to situation types that are **durative**: they are perceived as taking up time. These durative situations have a temporal contour whereas the final one (*drop a pencil*) does not. We will say that *drop a pencil* is **punctual**, and we will use the parameter **duration** to explain that *draw a tree, draw, work* and *like* all have something in common: they are 'plus duration' (or + duration). *Drop a pencil* does not share this feature: it is 'minus duration' (or – duration).[5]

---

[5]From a strictly scientific point of view, of course, any situation takes up time. What we are interested in here is the speaker's perception of situations that are not felt to last in time or her intuition that certain situations cannot be extended in time.

Another parameter we can use to characterize situation types is **dynamicity**. If the situation represented is dynamic, it presents something as happening. The input is not always the result of an agentive 'doer': when we say *It's raining*, there is no animate agent[6] responsible for the input, but the situation is none-theless dynamic. Another way of characterizing dynamicity is to consider that there is some potential for change or development. This entails that a dynamic situation has an energetic contour, whereas a non-dynamic situation exists as a static state or condition. There is no fail-proof test for determining whether a situation is dynamic. However, one test that often works is the possibility of using the verb in the imperative. If you can command or request someone to do something, it means that a certain amount of input of energy will be nec-essary to bring about the situation in question. Another helpful test involves checking whether the verb or VP can be used as a complement of *stop*. If it is possible (*stop asking silly questions* but not **stop being tall*), the situation type is most likely dynamic. Put differently, we can say that a situation type is '+ dynamic' or '– dynamic'. If it is + dynamic, it 'does'; if it is – dynamic, it 'is'.[7]

A final parameter is that of **inherent endpoint**: some situations are repre-sented as having an inherent endpoint beyond which they cannot continue. Take a couple of examples: there is no endpoint inherent in the linguistic expression used to represent the act of drawing, working or liking (which is not to say that in the actual world, there may not be a factual endpoint to a sit-uation of drawing, working or liking). There is, however, an inherent endpoint to *draw a tree* and *drop* (which is not to say that in the utterance, the situation is always represented as actually reaching that endpoint). The moment a situ-ation is conceptualized and represented as that of drawing a tree, an inherent endpoint is contextually given. In other words, it is clear that the situation of drawing a tree can potentially reach its culmination and cease to be the case. Another way of looking at it is that with the situation *draw*, there is no notion of intended or expected final result; with the situation *draw a tree*, however, there is (namely, a completed picture of a tree). This is true even if Jennifer stops drawing before she has a chance to finish, meaning that the situation *draw a tree* is the same situation type whether we say *Jennifer **drew** a tree* (where a finished product is explicit) or *Jennifer **was drawing** a tree* (where it is not said whether or not Jennifer finished her drawing). The same can be said

---

[6]See Chapter 2 (Section 5.3) for a discussion of the concept of agent.

[7]Anticipating the discussion somewhat (see p. 191), there are some non-state verbs that intuitively have a stative feel about them. So-called **verbs of stance** (e.g. *sit, lie* and *stand*) are not likely to be perceived as dynamic. Note, though, that in many contexts, they can be put into the imperative (*Sit still! Lie down! Stand still!*) and this reveals that input of energy is required by the situations they refer to.

of *drop*. Even though it is perceived as having no duration, there is an inherent endpoint beyond which the situation captured by *drop* is no longer the case. There is no such inherent endpoint that is linguistically expressed in *draw, like bright colours* and *work hard*.

On the basis of the three parameters introduced, we can distinguish four situation types:

Table 4.1 Features of situation types

	State	Activity	Accomplishment	Achievement
Duration	+	+	+	−
Dynamicity	−	+	+	+
Inherent endpoint	−	−	+	+

Table 4.1 shows that the four situation types differ in minimally one feature. The feature distinguishing the situation type **State** from all other situation types is that a State is not dynamic. The situation types **Activity** and **Accomplishment** differ in that an Activity is not associated with an inherent endpoint whereas an Accomplishment is. The situation types Accomplishment and **Achievement** differ in that an Accomplishment has duration whereas an Achievement does not.

In (5) through (8) below, you will find a list of examples that illustrate the different situation types. It is possible to make subdistinctions within each category. We have only introduced additional classes if they are important for usage issues addressed in this book:

(5) **State**
 – **Verbs of cognition**: *admire, agree, assume, astonish, believe, consider, despise, detest, disagree, dislike, doubt, esteem, expect, forget, forgive, frighten, imagine, know, like, love, mind, miss, please, realize, suggest, suppose, suspect, think, trust, understand* …
 – **Verbs of the senses**: *feel, hear, see, smell, taste*
 – **Others**: *be, belong to, concern, consist of, contain, cost, depend on, deserve, differ from, equal, exist, fit, have, include, interest, involve, lack, matter, mean, need, owe, own, possess, remain, require, resemble, satisfy, suit, tend, weigh* …

(6) **Activity**
 work/function well (for a machine, a car etc.)
 write, eat, draw, drink, paint, read, knit, play chess …
 write letters, eat cake, draw pictures, drink wine …
 rain, snow, hail, blow (the wind) …

(7) **Accomplishment**: *write a letter, eat an apple, draw a tree, drink a glass of wine, paint one's kitchen, read an article, knit a sweater, play a game of chess, push the car into the garage, travel to Paris, drive back home* …

(8) **Achievement** (**punctual** verbs): *knock at the door, explode, blink, jump the fence, drop a pencil, break the window, sneeze, cough, hit someone, kick a ball, stab someone, strike someone, throw a stick, catch a ball, bang one's head, thud, fire/shoot a gun* …

This overview shows that in some cases, the verb itself indicates the situation type: this is most often the case with States, where the meaning of the verb alone tells you that the situation type it refers to is non-dynamic and durative. A similar observation applies to Achievements, where the lexical meaning of the verb makes it clear that the situation is dynamic and non-durative. In the case of durative dynamic situations, however, the other constituents in the sentence are often crucial to determining the situation type. Whereas *drink* and *drink green tea* are Activities, *drink a cup of green tea* is an Accomplishment. Likewise *walk around town* is an Activity, but *walk to the station* is an Accomplishment. It follows from this that particular verbs are compatible with different situation types depending on the context in which they are used. Language is malleable, and the examples in (9) show in which ways this applies to situation types: contexts, in other words, forge and force meanings, the result being that a verb can belong to different situation types depending on the clause in which it occurs (see Section 2.2.3):

(9) He *hated* the idea of having to leave his family behind. (State)
He said that camp was fun, but actually he *was hating* every minute of it. (Activity)

I *rented* a car as soon as I got to the airport. (Accomplishment)
We*'ve been renting* this car for about six months now. We can't afford one of our own. (Activity)

Now that you are familiar with these four situation types, the mechanics of the progressive will be much easier to understand.

2.2 Basic aspects of meaning of the progressive

Two straightforward labels capture the basic meanings communicated by progressive aspect: **ongoingness** and **limited duration**.

2.2.1 Ongoingness
The most general characterization of the progressive is that it represents a situation as being in progress or as ongoing. The speaker uses progressive aspect to make it clear that a situation is taking place at the time of reference. It can be

ongoing at the moment of speech (*he's sleeping*), at a moment anterior to the moment of speech (*he was sleeping*) or at a moment posterior to the moment of speech (*he'll be sleeping*). The perspective the speaker adopts is that of presenting a situation as happening rather than presenting it as a discrete event. This is expressed linguistically through the use of the progressive marker:

(10) She*'s wórking* on her thesis this summer.
They *were driving* in Spain when the car broke down.
We*'ve been thinking* about you a lot lately.
I*'d been sleeping* for hours when I was suddenly jolted awake.
Don't bother her between 6 and 7 – she*'ll be reading*.

It follows from this basic characterization that it will generally not be possible to combine progressive aspect with the situation type we call a State (but see Section 2.2.3). The ongoingness communicated via progressive aspect implies dynamicity:

(11) *These shoes *are costing* too much.
*People in that town *were knowing* each other well.
*How long *has* she *been* owning her car?
*The old bottles *had been containing* medicine.
*In only a few weeks, Sam *will be having* a baby sister.

When the progressive combines with an Accomplishment, the beginning and end of the situation are out of focus. The speaker focuses on the middle of the situation. Even though the inherent endpoint may well be reached in the real world, this is not something that the speaker says anything about in the sentence:

(12) I*'m doing* my biology homework.
She *was making* a cake when I arrived.

Progressive aspect also interacts closely with numerical NPs (an NP in which the determiner is a number) functioning as DO. In most cases it is not possible to combine the progressive with such a constituent:

(13) (a) Look! ?He*'s smoking* <u>one</u> cigarette!
(b) Look! *He*'s smoking* <u>five</u> cigarettes![8]

In order to understand why numerical NPs are often incompatible with the progressive, start by considering that a number is the result of a counting process. Counting can only be completed when a situation is over, so unless a

---

[8]We are focusing here on the sequential interpretation of the numerical NP (one after the other) and disregard the other possible reading in which the Subject referent is smoking five cigarettes at the same time.

particular number is fixed as a (predetermined) target, a numerical NP is not likely to be considered an *inherent* endpoint. The difference in 'inherent end-point potential' of the NP becomes particularly clear when we consider the set of progressive dynamic sentences with a DO NP in (13a) and (13b) above with those that follow:

> (14) (a) Look! He*'s smoking* a cigarette! (I thought he didn't smoke.)
> (b) Look! He*'s smoking* the cigarette! (e.g. the one he has been fiddling with)

The determiner is a number in (13a) and (13b), an indefinite article in (14a) and the definite article in (14b). In (13a) and both examples in (14) the NP has a single referent; in (13b) there is reference to more than one cigarette. The question is whether the referent of the NP in each case does or does not constitute a potential inherent endpoint. The moment we have some kind of evidence (for instance, if we observe someone take out a cigarette and a lighter), we will quite naturally conclude that the process about to be started is that of smoking a cigarette. In other words, it is taken for granted that the situation *smoke the cigarette* or *smoke a cigarette* has an inherent endpoint. But seeing someone take out a lighter and a cigarette will not likely lead us to conclude that the person is about to smoke exactly one cigarette or exactly five cigarettes. We will be aware that the situation is that of *smoking five cigarettes* only when it is made clear from the beginning that this number is a target to be reached ('I dare you to smoke five cigarettes in a row'). *Five cigarettes* does not constitute an inherent endpoint in a context where, once the situation of smoking is over, we count the cigarette stubs and conclude: *John smoked five cigarettes*. In this case, *five cigarettes* is the result of an after-the-fact counting process. Similarly, *one cigarette* is associated with an after-the-fact counting process whereas *the cig-arette* or *a cigarette* is not. It should now be clear why the progressive is often not compatible with a numerical NP. The number indicates a factual (rather than an inherent, contextually given) endpoint whereas the function of the progressive is to leave the beginning and end of the situation out of focus. In other words, there is incompatibility in the examples in (15) between, on the one hand, an item that refers to a boundary and, on the other hand, a marker whose primary function is to defocalize the boundary:

> (15) *John *is smoking* <u>ten</u> cigarettes.
> *The waiter *has been breaking* <u>three</u> glasses.
> *John *is running* <u>five</u> kilometres.[9]

---

[9]Note that, especially with an Adjunct indicating future time, this sentence is fine with progressive aspect when five kilometres is a predetermined goal, as in 5K race. In that case, the situation is located in the post-present time-sphere: *He's running 5 kilometres next weekend.*

Progressive aspect becomes compatible with a numerical NP as soon as it becomes clear from the context that the number constitutes a predetermined *inherent* numerical endpoint, as in (16):

> (16) Look at John. He's *smoking* <u>ten</u> cigarettes in a row. He's trying to break a record.
> Look, the groom *is breaking* <u>three</u> glasses in front of the bride. It's a local tradition.
> John *is running* <u>five</u> kilometres as fast as he can. And then I'll try to beat his time.

2.2.2 Limited duration

The characterization of the progressive in terms of ongoingness summarizes the basic meaning of this linguistic marker, but it is useful to add another characterizing label, that of 'limited duration'.

2.2.2.1 Limited *duration*: punctual verbs

The progressive has communicative effects which at first sight appear to be contradictory. On the one hand, the ongoingness associated with the progressive is closely connected to duration. On the other hand, the progressive can be used to limit duration. It is here that the importance of situation types comes to the fore. Combined with Achievements, which inherently take up little time, the progressive has the effect of giving duration to the situation. This translates into one of two interpretations. The first is a slow-motion effect, whereby the temporal contour of the punctual situation gets extended through the use of the progressive. More specifically, there is focus on the stretch of time directly preceding the non-durative event referred to by a verb such as *arrive* or *leave*:

> (17) His train *was* just *arriving* when I got to the station.
> The bus *was leaving*, so I had to hurry.

This interpretation is common for situations with verbs for which the stretch of time immediately preceding the Achievement can be perceived before the actual event occurs.

The second interpretation is repetition of the punctual situation, which equally results in the situation becoming durative (as in (18)):

> (18) Someone's *knocking* at the door. Will you please go and see who it is?
> The neighbour's dog *was barking*, so I finally had to complain.

It should now make sense why a sentence like *She was breaking her arm* will not usually be used: neither a slow-motion effect nor the effect of repetition is a possible interpretation for the situation *break one's arm*.

2.2.2.2 *Limited* duration: activities, habits, tentative statements

We get the opposite effect with situations that inherently take up time, such as Activities. The progressive in combination with an Activity can have the effect of restricting the duration rather than extending it, as above; the speaker may want to convey that the situation is temporary:

(19) She's fifty years old and still *lives* with her parents.
but She's *living* with her parents until she finds a place of her own.
She *colours* her hair. It's obvious she's not a natural redhead.
but The role of Vera is a redhead; she's *colouring* her hair until the end of the run.

It follows from this observation that the progressive does not normally combine with adverbs that express frequency or repetition, such as *always, forever* and *eternally*: these are incompatible with the idea of *limited* duration. However, such adverbs can combine with progressive aspect, and when they do, a meaning emerges that is not related to any of the typical progressive features mentioned thus far. The communicative effect is that of expressing one's affective stance with respect to the habitual nature of the situation. We call this use of progressive aspect the **progressive of affect**:

(20) My sister *is constantly embarrassing* me in front of my friends.
His assistant *is forever coming up* with excuses to extend deadlines.
You're *always working* late. You should spend more time at home.

Although the emotion expressed is very often one of irritation, the sentiment conveyed by the progressive of affect is not necessarily negative as in the sentences above. In the following examples, the tone is the opposite – rather than critical, it is laudatory:

(21) Sarah's a great mother. She's *always putting* her kids first.
Despite working long hours, my husband *is constantly helping* me around the house.
Judith *is forever volunteering* her time to help others in need.

The meaning expressed by the progressive of affect occurs only when the progressive is used in combination with an adverb that implies repetition. If there is anything irritable or laudable about the examples in (22), it is not expressed linguistically. These sentences are simply dispassionate statements of fact:

> (22) I'm *working* long hours (e.g. this week).
> My parents are *looking* after my children (e.g. today).

The observation that the progressive can bring out the temporary nature of a situation also helps to account for why the progressive is sometimes used to render a statement tentative. We put less pressure on the hearer when we say *I am hoping you might have some time* (and even less so when we say *I <u>was</u> hoping you might have some time* (see Section 3.3.3)) than when we say *I hope you (might) have some time*. In the latter case, the speaker leaves less room for a negative response. The effect of tentativeness is related to the fact that the progressive expresses limited duration. By communicating the idea that the hope is temporary, the statement leaves much more space for refusal than when the non-progressive is used, which refers to a present hope without the idea of limitation in time. The following examples are similar:

> (23) I'm (I was) *thinking* you might be able to share some of the expenses with me.
> I'm (I was) *wondering* if you could help me move house next weekend.
> We're (We were) just *wanting* to know if you've made a decision yet.

2.2.3 Fuzzy borderlines

We pointed out in Section 2.1 that it is not always possible to classify a non-finite VP in terms of situation type out of context. For instance, *be* would clearly seem to be a State verb, and this explains why it should not be possible to combine it with the progressive. However, it is possible to say to someone *You're being childish!* Since *be childish* means *behave childishly* in this sentence and is therefore dynamic in nature, it is compatible with the progressive. Another example concerns the verb *have*. As we saw in Chapter 2, Section 2.4, *have* can be used as a State verb as in *have brown hair, have a car* or *have a twin sister*. In these cases, the progressive is not possible (**He's having brown hair/a car/a twin sister*). But *have* can also be dynamic, in expressions such as *have a cigarette, have a wonderful time* or *have dinner*. Accordingly, there is nothing exceptional about sentences like the following:

> (24) I was *having* a cigarette on my front porch when my Mom drove up.
> (postcard) We're *having* a wonderful time in Italy! Wish you were here!
> Sorry, but we'll *be having* dinner then. Can you call later in the evening?

Similarly, certain verbs of cognition can be combined with the progressive if there is reference to a gradual mental process, as in the following examples:

(25) I find I'm *understanding* English grammar <u>better and better</u>.
Nutritionists *are* <u>increasingly</u> *doubting* the benefits of a low-carbohydrate diet.

In these contexts the progressive clearly forces a dynamic reading; accordingly the verbs no longer represent States but rather Activities. However, while many State verbs can be used dynamically, not all of them can. *Know*, for instance, is a verb which strongly resists a dynamic interpretation in any context. You are not likely to come across *know* with progressive aspect. The verbs in (5) above (p. 182), especially those in the category 'Others', are ordinarily only compatible with a State reading and are therefore used with non-progressive aspect.

The verbs of the senses *feel, hear, see, smell* and *taste* are worth mentioning in this context. These are State verbs when they refer to an involuntary sensation happening to a Subject referent (the (a) examples in (26)), but they can also be used dynamically when they refer to a Subject referent voluntarily acquiring a sensation (the (b) examples in (26)). In the case of *hear* and *see*, the different readings result in different lexical items being used. The point that is of particular interest to us is the following: when they have a dynamic reading, these verbs can combine with the progressive, but not when they have a State reading.[10] Note that the verbs of the senses can also be used intransitively, in which case they communicate States (the (c) examples in (26)). When used intransitively, *smell, taste* and *sound* are not ordinarily used in the progressive (but see (27) below); *look* and *feel*, however, quite commonly are:

(26) (a) I (can) *smell* something burning. Is there something in the oven?
(b) I *was smelling* the soup and burned the tip of my nose.
(c) The flowers from your garden *smell* wonderful. (cf. ?are smelling)

(a) Do you (can you) *taste* the cinnamon in these biscuits?
(b) The chef *is tasting* the sauce to see if it's ready.
(c) This roast *tastes* a lot like my grandmother's. (cf. ?is tasting)

(a) I (can) *hear* music coming from the park. What's going on over there?
(b) I'm *listening* to my new CD and have to admit I'm a bit disappointed.
(c) It *sounds* as though you've been working hard lately. (cf. ?is sounding)

---

[10]Note that, in certain contexts, it is the modal auxiliary *can* that conveys the idea of ongoingness at the moment of speech with verbs of the senses when they express involuntary sensation (i). In other (habitual or repetitive) contexts, this is not the case (ii):
(i)   Quiet – I *can hear* someone coming. Don't move.
(ii)   Every morning, I *can hear* the birds singing in my garden.

(a) If you squint, you (can) *see* England from here.
(b) Did you get the photo I sent you? – Yes, I'*m looking* at it right now.
(c) She *looks/is looking* good these days. Has she lost weight?

(a) Do you (Can you) *feel* that draught of cold air?
(b) The old man *was feeling* the texture of the fabric to judge its quality.
(c) I *feel/am feeling* a bit under the weather.

We mentioned above that *smell, taste* and *sound* could not be used in the progressive when used intransitively. This is a very helpful rule of thumb that can help to avoid producing unnatural sentences such as ?*This soup is tasting really good.* However, you will occasionally come across examples such as those in (27), where this rule seems to be broken:

(27) (a) The sun is out, the beers are open and the BBQ *is smelling* heavenly. (www)
(b) The proprietor [...] not only brings your food out but makes sure to come around and ask how everything *is tasting*. (www)
(c) The backstage teams are working equally hard on costume and set and the music *is sounding* better and better as each rehearsal goes by. (www)

As we mentioned earlier, contexts forge and force meanings: these are not exceptions to any rule. They are simply cases where, contextually, the speaker can force what is usually a State into a dynamic reading, effectively turning it into an Activity. Note that the contexts where she can do this are constrained: the activity necessarily has to be temporary or changing at the moment of speech. If you compare the sentences in (27) to the sentences in (28) below, you'll get a better idea of how important context is in determining whether progressive aspect is likely to be possible with these verbs of perception. Here, there is nothing really temporary or changing about how the Subject referent smells, tastes or sounds; consequently, the progressive is at best odd, if not impossible:

(28) (a) There's nothing wrong with this meat. It *smells* (?*is smelling*) perfectly fresh.
(b) These aubergines *taste* (?*are tasting*) as though they've been cooked in olive oil.
(c) Whoever's playing the piano *sounds* (?*is sounding*) like a professional.

It should now be clear that some knowledge about situation types combined with a basic insight into the meaning of the progressive unveils a logical system and eliminates the need to learn lists of rules by heart and sets of exceptions to each rule. Once you have grasped the basics, the system emerges and the larger picture becomes much clearer.

To conclude this section on situation types and aspect, we would like to address the status of verbs such as *sit, stand, lie* and *hang* and also *wait, stay* and *live*. These verbs all refer to the static location of something and, as such, would intuitively seem to refer to States – after all, they do not refer to dynamic processes like *run, work, cook* or *drive*. However, these verbs are perfectly compatible with progressive aspect, which is not possible for States:

(29) *I'd been waiting* for hours when he finally arrived.
The policeman told us that we shouldn't *be sitting* on the sculpture.
She *was* just *standing* there, staring straight ahead.

Rather than consider the above examples exceptional, we consider that the verbs are in fact '+ dynamic' insofar as they meet the criterion we established for dynamicity, namely, potential for development and input of energy by the Subject referent. The Subject referents in the above examples can interrupt or stop what they are doing. They can decide to do it or decide not to do it. In other words, they require some active input by the agent, or the 'doer'.

We are forced to concede that the sentences in (30) below are a bit more problematic:

(30) The books *are lying* on the dining room table.
Two large oak desks *were standing* in the middle of the office.

Any proficient speaker of English will confirm that there is nothing unusual about these sentences. And yet it is more difficult to apply our criterion for dynamicity to get the '+ dynamic' value necessary to distinguish these from State verbs. In such cases, we simply have to consider that the linguistic system obeys a logic that does not correspond the logic we adopt in our understanding of the real world. We saw other examples of this in Chapter 3 in our discussion of countability.[11]

2.2.4 States and stative situations
It is useful to make a final terminological distinction at this stage. So far we have been talking about situation types, a State being one of the four situation types traditionally distinguished. A State should not be confused with a **stative situation** (a characteristic of an extra-linguistic situation). Take the following pair of examples:

---

[11]The noun *furniture*, as we saw in Chapter 3, would appear to defy logic by being grammatically uncountable (i.e. we cannot say *many furnitures, *a furniture, *a few furnitures), although nothing prevents us in the real world from counting tables, chairs, desks and the like.

(31) (a) The tree *lost* its leaves in October this year.
(b) The old tree they cut down always *lost* its leaves in October.

While the situation type *lose its leaves* is an Accomplishment in both (31a) and (31b), the fact that there is reference to a situation that is repeated leads us to say that the sentence in (31b) refers to a stative situation. Any habitual situation (in fact, any regularly recurring situation that is unlimited in time) is a stative situation, regardless of whether it is located in the past, the present or the future, and irrespective of the situation type it represents. It is therefore important to bear in mind that qualifying a sentence as referring to a stative situation is not the same as saying that the situation type is a State. Similarly, any Activity represented as a (permanent) habit remains an Activity. The perception that there is something State-like about these situations stems from their being stative situations, not States:

(32) Many people still *drink* only red wine with beef.
She *freelances* as a camera operator and video editor.

3. Tense

3.1 Time-spheres, tenses and temporal relations

As pointed out in the introduction, tenses are forms of the verb that are primarily used to communicate temporal information about situations. More accurately, the addition of tense markers[12] to the verb base has the effect of locating situations (as they are represented in clauses)[13] in time. The basic temporal division that is made by a speaker is that between the past and the non-past. The non-past includes the moment of speech, which we refer to as NOW. The non-past divides into three **time-spheres**: the present (which coincides with the moment of speech), the pre-present and the post-present. It

---

[12]Except for the third-person singular form (e.g. *she dances*), it is the absence of any overt marker that signals the present tense. Compare this to the active and passive voice as discussed in Chapter 2: whereas the passive is signalled by the passive marker *be* (or sometimes *get*) combined with the past participle of a (di)transitive verb, it is the absence of any overt marker that signals the active voice.

[13]We explained in Section 2.1 that any representation of a situation in a sentence is indicative of the speaker's perception and subjective choice of how to represent it (see example of Jennifer drawing on p. 180). From this it follows that it is not a situation as such that is represented in a sentence, but rather, the particular way in which it is perceived by the speaker. From now onwards, we will use 'situation' as a shortcut for the more accurate (but wordier) 'the situation as it is represented in the clause'.

follows from these basic temporal divisions that we need at least four tenses: one to locate a situation in the past time-sphere, one for the pre-present, one for the present and one for the post-present. In Figure 4.2 we can see how such a timeline might appear.

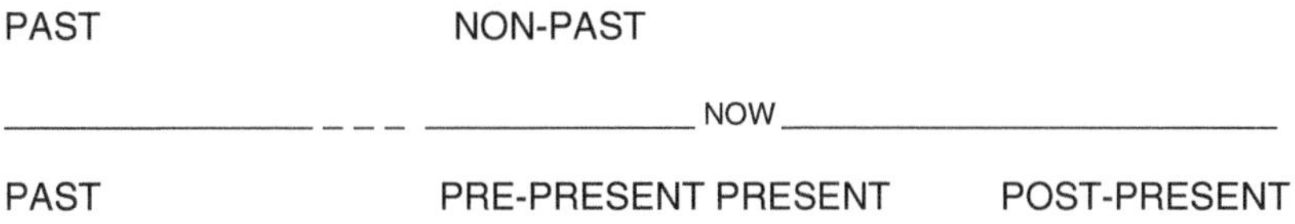

PAST   NON-PAST

_____ _ _ _ _____ NOW _____

PAST   PRE-PRESENT PRESENT   POST-PRESENT

Figure 4.2 Representation of the timeline.

Apart from locating situations in time, tenses can also express temporal relations between situations. For instance, in *He said he had just heard the news*, the past perfect *had heard* represents the situation of hearing the news as **anterior** to (i.e. temporally located before) that of saying. In *He said he would trim the hedge the next day*, the past future *would trim* represents the situation of trimming the hedge as **posterior** to (i.e. temporally located after) that of saying.

Table 4.2 reveals how the forms of the eight tenses unambiguously indicate the temporal information they convey. This information is made explicit by the presence or absence of three features:

1. +/− -ED
2. +/− *will*
3. +/− *have*

The first feature is straightforward: the verb form either carries a marker for past time or does not. The second feature refers to the presence or absence of *will*, that is, the presence or absence of a form that expresses a relation of posteriority. *Have* signals a relation of anteriority, which can be combined with a past time marker, a present time marker or a future time marker. Table 4.2 shows how the tenses are composed of a combination of three temporal markers.

It is inherent in any perfect tense – all of which have the marker *have* – that the situation referred to is anterior to some moment in time: with the present perfect, the situation is anterior to the moment of speech; when the past perfect is used, the situation is anterior to some moment in the past, and to some moment in the future when the future perfect is used. *Will* signals in every case that the situation is posterior to some moment in time. It is posterior to the moment of speech with the future and the future perfect tenses. When

Table 4.2 A feature analysis of the English tenses

Temporal features			Tense	Aspectual choice	Example
-ed	*will*	*have*		progressive	
−	−	−	Present	−	He does it
−	−	−		+	He is doing it
+	−	−	Past	−	He did it
+	−	−		+	He was doing it
−	+	−	Future	−	He will do it
−	+	−		+	He will be doing it
+	+	−	Past Future	−	He would do it
+	+	−		+	He would be doing it
−	−	+	Present Perfect	−	He has done it
−	−	+		+	He has been doing it
+	−	+	Past Perfect	−	He had done it
+	−	+		+	He had been doing it
−	+	+	Future Perfect	−	He will have done it
−	+	+		+	He will have been doing it
+	+	+	Past Future Perfect	−	He would have done it
+	+	+		+	He would have been doing it

will is marked by it -ED (= *would*) to form the past future and the past future perfect, it refers to a situation posterior to a moment in the past time-sphere.

In Sections 3.2 to 3.7, we will discuss each of the eight tenses illustrated in Table 4.2. For each tense, we will also comment on the effect progressive aspect has on the meaning.

3.2 The present tense

3.2.1 The present tense and situation types

The present tense is used to locate a situation in the present time-sphere, which is the time-sphere that coincides with the moment of speech:

> (33) He *works* at his father's company.
> They*'re working* on an important project this week.
> A return flight to Vienna *costs* only £100 if you take an early flight.
> It*'s costing* more and more to send one's children to college.

Water *boils* at 100 degrees Celsius.[14]
Careful, the water*'s boiling* – don't burn yourself.

The examples in (33) illustrate the present tense with non-progressive and progressive aspect. We need to make an important observation concerning the situation types that can be referred to by a non-progressive present tense form: (i) as explained in the introduction to this chapter, non-progressive aspect represents a situation in its entirety; (ii) the moment of speech is perceived of as a point in time. It follows from this observation that it is not possible to use a non-progressive form to refer to a present ongoing Accomplishment (e.g. **I eat an apple now* (cf. *I'm eating an apple now*)) or a present ongoing Activity (**I eat now* (cf. *I'm eating now*)): a situation with an inherent temporal contour that is referred to as a complete unanalysable whole cannot coincide with a point in time. When an Accomplishment or an Activity is represented as ongoing through the use of the progressive, there is no such incompatibility, since an ongoing situation can be the case at a point in time. Summing up, to represent a dynamic situation as ongoing at the moment of speech, we use progressive aspect.

The present (non-progressive) tense is commonly used to refer to States as well as stative situations. It typically refers to a permanent characteristic (34a) or to a present habit (34b). Present habits are nothing more than one kind of stative situation (see 2.2.4):

(34) (a) The Trans-Siberian railway *stretches* almost 6000 miles from Moscow to Vladivostok.
Water *freezes* at zero degrees Centigrade.
(b) She *works* as a nurse at the local hospital.
I *take* the metro to work every day.

3.2.2 The present progressive
Given the appropriate situation type, the present tense can combine with progressive aspect. The meaning will be that of ongoingness at the moment of speech, as in (35), of 'present temporary duration', as in (36), or of 'present temporary habit', as in (37):

---

[14]As will be pointed out below (Section 3.6.2), sentences like this are said to be omnitemporal. The situation is of course valid at the moment of speech, but it is also valid in the past and the future. In other words, it is always true that water boils at 100 degrees Celsius, not only in the present time-sphere.

(35) Have you seen John? – Yes, he *is working* in the garden.

(36) He *is living* in Brussels. (= 'for the time being' or 'until he moves')
(cf. He *lives* in Brussels.)

(37) He*'s walking* to work this week because his car is at the garage.
(cf. His office is only about fifteen minutes away, so he *walks* to work.)

If a situation happens regularly and if the speaker wants to give a more subjective (appreciative or depreciatory) view of the situation, she can use the progressive of affect – the progressive in combination with an adverb of repetition or frequency, as in (38) and (39). Recall that the negative emotive value this construction is often claimed to convey is not the only one possible, as shown in (39):

(38) I have a user in my office who *is constantly forgetting* to save his files. Due to his nearly complete incompetence, he sometimes loses a full day's work [...]. (www)

(39) Dion has been tremendous towards me. On the pitch he is like a big brother. He *is always helping* me. He *is always lifting* me and *keeping* me going at 100 per cent. (*The Independent*, 22 November 2002)

There are some contexts which seem particularly suitable for the progressive but in which progressive aspect is not used. In sports commentaries, for instance, in which journalists are commenting on events that are happening while they are speaking (40a), or in a commentary that accompanies a demonstration of the different steps of a process (40b), non-progressive aspect is used even though there is reference to dynamic situations that are ongoing at the moment of speech:

(40) (a) Jesperson *runs* with the ball, he *passes* it to Cleave … Reams *intercepts* it …
(b) So watch closely: I *select* the text I want to move, I *drag* it up, I *release* the mouse button, and I *resave* the document.

It is usually not possible to use the progressive with **performative verbs** (used only with first-person *I*, and occasionally with *we*):

(41) I now *pronounce* you husband and wife.
I solemnly *swear* to uphold the standards of this organization.
We *order* the defendant to vacate the property within thirty days.

With performative verbs, the very fact of uttering the clause in question creates the situation it refers to. Although the situation referred to is ongoing at the moment of speech, the progressive is not used. It may well be that these verbs are interpreted as referring to punctual situations whose durational contour it is impossible to extend. This is precisely one of the effects of the progressive when it combines with an Achievement (see (17) and (18) above).

3.2.3 The present to refer to the future

The present tense can also be used to refer to time-spheres other than the present. The non-progressive form can be used to refer to a situation located in the future (what we call the post-present time-sphere) provided the situation located in the future is seen as fixed and unalterable. (The (b) examples below show that the same form can also refer to stative situations located in the present time-sphere):

(42) (a) My train *leaves* tomorrow at 8. Can you take me to the station?
    (b) cf. The train I take to work every morning *leaves* at 8.

(43) (a) Sorry, I *work* on Saturday. Can we meet on Sunday instead?
    (b) cf. I *work* on Saturdays. Can we meet on a Sunday instead?

(44) (a) The sun *rises* at 5.18 tomorrow morning.
    (b) cf. The sun *rises* early in this part of the country.

This use is sometimes called a timetable future. A timetable is seen as fixed and not subject to change. Future time situations that involve something comparable to a timetable can often be referred to by means of a non-progressive present tense. Sentences that describe future scientific certainties also belong to this category, as the speaker considers that she cannot control or prevent the future situation. For instance, the example in (43a) could signal that working on Saturday is a requirement of the Subject referent's employer rather than an arrangement that the Subject referent has made herself. The example in (44a) refers to a natural rather than man-made situation.

The progressive form of the present can also be used to refer to the future, but only when the situation that is located in the future is the result of a present plan on the part of the Subject referent, something akin to an arrangement in the Subject referent's schedule:

(45) I'm *having* dinner with Jane <u>next week</u>.
She's *defending* her thesis <u>later this afternoon</u>.
They're *leaving* <u>early tomorrow morning</u>.

The examples in (42) to (45) illustrate that the present tense locates a future situation in the post-present time-sphere only when there is clear reference to future time. This usually comes in the form of a future-time temporal Adjunct in the clause itself (underlined in the examples above). It can also be established contextually as in (46), where future time is established in the question and understood to apply in the answer:

(46) Any plans for <u>tomorrow</u>? – No, I'm just *hanging out* and *relaxing*.

Further examples of the present used to refer to future time can be found in the sections on future time reference (Sections 3.6.2 and 3.6.3).

3.2.4 The present to refer to the past

The non-progressive present can be used with **verbs of communication** (such as *talk, say, report* and *inform*) to refer to a situation that is located before the moment of speech:

(47) I *hear* you're getting married. When's the big day?
John *says* that the results of the election are bound to be interesting.

Clearly, the Subject referents in (47) have heard (or said) the information before the moment of speech; one might just as well have said *I've heard* (or *John's said*) or even *I heard* (or *John said*). The effect of using the present here is often to invite the hearer to confirm or even just to react.

The present tense also has past time reference when it is used in newspaper headlines or in captions in which past events are referred to. In this case, the present tense makes the account more direct and, as with the verbs of communication addressed above, can serve to draw the reader in:

(48) President *Meets* Queen
Unemployment *Drops* 1 Per Cent
Hurricane *Devastates* Coast

Finally, the speaker will often use present forms, both progressive and non-progressive, to tell a story having past time reference. This is often referred to as the **narrative present**:

(49) Did I tell you what happened to me yesterday? So I'm *sitting* in my office when my boss *comes* in and *asks* if she can sit down for a minute …

Such a story can of course always be told using the past tense as well:

(50) Did I tell you what happened to me yesterday? So I *was sitting* in my office when my boss *came* in and *asked* if she could sit down for a minute ...

In Chapter 1 it was pointed out that a given constituent can perform different functions in the clause (see 3.3). We observe a similar phenomenon here, where one particular form (the present tense) can perform different functions: its unmarked function is to establish present time reference, but it fairly regularly refers to another time-sphere in ways that are predictable and generalizable.

3.3 The past tense

3.3.1 The past tense: non-progressive versus progressive

The past tense is used to locate a situation in the past time-sphere:

(51) My favourite uncle *died* in 2011.
The worker *fell* off the ladder and *was taken* to hospital.
I *worked* hard all day yesterday and *slept* well last night.

As with the present tense, the progressive marker can be added given the appropriate context, namely one in which there is reference to a dynamic situation that was ongoing at a past moment in time. Pay particular attention to the Adjuncts in brackets in the examples in (52):

(52) (a) I *was walking* out the front door [when you arrived].
(b) We *were (still) having dinner* [at 7] – we missed the beginning of the film.
(c) She *was working* at her computer [all day long].
(d) [When I woke up], the wind *was blowing* and it *was raining*.
(e) I *was reading* and Sarah *was taking* a nap – neither of us heard him walk in.

In the first two sentences, there is reference to a dynamic situation that is ongoing at a moment in time that is specified in the sentence. In (52a) the ongoing situation was interrupted, whereas in (52b) the situation was ongoing both before and after the time specified by the Adjunct. In (52c) the situation holds throughout the time referred to by the Adjunct. Example (52d) offers a description of a scene. Indeed, the progressive is often used to provide background in a narrative, against which the actual events of the story (the foreground) will be referred to with non-progressive aspect: here, the event is *I woke up*. Finally, in (52e) there is reference to two dynamic situations that are ongoing at the same time in the past. This is similar to what we find in sentence (52d), only here the background situations of reading and nap-taking are more clearly understood as explaining why he was not heard when he walked in. This is not necessarily the case in (52d).

It is interesting to observe the effect of a change from progressive to non-progressive:

(53) (a) I *walked* out the front door [when you arrived].
(b) We were hungry, and so we *had dinner* [at 7].
(c) She *worked* at her computer [all day long].
(d) The wind *blew* through the trees and the rain *poured* down.
(e) ?I *read* my book and Sarah *took* a nap – neither of us heard him walk in.

In (53a) there is reference to a sequence of events: your arrival is followed by (and is perhaps even the cause of) my leaving. In (53a) and (53b), the time specified by the Adjuncts is the point at which the situation referred to in the main clause starts. This is especially clear in (53b), since *have dinner* has a clear starting point: it is an Accomplishment. It is less obvious in (53a), since *walk out the door* is an Achievement: the beginning of the situation coincides with the end. In both sentences, the complete situation (*walk out the door* or *have dinner*) is presented as a single unanalysable whole.

The difference between the non-progressive and progressive versions of the sentences in (52c) and (53c) is less considerable than between the non-progressive and progressive versions of (52a)/(53a) and (52b)/(53b). The progressive in (52c) emphasizes the duration and communicates more explicitly the idea that she worked for a long time than when the non-progressive form is used. In (52d), reference is made to two dynamic situations that are taking place simultaneously. Such a context illustrates the core meaning of the progressive: it is typically used to refer to a situation (here, two situations) as ongoing. Although the non-progressive form in (53d) is theoretically possible, the sentence sounds more natural when the progressive form is maintained. It is unlikely that non-progressive forms would be used here when they serve as a background to a foregrounded event such as [When I woke up], which you will notice is not included in (53d). In (53e), finally, using progressive instead of the non-progressive aspect impacts on the temporal order that is communicated. The core meaning of the non-progressive – that of representing a situation as a single, unanalysable whole – has the effect of changing the temporal relation of simultaneity into one of sequence: the two Accomplishments are interpreted in the order in which they are mentioned (that is, the second is located after the first, chronologically). Accordingly, (53e) will not be used to describe the scene communicated in (52e).

As is the case with the present, the progressive of affect can be used with the past tense provided the sentence contains a verb that expresses repetition or frequency:

> (54) [H]e *was always doing* nice things, like one day I'd be eating a Galaxy Ripple and the next day he'd bring round a pack of them. (www)
> Moralists *are always complaining* about our lack of self-knowledge, but how can we be expected to know ourselves when it's so difficult for us to see ourselves? (www)

3.3.2 The past to refer to a future in the past

Like the present non-progressive, the past non-progressive can be used to refer to a timetable future, the difference being that the posterior moment is looked at from the past:

> (55) He told me he was sorry, but that he *worked* on Saturday and was unavailable. (Note that this is not the same as *He told me he worked on Saturdays*, where *worked on Saturdays* is a stative situation.)
> She told me that her train *left* at 8 and asked me to take her to the station. (Again, this is not the same as *She told me that her train left at 8 every morning*.)

The posterior situation is not necessarily located in the past time-sphere – the situations *work on Saturday* and *leave at 8* can be located anterior to or posterior to the moment of speech.

Similarly, just as the present progressive can be used to refer to a future situation that is the result of a present plan, the past progressive can be used to refer to a planned future in the past:

> (56) I *was having* dinner with Jane the following week.
> She *was defending* her thesis later that afternoon.
> They *were leaving* early the next morning.

3.3.3 The past progressive to refer to a present situation

We explained in Section 2.2.2.2 a side-effect of the meaning of limited duration communicated by the progressive, namely that it can make a hope or wish more tentative. This effect can be enhanced by combining the progressive with a past tense, even when there is reference to a present hope or wish:

> (57) We *were hoping* to see the doctor this afternoon.
> I *was wondering* whether you've finished the report.

The speaker not only presents the situation of wondering or hoping as temporary (through progressive aspect) but also gives it more distance by locating it in the past. In this way, there is more ample space for disagreement. The addition of, first, the progressive marker and then the past tense makes the situation incrementally more tentative:

> (58) I hope you can stay.
> I'm hoping you can stay.
> I was hoping you could stay.

Examples like these illustrate the interaction of tense markers and aspect markers as having an impact on meaning that is related to their usual unmarked meaning.

3.4 The present perfect tense

3.4.1 The present perfect and the pre-present time-sphere

The present perfect is another tense in English that can be used to locate a situation before the moment of speech. This tense locates a situation in the **pre-present time-sphere**, which is distinct from the past time-sphere. It establishes a different relationship between the moment of speech and the situation referred to in the clause: this tense refers to a situation that either happened or started happening (or, if the situation is a State, either was the case or started being the case) before the moment of speech, but without reference to a specific past time.[15] In other words, the present perfect expresses a relationship of anteriority between now and a situation before now:

> (59) I've *given up* smoking. (= I gave up smoking sometime before now (= the moment of speech), without stating when. I am no longer a smoker.)
> It's *been raining* for three days. (It started raining three days before now (= the moment of speech). It's still raining now.)
> She's always *considered* Jim her best friend.

To grasp the difference in meaning between the past tense and the present perfect tense, it is necessary to take a closer look at the way in which the time-sphere preceding the present can be conceptualized. The **past time-sphere**

---

[15]As pointed out in Section 1, we adhere to the view that the perfect constitutes a temporal marker rather than an aspectual marker. In other words, we hold that the present perfect is a tense in its own right and not an aspectually marked present tense. Not all linguists share this point of view.

may be thought of as completely disconnected from the present, as in the visual representation of the timeline given in Figure 4.3 below.

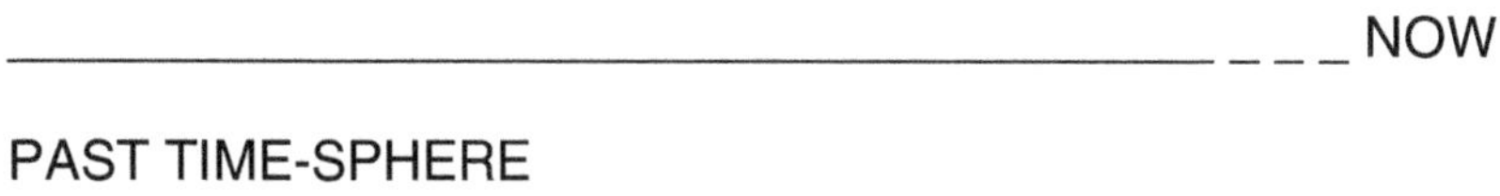

_ _ _ NOW

PAST TIME-SPHERE

Figure 4.3 Representation of the past time-sphere on the timeline.

Alternatively, situations located before now may be thought of as being connected with the present, in which case we use the label pre-present time-sphere, shown in Figure 4.4.

NOW

PRE-PRESENT TIME-SPHERE

Figure 4.4 Representation of the pre-present time-sphere on the timeline.

In both cases, the time referred to lies before the moment of speech. When the present perfect is used, however, a link with the present – one which is absent when the past tense is used – is expressed linguistically. The use of the past tense implies that the situation is perceived as being severed from the present. Just as a situation may be described in different ways (see Section 2.1), the speaker may also represent a situation that occurred or 'was the case' before now in different ways. Imagine a situation in which a speaker made a trip to China in 2017. To refer to the trip, she could say either of the following:

(60) I *went* to China in 2017.
I've *been* to China (before).

In both cases the speaker may be thinking of the same situation, but in the first case, she focuses on the year 2017, which is disconnected from the moment of speech. In the latter case, she locates the visit in a period of time that starts before now and leads up to now without specifying exactly when she visited China. The sentence will give rise to inferences such as 'The speaker knows about traveling in China, or can recommend hotels, or does not need any further advice about travel in China'. This is not to say that when the first sentence is uttered, these same inferences cannot be equally the case: *I went to China in 2017* can also imply that the speaker has some familiarity with the country, but the link between now and then is not an element of meaning overtly communicated by the past tense. In other words, it is not expressed linguistically. The present perfect in contrast explicitly tells the hearer that there is a link of some sort between now and before now. Put somewhat more technically, when the present perfect is used the moment of speech and the reference time (i.e. the point of view from which you look at the situation) coincide. When the past tense is used, the speaker first moves away from the present and views the past situation from a past reference time, a point of view within the past time-sphere. The representation in Figure 4.5 may help you to visualize this generalization.

For the analysis of any tense, it is useful to appeal to three time points: the **moment of speech (S)**, the **reference time (R)** and the **event time (E)**. The event time (E) is the time of the situation that is referred to in the clause. The reference time (R) is the vantage point from which we look at a situation. As we will see below, the claim that there are three time points inherent in the past perfect, for example, is uncontroversial: it is intuitively easy to understand that there is reference to a situation (E) that lies before a reference time (R) (in this case, a past moment) which itself lies before the moment of speech (S): E–R–S. At first sight, one might be inclined to think that only two points in time are referred to when the past tense or the present perfect is used: the speech time ('now', S) and the time of the situation (E), which lies before now. However, the inclusion of R in the analysis of the present perfect and the past tense is crucial. The inclusion of R in the analysis of these tenses makes explicit – in a different way – the idea that when the present perfect is used, a situation lies in the pre-present time-sphere, thus establishing a link between a situation before now and now: we will say that R coincides with S when the present perfect is used. When the past tense is used, R coincides with E: the vantage point

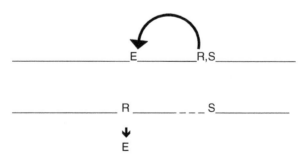

Figure 4.5 Representation of the present perfect and the past tense in terms of S, R and E.

from which the situation is conceptualized does not coincide with the moment of speech in this case. Rather, it lies in the past time-sphere. In other words, if we are to capture the meaning of the tenses, we also need three time points for tenses that, at a superficial level, may seem to involve only two time points.

It follows from these observations that a past situation referred to by a present perfect is not necessarily closer in time to the moment of speech than a past situation referred to by a past tense, as is shown in the following examples:

> (61) I've seen the Great Wall of China before. It was during my first visit twenty-five years ago.
> I saw him five minutes ago, so he must be around here somewhere.

These examples show that the present perfect does not on its own refer to a recent past. Such a generalization does not capture the basic difference between the past tense and the present perfect.

3.4.2 Different types of present perfect and the progressive

The temporal frame inherent in any use of the present perfect might be paraphrased as follows: 'in a period of time starting before now and leading up till now (the moment of speech), something happened (or was the case) or started happening (or started being the case)'. We include 'was/started being the case' as part of our paraphrase because States, which do not refer to something happening, are compatible with the present perfect. The link between 'before now' and 'now' is inherent in the very idea of pre-present time-sphere and may take different forms.[16]

3.4.2.1 The continuative present perfect

The present perfect can be used to refer to a situation that started before the moment of speech and still holds at the moment of speech. We will use the label **continuative present perfect** to refer to this kind of perfect subtype:

> (62) (a) We've been looking forward to this day for months.
> (b) We've looked forward to this day for months.

---

[16]Although we concentrate here on the present perfect, the generalizations concerning perfect types hold for all the perfect tenses. It will ultimately be clear how the perfect tenses, be they present, future or past, with non-progressive aspect or with progressive aspect, always have the same basic characteristics.

In (62) the situation type is an Activity, so progressive aspect is common (62a). Its effect will be that of focusing on the duration of the situation. Indeed, a continuative present perfect is often used in conjunction with a temporal Adjunct that refers explicitly to duration (a *for*-Adjunct or a *since*-Adjunct; see Section 3.4.3). Non-progressive aspect is possible as well (62b), but this results in a more matter-of-fact interpretation. The duration of the situation (which is nonetheless indicated by the temporal Adjunct), and hence the intensity of the feeling expressed, is de-emphasized. In (63), it is not possible to use progressive aspect to focus on duration since the situation is a State.

> (63) They*'ve known* each other since they were kids.
>   *They*'ve been knowing* each other since they were kids.

3.4.2.2 The indefinite present perfect

The present perfect can also refer to a situation located entirely before the moment of speech. The present perfect here is an **indefinite perfect**: the situation does not continue until the moment of speech. The link with the moment of speech has the following paraphrase: 'in a period starting before now and leading up to now, something happened or was the case'. In other words, the temporal frame the situation is located in establishes a link with 'now'.

The indefinite present perfect is compatible with different situation types:

Indefinite present perfect combined with an Activity
Consider the following example:

> (64) I*'ve studied* progressive aspect in English.

The speaker has chosen to use the present perfect because she wants to indicate explicitly that the pre-present situation is somehow relevant to the present. In this particular case, she may want to inform us that she now knows more about the subject than before.

When the progressive marker is added, the focus is more on the activity that the speaker has been engaged in before the moment of speech. This is not surprising given that the basic meaning of the progressive is ongoingness:

> (65) I*'ve been studying* progressive aspect in English.

One context with which the present perfect progressive is especially compatible is when the sentence informs the hearer of the Subject referent's recent activities. Very often, a present progressive sentence sounds like an answer to the question *What have you been doing recently?* In these contexts, we are more interested in the progression of the Activity that the Subject referent has been engaged in and less in the present results of that Activity.

There is a much clearer insistence on present time results when the present perfect with non-progressive aspect is used than when the present perfect progressive is used. Note however that when the result produced by the Activity is explicitly mentioned, there is a tendency to use the progressive marker, especially if the effect on the present follows from the fact that the situation was ongoing:

> (66) You look exhausted. – I am. I*'ve been working* in the garden all day.
> (being exhausted follows from working in the garden)

The present perfect non-progressive will sound much less natural in this context (see (67a)). The reason for this is that the result referred to (exhaustion) is linked up with the ongoing activity phase preceding the moment of speech. In contrast, the non-progressive perfect brings to the fore results associated with the end of the activity. In (67b), non-progressive aspect is more likely than progressive. This is precisely because the speaker is interested not in the ongoing phase of the activity but in the result of that activity:

> (67) (a) You look exhausted. – I am. ?I*'ve worked* in the garden all day.
> (b) I*'ve worked* enough for today. I'll finish up the weeding tomorrow.

When the indefinite present perfect combines with an Accomplishment rather than an Activity, the difference in effect between the present perfect progressive and the present perfect non-progressive is much more considerable.

Indefinite present perfect combined with an Accomplishment

The sentences below illustrate Accomplishments. Recall that one of the defining features of an Accomplishment is that there is an endpoint inherent in the situation. When an Accomplishment is used in the present perfect non-progressive tense, the sentence communicates that the endpoint inherent in the situation has been reached and that there is a result at the moment of speech:

> (68) (a) I*'ve painted* the kitchen walls yellow.
> (b) Their prices *have increased* by 15 per cent.
> (c) Their prices *have increased* recently.

The result communicated by each of these sentences is related to the endpoint inherent in the Accomplishment and can be paraphrased as follows:

(69) (a) The kitchen walls are yellow.
  (b) Their prices are currently 15 per cent higher than before.
  (c) Their prices are currently higher than before.

On top of the results inherent in the situation type (shown in (69a) to (69c)), other kinds of present effects may be communicated. In (70a) to (70c), we give some examples of the kinds of present effects that might accompany the present perfect sentences in (68a) to (68c):

(70) (a) We should pick out linoleum that matches.
    Let's use a different colour for the bedroom.
    etc.

  (b) and (c) We can spend less now than before.
       They are taking advantage of consumers.
       This must be a reflection of the current economic situation.
       etc.

An obvious question is whether we can add the progressive marker to the indefinite present perfect sentences in (68):

(71) I've *been painting* the kitchen walls yellow.
  (cf. I've *painted* the kitchen walls yellow. (68a))

In (71), the progressive highlights the situation in its progression. Recall that with progressive aspect, the beginning and end of the situation are out of focus. As a result, the basic message communicated by the speaker is that, in a period starting before now and leading up to now (perfect meaning), she has been engaged in painting the kitchen yellow (progressive meaning). The link that the present perfect establishes with the moment of speech may imply that she would like the hearer to draw some conclusion(s) about the effect of the situation on the present. The following are among the possible inferences:

(72) *Present time result follows directly from the Accomplishment*:
      Some (or parts) of the walls are yellow.
   Present time results not inherent in the Accomplishment:
      I'm tired.
      I'm covered in paint.
      I'm becoming an expert painter.

Let us take a look at the other two examples in (68). Compare (73a) and (73b) to (68b) and (68c), above:

(73) (a) *Their prices *have been increasing* by 15 per cent.
　　　(cf. Their prices *have increased* by 15 per cent.)
　　(b) Their prices *have been increasing* recently.
　　　(cf. Their prices *have increased* recently.)

We saw in Section 2.2.1 that numerical NPs are very often incompatible with the progressive because of the tension created between a marker that imposes a boundary (numerical NP) and one that defocalizes the boundary (the progressive). Example (73a) is another case in point: it is not possible to use the progressive unless it is used in a context in which there is a spiral series of increases by 15 per cent that continue to happen. For the progressive to be used here, the meaning would have to be 'Their prices have increased several times recently, and each time they have increased by exactly 15 per cent', a situation that is perhaps not impossible but is highly unlikely. Consequently, it is just as unlikely that one would try to represent such a situation linguistically.

The progressive in (73b) is straightforwardly understood to refer to a dynamic situation whereby prices have either repeatedly increased or started to increase at some point before now and have not stopped increasing. In other words, the progressive has its unmarked meaning and serves to highlight the duration of the situation. In this particular case, the notion of duration is brought about in the same way as in sentences with an Achievement, in which the use of the progressive may also result in a repetitive reading (see examples in (18)).

Indefinite present perfect combined with a State
The indefinite present perfect can combine with a State. In this case, we very often get an **experiential reading**, as in the following:

(74) He*'s owned* a restaurant before.
　　I*'ve been* to South America.

In examples like this, the idea is 'in a period starting before now and leading up to now, the Subject referent has experienced something *at least once*'. This experiential reading is also possible with other situation types:

(75) She*'s travelled* around South America (before). (indefinite perfect, Activity)
　　He*'s run* a 10K ((at least) once). (indefinite perfect, Accomplishment)
　　It's not the first time you*'ve broken* a plate. (indefinite perfect, Achievement)

We have put the Adjuncts *before* and *at least once* in brackets: although these Adjuncts are not necessary for the sentences to have an experiential reading, such sentences are often found with adverbs of this kind. The Adjuncts correspond to the adverb *ever* found in experiential interrogatives, such as the following:

(76) *Have* you ever *been* to Mount Rushmore?

We can also account for these commonly used adverbs in experiential perfects given that they can often serve to disambiguate a non-experiential reading from an experiential reading:

(77) He's (just) *had* a heart attack.
　　(= He's on his way to hospital – non-experiential)
　　He's *had* a heart attack (at least once) before.
　　(= He can tell you what the symptoms are – experiential)

Indefinite present perfect combined with an Achievement

It is possible to get an indefinite perfect reading in a sentence with an Achievement. If the non-progressive form is used, the meaning will be that the situation referred to happened just once:

(78) He's just *coughed*. That's the cue for us to get up and leave.
　　Last year's star player *has kicked* the ball – the season has officially begun.

Adding the progressive markers brings about a repetitive reading:

(79) He's *been coughing* a lot lately.
　　She's *been kicking* that ball around all morning.

Note that the progressive can only be used if the lexical content of the clause is compatible with a repetitive reading. This is not the case in an example like the following:

(80) He's *broken* his finger.

The result referred to that is inherent in the Achievement is 'His finger is broken.' The hearer may associate additional results with the sentence such as 'He is in a lot of pain', 'He can't participate in the swim meet' or 'That's why his handwriting is so bad.' The addition of the progressive results in an unacceptable sentence:

(81) *He's *been breaking* his finger.

It is unlikely that this sentence can be used in a meaningful way, since it implies that someone either has repeatedly tried to break a finger or has been in the process of breaking a finger, but that the process has not reached completion.

3.4.2.3 The repetitive present perfect

A third and final type of present perfect is called **repetitive**. It is in some ways a cross between a continuative and an indefinite present perfect.

The repetitive perfect shares with any present perfect sentence the idea of 'in a period of time starting before now and leading up to now, something happened (or was the case) or started to happen (or be the case)'. Here, though, the 'something' is a series of situations. On the one hand, the repetitive perfect shares with the indefinite perfect the fact that the final occurrence of the series lies completely before the moment of speech. On the other hand, the repetitive perfect shares with the continuative perfect the fact that the event may well be repeated after the final occurrence; from that point of view the situation might be seen as still continuing at the moment of speech.

The present perfect non-progressive may communicate repetition with any situation type provided it is clear from the context that there were several instantiations of the same situation:

> (82) I've had several headaches this past month. (State)
> That group has performed in Toronto several times. (Activity)
> Our dog has bitten the postman more than once. (Achievement)
> The trade unions have demanded higher salaries many times. (Accomplishment)

The progressive can also bring about this reading even in the absence of adverbials or determiners signalling repetition:

> (83) That group has been performing in Toronto.
> Our dog has been biting the postman.
> The trade unions have been demanding higher salaries.

In the examples in (83), it is the progressive that brings about the repetitive reading.

Given the incompatibility of numerical NPs and the progressive, it should be clear why the progressive is ungrammatical in the following sentences:

> (84) *That group has been performing twice in Toronto.
> *Our dog has been biting the postman three times.
> *The trade unions have been demanding higher salaries on several occasions.

The function of the numerical NPs is to put a boundary to the situation. These numerical NPs are thus incompatible with the progressive, whose function is (in this context) to leave the end of the (repetitive) situation out of focus.

3.4.3 Temporal adjuncts

Our characterization of the present perfect implies there will be constraints on possible combinations of this verb form with adverbial Adjuncts. These constraints follow quite naturally from the meaning of the present perfect as a tense which locates a situation in the pre-present time-sphere and not in the past time-sphere.

Adjuncts that refer to periods of time that are located in the past time-sphere are predictably incompatible with the present perfect. In such cases, the past tense is used:

> (85) *I*'ve seen* her <u>yesterday</u>.
>   (cf. I saw ...)
>   *Julia *has heard* from him <u>an hour ago</u>.
>   (cf. Julie heard ...)
>   *Their first book *has* first *been published* <u>in 2012</u>.
>   (cf. Their first book was published ...)
>   *I*'ve spoken* to her about the exams <u>last week</u>.
>   (cf. I spoke ...)
>   *I*'ve hated* spinach <u>when I was a kid</u>.
>   (cf. I hated ...)

Adjuncts that refer to periods of time that are connected with the present predictably combine with a present perfect:

> (86) I*'ve been reading* for <u>two hours now</u>.
>   I*'ve been sleeping* badly <u>lately/recently</u>.
>   She's *just* *left*. You can still catch her.
>   They*'ve worked* together <u>since 1990</u>.

Some Adjuncts are compatible with both a past tense and a present perfect tense. The choice of tense will ultimately depend on the (shade of) meaning the speaker wants to communicate. The present perfect (the perfect tenses in general, in fact) very often combines with *already, before, just* (when *just* means 'very recently'), *not ... yet* (and *yet* with an interrogative clause), *since, lately, ever* and *never* provided these adverbs express the idea of 'period up to now':[17]

---

[17]It is common in North American English to combine a past tense with adverbs such as *just, already, ever, never* and *(not) yet*. The present perfect is always possible as well.

(87) I've already *read* this book.
   The committee *has* not yet *decided* if the proposal will be approved.
   Have you (ever) *heard* such a ridiculous story (before)?
   I *have* never *been* so insulted in my entire life.

The following sentences show that some of these adverbials do not always convey this meaning:

(88) (a) I *have* never *spoken* to a professor. (= I'm still a student.)
         I never *spoke* directly to a professor. (= I'm not a student any more.)

   (b) *Have* you ever *beaten* him at chess? (= You still play chess from time to time.)
         Did you ever *beat* him at chess? (= You don't play chess with him any more.)

   (c) My great-aunt *has* never *left* her hometown. (= She's still alive.)
         My great-aunt never *left* her hometown. (= She's no longer alive.)

Similarly, adverbs like *today, this morning (afternoon/week/month/year)* and *recently* are found with both the past tense and the present perfect. If the time of the Adjunct is or is considered to be in the past time-sphere, the speaker will tend to choose the past tense. If on the other hand the time of the Adjunct is or is considered to be in the pre-present time-sphere, the speaker will most likely choose the present perfect:

(89) (a) *Did* you *see* John this morning? (moment of speech = 3 pm)
   (b) *Have* you *seen* John this morning? (moment of speech = 9 am)

(90) (a) *Did* you *work* hard this week?
   (b) *Have* you *worked* hard this week?

(91) (a) I've *seen* him recently.
   (b) I *saw* him recently.

In the first case, the choice of tense is determined by the time of day at which the sentence is uttered: the utterance in (89a) takes place in the afternoon, so any question about events in the morning will be located in the past time-sphere. In (89b), however, the speaker locates her question about the past in the pre-present time-sphere since, when she asks it, it is still 'this morning'. In (90a) and (90b), the speaker can impose her own subjective view of the week a bit more freely: whether the week is considered close enough to its end to be located completely in the past time-sphere (90a) or considered to be pre-present (90b) is more a matter of a given speaker's point of view at the end of the week. On a Friday afternoon when the speaker doesn't think she's going to do much work before the weekend, she might be more likely to say *I worked hard this week*: it is as though her eagerness for the week to be over is so strong that she considers it to be over before it actually is. The opposite is equally possible. A diligent worker may well consider the workweek not to be over until Saturday morning. Likewise, in the examples in (91), the temporal Adjunct *recently* is interpreted differently: in (91a) the speaker has no specific past moment in mind, whereas in (91b) the speaker has in mind the specific past moment when the meeting took place.

No discussion of the present perfect is complete without an account of *since* adverbials and *for* adverbials. When combined with a present perfect, both explicitly establish reference to a period of time 'starting in the past and leading up to now'. However, whereas a PrepP or a past tense subclause with *since* defines the pre-present period by referring to the point of departure in a stretch of time, the PrepP with *for* does so by indicating the entire duration:

(92) Thomas *has been* away <u>since two o'clock</u>.
Thomas *has been* happy <u>since he left his job</u>.
Thomas *has been* away <u>for three hours</u>.

The present perfect is always used in the clause that contains the *since*-Adjunct, regardless of whether the Adjunct has the form of a PrepP (e.g. *since two o'clock*) or a subclause (e.g. *since he left his job*). *For*-Adjuncts are always PrepPs (e.g. *for three hours*).

If the *since*-Adjunct is a clause and if the *since*-clause refers to the beginning of a period, the past tense will be used in the *since*-clause (93). If the *since* Adjunct is a clause and if the *since*-clause refers to the whole period ('starting before now and leading up to now (and still the case now)'), the present perfect will be used in the *since*-clause (94):

(93) I've *been working* freelance <u>since I graduated from university</u>.
I've only *spoken* to him once <u>since he accepted the job offer</u>.

(94) I've *been working* freelance <u>since I've lived in France</u>.
I've *spoken* to him only once since <u>he's been living with his girlfriend</u>.

Note that, unlike a *since* adverbial, a *for* adverbial can be used with a past tense if the period of time referred to lies in the past time-sphere:

(95) Thomas *was* away <u>for three hours</u>.

Finally, the present tense can be used instead of the present perfect in clauses of the type *it has been* + period of time + *since*. It seems that (96a) can be used by all speakers of English, whereas (96b) is much less common in North American English and with younger speakers in general:

    (96) (a) It *has been* three years <u>since we last saw each other</u>.
           (b) It's three years <u>since we last saw each other</u>.

3.4.4 Summary of the present perfect

The visual representation in Figure 4.6 of the three different types of present perfect will help to bring out even more clearly what unites and what separates the three types.

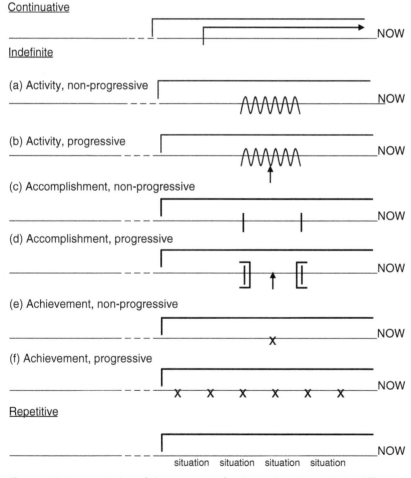

Figure 4.6 Representation of the present perfect in combination with the different situation types.

We have paid considerable attention to the perfect for the following reason: once you have understood the meanings of the present perfect, there is little to be added when dealing with the other perfect tenses. The only difference is that the time from which one looks back (i.e. what we call the reference time (R)) is located in a different time-sphere. As pointed out on Section 3.1, the temporal meaning conveyed by *have* is that it refers to an anterior situation. The point from which we look back is (i) the moment of speech (present perfect), (ii) a moment in the past (past perfect), (iii) a moment in the future (future perfect) or (iv) a moment posterior to a past moment in time (past future, as in *He said he would have finished the assignment before the deadline*).

The approach we have taken should give you a better insight into the difference between the past tense and the present perfect and help you to understand why the following (fairly commonly found) rules are not entirely accurate:

- the present perfect is used to refer to a recent past
- the present perfect is used when the speaker wants to communicate a present result

You should now also have a clearer view on the delicate interaction between the situation type, the kind of perfect and the result communicated.

3.5 The past perfect tense

3.5.1 Meaning

The past perfect has the same uses as the present perfect, the crucial difference being that rather than looking back to a situation from a present point of view (E–R,S), the speaker looks back from a past point of view (E–R–S). Visualized on the timeline, the temporal constellation communicated by the past perfect is shown in Figure 4.7.

Figure 4.7 Representation of the past perfect in terms of S, R and E.

Put differently, the past perfect communicates anteriority in the past time-sphere: there is reference to a situation that happened before a past moment in time.

The reference time (R) may be given contextually, as in (97), or it may be mentioned in the sentence or a preceding sentence, as in (98):

(97) Jane got that job she interviewed for. – I'*d been wondering* about that. Good
for her.

(98) (a) By the time I arrived, everyone else *had* already *left*.
(b) It wasn't till I got to my office that I realized I'*d left* my lunch at home.
(c) I ran into John. He'*d* just *been* to the dentist and could hardly talk.

In (97), the moment at which the second speaker thought about Jane is anterior to a moment that is not specified, yet it is clear from the context that
it lies in the past time-sphere. In (98), the situations referred to by the past
perfect lie before the moment the speaker arrived (98a), before the moment
the speaker realized something (98b) and before the moment the speaker ran
into John (98c).

3.5.2 Different types of past perfect and the progressive

The past perfect can be indefinite, continuative or repetitive. The visual
representations of the different kinds of present perfect also apply to the
past perfect. The only difference is that rather than taking the moment of
speech as a reference point, the point of reference is in the past time-sphere.
The constraints on the combination of the progressive and the past perfect
are also the same as those on the combination of the progressive and the
present perfect. The examples in (99) to (101) below will seem familiar: by
comparing them to the examples in Section 3.4.2 above and studying them
together, you will get a clear idea of how 'perfect-ness' is exactly the same
– it is only the time-sphere (and, hence, the 'point up until which') that
changes.

3.5.2.1 The continuative past perfect

The paraphrase associated with the continuative past perfect is as follows:
'a situation started happening, or started being the case, in a period of time
starting before a past moment in time and leading up to that past moment
in time'. This explicit paraphrase, though wordy, corresponds to an intuitive
understanding of the meaning of the past perfect:

(99) (a) We *had been looking* forward to that day for months (and so we were excited
when that day finally came). (cf. 62a)
(b) They had known each other since they were kids (and this explains why their
collaboration was successful). (cf. 63)

3.5.2.2 The indefinite past perfect

In the following examples, we have transposed the present perfect examples listed in 3.4.2 to the past time-sphere. There is reference to a situation that is finished before a reference point in the past:

(100) I *had studied/had been studying* progressive aspect in English, and so I passed the grammar exam easily. (Activity) (cf. (64), (65))

I'd *painted/had been painting* the kitchen walls yellow. (Accomplishment) (cf. (68a) and (71))
Their prices *had increased/*had been increasing* by 15 per cent. (Accomplishment) (cf. (68b) and (73a))
Their prices *had increased/had been increasing recently*. (Accomplishment) (cf. (68c) and (73b))

He had *owned* a restaurant before, so he knew how to start a business. (State) (cf. (74))
I *had been* to South America, so I could already speak a little Spanish. (State) (cf. (74))

He *had* just *coughed*. That was the cue for us to get up and leave. (Achievement) (cf. (78))
He'*d been coughing* a lot lately, so I told him to see a doctor. (Achievement) (cf. 79)

3.5.2.3 The repetitive past perfect

In examples with a repetitive past perfect, there is reference to a sequence of situations, each of which lies before the reference point in the past:

(101) The trade unions *had demanded* higher salaries many times. (cf. (82))
The trade unions *had been demanding* higher salaries. (cf. (83))
*The trade unions *had been demanding* higher salaries on several occasions. (cf. (84))

The final example is ungrammatical because of the incompatibility between the progressive marker, which leaves the end of the situation out of focus, and the numerical NP *on several occasions*, which puts an explicit boundary to the situation.

3.5.3 Tense simplification

When a situation inherently communicates an unambiguous temporal relation of anteriority, it is not necessary to use the past perfect to render explicit that relation. This phenomenon is sometimes called **tense simplification**:

(102) (a) <u>After</u> we *finished/had finished* the meeting, we all went out for a drink.
  (b) I wrote back to her <u>as soon as</u> I *received/had received* her letter.
  (c) She was reading the book she *was given/had been given* for her birthday.

The conjunctions *after* (102a) and *as soon as* (102b) impose a temporal order in the sense that their meaning implies that the situation in the time clause happens before that in the main clause. In (102c), it is our knowledge of the world that imposes a temporal order: it is only possible to read a book after one is in possession of the book. From that perspective, 'giving a book' necessarily precedes 'reading a book'. In cases like these, there is no need for a verb form that confirms the temporal order (relation of anteriority) between the situations, although the past perfect remains possible. In other words, the speaker can choose to use the past rather than the past perfect when she does not feel it is necessary to express the relationship of anteriority twice: since the sentence implies a temporal order, confirmation of that order through a tense is not necessary. However, when the lexical semantics of the sentence or our world knowledge does not naturally imply a temporal order, it is generally not possible to use the past rather than the past perfect without changing the meaning:

(103) (a) She told us that the police *had been* there.
  (b) She told us that the police *were* there.

(104) (a) When I got there, she and her husband *had been arguing*.
  (b) When I got there, she and her husband *were arguing*.

In the (a) examples in (103) and (104), the situation referred to by the italicized form is anterior to the other situation. In the (b) sentences, the situations are simultaneous.

3.6 Future time reference

There are a number of forms that can be used in English to establish future time reference. These forms locate the situation in what we have called the post-present time-sphere, the stretch of time that lies after now. We choose to refer to a post-present rather than a future time-sphere to highlight that, like the pre-present, there is often a link with the present moment of speech and the situation located after (or posterior to) it. Indeed, we have already observed that the present tense (both non-progressive and progressive) can be used to establish future time reference. In this section, we will also discuss some additional ways to situate events in the post-present time-sphere: (i) the future tense (*will* + verb base), (ii) *be going to* and (iii) *be to*. The final form discussed in this section, the future perfect, is somewhat different: its structure includes reference to the future (through the use of *will*), but it also communicates, through the inclusion of *have*, a relationship of anteriority. This combination results in a meaning that cannot be captured as straightforwardly as 'reference to a post-present situation.'

3.6.1 Future tense (will + verb base)

The future tense is formed by combining the tense marker *will* (or, optionally, *shall* in the first person)[18] with the verb base: *He will be here tomorrow.*

It should be obvious that future situations are by their nature very different from present situations or past situations. Any situation that is located in the future has not yet occurred. Another way of saying this is that the situation has not yet **actualized**. Seen from this perspective, we are in fact making a prediction whenever we refer to the future. There does not seem to be a definitive answer to the question of whether the use of *will* primarily implies that the speaker is predicting or whether it means that she is simply locating a situation in the future (see footnote 1, Chapter 5).

When the speaker uses the future tense, she communicates an assumption that something will happen. The speaker does not represent the future situation as depending on the volition or intention of the Subject referent of the sentence:

(105) You*'ll understand* why I reacted that way once you've calmed down.
Put this jumper on under your coat. You*'ll be* warmer.
Dora *will be* almost 50 by the time she finishes writing that book.
Do young girls really wonder who they *will end up* marrying someday?
His new job *will require* him to travel more than he's used to.

The future tense (*will* + verb base) is not ordinarily used to talk about arrangements or intentions, which are typically more connected with the Subject referent:

(106) Any plans for the weekend? – ?Yes, I *will have* dinner with friends.
Sorry, I can't accept your invitation: ?I*'ll spend* Christmas with my girlfriend.[19]

---

[18]*Shall* can be used with a first-person Subject. It is a formal alternative for *will* and is only rarely used. We will discuss *shall* in the chapter that deals with modality. Note that both *shall* and *will* are often abbreviated to *'ll*.

[19]Note that this sentence is only strange in a context where the second speaker is supposed to be talking about previously arranged personal plans. If during the exchange he spontaneously makes the decision to spend Christmas with his girlfriend, the sentence *I'll spend Christmas with my girlfriend* is perfectly fine.

Will often conveys meaning which has more to do with various shades of volition (most often willingness of lack of willingness) than with actual future time. Furthermore, *will* can convey the likelihood that something is the case. These kinds of meaning are called **modal** and are discussed in greater detail in Chapter 5. In the meantime, here are a few uses where the modal meaning of *will* can be contrasted with what is more straightforwardly future (see (105) above):

(107) The doctor *will see* you now. (willingness)
She *won't eat* uncooked vegetables. (refusal, absence of willingness)
I don't care what you say, I *will tell* him what I think. ((obstinate) insistence)
Who's that at the door? – That *'ll be* Lee. He always stops by after work. (probability)
Some salesmen *will resort* to anything just to make a sale. (typical behaviour)

Volitional-modal *will* and the future use can be hard to tease apart. For instance, a question such as *Will he help us?* is ambiguous. It can request information about the future, but it can also ask whether he is willing to or agrees to help us at the moment of speech. In fact, it is not inconceivable that the question can have both future and volitional-modal meaning at the same time.

Since *will* + verb base can in some contexts be misinterpreted as expressing willingness (when the sentence is affirmative) or refusal (when the sentence is negative) rather than straightforward future time, the future progressive is a common alternative that ensures that nothing more than a prediction about the future is being made. In examples of this type, there is sometimes reference to the preparatory phase or activity that is prior to the expected event:

(108) Within the next few days, you*'ll be receiving* our newsletter.
Our guests *will be arriving* sometime this afternoon.
Jill *will be working* next Saturday, so she *won't be joining* us for lunch.
Will you *be using* the computer today?
I *won't be going* to the party after all. I've got too much to do.

The future progressive in the sentences in (108) does not necessarily communicate the unmarked meaning of the progressive, that is, to inform the hearer that at a future moment in time a particular situation will be ongoing. Rather, the speaker makes a prediction without a foregrounded plan or an intention. She informs the hearer that what will happen is the expected pattern of events, the normal routine. In some cases, the preparation of the future situation is hinted at. For example, we can predict you will be receiving our newsletter because we are working on it now. The following non-progressive versions of the sentences in (108) show how the most natural interpretation of *will* is often connected to willingness (or absence of willingness) rather than future time reference:

(109) Just send in this form, and you'll *receive* our newsletter. (promise)
Don't worry, our guests *will arrive* sometime this afternoon. (promise)
Jill *will work* next Saturday, so you needn't worry about finding someone else.
(willingness)
Will you (please) *use* the computer next time instead of writing everything out
by hand? (willingness)
Sorry, but I *won't go* to that party: I'm not interested in wasting my time. (refusal)

This does not mean that the future progressive cannot have its unmarked meaning of ongoingness:

(110) If you come at 3, the baby *will be* sleeping. Can you come a little later?
This time next week, I'll *be lounging* on some beach in Barbados!

A peculiarity of the English tense system is that it is not possible to use a form of *will* (or *would*, as we will see below) in a time clause or in an *if*-clause when it has future time reference. In time clauses and *if*-clauses, we use the present tense, the present perfect or the past perfect. Many other languages allow the use of the future tense in these contexts:

(111) I'll tell you the whole story <u>when</u> you *get* here. (*will get)
<u>After</u> he *leaves*, we'll tell you what really happened at the meeting! (*will leave)
Tell me what you want for dinner <u>before</u> I *go* to the supermarket. (*will go)
<u>Once</u> you*('ve) finished* your homework, you can play with your friends. (*will
(have) finish(ed))
<u>If</u> it *rains*, we'll have to cancel tomorrow's school picnic. (*will rain)
Please call us <u>as soon as</u> you *arrive*. (*will arrive).

He told us to phone <u>as soon as</u> we *(had) arrived*. (*would (have) arrive(d))
I always thought I'd be a doctor <u>when</u> I *grew up*. (*would grow up)

3.6.2 The present non-progressive

We have already seen that the non-progressive form of the present can be used to establish future time reference provided the future situation is understood as unalterable (see Section 3.2.3). As the examples given show, a timetable future can refer to a variety of contexts not limited to actual timetables:

(112) Our train *leaves* at 7.15 sharp – don't be late.
The first-years *sit* their exams the week of the 6th.
The metro *stops* running in just under an hour – we'd better hurry.
The curtain *goes up* at 7 pm, so we should be in our seats before then.

It is important to understand what we mean by unalterable: trains can be late, and performances can be cancelled. Here, it is the speaker who holds the situation to be unalterable. As pointed out in Section 3.2, the idea that comes to the fore in examples of this type is that the situation has been scheduled and because of that is considered not to be subject to change. Compare this use of the non-progressive with the use in examples such as those in (113) and (114), which are unalterable in the strictest sense of the word. In (113), the situation has future-time reference, whereas in (114) the situations are omnitemporal – they are always valid:

(113) The first day of Ramadan *falls* on 11 August next year.

(114) The sun *rises* in the east and *sets* in the west.
Water *contains* hydrogen and oxygen.
Blue mixed with yellow *makes* green.

3.6.3 The present progressive

We have also seen that when the present progressive is used, the future situation is most often represented as resulting from a present plan or arrangement (see Section 3.2.3). Unlike in the case of the non-progressive present, the present progressive generally implies that the Subject referent can exercise control over the situation:

(115) We*'re having* friends over for dinner on Saturday night.
Richard and I *are meeting* in front of the cinema at 9.
His band at school *is organizing* a raffle next week to raise money for new uniforms.

The difference in meaning between the progressive and non-progressive can be seen in the following pair of examples:

(116) (a) Jennifer *is staying* home tomorrow night. She's too tired to go out.
(b) Sorry, but Jennifer *stays* home tomorrow night. She's being punished.

In (116a) it is Jennifer's own personal plan to stay home, whereas in (116b) we are more likely to understand that an outside authority (e.g. her mother) has imposed it. Accordingly, in the latter case the situation is presented as being unalterable and not open to negotiation.

In contexts where the Subject referent clearly has no control over the situation, *be going to* or the future tense is generally used:

(117) The stock market *is going to take/will take* (*is taking) a turn for the worse next quarter.
According to the forecast, it*'s going to snow/will snow* (*is snowing) tomorrow.

Finally, progressive aspect with a present tense is sometimes used to announce a spontaneous decision to do something. This is different from the context of a pre-arranged personal plan as exemplified in (115) above:

(118) Goodnight, everyone. I*'m going* to bed.

In (118), the speaker is not referring to a pre-arranged personal plan. The decision to retire corresponds exactly to the utterance announcing the decision. This is similar to, but not exactly the same as, the use of *will* in what is also often called a spontaneous decision:

(119) (telephone ringing) I*'ll get* it!
Sorry, the director isn't in his office. – All right, I*'ll stop by* later.

In (119), the decision to answer to phone or to stop by later is also conceived and announced simultaneously. The difference lies in the fact that here, something in the immediately preceding discourse triggers the decision (e.g. hearing the phone ring or learning that the director is unavailable): these decisions could not have been made a moment before. In (118), on the other hand, nothing external to the speaker's own intentions conditions her announced decision to go to bed.

3.6.4 Be going to + *verb base*

When combined with *be* to refer to future time, *going to* is very commonly reduced to *gonna* in spoken English. It is not considered standard to use the form in careful written English, however.

There are two contexts in which *be going to* is used. In the first case, *be going to* + verb base makes it clear that the future situation may be the result of a present intention:

(120) One of these days, I*'m going to learn* Russian.
How *are* you *going to explain* the situation to her?

The Subject referent has the present intention of doing something in the future: the first sentence implies that the Subject referent intends to learn Russian, even if there is no present arrangement to do so; the second example inquires into the hearer's current plan of action.

We have already seen that the present progressive can also refer to a future plan, which raises the question of the difference in communicative effect between the present progressive and *be going to*. Generally speaking, *be going to* is preferred when, at the moment of speech, there is not yet any definite personal plan to actually carry out the intention. If arrangements have already been made, speakers will often prefer the present progressive. That said, the difference between an intention and a personal plan is in many cases obscured, rendering both possible in a given context:

(121) (a) Thomas *is going to do* a Dutch course
      (b) Thomas *is doing* a Dutch course.

The temporal Adjuncts we could add to each of these sentences will be different, however. In (121a) we might say *someday* or *one of these days*, whereas in (121b) we are much more likely to give precise information such as *in November* or *next summer*, which implies that he has already registered for the course – it is a definite plan. Note additionally that the second example could refer to a present ongoing situation, and take an Adjunct such as *this week*.

The second typical context of use of *be going to* + verb base is one in which a future prediction is made on the basis of present evidence. In the most striking case, the present evidence is immediately perceivable. The examples in (122) illustrate this use:

(122) (thunder, lightning) Let's get inside, I think it*'s going to rain*.
      Careful, you*'re going to spill* that all over the place.
      Look, she*'s going to jump*! Quick, someone stop her!

Sometimes, the prediction is based not so much on what is immediately perceivable but on present knowledge or on the speaker's expectation, as in the following examples:

(123) I'm convinced that this decision *is going to have* long-term ramifications.
      I've heard he's found a better-paying job. I wonder if he*'s going to quit*.

Be going to + verb base is preferred to *will* + verb base when the speaker inquires into future actions of the hearer, especially in contexts in which *will* + verb base is more likely to be interpreted as expressing willingness (an invitation or a request). We have already seen another case in which a different form is preferable to *will* + verb base, when *will* seems to convey, first and foremost, volitional meaning. Compare the sentences in (124):

(124) (a) *Will* you *work* on the project over the weekend?
      (b) *Will* you *be working* on the project over the weekend?
      (c) *Are* you *going to work* on the project over the weekend?
      (d) *Are* you *going to be working* on the project over the weekend?

Although the question in (124a) could be understood as inquiring about the hearer's future plans, this is not the first interpretation we would intuitively assign to the utterance. The question asks the hearer whether he is willing to work on the project. If the speaker is the hearer's boss, (124a) could even be understood as a polite way of expressing an expectation ('I expect you to work on the project over the weekend.')

The three alternatives allow the speaker to avoid this volitional interpretation and to insist on future meaning: in (124b), the progressive is used; in (124c), *going to* + verb base is used; and in (124d), we find a combination of both forms. The nuances expressed in (124b), (124c) and (124d) are more or less subtle, depending on the speaker, but all three of them clearly have future meaning, in contrast to (124a), where the volitional interpretation almost invariably wins out over future meaning. The differences in shades of meaning might be captured as follows: in (124b) the speaker focuses on the future activity to be performed; in (124c) the focus is on the hearer's present intentions while in (124d) the speaker focuses simultaneously on the hearer's present intentions as well as on the activity to be performed.

The above observations have no doubt made it clear that *be going to* is in a way the mirror image of the present perfect in the sense that there is a clear link between the present and a future moment in time: with the present perfect, the speaker is looking at the past from a present point of view and with *be going to*, the speaker is looking at the future from a present point of view.

3.6.5 Be to + *verb base*

Like the present progressive, *be to* + verb base refers to a future that is the result of a plan. Unlike in the case of the progressive, which is generally associated with a personal plan, *be to* normally refers to an official plan or a schedule imposed by an external authority:

> (125) The new criteria *are to be applied* starting in January of next year.
> The CEO *is to address* the board at next week's annual meeting.

Apart from locating a situation in the future, *be to* + verb base can also express necessity.[20] Even more so than *will*, *be to* combines a temporal meaning with a modal meaning.

---

[20]Note that *be to* can also express possibility when it combines with a passive infinitive (i.e. *be* + past participle): *More information is to be found on our webpage* (= finding more information is possible).

3.6.6 The future perfect tense (will + have + past participle)[21]

The future perfect is formed by the marker *will* followed by *have* in the infinitive form followed finally by the past participle (i.e. a lexical verb, marked by -EN). Theoretically, this tense can locate a situation in any of the time-spheres. This is shown in Figure 4.8.

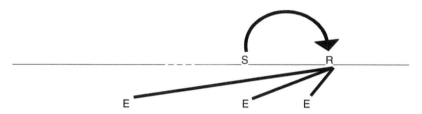

Figure 4.8 Representation of the future perfect in terms of S, R and E.

The main feature of the future perfect is that it refers to a situation that is anterior to some moment (or reference time (R)) in the post-present. In most cases, the situation is located in the post-present as well:

(126) Sarah *will have eaten* when she gets home later tonight.

In (126), 'later tonight' is a post-present reference time before which Sarah's eating – also located in the post-present – will take place. Although less common, the scenario in (127) – where Sarah's eating takes place before the moment of speech – is possible as well:

(127) There's nothing to eat, but Sarah *will have eaten* by now, so it's not a problem.

In this case, the temporal meaning is overlaid with some **epistemic** modal meaning: although the speaker has no factual evidence of Sarah's having eaten, she has every reason to believe the situation has actualized. We have already seen in our discussion of the future tense that, with *will*, modality and purely temporal relations can operate at the same time. We discuss this further in Section 4.1 of Chapter 5.

It is a comparatively rare scenario, but the future perfect can locate a situation in the present time-sphere:

---

[21]The label **perfect infinitive** is often used to refer to *have* + past participle when it combines with *will* or with other modals: *She may have done it, He might have forgotten* etc.

> (128) You *will have been* aware that Mrs Mayer has not been teaching your children since half-term. Unfortunately Mrs Mayer is quite unwell and at the present time is not expected to be back in school before the end of term. (www)

The most straightforward way of interpreting the location of the situation *be aware* in (128) is to consider that the parents' awareness coincides with the moment of speech (so, the present time-sphere) rather than before it or after it. A reasonable paraphrase might be 'you are (probably) aware now of Mrs Mayer's absence'.

It makes sense that the future perfect can refer to situations located in three different time-spheres: the only function of *have* is to indicate that there is reference to a situation that is anterior to the future reference point established by *will*. There is no specific time-sphere associated with a temporal relation of anteriority as such if the point in time from which one looks back lies in the future. This is obviously not the case when looking back from a present point of view to an anterior situation (present perfect), or from past reference time to an anterior situation (past perfect).

Predictably, we can distinguish three types of future perfect: a continuative future perfect (129a), an indefinite future perfect (129b) and a repetitive future perfect (129c). In each of these examples, both the reference time and the situation are located in the post-present:

> (129) (a) Soon they *will have been living* in Hungary for ten years.
> (b) By next month, the decision *will have been made* official.
> (c) We *will have seen* each other several times before the end of the year.

The same constraints that we have seen before hold concerning the use of the progressive, although it must be said the future perfect progressive forms are far less commonly used than, for instance, present perfect or past perfect progressive forms:

> (130) Next year, I'*ll have been divorced* for as long as I was married. (*will have been being)
> She *will have smoked* twenty cigarettes before the end of the evening. (*will have been smoking)

We will now turn to the two final tenses that we recognize in our system: the past future tense and the past future perfect tense.

3.7 Seeing the future from the past

The past future tense and the past future perfect tense share two temporal features: they are marked for past tense (-ED), and they also imply reference to a posterior situation (*will*). These two elements of meaning are linguistically expressed through the use of *would*, which is nothing more than *will* + -ED. *Would* + verb base is called the **past future** because there is reference to a situation that is posterior to a past moment in time. In other words, it expresses future in the past. The past future perfect is the past counterpart of the future perfect. As in the case of the future perfect, there are two temporal relations involved: one of posteriority (through the use of *would*) and one of anteriority (through the use of *have*). Unlike in the case of the future perfect, rather than looking forward from a present point of view (*will*), the starting-point of the temporal relation of posteriority is a point in the past time-sphere, hence the use of *would*. We will see that these two tenses are typically found in subclauses to express this kind of temporal information.

3.7.1 The past future tense (would + verb base)[22]

Would (*will* + -ED) + verb base is similar to the future tense in that it refers to a situation that is posterior to the reference time. In this case the reference time is located in the past time-sphere rather than coinciding with the moment of speech:

(131) **He said** he *would be sleeping* and told us not to disturb him.

The following are different contexts in which the sentence in (131) could be uttered. They show that the situation referred to by the past future tense can in principle be located in the past time-sphere (132a), the present time-sphere (132b) or the post-present time-sphere (132c):

(132) (a) Why on earth did you wake him up?
(The situation of (him) sleeping (like the situation captured by 'he said') is located in the past time-sphere, so before the moment of speech.)

(b) ... so, please keep your voice down.
(The situation of him sleeping is located in the present time-sphere: he is still sleeping at the moment of speech.)

(c) ... so please don't call between 5 and 8 tonight.
(The situation of him sleeping is located in the post-present time-sphere, after the moment of speech.)

---

[22] *Would* + verb base is often called the *conditional tense*. This creates a potential terminological confusion in that the term *conditional* refers to sentences of the type *I would talk to him if I were you*, where *would* + verb base does not refer to a future seen from the past. Conditional contexts will be dealt with in Chapter 5. To tease apart temporal relations from conditional contexts, we prefer to call *would* + verb base the *past future tense*.

The past future tense is visualized in Figure 4.9:

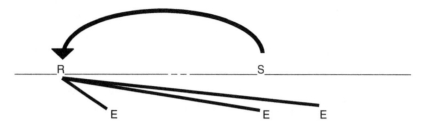

Figure 4.9 Representation of the past future tense in terms of S, R and E.

As in the case of the future perfect, it is the context of the utterance ((132a) to (132c)) rather than the past future tense itself that signals to the speaker in which time-sphere the situation is located. In other words, *would* + verb base signals that a situation (E) is posterior to a past moment in time (R) but as such does not give information about the time-sphere in which E is located. In many cases, the exact temporal location of the situation is vague. In (131), the verb of saying *said* is necessarily located in the past time-sphere, but the situation {*he – sleep*} can be located in the past (132a), the present (132b) and the post-present (132c) time-spheres.

The past future tense is found mainly in subclauses: the subclause in (131) above is underlined; the main clause begins with **He said** ..., in boldface. It is also found in contexts in which a specific type of narrative technique, called **free indirect speech**, is used.

> (133) The visitors were given strict instructions: before entering the old man's quar-
> ters, they were to lower their voices. The man *would be sleeping* and *would
> not want* to be awoken.

In this case, the narrator steps back and looks at situations from the perspective of one of the participants in the narrative. This translates into a very specific form with somewhat amalgamated features: from a formal point of view, it is a main clause (hence the use of the term *free*) but the tenses are typically those that would be used in a subclause embedded in a main clause such as *(s)he said* or *(s)he thought*. In other words, in free indirect speech the perspective changes from that of the narrator to that of someone who is part of the narrative being told: this is shown with the past future tense in (133) – the details about the man sleeping and not wanting to be awoken come not from the narrator but from whoever gave the visitors the instructions.

Would + verb base can also refer to a future (in the past) presented as determined by fate, as in (134):

> (134) Years later, this relatively unknown scientist *would win* the Nobel Prize.

The speaker presents a past fact as a prediction. She knows perfectly well that the scientist won the Nobel Prize, but rather than present that as a fact (*Years later, the scientist won the Nobel Prize*), she turns it into an actualized prediction. This kind of sentence is often used in written narratives of the biographical or encyclopedic type. The speaker can effectively create dramatic tension by making a prediction while at the same time confirming with authority that the prediction came true: this rhetorical technique prompts us to ask a question ('Did he win that Nobel Prize as you predicted?') while at the same time providing the answer to the question ('He won the prize').

In addition to its purely temporal meaning, *would* + verb base can also communicate all the modal meanings associated with *will* (see (108) above):

> (135) I was told that the doctor *would see* me immediately. (willingness)
> As a child, she *wouldn't eat* uncooked vegetables. (refusal, absence of willingness)
> I made it clear that I *would tell* him what I thought regardless. ((obstinate) insistence)
> Someone knocked. He knew it *would be* Lee. He always stopped by after work. (probability)
> I should have known he *would resort* to anything to make a sale. (typical behaviour)

Would + verb base is also commonly used in hypothetical contexts (see footnote 22). It is used in the main clause representing a situation which is contingent on another situation, found in an *if*-clause:

> (136) It *would make* the authors very happy if the book *received* favourable reviews.
> If you *hired* an assistant, it *would save* a lot of time.

3.7.2 The past future perfect tense

The past future perfect tense makes use of the three main tense markers we have seen. It is formed with *will*, to which is added the past-time marker -ED (= *would*). This is followed by the perfect marker *have* (here, in its infinitive form) followed finally by the lexical verb, which is marked by -EN. The (non-progressive) past future perfect of the situation {*we – finish by then*} is *we would have finished by then*.

The past future perfect is the past counterpart of the future perfect (*we will have finished*). In both cases, *have* (in conjunction with a past participle, that is, lexical verb + -EN) expresses a relation of anteriority. This, as we have shown, is the case for any perfect tense. In the case of the future perfect (*will have finished*), the situation is anterior to the time referred to by *will*; in the case of the past future perfect (*would have finished*), the situation is anterior to the time referred to by *would*. And while *will* in the future perfect expresses posteriority with respect to the moment of speech, the relation of posteriority communicated by *would* in the past future perfect starts from a point in the past time-sphere. In contrast to the future perfect, however, which can occur freely in a main clause, the past future perfect is typically used in a subclause. In this section, we highlight examples of the past future perfect by underlining the subclauses that contain a past future perfect. Contrast (137) and (138), below:

> (137) I *will have heard* from the interview committee by the end of the week.
> (The future perfect is used in a main clause.)

> (138) **They said** <u>I *would have heard* from the interview committee by now</u>. But I'm still waiting.
> (The past future perfect is typically found in a subclause.)

Note in (138) that, in contrast with the past-time situation *They said*, the subordinated clause *I would have heard ...* is not located in the past time-sphere. The context ('I'm still waiting') makes it perfectly clear here that, at the moment of speech, the speaker has not yet heard from the committee. (The actualization of that situation – if it even occurs – will necessarily be located in the post-present, after the moment of speech.)

Given the interplay between anteriority and posteriority, it is easier to get a handle on what exactly the past future perfect communicates when we take a look at an authentic example with some greater context. What is particularly illustrative about the example in (139) from BBC NEWS is that (i) the past future perfect *we would have learnt enough Spanish* is nestled among examples of the past future (*migrants would be given legal status; it would take months; we would be able to pretend*); and (ii) it is very clear where these situations are located with respect to the past-time situations with *said*:

> (139) In 2001, a huge number of illegal immigrants went on hunger strike in Spain demanding legal status. Among them were many Pakistanis, Bangladeshis and Indians who had taken refuge in churches. Finally, the Spanish government said

migrants residing and working illegally in Spain for many years would be given legal status. On hearing the news, my friend suggested we go to Spain. He said it would take months, or even years, for the authorities there to interview us. By that time, **he said**, we *would have learnt* enough Spanish to communicate and we would be able to pretend we had been in the country for a long time. (www)

It should be clear that the past future perfect situation referred to by *we would have learnt enough Spanish* is <u>anterior to</u> 'by that time' (a future time to which the past future situations *it would take months* and *we would be able to pretend* also refer) and that all three situations are <u>posterior to</u> the situation *he said*.

As with the three other perfect tenses we have seen thus far, it is possible to distinguish three types of past future perfect:

(140) **He said** that <u>by then we *would have learnt* enough Spanish to communicate</u>. (indefinite perfect)
He said that <u>by then we *would have lived* there long enough to pass for natives</u>. (continuative perfect)
He said that <u>by then we *would* probably *have been hired* illegally more than once</u>. (repetitive perfect)

And, of course, progressive aspect can combine with the past future perfect as well. Consider the following example, where a married couple's future life plans are evoked retrospectively after the woman's husband has died:

(141) **[T]hey were imagining** that <u>she *would have finished* her master's in physiotherapy and *would have been working* for a few years by then</u>; a chunk of the mortgage on their flat would have been paid – and her husband would be alive.

Notice how the system – making use here of (i) a past future perfect Achievement (of the type indefinite: *she would have finished her master's*) and (ii) a past future perfect Activity with progressive aspect (*she would have been working for a few years*) – communicates the same basic temporal information, namely a situation X is anterior to a situation Y (*her husband's death*) which itself is posterior to situation Z (*they were imagining*), the different situation types making for different aspectual contours.

The following example shows free indirect speech (cf. (133)):

(142) They decided that the best solution was to go to Spain. It would take months, or even years, for the authorities there to interview them. By that time, they *would have learnt* enough Spanish to communicate.

Finally, as we saw with the past future and the future tenses, the past future perfect cannot occur in subordinate time clauses introduced by conjunctions such as *when, as soon as* and *once*. The past perfect (or the past – see tense simplification in (102)) is used instead:

> (143) He told us to phone as soon as we *(had) arrived*. (*would have arrived)
> I knew that once he *(had) read* (*would have read) the book, he'd want to read the sequel.

The past future perfect as described above conveys strictly temporal information. But *would* + *have* + past participle can also refer to a counterfactual situation located in the past time-sphere. The situation is contingent on another counterfactual situation located in the past time-sphere and represented in an *if*-clause:

> (144) (a) She *would have installed* the software for you if you *had asked* her.
> (Both clauses are past time counterfactual situations: she did not install the hardware; you did not ask her to.)
>
> (b) She *wouldn't have installed* the software if she *had known* it was damaged.
> (Again, both clauses are past time counterfactual situations: here, she did in fact install the hardware; she did not know it was damaged.)

Note that in these counterfactual sentences, *would* + *have* + past participle is used in the main clause, and a modal past perfect (see Chapter 5, Section 8) is used in the *if*-clause. The same restriction applies to *would* + *have* + past participle in an *if*-clause in counterfactual conditional sentences as in subordinate time clauses:

> (145) If I'd *known* (*would have known), I wouldn't have said anything.

We will have the occasion to examine conditional sentences in Chapter 5.

4. Conclusion

Our aim in this chapter was to discuss how temporal and aspectual markers conspire to show how situations are perceived by speakers and how they are located in time. We began by giving an overview of aspect before zooming in on situation types, as they determine to a considerable extent whether the progressive marker can be added or not and what effect it has if it is used. We then laid out a tense system in which three temporal features, -ED, *will* and *have*, combine to locate situation in four different time-spheres, organized around the moment of speech. We saw how, within and between these time-spheres, one situation can be seen as anterior to or posterior to another. We hope that the discovery of the system of interaction between these different factors has convinced you of the following:

- there are similarities between the forms that locate situations in different time-spheres (e.g. present perfect, past perfect, past future perfect, future perfect; e.g. future tense and past future tense);

- progressive aspect cannot be fully mastered without taking into consideration the effect of situation types as well as other factors, including numerical NPs;

- the choice of tense is not determined by a set of independent rules. Rather, the 'rules' follow from a few basic generalizations related to how time is perceived in English.

Exercises

Exercise 1. Identify the tenses that are italicized, specifying whether the verb form has progressive or non-progressive aspect. Then identify the situation type of the relevant clauses.

1. She *was* slowly *backing* her car into the garage.
2. They*'ve known* each other for years.
3. The bomb *exploded* right in the middle of the market.
4. Henry *draws* pictures in his room every afternoon.
5. *Is* someone *knocking* at the door?
6. How much *will* that new computer *cost*?
7. The kitten *had lapped up* the bowl of fresh cream.
8. My students *have been reading* more than usual.

Exercise 2. Complete each sentence below with one of the eight tenses on page p.179, using either progressive or non-progressive aspect. There may be more than one possible answer, and all eight tenses will not be used. Formulate, using the concepts introduced in this chapter, why in each case the form you choose is best given the context of the sentence. Finally, identify the situation type exemplified in the clauses corresponding to each of your answers. Explain your choice in terms of the variables *duration, dynamicity* and *inherent endpoint*.

break	live	play	cough	contain	own
lie	love	change	learn	drive	shatter
be	write	sneeze	sleep		

1. This bottle of juice ____ six servings of 250 millilitres.
2. Every autumn, the leaves of this tree ____ colour.
3. When she dropped the mirror, it ____ into thousands of shards of glass.
4. She ____ a Chopin nocturne on the piano when I walked in.
5. I didn't really feel like going to Rome because I ____ there before.
6. If I have time tomorrow, I ____ him a short letter.
7. Oh, no! Sorry, I ____ (just) one of your beautiful china plates!
8. This time next week, we ____ on a sandy beach in Greece.
9. We ____ our house for twenty years next month. How time flies…
10. If there's a train strike tomorrow, we ____ to Paris.
11. Whenever there's a lot of pollen in the air, I ____ uncontrollably.
12. They ____ in that house for the past twenty five years. They love it there.
13. The average baby ____ sixteen hours a day.
14. Our son ____ for several days, so we brought him to the doctor's.
15. Our children ____ Mandarin Chinese at school. It's their favourite subject.
16. I absolutely ____ pizza. It's my favourite food. I could eat it every day.

Exercise 3. Read the following extract from the English-language press. Identify the tenses that are italicized, specifying whether the verb form has progressive or non-progressive aspect. Then identify the situation type of the relevant clauses.

Crocodile suspected in disappearance of Scottish man at Australian campsite
Search continues for 63-year-old who was camping with his wife on
river in northern Queensland

A Scottish man (1) *is believed* to have been killed by a crocodile next to a remote river while camping in north-east Australia. Arthur Booker, 63, who (2) *was born* in Banffshire, (3) *had been camping* with his wife, Doris, near the Endeavour river, five miles north of Cooktown […]. The couple, who (4) *lived* in Logan near Brisbane, (5) *had been travelling* around the country in a caravan. […] Booker [allegedly] (6) *went* to the river to check crab pots for the day's catch at around 8.30am yesterday. Booker's wife (7) *raised* the alarm when he (8) *had not returned* to the camp after two hours. […] 'No sign of the man (9) *has been found* and police strongly (10) *suspect* a crocodile attack,' a rangers spokesman said. 'They (11) *were searching* the river and a small creek from where Mr Booker (12) *was taken*, looking under logs in case the big croc (13) *had stashed* the body in there.' The local environmental protection agency (14) *will set up* crocodile traps near the campsite. Endeavour river (15) *has* a large population of saltwater crocodiles. Warning signs (16) *are dotted* throughout the campsite. (www)

Exercise 4. Complete the following sentences with the present tense of an appropriate verb from the list below. Use the same verb for each sentence in the pair, using progressive aspect for one and non-progressive for the other, as appropriate. Finally, decide if any other aspectual choice is possible, and explain why.

understand	cost	taste	feel	consider
depend	hate	doubt	have	enjoy

1. (a) Only six months into the job, and I _____ (already) it.
   (b) I hope they don't serve us salmon again. I _____ (absolutely) fish.
2. (a) I _____ a chemistry class on Thursday mornings. Can we meet at another time?
   (b) Sorry, I _____ breakfast. I'll call you back in twenty minutes or so.
3. (a) I really did believe her at first. I now find I _____ (seriously) a lot of what she says.
   (b) I'm sorry, have we met? – I _____ we have, I've only just started working here.
4. (a) I'm only in Liverpool for about six months, but so far I _____ it here a lot.
   (b) I _____ (really) Judith's company and would like to spend more time with her.
5. (a) What is this bag is made of? – I'm not sure, but it _____ like denim.
   (b) She _____ a little down now that her boyfriend's gone back to Sweden.
6. (a) I want to change suppliers, and so I _____ (currently) a range of local cheeses.
   (b) There's something strange about the way this soup _____. What did you put in it?
7. (a) It _____ a lot to take the Eurostar to London if you don't buy a ticket in advance.
   (b) It _____ less and less to eat and live healthily these days.
8. (a) I _____ your wanting to wait, but time's running out. We should make a decision soon.
   (b) At first I found Dutch complicated, but as time goes by, I _____ it more and more.
9. (a) We _____ the offer on our house, but frankly we'd hoped to get more for it.
   (b) Many people _____ it very rude to show up at someone's house empty-handed.
10. (a) Reduce, reuse and recycle! Future generations _____ on you!
    (b) I'd love to come with you, but it _____ (really) on what time I'm able to leave work.

Exercise 5. Put the verbs in the following sets of sentences in the present tense, paying particular attention to aspect. What generalizations can you make about progressive versus non-progressive here? What does this tell us about different situation types?

1. My sister-in-law (*see*) an acupuncturist to help her quit smoking.
   You/(interrogative) (*see*) what I mean? There's nothing to be done about it.
2. The magistrate (*hear*) the appeal next month, but his lawyers are anything but optimistic.
   They/(interrogative) (*hear*) the traffic from their tenth-storey flat?

3. This fabric (*feel*) like silk. Is it genuine or fake?

   We all (*feel*) like going for Chinese tonight. Do you want to come?

   My colleagues and I (*feel*) a lot of pressure from the upper echelons of the firm.

4. Why/that man/(interrogative) (*look*) at us like that? Do we know him? Does he know us?

   It (*look*) as though it could rain later. Let's take the umbrella just in case.

   What an odd dog. It (*look*) like a mix between a dachshund and a pit bull.

   I ran into Sonia last week. She (*look*) great!

5. The soup (*taste*) really good. What's in it?

   I just (*taste*) the soup to see whether it needs seasoning. Then we can eat.

   Now that they're roasting the beans onsite, their coffee (*taste*) better than ever.

Exercise 6. Choose the appropriate pair of verbs to complete each sentence. Use the past tense in both cases, paying particular attention to non-progressive and progressive aspect. The verbs are not necessarily in the same order in the sentences. Negative forms may be necessary. If both aspects are possible, explain: are there any cases in which the choice fundamentally changes the meaning of the sentence?

sit – open	stand – come	respond – think	open – blow
listen – catch	diet – suggest	be – live	read – work
read – lend	hope – lose	start – complain	work – meet
notice – snow	leave – stay	walk – chat	

1. Sorry, I _____ everything you said. I _____ very closely to your explanation.
2. As soon as I _____ the window, a gust of wind _____ out all the candles.
3. The entire staff _____ up when the CEO _____ into the room.
4. He _____ down and then quietly _____ his book.
5. Ruth _____ we order the dessert, but I _____ at the time and said no.
6. My students (always) _____ about the homework I gave them, so I _____ giving them less.
7. She _____ me the book last month, but I _____ it until last weekend.
8. The kids _____ in their room and my husband _____ in the garden: the house was silent.
9. My sister _____ for England early the next morning, so she _____ very long at the party.
10. The first thing he _____ when he got outside was that it _____ hard.
11. I _____ in Europe when the president _____ elected.
12. When my parents _____ (first), they _____ (both) for the same insurance company.
13. I _____ you might be able to help me. I _____ my mobile and need to call home ASAP.
14. Everyone _____ away mindlessly when the teacher _____ into the classroom.

15. I _____ you might want to ring her up and talk to her. She _____ well to the bad news.

Exercise 7. Complete the sentences with these pairs of verbs. Note that the verb pairs are not always in sentence order. Choose the most appropriate tense – present perfect or past – paying close attention to the *since*-clause.

live – work	regret – move	be able – publish	fail – not be
be – come	work – enjoy	change – be	see – know

1. John _____ enthusiastic about his studies since he _____ his first-semester exams.
2. Since I _____ here, I _____ every single day. I really love my job.
3. Ever since the day he first _____ to Rome, he _____ it. It's just too far from home.
4. So much _____ since I _____ last here. There's much more traffic and more tourists.
5. Since he _____ his first book, he _____ to write another word: he's got 'writer's block'.
6. Ever since they _____ in the neighbourhood, they _____ closely with the community.
7. Since I _____ you, I _____ (rarely) you so down-hearted and depressed.
8. He _____ a dictator since he _____ (first) to power following the military coup.

Exercise 8. Complete the following sentences with an appropriate verb from the list below. Use the same verb for each sentence in the pair. Choose the past tense for one sentence and the present perfect tense for the other. Use non-progressive aspect, but indicate whether progressive aspect is also possible. Comment in each case on your choice.

regret	cut	read	receive	drive
speak	sell	become	know	grow

1. (a) In 2017 alone, our company _____ an average of 1000 e-mails a month.
   (b) Our company _____ so many e-mails lately that we're thinking of expanding our website.
2. (a) I first _____ aware that my baby was moving when I was about 18 weeks pregnant.
   (b) We _____ increasingly concerned these past months about the level of absenteeism.
3. (a) I _____ Cathy for forty years. She's a good neighbour, and I'm happy to be her friend.
   (b) She _____ within weeks that she'd rushed into the situation blindly and naively.
4. (a) Financially speaking, her parents _____ her off completely. She's on her own now.
   (b) His father _____ him out of his will when her learned of his son's reckless spending.
5. (a) He _____ buying that car since the day he bought it. It breaks down regularly.

  (b) She _____ (long) her decision to quit her job. But now she realizes it was a wise decision.

6. (a) Wow, you _____ since the last time I saw you! You're such a big boy now!

  (b) My son _____ out of his last pair of shoes in what seemed like a matter of weeks.

7. (a) I _____ *Oliver Twist* in high school and then in college. I've never been a Dickens fan.

  (b) I'm sure I _____ somewhere that you should never use a second-hand car seat.

8. (a) I _____ to my boss about a promotion not that long ago, and he seems optimistic.

  (b) My boss _____ to his boss about my long-term potential and says I'll be promoted soon.

9. (a) They _____ thousands of copies of the book before realizing key pages were missing.

  (b) They _____ as many copies of the book this past week as they'd normally sell in a month.

10. (a) Kim _____ in England before. She can tell you what's it like to drive on the left side.

  (b) I _____ (once) all the way from London to Edinburgh non-stop by myself.

Exercise 9. Complete the following sentences with the present perfect tense of an appropriate verb from the list below. In each case, decide whether progressive and non-progressive aspect is possible. If only one is possible, explain why. If both are possible, explain the semantic effects that fall out from the choice.

paint	study	announce	break	see
fall	change	plant	visit	work

1. Temperatures _____ rapidly since last Monday, they're now predicting snow later today.
2. The CEO _____ that twenty-five employees will be made redundant before December.
3. I _____ him three times this week already and am getting a little sick of his company.
4. My sister _____ French for two months now. She's ready to come to France to practise.
5. She _____ more than usual lately. Let's wait until after Christmas before inviting her over.
6. Now that they _____ their kitchen, they can do the living room and bathroom.
7. A 23-year-old Swiss man _____ the world record for swimming across the English Channel.
8. Is this the first time they _____ the north of France?
9. Look at your hands! – I know, I _____ tulip bulbs in the garden. I'll wash them now.
10. You _____ so much since I last saw you! I almost didn't recognize you!

Exercise 10. First, identify the present perfect forms in the following sentences and identify the situation type they represent. Then, identify and comment on the verbal aspect of the present perfect, pointing out any effects it has: can it be changed from progressive to non-progressive or from non-progressive to progressive? Finally, identify the kind of present perfect it is (continuative, indefinite or repetitive).

1. How long have you suspected him of doctoring the accounts?
2. She's been watching that five-part documentary on the First World War. She's enjoying it.
3. I've been calling that number all morning, but no one's answering.
4. I've written letters to the editor of our local paper to raise public awareness.
5. People have been complaining about the noise coming from the nightclub.
6. Sorry, I've already had dinner. But I'd love to join you for coffee and dessert.
7. I've been working with the same group of people for almost twenty-five years.
8. I think I must be in love. I've never felt so happy and confused at the same time.
9. Has someone dropped something on my antique table? There's a huge gash in it!
10. You've been coughing a lot lately. Shouldn't you go and see the doctor about that?
11. Ever since I spilt coffee on my computer, it hasn't worked very well.

Exercise 11. Take a look at the following scenarios. (i) Give the correct form(s) of the verbs. Sometimes you have to choose the correct verb to use. If more than one form is possible, give both forms and explain why this is possible. If you use a present perfect, explain what kind of present perfect it is (continuative, indefinite or repetitive). (ii) Complete the Adjuncts in brackets {} using *for, since, ago* or *in.*

1. Peter is American, but he _____ (*live*) in London.
   He _____ (*live*) in London {2010}/{almost ten years}.
   He _____ (*move*) to London {2010}.
   He _____ (*move*) to London {about ten years}.

2. Elaine's an interior designer. She _____ (*redecorate*) people's homes.
   She _____ (*redecorate*) people's homes {she _____ (*finish*) university}/{nine or ten years}.
   She _____ (*start*) redecorating {nine or ten years}.

3. Sylvie _____ (*work*) for a local internet provider.
   She _____ (*work*) for the company {six months or so}/{February}.
   She _____ (*be hired*) {February}/{six months}.

4. Ruth _____ (*run*) a sandwich shop.
   Her family _____ (*run*) the sandwich shop {she _____ (*be*) a kid}/{quite some time}.
   Her grandfather _____ (*first/open*) the shop {the 1940s}/{six decades}.

5. Kim loves to travel. She _____ (be/go) to China, Australia, Russia and many other places.
   She _____ (travel) {she _____ (first/catch)} the travel bug {about ten years}.
   She _____ (travel) as much as she can.
   She _____ (travel) {I _____ (know) her}/{I _____ (first/meet) her in 1998}.
   She _____ (be/go) to Rio de Janeiro for the Olympics in 2016 …
   … but she _____ (never be/never go) to Egypt.

6. Brian is quite wealthy. He _____ (own) a yacht.
   He _____ (own) the yacht {he _____ (retire) at age 50}.
   He's still in his early 50s, so he _____ (not own) it {very long}.
   He _____ (buy) the yacht {a few years}/{2015}.

7. Sarah is a teacher. She _____ (teach) at a local high school.
   She _____ (teach) {she _____ (finish) university at age 23}.
   She's 55, so she _____ (be) a teacher {more than 30 years}.
   She _____ (start) teaching {1987}/{a long time}.

8. Henry is a musician. He _____ (play) the piano.
   He _____ (play) the piano {he _____ (be) six or seven years old}.
   He's 11 now, so he _____ (play) the piano {four or five years}.
   He _____ (start) learning how to play {2015}/{a few years}.

Exercise 12. Paying attention to the Adjuncts, find a way to express sentences 1 to 10 using the present perfect. While the point of view will change, each sentence should have the same basic meaning as the original. You will need to make other changes in the sentence. This may include the verb you use, using a negative instead of an affirmative form, etc. (Note that there may be several possibilities. If you can think of more than one possible way to recast the sentence, give all possibilities.)

Example:
   Rebecca moved to Dublin in 1998.
      > Rebecca has lived (has been living) in Dublin since 1998.
   Rebecca moved to Dublin many years ago.
      > Rebecca has lived (has been living) in Dublin for many years.

1. My mother-in-law arrived at the beginning of last week.
2. The last time I spoke to Matilde was on the day of her wedding.
3. It's more than six months since anyone's lived in that house.
4. Henry moved to Boston ten years ago.
5. I quit studying Japanese when I moved back to the States.

6. The drain in the kitchen sink started leaking a week ago. I can't get hold of a plumber.
7. Thomas got his current job as a project manager last May.
8. The last time he sent me an e-mail message was at least six months ago.
9. He got his driving licence when he was only sixteen.
10. They moved to Singapore as soon as they graduated.

Exercise 13. Complete the following sentences with the present perfect tense or the past perfect tense of an appropriate verb from the list below. In each case, decide whether progressive or non-progressive aspect is possible. If only one is possible, explain why. If both are possible explain the semantic effects that fall out from the choice. You may need to use the negative form of the verb or an interrogative form.

date	start	live	work	lie	run
decide	read	smoke	arrive	speak	take

1. Peter _____ harder than ever that year, so he decided to take a longer vacation.
2. _____ (you)? You're all out of breath – Yes, I didn't want to be late for the meeting.
3. It was obvious that Tom _____ again – his breath stank of tobacco.
4. Last time I saw you, I don't think I _____ my new job yet.
5. Jane _____ Chinese lessons for years now, but she still can't speak it very well.
6. _____ (you) to John this morning? – No, not yet, but I think he's in his office.
7. I _____ a book on ancient Greek mythology. So far, it's really interesting.
8. By the time I got to the party, all of the other guests _____ and were busy talking.
9. She's still adjusting to her new job in Shanghai. She _____ there for very long at all.
10. They _____ in the sun for hours when they finally realized how sunburnt they were.
11. My parents _____ if they're going to do anything special for their anniversary this year.
12. How long _____ (you) when you finally met his family for the first time?

Exercise 14. Using one of the verbs below, complete the following sentences using the past perfect. Negative forms may be necessary. Then decide in which sentences the past perfect can be replaced by the past. Explain your choices. Are there any cases where the change entails a difference in meaning?

see	set	read	finish	forget
save	try	do	find	cheat

1. By the time I got round to buying the book, all of my friends (already) _____ it.
2. The waiter took away my plate before I _____ my meal. I hate it when they do that.

3. As soon as they _____ enough money, they made a down payment on a new house.
4. Until recently, I _____ (never) the film *Citizen Kane* in its entirety.
5. She told her son she wouldn't help him with his homework until he _____ to do it himself.
6. The teacher asked us if we _____ (ever) in a test. No one knew what to say.
7. Matt's mother told him to clean his room; in fact, he _____ (already) it.
8. It wasn't until I arrived at work that I remembered I _____ to lock the front door.
9. Once they _____ a quaint hotel to stay at, they decided to purchase their train tickets.
10. When my sister asked where her keys were, I told her I _____ them on the kitchen table.

Exercise 15. Put verbs in the following sentences into the past tense, the present perfect tense or the past perfect tense. Determine in each case whether progressive or non-progressive aspect (or both) would be used, and comment on any semantic effects that this choice brings about. Finally, complete the adjuncts in brackets ({}) using *for, since* or *ago* as appropriate. What generalizations can you make about the use of *for, since* and *ago* with respect to these tenses?

1. She (*live*) in London {a while} in the early 1990s.
2. They (*work*) on the case {a couple of weeks}; I'm sure they'll finish it by tomorrow.
3. We (*know*) each other {last March}. We're now quite good friends.
4. I (*stand*) here waiting {about an hour}; is he going to show up or not?
5. She (*not see*) her parents {Christmas}, so she decided it was time to give them a ring.
6. My sister (*be*) in the bathroom {half an hour this morning}, so of course I was late.
7. I (*finish*) my master's degree {five years}.
8. You (*not do*) a thing {nine o'clock}; isn't it time you got down to work?
9. We (*be*) married {more than ten years}; amazing how time flies, isn't it?
10. We (*get*) married {more than ten years}, and yet it seems like only yesterday.

Exercise 16. Put the verb in brackets into an appropriate present perfect, past perfect or future perfect tense. Choose a perfect tense even if another *non*-perfect tense is possible. If both aspects are possible, give them both. If both are possible, indicate whether there is a fundamental difference in meaning between the two. Indicate the situation type of the relevant clause, and indicate what kind of perfect is being used. Finally, specify what the reference time (R) is.

1. Can you believe that next month I _____ (*have*) this car for fifteen years?
2. Can we meet at 8 ? – No, I _____ (*exercise*) just before that. I'll want to have a shower first.
3. We're going to Paris in six months. I _____ (*study*) French for a whole year at that point.
4. A year from now, you _____ (*work*) enough to have the necessary experience.
5. I _____ (*have*) this car for far too long. It's time to buy a new one.
6. I couldn't understand a thing. At that stage, I _____ (*study*) French for only a year or so.
7. When they saw I _____ (*work*) with kids before, they offered me the position on the spot.
8. Ten o'clock? But the train _____ (*leave*) by then! We have to leave earlier.
9. _____ (*you/ever/work*) with young children before? Experience is very important.
10. She finally realized that she _____ (*sneeze*) because of the cat – she's allergic.
11. I _____ (*clean*) the entire house. It's time to make myself a cup of tea.
12. I _____ (*take*) this online test four times. I'm not going to take it again.
13. I could tell that she _____ (*sleep*) when I phoned. She didn't sound very coherent.
14. The last train _____ (*leave*). We had no choice but to rent a hotel room.
15. I _____ (*study*) French for a year. It's still hard for me to follow when people speak quickly.
16. By the time I finish this course, I _____ (*take*) the test three times.
17. It was time to buy a new car. I _____ (*have*) the same one for too long.
18. By the time he got home, I _____ (*clean*) the entire house.
19. Sorry, but the train _____ (*leave*). You'll have to take the next train.
20. I _____ (*sneeze*) a lot lately. I think I'm getting a cold.
21. By the time you get home, I _____ (*clean*) the entire house.
22. He decided not to take the test again. After all, he _____ (*take*) it several times before.
23. I _____ (*cry*). That's why my eyes are red. Don't worry, it's nothing serious.

Exercise 17. Complete these sentences with one of the verbs provided. Use the present tense, the past tense or any of the perfect tenses. Choose in each case progressive or non-progressive aspect as required by the context. Notice that in this exercise, you will have to use forms of the future <u>perfect</u> tense. However, do *not* use the future tense (e.g. do not use *I will do it* (future, non-progressive) or *I will be doing it* (future, progressive)).

| work | leave | read | drive | break | live | snow |
| fall | warn | be | take | lose | fly | |

1. When the students take the exam next week, they _____ the chapter on verb tenses several times. They should have no trouble getting a good mark.
2. I _____ one of my grandmother's beautiful crystal wine glasses last night while doing the washing up.

3. Sorry, but could you keep your voices down, please? The children _____ a nap.
4. I _____ you more than once not to drive too fast on this road. If you get a speeding ticket, it'll be no one's fault but your own.
5. At age 13, he was already a seasoned traveller. In fact, he (already) _____ across the Atlantic four or five times.
6. John is Australian, but he _____ for a multinational corporation based in Dubai.
7. As of June the first, she _____ in Portugal for exactly ten years.
8. She _____ non-stop for several hours when the tragic accident occurred.
9. My grandparents _____ married for many years. They do quarrel sometimes, but by and large they get on just fine.
10. Looking out the window that morning in April, I couldn't believe my eyes – it _____!
11. I _____ my glasses again. I can't find them anywhere. Do you have any idea where they might be?
12. (*in the car*) The kids are exhausted. I'm sure they _____ asleep by the time we get home.
13. I got to the bus stop on time – or at least I thought so. But the bus (already) _____, so I ended up having to walk all the way to work.

Exercise 18. Comment on how future time is expressed in the following sentences. Are there any sentences where future time is less prominent than another modal-like meaning?

1. Congratulations, you have won the contest. You'll be receiving your prize within a week.
2. I'll pick the kids up from school if you have to work late.
3. Listen, I'm about to leave. Can I ring you back in a couple of hours?
4. They're going to Portugal next summer.
5. I'll be back in a minute – just wait for me here.
6. October 31st, and it's already freezing: it's going to be a long, cold winter, I think.
7. In another month or so, I'll have been working on this project for a year.
8. The concert begins at 8 o'clock sharp. Don't be late.
9. Boys will be boys.
10. You will do as I say. Otherwise, there's going to be trouble.
11. John Perry is to play George Washington in a new West End play next season.
12. Sorry, but I work this weekend. We'll have to get together next week instead.

Exercise 19. Complete the sentences below with the correct form of one of the verbs given. Use the present progressive or *be going to* (+ verb base) to refer to future time. Either form may be possible in a given context. If so, make explicit the difference in meaning. Be able to justify your choices.

meet   take   realize   cut   faint   talk   start   tell

1. One of these days, he _____ that he shouldn't have got married so young.
2. I'm starving. I think I _____ (actually) if I don't get something to eat soon.
3. The two CEOs _____ late this afternoon to discuss the merger of the two companies.
4. As soon as the boss gets back, John _____ to her about changing positions.
5. _____ (he) his girlfriend the truth about why he's decided to break up with her?
6. Patricia _____ looking for a new job next autumn. She feels it's time for a change.
7. *The Tribune* _____ its writing staff by 25 per cent. It's a dark time for journalists.
8. I've been reading for too long. I can't concentrate any more. I think I _____ a short walk.

Exercise 20. Complete the sentences below with the correct form of one of the verbs given. Use the future tense or *be going to* (+ verb base) to refer to future time. Be able to justify your choices.

finish   get   explain   love   answer   host

1. I'm sure Ms Citron _____ what to do to make up for the homework you didn't do.
2. We _____ a Christmas party again this year. Loads of people you know will be there.
3. Do try that restaurant sometime soon. Whatever you order, you _____ the food there.
4. If you dial this number, the receptionist _____. Ask her to put you through to me.
5. There's no way we can complete this report today. – Don't worry, we _____ it tomorrow.
6. Have you heard the latest? Kim and Chris _____ married late next summer.

Exercise 21. Complete the following sentences using a verb of your choice with a form (including, but not limited to, the future tense) that can logically be used to express future time. If more than one form is possible, explain. Are there any cases where future time and a more modal reading with *will* are both present?

1. The last train for Rome _____ at 8 pm. Perhaps we should try to book our tickets now.
2. One of these days, Jim _____ his novel. Who knows, maybe it'll be a best seller.
3. I'd love to come, but I can't. I _____ friends that night for drinks and dinner.
4. Just think, in another couple of months, we _____ each other for ten years! Amazing!
5. There are no job openings at this time, but we _____ you if something comes up.
6. By the time he's thirty, he _____ for his father for more than half his life.

7. I _____ the Easter holiday in Athens with my parents, so we'll have to meet after that.
8. The film _____ at half past seven, so let's meet a little earlier in front of the cinema.
9. Why don't you call Eric if you need a hand? I'm sure he _____ if you ask nicely.
10. In two months' time, my parents _____ married for thirty years.
11. We can't make it on Saturday – we _____ to a new house and we'll be too tired to come.
12. The play _____ at 8 o'clock sharp, and I don't want to miss the beginning. Don't be late.

Exercise 22. Choose a verb that can complete both sentences in the pair ((a) and (b)). Use *will* + verb base, choosing progressive aspect in one case and non-progressive aspect in the other. Negative forms may be needed. Explain your choice in each case: does futurity or modal meaning come to the fore? Is it accurate to say that *will* + verb base does not always correspond to the future tense?

travel   help   read   start   check

1. (a) I _____ this book anytime soon, so feel free to borrow it if you like.
   (b) I _____ this book until you've bought a copy. We can read it together.
2. (a) I _____ you choose a dress for the wedding. How about next weekend?
   (b) I can't work next Saturday after all. I _____ my sister move house that day.
3. (a) His car _____. Do you think we should call a mechanic?
   (b) Ladies and Gentlemen, the play _____ in just a few minutes. Please be seated.
4. (a) Our plane lands at 9 pm so tell the hotel we _____ in late.
   (b) We _____ in early if you want, but it's not a very busy airport.
5. (a) The service was awful. I _____ with this airline ever again.
   (b) The president _____ to that country if and only if he receives an invitation.

Exercise 23. Complete each sentence below with one of the eight tenses on page 179, using either progressive or non-progressive aspect. Use each tense~aspect combination only once. If two choices seem possible, choose your answer in light of what works best in the other sentences. Making use of the concepts introduced in this chapter, explain in each case why the form you choose is best given the context of the sentence.

listen   work (x 2)   recognize   sleep (x 2)   arrive   wear   have
cancel   rain   know   see   finish (x 2)   be

1. She _____ when we phoned her. The call woke her up.
2. It struck me that, at the end of the month, we _____ together for ten years.
3. What awful weather this is. It _____ for two days.
4. John _____ for Microsoft©. It's his permanent job.

5. If it rains, we ____ the picnic.
6. Quiet please, I ____ to the radio.
7. I knew that, by the end of the week, he ____ the project.
8. They got married in 1973. In 2023, they ____ married for fifty years.
9. He ____ for several hours when I woke him up.
10. They ____ at our place at 8 o'clock sharp yesterday.
11. She didn't come with us because she ____ the film already.
12. Don't call between 7 and 8 – we ____ dinner.
13. They're late, as always. By the time they get here, we ____ dinner.
14. I ____ John for twenty-five years. He's my best friend.
15. He said not to worry, (that) he ____ a red hat, ...
16. ... and (that) I ____ him immediately.

Exercise 24. Using the prompts in A and B below, make a complete sentence beginning with the word or words given. A and B are not necessarily in the correct order. Use *will* or *won't* in the other part of the sentence.

A	B
1. you/at least try to guess *Until* ...	I/tell you the answer to the question
2. the committee's choice/made official *Provided* ...	she/be able to start working immediately
3. I/proofread it carefully for mistakes *After* ...	my official translator/send me the document
4. we/show them to our lawyer *Before* ...	we/sign the papers
5. something miraculous/happen soon *Unless* ...	we/be able to pay off our debts
6. he/call me back *Just in case* ...	I/leave you my mobile number
7. she/answer the phone *If* ...	she/think it's a telemarketer

Exercise 25. Give the progressive counterpart of the following sentences. Are there any cases where progressive aspect renders the sentence ungrammatical or semantically odd? What are the different effects brought about by the progressive ~ non-progressive dichotomy?

1. She listens to the morning news on the radio.
2. She listened to the morning news on the radio.
3. She likes/enjoys listening to the morning news on the radio.
4. He always/never complains about the weather.

5. He takes the number 52 bus to get to work.
6. He always takes/never takes the number 52 bus to get to work.
7. I've read the book you lent me.
8. I've just read the book you lent me.
9. I've already read the book you lent me.
10. I read (/red/) the book you lent me.
11. I read (/ri:d/) the books you lend me.
12. I've read that book before.

Exercise 26. Give the progressive counterpart of the following sentences. Are there any cases where progressive aspect renders the sentence ungrammatical or semantically odd? What are the different effects brought about by the progressive ~ non-progressive dichotomy?

1. They won't spend the holidays with us this year.
2. I leave at 8 o'clock tomorrow morning.
3. The last train leaves the city centre at around midnight.
4. We will send you our catalogue free of charge.
5. She lives with her grandmother on the Upper East Side.
6. I wonder if we could meet sometime next week.
7. What does your brother-in-law do?
8. I missed my plane and had to take a later flight.
9. Christine sprained her ankle last week.
10. He worked as an administrative assistant.
11. He works as an administrative assistant.
12. We both felt a bit peckish, and there was nothing to eat.

Exercise 27. Give the progressive counterpart of the following sentences. Are there any cases where progressive aspect renders the sentence ungrammatical or semantically odd? What are the different effects brought about by the progressive ~ non-progressive dichotomy?

1. Walking into the house, I smelled my mother's vegetable soup cooking.
2. Standing in front of his steaming pot, the chef proudly smelled his soup.
3. If I had known the answer, I would have passed the test.
4. It had rained the day before, and the ground was wet and muddy.
5. John, will you stay for dinner?
6. You are ridiculous./He is really unreasonable./She is 100 per cent French Canadian.
7. My husband works this weekend, so I'll take care of the kids.
8. He must work harder at learning his irregular verbs.
9. I think Christine has sprained her ankle. Get some ice.
10. William had read the book when the film came out.

11. The day of his interview, William hadn't felt well for several days.
12. They will send us the documentation we requested.

Exercise 28. In two of the following sentences, *would* + verb base has meaning which, when compared to the other sentences, is more closely associated with straightforward future time reference. In the other sentences, however, *would* + verb base has meanings which are less future-like and more modal. These include the following modal meanings:

    a. narrative flash-forward

    b. probability

    c. typical behaviour

    d. refusal

    e. promise

    f. willingness

Indicate which two sentences are more oriented to future time reference; for the other six sentences, indicate which type of modal meaning comes to the fore, using (a) to (f) above. Each of the modal meanings is used only once.

1. I assured him that I *would do* everything according to his instructions.
2. The secretary said that they *would be sending* the package before closing time.
3. Patricia McGillen was born into a poor family and did not even graduate from high school. She *would* later *become* one of the greatest mystery writers of the twentieth century.
4. Do you need my help on Sunday? – No, thanks. I asked John and he said he *would help*.
5. We told her we were busy, but she *wouldn't take* 'no' for an answer.
6. The paper said the tide *would come in* at 6.34 pm tonight.
7. At exactly 5 pm, the phone rang. I was sure it *would be* Lee. In fact, it was my mother.
8. My sister forgot my birthday. – Yeah, well she *would*. She never remembers anything!

Exercise 29. Complete the following narrative using the correct tense of the verbs in brackets. In some cases, you will have to incorporate other functional words, also given in brackets. Pay close attention to aspect (progressive vs. non-progressive). Be able to justify your choices.

An Unexpected Encounter

I _____ (*walk*)[(1)] down the street the other day when I _____ (*see*)[(2)] a girl I _____ (*go*)[(3)] to high school with. She _____ (*stand*)[(4)] on the corner, talking to another woman. I

_____ (*not set*)⁽⁵⁾ eyes on her for thirty years or so, so I wasn't absolutely sure it was her at first. But then I _____ (*hear*)⁽⁶⁾ her voice and laughter, and there could be no mistake: it was Jenn Kenny, my very first high school crush.

I should probably mention that, nowadays, I _____ (*not see*/really)⁽⁷⁾ anyone from high school any more. I _____ (*not keep*)⁽⁸⁾ in touch with anyone at all since we _____ (*graduate*)⁽⁹⁾. After high school, my fellow classmates _____ (*go*/all)⁽¹⁰⁾ on to do exciting things. I on the other hand _____ (*have*)⁽¹¹⁾ a string of boring jobs, none of which I _____ (*seem*)⁽¹²⁾ to keep for very long. (In fact, I _____ (*lose*)⁽¹³⁾ my most recent job a month ago and _____ (*not find*/still)⁽¹⁴⁾ anything else. So now I _____ (*live*)⁽¹⁵⁾ with my parents until I _____ (*find*)⁽¹⁶⁾ a new job – an awkward set-up since they _____ (*tell*/always)⁽¹⁷⁾ me I _____ (*need*)⁽¹⁸⁾ to stop watching television and spend more time looking for employment.) Anyway, in spite of my low self-confidence, I _____ (*decide*/finally)⁽¹⁹⁾ to approach Jenn and say hello. When I _____ (*step*)⁽²⁰⁾ up to her, the two friends _____ (*talk*/still)⁽²¹⁾ to each other.

'Hello,' I said. She _____ (*not say*)⁽²²⁾ anything. I continued. 'It's me, Jake. _____ (*you*/remember*)⁽²³⁾ me? We _____ (*go*)⁽²⁴⁾ to high school together.'

At that point, her friend said 'Listen, I _____ (*meet*)⁽²⁵⁾ a friend for lunch in half an hour, so I've really got to get going.' And she was off.

I was now alone with my high school crush. 'Erm, yeah, of course,' she said. 'But it _____ (*be*)⁽²⁶⁾ a long time, though. How _____ (*you*/be*)⁽²⁷⁾ since high school? What _____ (*you*/be*)⁽²⁸⁾ up to since we _____ (*see*/last)⁽²⁹⁾ each other? _____ (*you*/live*)⁽³⁰⁾ here all his time? I think this is the first time we _____ (*run*)⁽³¹⁾ into each other. Where _____ (*you*/work*)⁽³²⁾?'

It was so painfully obvious that Jenn _____ (*not have*)⁽³³⁾ any idea who I was. I suddenly _____ (*find*)⁽³⁴⁾ myself tongue-tied and _____ (*not know*)⁽³⁵⁾ what else to say. I thought about her friend who _____ (*leave*/just)⁽³⁶⁾ a moment before. 'You know, Judy, I _____ (*meet*)⁽³⁷⁾ some friends for a drink in a bit, so I _____ (*have*)⁽³⁸⁾ to say goodbye. See you soon!' And I _____ (*walk*)⁽³⁹⁾ away as quickly as I could.

How humiliating. I _____ (*hope*)⁽⁴⁰⁾ I _____ (*see*/never)⁽⁴¹⁾ her again. If I do, believe me, I _____ (*keep*)⁽⁴²⁾ walking. I _____ (*look*)⁽⁴³⁾ the other way. Then again, who _____ (*know*)⁽⁴⁴⁾ – I _____ (*not stop*)⁽⁴⁵⁾ thinking about her since our paths _____ (*cross*)⁽⁴⁶⁾ that day.

Exercise 30. Read each of the three sets of four sentences (1–4; 5–8; 9–12) and decide which description (a-d; e-h; i-l) corresponds to each one. As you respond, put the verbs into the correct form.

1. Interest rates (*rise*) dramatically. Fewer people are taking out real estate loans.
2. Listen to that thunder. It (*rain*) soon.

3. Elizabeth George? Yes, I (*read*) quite a few of her books. They're great.
4. I immediately reminded him that I (already/*call*) him the day before to explain the situation.

    a. a past situation that took place before (= is anterior to) some other situation in the past
    b. a repeated pre-present situation which may happen again, but not necessarily
    c. a pre-present situation that is explicitly shown to affect the general situation now
    d. a future prediction based on some present evidence

5. My plane (*leave*) at 5 sharp next Tuesday. Can you drop me off at the airport?
6. I (*work*) for a temp agency until I find a steady job.
7. Glad you'll be spending the holidays with us – the children (*be*) thrilled when they hear.
8. We (already/*finish*) the work by the middle of the week, so we took Friday off.

    e. a past situation that took place before (= is anterior to) a particular time in the past
    f. a present situation that is presented as being temporary
    g. a post-present situation that is part of some unalterable or timetable arrangement
    h. a future prediction based on knowledge or previous experience

9. I (*leave*) next week for Portugal. I've never been there, and I can hardly wait!
10. John (*started*) his new job sometime last week. So far, he quite likes it.
11. We can leave now. Dad (*find*) the roadmap he was looking for.
12. 'How was your weekend?' 'Splendid. We (*go*) to the seaside with the kids.'

    i. a past situation with a time Adjunct indicating when it happened
    j. a past situation without a time Adjunct in the clause but with an obvious understanding of when it occurred
    k. a recent pre-present situation that is shown to affect the immediate present
    l. a future personal plan that has already been arranged

Exercise 31. Explain the use of the italicized tenses in the following quotes.

1. 'These people's lives *will* never be the same. This is a life-altering event. When I *meet* the families of burn victims I tell them we *are going to become* very good friends, because you *will be coming* back here for years.' Dr. Bill Cioffi, chief of surgery at Rhode Island Hospital, on patients burned in the West Warwick nightclub fire. (*New York Times*, 23 February 2003)
2. 'Prisoners *are being taken*, and intelligence is being gathered. Our decisive actions *will continue* until these enemies of democracy *are dealt with*.' (*New York Times*, 11 April 2004)

3. Dr. Abdel Aziz Rantisi *assumed* the post just last month after a similar attack *killed* the group's founder, Sheik Ahmed Yassin. (*New York Times*, 18 April 2004)

4. A woman kidnapped a newborn six years ago, set fire to the mother's house to make her believe that the baby *had died* in the blaze, and then raised the child as her own. (*New York Times*, 3 March 2003)

5. The outgoing superintendent apologized for the damage the academy *had suffered* as a result of a scandal involving sexual assault of cadet women. (*New York Times*, 1 April 2003)

6. Hoping to counter the sway of conservative Christian groups, a coalition of moderate and liberal religious leaders *is starting* a political advocacy organization. (*New York Times*, 17 November 2003)

7. 'I don't eat ice cream now. I *eat* spinach leaves and vegetables'. Anastasia Vlochkova, one of Russia's best-known ballerinas, who was fired by the Bolshoi Theater, which said she *had become* too fat. (www)

8. The soldier *has been missing* for a week, and a voice on the tape said he *was being held* to trade for Iraqi prisoners. (*New York Times*, 17 April 2004)

9. 'SARS *has been* our country's 9/11. It *has forced* us to pay attention to the real meaning of globalization'. (*International Herald Tribune*, 14 May 2003)

10. The U.N. proposal *would dissolve* the Iraqi Governing Council and replace it with a caretaker government regime. (*New York Times*, 16 April 2004)

Exercise 32. Read the text in Exercise 1 again. Comment on the forms used to communicate aspectual and temporal information.

Exercise 33. A key statement in Chapter 1 is that functions can be expressed by more than one form and that one form can perform more than one function. Can you illustrate both statements with examples from Chapter 4?

5

Modals and modality

1. Introduction: Modal meaning

We have already paid a great deal of attention to verbs in this book. Chapter 2 dealt with auxiliaries versus lexical verbs, particle verbs versus prepositional verbs and verb complementation. Chapter 4 focused on how temporal information and aspectual distinctions are communicated in finite clauses. And yet there is an important issue relevant to the verb phrase in English that we have not yet addressed. So far, we have mainly looked at ways in which factual situations are represented – how, for instance, we refer to a present habit, or refer to a situation that is ongoing at the moment of speech, or refer to a past experience. A topic that still needs to be covered is how we use verbs to represent situations as *non*-factual, that is, as possible or necessary (or as impossible or unnecessary), or as hypothetical or counterfactual.

When situations are no longer represented as facts but as possible or necessary, we say that they are represented as **modal**.[1] The exact definition of **modality** is the source of debate among linguists. In the context of this grammar, we will define modal sentences as sentences that do not represent situations as facts. There are several forms that can be used to express modal meaning. These include modal auxiliaries, such as *may, could, must* or *can*:

(1) Listen, I *may* be late. *Could* you wait for me?
There *must* be some mistake – this *can't* be what I ordered.

Other verbal forms besides modal verbs can represent situations as non-factual as well:

(2) (a) If he *had listened* (= *Had* he *listened*) to me, he would understand.
(b) I wish you *were* more respectful of other people's opinions.
(c) What would you do if you *saw* someone stealing something from a shop?
(d) The president decreed that no more soldiers *be* sent to the front.

The italicized forms above all contribute to a situation being represented as less than factual. In fact, the examples in (2a) and (2b) represent a situation as **counterfactual** (i.e. the situation was not (2a) or is not (2b) the case): *had listened* is a **modal past perfect**, and *were* is a **modal past**. *Saw* in (2c) is also a modal past, but in this case the situation is presented as **hypothetical** rather than counterfactual. *Be* in (2d) is called a **subjunctive**.

There are also ways of expressing varying shades of modality that are not verbal: adverbs such as *perhaps* and *maybe* express modal meaning, as can adjectives such as *likely* and *possible* (as in *It's likely/possible that …*). These relatively transparent expressions of modal meaning are not treated in this chapter. Rather, we will look closely at the ways our definition of modality can be expressed verbally, starting with those forms that are perhaps most typically associated with modal meaning in English: the modal verbs themselves.

---

[1] From this point of view, any situation located in the future is modal. However, we argued in Chapter 2 that the post-present (or future) is also a time-sphere. Since we use particular forms to locate situations in the post-present, we stick to the view that a future tense exists. However, we do not question the fact that the nature of future time situations is inherently different from that of (factual) present time and past time situations. And we also acknowledge the often overlapping realms of futurity and modality (see Section 3.6.1 in Chapter 4).

2. Modal verbs

2.1 The central modal auxiliaries

Can, could, may, might, shall, should, will, would and *must* are the **central modal auxiliaries**. Their syntactic behaviour is characterized by direct *not*-negation, Subject-auxiliary inversion and ellipsis as discussed in Chapter 2, Section 2.2:

(3) *Should* I get her a present? – No, you *shouldn't*.
You *mustn't* forget to bring her a present.
He *may* not be at home. Then again, he *may*. I really don't know.
She *can't* swim, *can* she?

What differentiates these verbs from the auxiliaries *be, have* and *do* is that they do not have a special inflected third-person singular form (*she may* and *he can*, not **she mays* or **he cans*) and that they do not have non-finite forms such as **to should* or **musting*.

Whereas the past tense forms of the auxiliaries *be, have* and *do* very regularly establish past time reference, establishing past time reference with modal auxiliaries is more elusive. To appreciate this, recall that discussions of modality often present the central modals in pairs: *can ~ could, may ~ might, shall ~ should* and *will ~ would*. Given the following pairs, where (4a) and (5a) are situated in the present time-sphere and (4b) and (5b) in the past time-sphere, one might initially conclude that the second modal of each pair is the past tense of the first:

(4) (a) I *can* run really fast now that I've trained.
(b) I *could* run really fast when I was younger.

(5) (a) Some children *may* spend years on a waiting list before a spot opens up at that school.
(b) Back in those days, a child *might* spend an entire day labouring in the fields.

This would be too hasty a conclusion; although *could, might, should* and *would* are morphologically past tense forms of present *can, may, shall* and *will*, they very often do not locate a situation in the past time-sphere:

(6) I *could* help you (= today, tomorrow) if you like.
**I *could* help you yesterday if you like.

He *might* give us a hand (= now) (if we asked him).
**He *might* give us a hand last week.

For that reason, it will be useful throughout this chapter to bear in mind the important distinction between the **past form** of a modal and actual **past time reference**. As we saw in our discussion of aspect and tense in Chapter 4, the two do not necessarily coincide.

The modal auxiliary *need* is different from the central modals insofar as it is restricted to **non-assertive contexts**.[2] Auxiliary *need* is primarily found in the negative form (7a), and to a lesser extent in interrogative clauses (7b). It is not found in assertive contexts (7c):

> (7) (a) You *needn't* worry about me.
> (b) *Need* I say more?
> (c) *I *need* talk to you about something.

Because of this syntactic constraint, auxiliary *need* is not considered a central modal; it is sometimes called a **marginal modal**.

Having presented the principal formal characteristics of the central modal auxiliaries, we will now zoom in on the basic meanings they communicate. Modal auxiliaries tell us that a situation is either possible (8a) (or that it is possible for someone to do something (8b)) or that a situation is necessary (9a) (or that it is necessary for someone to do something (9b)):

> (8) (a) You *can* get coffee from the machine downstairs.
> (b) She *can* swim really well.

> (9) (a) Chapter 4 *must* be read by next Friday.
> (b) You *must* read Chapter 4 by next Friday.

Modal meaning, then, is often defined as being intimately involved with the notions of **possibility** and **necessity**. It is only with the modals *will, shall* and *would*, as in (10), that it is difficult to determine precisely in what ways possibility or necessity is being communicated (see Section 6):

> (10) I *won't* help you. (= I refuse to help you.)
> *Shall* I give you a hand? (= Do you want me to help you?)
> *Would* you mind taking the aisle seat?

Some of the meanings expressed by *will, shall* and *would* are more easily captured in terms of **volition** (see Chapter 4, Section 3.6.1). The extent to which volition is a part of non-factuality is not clear. We will nonetheless include

---

[2]We defined a non-assertive context in Chapter 3 as one that is either negative or interrogative in meaning (see Section 3.2.3.3).

these verbs in our discussion of the central modals since they have the same formal syntactic behaviour.

2.2 Lexical modal verbs

Not all modal verbs are auxiliaries: *need to* and *have to*, both of which are lexical verbs, communicate modal meaning (in this case, necessity) as well. These are called **lexical modal verbs**. Note the use of *do*-insertion in these examples:

> (11) I *need to* explain the situation to him.[3]
>> Do I *need to* say more?/You don't *need to* do anything.
>> I *had to/needed to* pick up Jennifer after school.
>> Why did he *have to* leave?/He didn't *have to* work yesterday.

Lexical verbs that express modal meaning are sometimes called **semi-modal verbs**.

2.3 *Ought to* and forms with *be*

The meaning of *ought to* is quite similar to that of *should*. It is neither a central modal auxiliary nor a lexical modal verb. It has all of the properties of the central modal auxiliaries except one: it is followed by *to*, a trait it shares with lexical *need to* and *have to*. *Ought to* is less common in contemporary English than *should*. This may be because the addition of direct *not*-negation and Subject-auxiliary inversion results in a rather cumbersome construction. The examples marked with the symbol $^\triangledown$ below are perfectly grammatical, but many people avoid using negative and inverted (and especially negative inverted) forms with *ought to*:

> (12) She *should* tell him the truth./She *ought to* tell him the truth.

>> She *shouldn't* tell him the truth.
>> $^\triangledown$She *oughtn't to* tell him the truth.
>> *Should* she tell him the truth?
>> $^\triangledown$*Ought* she *to* tell him the truth?
>> *Shouldn't* she tell him the truth?
>> $^\triangledown$*Oughtn't* she *to* tell him the truth?

---

[3]Note that the lexical verb *need to* (unlike auxiliary *need*) can be used in assertive as well as non-assertive contexts:

I *need to/don't need to* explain the situation to him.

The distinction in meaning between the lexical verb and the modal auxiliary is often quite small. We will return to these verbs in Section 5.3.1.3.

Given that in most cases (but not all – see Section 5.3.1.4) *ought to* is interchangeable with *should*, and that *should* is on the whole the more common of the two, a good rule of thumb is to use the central modal *should* systematically.

Be to is another form which can also express both necessity (13a) and possibility (13b):

> (13) (a) These packages *are to* be delivered to the following address.
> (b) Information about the conference *is to* be found on our website.

Be able to (expressing ability) and *be allowed to* (expressing permission) are sometimes used as alternatives (sometimes optionally, sometimes obligatorily) to the modal auxiliaries *can* and *could*. These **periphrastic forms** (combinations of words rather than a single grammatical form) also express modal meaning.

It should now be clear that we take a broad view of the modal expression of necessity and possibility insofar as we include in the category of modal verbs not only the central modal auxiliaries, but marginal modal auxiliaries, lexical modals and periphrastic expressions as well. While it is important to recognize potential nuances between modal auxiliary ~ lexical verb pairs with similar meaning (the classic example being *must* versus *have to* to express necessity), we will insist on the *potential* for a difference in meaning. Although *must* in certain cases is perhaps more likely than *have to*, there are also cases where insisting on a fundamental difference between the two is futile. The following example illustrates this point:

> (14) Please note that applications *must/have to* be submitted before the end of January.

3. Composition of a modal sentence

Before delving into modal meaning as expressed by modal verbs, we need to point out an important generalization concerning the **composition of a sentence with a modal verb**. Any modal sentence[4] necessarily consists of two parts: (i) a modal meaning of possibility or necessity (M) and (ii) a **proposition** (what is left of the sentence when the modality is taken away) representing a

---

[4]From now onwards, we will use **modal sentence** as a shortcut for 'a sentence with a modal verb' and **modal utterance** as a shortcut for 'the utterance of a sentence with a modal verb'.

particular situation (P). Take for example the sentences in (15) compared to the paraphrased sentences that follow each one:

(15) (a) You *may* be right about that.
   → It is possible (M) that you are right (P).
   (b) You *may* park in front of the garage.
   → It is possible (M) for you to park there (P).

Sentence (15a) is made up of two parts: the basic proposition {*you – be right about that*} and the modal meaning (possibility, expressed by *may*). Paraphrasing modal sentences as in (15) can help to tease apart M from P.

The compositional nature of a modal sentence has some important consequences. The first is that negation can bear either on the proposition, as in (16a), or on the modal meaning expressed, as in (16b). We call this phenomenon the **scope of negation** (see Chapter 3, Section 3.2.3.4). Scope of negation simply refers to whether it is M or P that is negated by *not*:

(16) (a) You *may* NOT be right about that.
   → It is possible (M) that you are NOT right (P).
   (b) You *may* NOT park in front of the garage.
   → It is NOT possible (M) for you to park there (P).

The sentences in (16) are the negative counterparts of (15). As shown, the scope of negation becomes clear when we paraphrase the sentence by teasing apart M from P. P is negated in (16a) whereas M is negated in (16b). Note that *not*, which is always positioned immediately after the modal auxiliary, is not a reliable indicator of whether the scope of negation is over M or P. It may be helpful in our discussion of negation to recall Section 2.2.1 of Chapter 2. We pointed out that auxiliaries have special negative forms in -*n't*, which we call short negatives. This also holds for modal auxiliaries. Thus, the modal verb can be followed by the negative adverb *not* or the special short negative form of the modal can be used. Neither, however, is an indicator of scope: in *You mustn't work too hard*, negation is built into the form of the modal verb, but the scope of negation is over P and not M. This becomes clear as soon as you create the paraphrase *It is necessary* (M) *for you **not** to work too hard* (P).

The basic insight that a sentence with a modal is composed of both M and P is also needed to accurately describe the temporal information contained in a modal sentence. There is a distinction between the temporal location of M on the one hand and the temporal relation between M and P on the other. The temporal location of M is straightforward when the modality is expressed by a lexical modal verb. Look at the sentences in (17), where P = {*she – be back by ten*} and M = *was/is/will be necessary to*. M can be situated in the past, present and post-present time-spheres:

(17) She *had to* be back by ten. (M (= necessity) in the past time-sphere)
She *has to* be back by ten. (M (= necessity) in the present time-sphere)
She *will have to* be back by ten. (M (= necessity) in the post-present time-sphere)

The examples in (17) are easy to grasp given that *have to* is a lexical modal verb. As such, it expresses temporal information via tenses, like any other (non-modal) lexical verb. When it comes to modal auxiliaries, however, the morphologically past form and past time reference often do not correspond. In other words, the past tense form often does not locate M in the past. We illustrated this in (6) above with the modals *could* and *might*, both of which can, but often do not, have past time reference in a main clause.

When they are embedded in a clause containing a past tense verb, all past time modals can locate M in the past. Contrast (18a), where the modals can have past time reference, with (18b), where they cannot:

(18) (a) **He said** we *should/must/might* do it.
(b) We *should/must/might* do it.

Note that the location of M in the past time-sphere is occasionally brought about by a perfect infinitive (= *have* + past participle):

(19) You didn't even attempt to contact me. You *might/could have tried*, at least.
(= It **was** possible for you to try.)

The effect of *have* is particularly clear when we compare the example in (19) with that in (20), in which *have* is absent:

(20) You never even attempt to contact me. You *might/could* try, at least.
(= It **is** possible for you to try.)

The upshot of all this is that the temporal location of modality is more straightforward with lexical modals like *have to* and *need to* than with past time modal auxiliaries.

The dual composition of a modal sentence implies that there is a second piece of temporal information communicated by a modal sentence: the temporal relation between M and P. We have already introduced the notions of anteriority, simultaneity and posteriority in our discussion of tenses in Chapter 4. There can also be a relationship of anteriority ('before'), simultaneity ('at the same time') or posteriority ('after') between M and P. Take a look at sentences in (21):

(21) She may be in her room. (M = *may*, P = {*she – be in her room*})
Simultaneity (it is possible (present possibility) that she is in her room at present)
M and P are simultaneous

She may be back by ten. (M = *may*, P = {*she – be back by ten*})
Posteriority (it is possible (present possibility) that she will be back by ten)
P is posterior to M

He may have missed his train. (M = *may*, P = {*he – miss his train*})
Anteriority (it is possible (present possibility) that in the past he missed his train)
P is anterior to M

In these examples, the perfect marker *have* after the modal is necessary to express the anteriority of P with respect to M. In the case of simultaneity and posteriority, the verb base is used: it is either the context in which the modal utterance occurs or the presence of a future-time temporal Adjunct (such as 'by ten') that enables us to interpret P as being posterior to M. Otherwise, P will often be understood as being simultaneous with M.

Later in this chapter, we will systematically address which forms are used to locate modal meaning in the present, past and post-present time-spheres. Be aware that the distinction between (i) the temporal location of M and (ii) the temporal relation between M and P explains why the temporal information communicated by modal sentences is of different types and, in a certain way, less explicitly communicated than in non-modal sentences.

4. Modal verbs expressing epistemic meaning

4.1 Definition of epistemic meaning

Sometimes a speaker wants to indicate the extent to which she believes a situation is likely to be true (or, more specifically, the extent to which it is possible or necessary). When a speaker has evidence enabling her to conclude that a situation is or is not the case, the sentences that are used to communicate this express **epistemic modality**. The word *epistemic* comes from the Greek word *epistēmē*, meaning 'knowledge': when a speaker uses her knowledge to conclude whether a past, present or future situation is true (possible or necessary), she is making use of epistemic modality. Such evidence, for example, might be that someone's car is in the garage. Based on this evidence, she can use her knowledge to draw conclusions or make deductions such as the following[5]:

> (22) (a) He *must* be at home.
>   (This is necessarily the case.)
>
>   (b) He *should* be at home.
>   He *ought to* be at home.
>   (He probably is – he's usually there when his car is in the garage.)
>
>   (c) He *may* be at home.
>   He *might* be at home.
>   He *could* be at home.
>   (Maybe he is, maybe he isn't; but his car in the garage means his being at home is possible.)

As the paraphrases demonstrate, there is a difference in strength of the modal meaning (necessity ((22a) and (22b)) or possibility (22c)) communicated by the modal verbs: *must* communicates that the speaker is entirely convinced – that it is necessarily the case – that the owner of the car is at home. *Should* and *ought to* are lower on the necessity scale than *must*, leaving more room for doubt, whereas when we use *may, might* or *could*, we simply want to say that the situation is conceivable or possible.

The difference in strength of epistemic necessity (22a) and (22b) is at least partially due to the fact that deductions made are of different types. Simplifying things somewhat, when we use *must* we are making a logical deduction based on what we know or perceive: because A is true (= the car is in the garage), we consider that B is necessarily true as well (= he must be at home). Of course, our deduction may well be totally off the mark. (For example, the owner of the car could be taking a walk and not be home at all.)

When we use *should* (or *ought to*), our deduction is based not so much on logic but rather on what is usually the case. For this sort of deduction, *should* and *ought to* are in practice almost always interchangeable, although *should* is more common.

In the scenario presented in (22) (*He must/should/ought to be at home*), both kinds of deduction are possible. Either we use *must*, logically concluding

---

[5]There is another possibility, which we do not include here: He *will* be at home (see examples (103a) and (107), below). Epistemic *will* often includes a feel of futurity that the other modals in (22) do not. Not all users of English use *will* in this way, and for those who do, there are constraints that we cannot explore fully here. We nonetheless address the use of the modal *will* to express epistemic modality in Section 6.

that a car in the garage means that the owner of that car is at home, or we use *should/ought to*, reasoning that the person is probably at home because they are usually at home when their car is in the garage. This does not mean that *should/ought to* is always interchangeable with *must*, however:

(23) (a) She hasn't eaten all day. She *must be* (*should be) hungry.
(b) Her interview was yesterday. She *should hear* (*must hear) from them soon.

The situation represented in (23a) involves a logical deduction: based on what the speaker knows about nutrition, she considers that hunger follows logically from not eating. In (23b) however, the speaker does not genuinely infer a conclusion. Rather, she refers to the normal course of events: it is a normal procedure to give feedback to candidates about the outcome of an interview. When there is reference to an expected state of affairs, *should* rather than *must* is used.[6]

Might and *could*, which convey epistemic possibility, usually feature lowest on the probability scale, although the difference between *may* and *might/could* in epistemic contexts is minimal. It is true that the past forms *might* and *could* add a touch of tentativeness not present in *may*; we have already referred to this effect in other contexts (see Chapter 4, Section 3.3.3), but the difference in the likelihood of the situation being the case is relatively small.

May, *might* and *could* can be used almost interchangeably in affirmative declarative sentences; in interrogatives, it is principally *could*, and to a lesser extent *might*, that are used to inquire into epistemic possibility. *May* is not used in this case:

(24) Bram *may/might/could* have caught swine flu at school.
*Could/(Might)/*May* Bram have caught swine flu at school?
James seems exhausted. It *may/might/could* be that he's working too hard.
James seems exhausted. *Could/(Might)/*May* it be that he's working too hard?

There is also a restriction with epistemic *may/might/could* with a negative sentence. In this case, however, it is *could not* that is less likely to be used, and *couldn't* is impossible:

(25) (a) The executive board *may/might/could* reach a consensus today.
(b) The executive board *may not/might not/?could not* (*couldn't) reach a consensus today.

---

[6]There is more to the distinction between these two ways of making a deduction than can be described here. This description helps to account for the most important difference between the two.

Although *could not* is unlikely to be used with an epistemic reading in (25b), it is possible with non-epistemic meaning (see Section 5.1): 'it was not possible for them to reach a consensus' (or 'they were not able to'):

(26) The executive board *could not* reach a consensus yesterday.

Note that on the non-epistemic reading in (26), M (the impossibility) is located in the past (= it **was** not possible for them to reach a consensus), whereas on the epistemic reading with *may not* and *might not* in (25b), M is located in the present (it **is** possible that they won't reach a consensus). The paraphrases also show that on the epistemic reading, a situation is not possible (*not* bears on the proposition (25b)); on the non-epistemic reading, the negative word *not* bears on the modality (26). We will address in more detail the impact of *not* on the meaning communicated in a modal sentence in the next section.

A noteworthy subcategory of epistemic possibility is found in cases such as the following:

(27) I *may* be your younger sister, *but* that doesn't mean you can tell me what to do. Britain *may* be an island; seafront property, however, is still at a premium.

These examples are said to be **concessive**: it is obvious that the meaning is not 'it is possible that I am your younger sister/that Britain is an island' – the situations are presented as being not only possible, but actually the case. The speaker concedes that, in spite of the fact that a situation A is true, a correlated situation B is not what one might expect. English uses *may* in conjunction with a concessive word such as *but* or *however* to express this somewhat different kind of epistemic possibility.

4.2 Epistemic meaning and negation

We can also express how *un*likely it is that a situation is the case or how likely it is that a situation is not the case. Let us now imagine that the evidence from which we form a conclusion or make a deduction is the fact that someone's car is *not* in the garage[7]:

(28) He *can't* be at home.[8] (It is not possible that he is at home.)
He *couldn't* be at home. (It is highly unlikely that he is at home.)

---

[7]*Epistemic* modality expresses how certain the speaker is about whether or not a situation is the case. This scale ranges from impossibility (*It can't be John*) to necessity (*It must be John*). Note, however, that the degree of certainty in both cases is the same.

[8]Again, we will save our discussion of epistemic *He won't be at home* for Section 6.

He *may not* be at home. (It is possible that he is not at home.)
He *might not* be at home. (It is possible that he is not at home.)

Notice that we did not list the negative counterpart of all the affirmative sentences given in (22). First, *shouldn't* and *oughtn't to* do not feature in the list. We'll explain why in Section 4.2.1. Another observation is that epistemic *must* does not make use of the corresponding short negative form *mustn't*: when we want to say that it is not possible that a situation is the case, we use *He can't be at home* rather than *He mustn't be at home.*[9] Notice too that *could* moves from quite low on the probability scale to quite high on the scale of improbability with the form *couldn't*. And, following what we showed above in Section 3, the paraphrases demonstrate that in the first two examples it is the possibility (M) that is negated (**impossibility**), whereas in the latter two it is the situation (P) that falls under the scope of *not*. The associated paraphrase 'it is possible that something is not the case' has led some people to use the label **negative possibility**. What all of this shows is that there is more to negation with modals than the simple observation that the addition of *not* has the effect of turning an affirmative statement into a negative statement. We'll address each of the points raised in more detail in the sections that follow.

4.2.1 should not (shouldn't)/ought not to (oughtn't to)

When *not* combines with *should* (or *ought to*), the modal meaning can change. While we are still in the realm of (absence of) necessity, it is not systematically of the epistemic kind:

(29) University fees are soaring. It *shouldn't* cost so much to put a kid through college.

In (29), the speaker is opposed to the actualization of P {*it* (= putting a kid through college) – *cost so much*}. In more technical terms, she refers to the necessary non-actualization of a situation. *Not* negates P, and in doing so establishes prohibition.[10] While it is still modal meaning that is communicated (i.e. a situation is represented as undesirable rather than as a fact), it is quite different from the process of inference associated with epistemic meaning. The speaker in (29) attempts to interfere in the actualization (the realization or 'happening') of a situation. The modality here has non-epistemic meaning, discussed in greater detail in Section 5.

---

[9]The epistemic interpretation of *must not* is addressed in Section 4.2.4.
[10]In other words, prohibition – a label commonly used in discussing modality – refers to the discursive function of the modal utterance.

In (30), however, where *not* also negates P rather than M, the meaning is epistemic. In other words, while *shouldn't* does not feature in the list of negative counterparts given above (in the example in (28), *shouldn't* would establish only non-epistemic meaning (He *shouldn't* be at home = I don't want him to be at home)), it can in other contexts be used to communicate epistemic meaning:

(30) It *shouldn't* cost too much if we do the work ourselves.

Example (30) can be paraphrased 'it is necessarily (= probably) the case (M) that doing the work ourselves will not be expensive (P)'.

4.2.2 may not (?mayn't)/might not (?mightn't)

Note first that it is not usual to use the short negative form with epistemic *may* or *might*[11]:

(31) The car isn't in the garage. He *may not/might not* be at home.
He *?mayn't/?mightn't* be at home.

This formal restriction might seem indicative of the scope of negation and suggest that *not* has scope over P rather than M in (31). Recall, though, that the choice between the adverb *not* and the short negative form of a modal verb is not a clue to the scope of negation: in sentences that express permission, for instance, the short negative form *mayn't* is not usual, even though in this case it is M rather than P that is negated:

(32) You *may not* enter the building. (It is not permitted/possible for you to enter the building.)
*?You *mayn't* enter the building.

4.2.3 cannot (can't) *and* could not (couldn't)

The sentence with *cannot (can't)* in (33c) is the negative counterpart both of epistemic necessity (33a) and of epistemic possibility (33b):

(33) (a) He *must* be at home. (epistemic necessity: {*he – be at home*} is necessarily the case)
(b) He *may/might/could* be at home. (epistemic possibility: {*he – be at home*} is possibly the case)
(c) – No, he *cannot/can't/couldn't* be at home. (epistemic impossibility: {*he – be at home*} is not possible)

---

[11]Many speakers of English never use the forms *mayn't* and *mightn't* at all, opting always for the forms with *not: may not, might not*.

In other words, when we want to communicate an inferred conclusion about a situation that is not the case (i.e. logical or epistemic *im*possibility), we use *can't (cannot)* or *couldn't*. With epistemic *can't/couldn't*, the scope of negation is over M.

Could not does not necessarily express the same meaning as *couldn't*. In theory, *not* may have scope over P, in which a negative epistemic possibility is communicated, or *not* may have scope over the modal, in which case epistemic impossibility is expressed. In the latter case, however, *couldn't* (rather than *could not*) tends to be used. This is an example where the impossibility to use the short negative form is in fact indicative of scope and, as a result, of the kind of modal meaning involved:

> (34) John *can't/couldn't* be at home. (scope over M: It is not possible that he is at home.)
> John *could* not be at home. (scope over P: It is possible that he is not at home./scope over M: It is not possible that John is at home.)

Note that there are constraints on the use of *could not* to express epistemic meaning (see (25)).[12] We will not examine these in more detail here: a useful rule of thumb is to use *couldn't* to express epistemic impossibility.

4.2.4 must not (mustn't)

When we use the short negative form of *must* (*mustn't*), it is less likely that we are expressing epistemic impossibility. An utterance with *mustn't* usually expresses prohibition ('it is necessary not to do something'). Compare *can't/couldn't* versus *mustn't* below:

> (35) (a) The car isn't in the garage. (I thus conclude that) he *can't/couldn't* be at home.
> (b) James *mustn't* be at home when her friends arrive. He doesn't like them.

The kind of modal meaning in these two sentences is not the same. In (35a), we draw an inference and conclude that a situation is not possible; in (35b)

---

[12]As pointed out in connection with example (25b), *could not* does not necessarily express epistemic meaning. *John could not be at home* can also mean that specific circumstances prevented John from being at home (for instance, because he had to work a late shift, it was not possible for him to be back in time to look after the children). *Could* here has past time reference (= it was not possible for John to be at home). This is a case of non-epistemic impossibility (see Section 5).

the speaker attempts to intervene in the actualization of a situation by pointing out that it is important for James not to be at home. As in the case of *shouldn't* in example (29) above, the modal meaning relates to the necessary (non)-actualization of situations. We use the term **non-epistemic modality** to capture this meaning, and it is non-epistemic necessity and non-epistemic possibility that we will address in Section 5.

Although *mustn't* is rarely epistemic (i.e. it almost always expresses prohibition, or 'necessity not to'),[13] the form *must not* can have an epistemic interpretation where the logical conclusion is of the type 'it is necessarily the case that P is not true' (negative epistemic necessity) rather than the conclusion 'it is not possible that P is true' associated with epistemic *can't/cannot*:

> (36) My logic is that if people complain about computer support/stability issues, they *must not* know how to fix it. (www)
>
> [S]ome people – who *must not* realise this is 2014 and not the medieval era – still take issue with a woman feeding her baby in a public space. (www)

In (36), the paraphrases are 'it is necessarily the case that people do not know how to fix it' and 'it is necessarily the case that (some) people do not realise this is 2014'; *not* here has scope over P rather than M, in contrast with epistemic *can't/couldn't* (cf. (33c)), where the scope of negation is over M: 'it is not possible that … '.[14]

Table 5.1 gives an overview of the epistemic and non-epistemic meanings with *not*. While the distinction between 'negative possibility' and 'impossibility' may be somewhat abstract, it should be clear that *He may not come* is ambiguous out of context.

The set of examples in (37) illustrates the meanings of each of the forms listed in Table 5.1. When the full forms with *not* are given in parentheses, it means that they are also possible without any change in meaning.

---

[13]Examples in which *mustn't* expresses epistemic impossibility can be found, as the following example illustrates. We maintain that such cases are rare and that they will be judged odd or impossible by many speakers:

> Can someone please raid Pharrell William's wardrobe and clear it of shorts? Pharrell regurgitated his Oscar's look from 2014 when he also wore shorts to a prestigious red carpet event. Sadly he *mustn't have realised* that it wasn't a good look then and isn't now. (www).

[14]This interpretation in terms of negative epistemic necessity, whereby *not* has scope of P, is the necessity counterpart of negative epistemic possibility, as on one reading of *He could not be at home* (example in (34)).

Table 5.1 Survey of modal meanings expressed by *must, should, ought to, may, might, can* and *could + not* (references are to the examples in (37))

	Epistemic impossibility	Epistemic negative necessity or possibility	Non-epistemic prohibition/ absence of permission
mustn't	−	−	+ (a)
must not	−	+ (b)	+ (a)
shouldn't	+ (c)	−	+ (d)
should not	+ (c)	−	+ (d)
oughtn't to	−	−	+ (e)
ought not to	−	−	+ (e)
may not	−	+ (f)	+ (g)
might not	−	+ (h)	−
can't	+ (i)	−	+ (j)
cannot	+ (i)	−	+ (j)
couldn't	+ (k)	+ (l)	+ (m)
could not	? (k)	−	+ (m)

(37) (a) You *mustn't* (*must not*) read with the lights off – it's hard on your eyes.

(b) Whoever said diamonds were a woman's best friend *must not* (**mustn't*) know how many beautiful and extravagant purses there are. (www)

(c) His plane has just landed. It *shouldn't* (*should not*) take him much time to get here.

(d) He *shouldn't* (*should not*) be up so late. Tomorrow's a school day.

(e) He *oughtn't to* (*ought not to*) be up so late. Tomorrow's a school day.

(f) He *may not* (**mayn't*) attend the meeting. If he's too busy, he'll have to miss it.

(g) You *may not* (**mayn't*) attend the meeting. It's for senior executives only.

(h) He *might not* (**mightn't*) attend the meeting. If he's too busy, he'll have to miss it.

(i) But she *can't* (*cannot*) be getting married – she met him only two weeks ago!

(j) She *can't* (*cannot*) get married until she's 18. Her parents won't allow it.[15]

(k) She *couldn't* (?*could not*) be getting married – she met him only two weeks ago!

(l) You *could* always *not* (*always *couldn't*) go if you don't want to.

(m) She *couldn't* (*could not*) get married until she was 18. Her parents wouldn't allow it.

---

[15]Note that in (j), M is located in the present time-sphere whereas it is located in the past time-sphere in (m).

4.3 Epistemic meaning, aspect and situation types

There can be important interaction between the type of modality the speaker intends to convey and the aspectual form of the verb following the modal. Similarly, there can be interaction with the situation type expressed in P. When considered out of context, the necessity modals are very likely to be interpreted as expressing epistemic meaning when followed by a progressive infinitive (as in (38)) or by a State verb (as in (39)). Otherwise, the hearer is likely to interpret the utterance as an order (as in (40)) rather than understand that the speaker is expressing her opinion about the likelihood of a situation:

(38) He's not at the office today. He *must* be working at home. (a logical conclusion regarding the P {*he – work at home*} – dynamic verb, progressive aspect)

(39) They spend six months a year in France – they *must* love it there. (a logical conclusion regarding the P {*they – love it there*} – State, non-progressive aspect)

(40) The contract states that he *must* work at home. They won't provide him with an office. (according to the contract, the P {*he – work at home*} is necessary – dynamic verb, non-progressive aspect)

In (38), it is hard to imagine a context where the speaker would be giving an order: here, progressive aspect establishes epistemic reading unequivocally. Conversely, non-progressive aspect in (40) is very closely associated with non-epistemic meaning. It is clear why this generalization is irrelevant when it comes to States. As you will recall, States are very seldom used with progressive aspect; in a decontextualized sentence such as *You must know the answer* (*know* being a State verb *par excellence*), it would seem that an epistemic interpretation is the most likely one (= you necessarily know the answer).

The unmarked link between aspect, situation type and modal meaning is not absolute: sometimes contextual information overrides the more usual modal ~ aspectual combinations. For instance, if we mention the fact that John is a full-time freelance writer, someone might very well deduce the following:

(41) He *must* work at home most days: most freelance writers do.

In spite of non-progressive aspect, the meaning in (41) is clearly epistemic. What is important here is that there is reference to a habit. Accordingly, even though the situation is an Activity rather than a State, there is reference to a stative situation. On the other hand, consider the following sentence:

(42) The children *must* be hiding.

Without a specific context, (42) will likely be interpreted as epistemic (= I logically conclude that they're hiding since I can't see them anywhere). Given the proper context, however, it can have non-epistemic meaning:

(43) The children *must* be hiding when grandma arrives; otherwise, it'll spoil the surprise.

These generalizations do not hold for possibility markers *may, might* and *could* when they locate M in the present time-sphere. Each of the following expresses epistemic meaning irrespective of situation type or aspect used:

(44) For all you know, he *may* love his job. What makes you think he doesn't?
(State, non-progressive aspect)

They *might* leave tomorrow. Then again, they might not.
(Achievement (dynamic), non-progressive aspect)

Sorry to spring this on you, but I *could* be leaving earlier than planned.
(Achievement (dynamic), progressive aspect)

In this section we have shown how modals can be used to reflect the degree of certainty that the speaker has about a situation being the case. We have analysed the impact of *not* on the meaning communicated, and we have shown that the short negative forms do not necessarily communicate the same meaning as the forms with *not*. We have also highlighted the interaction between modal meaning on the one hand and aspect and situation types on the other. We will now address non-epistemic modality and comment on the forms used to express non-epistemic possibility and non-epistemic necessity.

5. Modal verbs expressing non-epistemic meaning

5.1 Non-epistemic meaning

Modal verbs do not always indicate how likely we believe it is that a situation is (or is not) the case. We also use modal verbs to communicate an entirely different message, one where we want to say that it is necessary or possible for a situation to occur or that it is necessary or possible for someone to do something. In this case we are dealing with the necessity or possibility of the actualization of situations. We call this kind of modal meaning **non-epistemic**.[16] We provide some examples below:

(45) You *must* be back by twelve at the very latest.
   Whales *must* surface in order to breathe.
   She *has to* work harder if she wants to pass her exams.
   If you don't like the neighbourhood, you *ought to* consider moving.
   You *should* take more exercise. It'll help you lose that extra weight.
   Our proposal has been refused. We're all fired. *Need* I say more?
   Foreigners *need to* have lived in France for several years to be naturalized.
   You *are to* read the first two chapters before next week.

   Drinks *can* be bought from the machine downstairs. (mere possibility)
   Epileptic seizures *may* be brought on by strobe lights. (mere possibility)
   He *could* swim at the age of 3. (ability)
   She *can* play the clarinet extremely well. (ability)
   You *can* have two biscuits if you like. (permission)
   Thank you for your help. You *may* leave now. (permission)

You are probably used to referring to non-epistemic necessity and non-epistemic possibility in more transparent terms such as ability and permission rather than in terms of non-epistemic modality. But clearly, when you give someone permission to do something, this presupposes that you believe the action referred to can in theory actualize: permission presupposes possibility. In the same way, if you have the ability to do something, this means that your physical or intellectual state is such that it is possible for you to bring about a situation. In the examples of mere possibility with *can* and *may*, we are not saying much else than that a situation is possible. In all cases we are saying that a situation is possible or necessary or that it is possible or necessary for the Subject referent to do something. The paraphrases that follow make it clear that this characterization captures the core of meaning of all the examples in (45):

(46) It is necessary for you to be back by twelve at the very latest.
   For whales to breathe, it is necessary for them to surface.
   etc.

   Buying drinks from the machine downstairs is possible.
   It was possible for him to swim at the age of 3.
   It is possible for you to have two biscuits if you like.
   etc.

---

[16]**Root modality** is a term that is also commonly used to refer to non-epistemic meaning.

While the subclasses of non-epistemic modality illustrated in (45) seem to be clear-cut, meanings can overlap, as will be clear from the following examples:

(47) Thanks to the new machine, we *can* assemble 100 cars per hour. (ability and mere possibility)
The dose *can* be doubled to last through the night or for long car journeys. (permission and mere possibility)

We use the term 'non-epistemic possibility' as a general term that distinguishes this kind of modal possibility meaning from epistemic possibility. Non-epistemic possibility is made up of three discrete categories: ability, permission and mere possibility. For the sake of clarity, we will always add 'mere' to 'possibility' when we refer to this subclass of non-epistemic possibility. The term 'mere' here is neutral. It simply indicates that the idea of possibility is the only one communicated. In other words, it refers to the notion of possibility where the notion of ability or permission is absent.

We will now address each of the non-epistemic meanings and comment on the forms used to express them.

5.2 Non-epistemic (im)possibility

5.2.1 Permission
5.2.1.1 Can and may

Granting **permission** (the act whereby a speaker's utterance results in the hearer's being allowed to do something) as in (48) is usually expressed by the modals *can* and *may*.

(48) You *can* throw away those old shoes if you want to.
You *can* have as many helpings of this as you'd like.
If you promise to behave, you *may* sit at the table with the grown-ups.

In (49), the examples illustrate a speaker asking for permission:

(49) I've been working on this for hours. *Can* I stop now?
Can I park on this street if I don't have a local resident sticker?
May I have your full name and date of birth, please?

Can is the unmarked form used to express permission. *May* is used in more formal contexts or in contexts in which the speaker wants to highlight the difference between the hierarchically superior party granting permission and the hierarchically lower party to whom permission is granted. For reasons of politeness, speakers will sometimes avoid the use of linguistic signs that are indicative of differences in status when giving permission. This is less the case when it comes to asking for permission, where the use of *may* can be indicative of a politeness strategy enabling the speaker to show respect. Put more simply, it is always possible to use *can*, whereas the use of *may* can seem odd in contexts where social hierarchy is not important.

May has come to be used in fixed expressions such as *if I may* or *if I may say so*:

(50) Let me explain, if I *may*, why your solution won't work.
If I *may* say so, I think that's a very bad idea.

Although they literally mean *if you will allow me to* or *if you will allow me to say so*, these expressions are no longer understood as genuinely asking for permission. In the same way, a waiter saying *May I suggest the sea bass?* is not really asking a customer for permission, but simply wants to show respect. Indeed, by asking the question the waiter has already made the suggestion.

Be allowed to is generally not possible when the permission given is of the speaker ~ hearer type. In other words, *Can I smoke here?* can be used either to ask the hearer for his permission or to inquire whether it is generally allowed. With *Am I allowed to smoke here?* the speaker is not asking the hearer for permission; she wants to know if there is a rule or a law forbidding smoking.

Note that *could* (and, to a lesser extent, *might*) can also be used to request present-time permission:

(51) *Can/May/Could/Might I sit here?*

Could and *might* cannot be used to grant or refuse permission, however:

(52) *Yes, you can/may/*could/*might.*

This makes sense: in Chapter 4, we saw that past forms can be used to be less direct and to convey tentativeness in the present time-sphere (see Sections 2.2.2.2 and 3.3.3). In (51), the use of *could* or *might* conveys tentativeness on the part of the speaker asking for permission. The paraphrase 'Would you *possibly consider* giving permission?' helps to make this effect more transparent. An explanation for why *might I ... ?* as a more tentative form of *may I ... ?* is less common than *could I ... ?* for *can I ... ?* is that *may I ... ?* is already a polite form: the addition of tentativeness is not felt to be necessary outside the most formal of contexts. In short, when the past form *might/could* is used in a request for permission, there is an overlay of epistemic meaning: 'perhaps permission will be granted'. The notion of 'perhaps' is what makes the request for permission tentative. When it comes to giving permission, however, there is no need for a similar mitigating strategy: permission is granted or refused (i.e. with positive permission (you are allowed to) or negative permission (you are not allowed to)).

5.2.1.2 Absence of permission

As shown in (53), absence of permission is communicated by negating *can* or *may* with *not* (*cannot* or *may not*) or with the short negative form *can't*. The use of *may not* again highlights the hierarchical difference between the authority refusing permission and the hearer in the same way as it does in an affirmative clause giving permission:

(53) No, you *may not* sit at the table with the grown-ups.
No, you *cannot* throw those shoes away – they're as good as new.
Can't I park on this street if I have a local resident sticker?

Not has scope over the modal (see Section 3: it is not possible for you to do it).

As pointed out in Chapter 2 (Section 3.1), negative interrogatives have a specific rhetorical effect. The use of a negative interrogative clause to request permission has the effect of putting additional pressure on the hearer to grant permission. For example, a speaker might choose to use *can't I* instead of the more neutral *can I* to follow up on or reformulate a request when permission has already been denied. It has a more persuasive feel to it than the corresponding affirmative forms:

(54) (teacher) Put away your phone, please. You can't use it in class.
(student) But I'm not texting. *Can't* I use it to see what time it is?

In (54), the student has already been denied permission and tries to tip the scales in favour of a 'yes' by using *can't*. Here, for example, it will be interpreted as a kind of counterproposition.

5.2.1.3 Past permission or absence of permission

When we want to refer to (absence of) permission in the past, *could* (*could not/couldn't*) is used, or a paraphrase with the past tense form of *(not) be allowed to* or *(not) be permitted to*. *Might* is not used to express past permission.

(55) Only a few generations ago, women often *couldn't/weren't allowed to* go to college.
At that time, foreigners *could/were permitted to* visit the country without a tourist visa.
As a child, I *couldn't/wasn't allowed to* play outside until I'd done my homework.
Was there ever a time when you *could/were permitted to* park your car wherever you wanted?

What is important to understand in the examples in (55) is that there are no temporal boundaries to (the lack of) permission in the past time-sphere. This is often referred to as 'general permission', 'unlimited permission' (unlimited in time, that is) or 'theoretical permission': it results either from the use of a State or from the fact that there is reference to a (potentially) repeated situation (i.e. there is reference to a stative situation).

If we want to refer to a specific situation in which permission was granted or refused, we use a form of *be allowed to* or *be permitted to*. *Could* is not used in this case:

> (56) When I first asked to record the concert, my request was refused. But in the end, they changed their mind, and I *was allowed to/permitted to* (*could) bring my recording equipment with me.

In the examples expressing general past permission in (55), *could* is also possible in addition to *be allowed to* and *be permitted to*. *Could* cannot be used in (56), however. This is because the situation 'bring my recording equipment' is explicitly represented as having actualized. In (55), in contrast, there is reference to situations that were (potentially) repeated in the past without any specific actualization being referred to. Similarly, the sentence in (57) says what concert-goers were allowed to do, but nothing about what they actually did (although we might infer that such situations did in fact actualize in the past):

> (57) Not long ago, concert-goers *could/were allowed to/were permitted to* bring their mobile phones into the venue. It wasn't until recently that artists started banning such devices.

5.2.1.4 Future permission or absence of permission

In order to refer to future time (absence of) permission, we use *will (not) be allowed to* (or, less commonly, *will (not) be permitted to*):

> (58) The actress's son is serving a twenty-year prison sentence but *will be allowed to* attend his mother's funeral next week.
> Starting on Monday, drivers *won't be allowed to* make a right turn at the intersection between 7 am and 7 pm.

At first sight, it might seem that *can* and *may* can also be used in similar future time contexts:

> (59) You *can* spend the night at your cousin's next Saturday as long as your aunt agrees.
> Students *may not* remain in the residence halls during the upcoming winter holiday.

Note, though, that in (59), the permission itself (M) is situated in the present time-sphere (with reference to a posterior situation (P)); with *will (not) be allowed (permitted) to* (58), both the permission (M) and the event (P) are located in the post-present time-sphere.

5.2.2 Ability
5.2.2.1 Can

In addition to expressing permission, *can* also communicates ability in the present. **Ability** refers to the physical, intellectual or perceptual capacity to do something:

> (60) He *can* run a marathon in under two and a half hours.
> *Can* the interpreters speak any non-European languages?
> I *can* see the mountains from here. *Can* you, too?

In much the same way as *be allowed to* can in some instances paraphrase *can* with reference to permission, the periphrastic expression *be able to* is sometimes used to express ability, but not without certain constraints. For example, when we refer not to general ability but ability in the process of being actualized at the moment of speech, *be able to* is generally not used:

> (61) I *can/am able to* swim 30 laps without stopping even once.
> Hey, look at me! I *can* (*am able to) swim without armbands!

Manage to is an alternative form for *be able to* and is often used when there is more explicit reference to an obstacle to overcome for the situation to actualize. As a result, the (exceptional) skill of the Subject referent is brought to the fore. It is interesting to observe how, in (62b), the same observation holds, although given the meaning of *fail*, it is the (exceptional) lack of skill here that is highlighted:

> (62) (a) How *do* you *manage to* get so much done with a full-time job?
> (b) How on earth *did* you *manage to* fail such an easy exam?

The category of ability includes examples with inanimate Subject referents or Subject referents that do not have the potential to consciously perform an action:

> (63) If the conditions are right, a virus *can* mutate very rapidly.
> Our deluxe conference room *can* comfortably seat up to 100 participants.

The examples in (63) do not have Subject referents that can intentionally make use of a skill. However, since there is reference to an inherent characteristic or an inherent capacity that is predicated of the Subject referent – and since it is the nature of the Subject referent that lies at the origin of the characteristic referred to – we consider that they belong to the ability class as well.[17]

We pointed out in Sections 3 and 5.2.1.1 that the past tense forms of the modal auxiliaries do not always establish past time reference. In such cases, M may be located in the present, the past form having the effect of making the utterance more tentative. When *could* is used to communicate ability in declarative sentences, however, it has past time reference and does not convey tentativeness. Tentativeness strategies do not seem to be compatible as such with the idea of ability: one either has or does not have the innate or learned skills to do something, meaning there is no need for a form that expresses 'tentative ability'.

Could expressing ability can have present time reference but only in two specific contexts. The first is with an interrogative clause which functions as a request:

(64) *Could* you lift this box, please?

The issue is not whether the hearer is physically capable of lifting the box or not, but rather whether he is willing to do so. A paraphrase makes it clear that *could* establishes present time reference: 'is it possible for you to … ?' 'do you have the ability to … ?' So while at the literal level the inquiry is into ability, the speaker is actually understood to be inquiring into the hearer's willingness to lift the box. There is once again (see p. 276) an overlay of epistemic meaning (Is it *maybe* possible for you to lift the box?). In other words, the example in (64) illustrates a politeness strategy since the utterance leaves space for a response to the literal meaning of ability: 'I'm afraid I can't' means 'I do not have the physical ability to lift the box'. Refusal to do so is communicated only indirectly. In fact, it is not always possible to know whether the negative reply is motivated by physical inability or by unwillingness. Note that the short answer *I'm afraid I couldn't* is not appropriate here. As pointed out before, there are only two possibilities when it comes to ability: one either has the ability (*I can*) or not (*I can't*).

In the second case, *could* has present time reference when it is explicitly clear that there is reference either to potential actualization of ability in a hypothetical context (as in (65a)) or to counterfactual ability (as in (65b)). In other words, the person either has the present ability but is not making present use of it (65a) or does not have the present ability now (65b):

---

[17]Given that *may* is sometimes used instead of (the more usual) *can* in cases such as the examples in (63) above, a mere possibility interpretation (see 5.2.3 below) is not impossible here.

(65) (a) If you *could* just explain it in English, I might understand what you mean.
So, will you say it again, please, but in English?
(b) If only she *could* explain it in English, I might understand what she means.
Unfortunately, she doesn't speak English.

5.2.2.2 Inability

As in the case of absence of permission, inability is communicated by negating *can*:

(66) (a) He *can't* run a marathon in under two and a half hours.
(b) *Can't* the interpreters speak any non-European languages?
(c) I *can't* see the mountains from here. There's too much fog.

Notice (66b), which is not unlike the permission example in (54). Again, the negative interrogative communicates the speaker's stance with respect to the question: she deems that an affirmative answer is the only reasonable one (= 'I'm sure they can', or 'they should be able to'). For this reason, such an utterance is often used to convey surprise or reproach: there is an expectation that the interpreters can or should be able to speak non-European languages, and the speaker considers that this expectation is being challenged (see Section 5.2.1.2).

5.2.2.3 Past (in)ability

Past ability is communicated by *could* or a past form of *be able to*:

(67) At that time, he *could* run a marathon in under two and a half hours.
Couldn't the interpreters speak any non-European languages?
There was no fog that morning. I *could* see the mountains perfectly.

The examples just given all illustrate 'general ability', or 'unlimited ability' (unlimited in time) or 'theoretical ability', with reference to a State or to a stative situation. If the speaker wants to refer to a situation in which the ability actualized (i.e. in which the Subject referent made use of his skills to do something), a past form of *be able to* or *manage to* has to be used unless the verb is a verb of perception (*see, hear, taste, feel*), in which case *could* is possible as well. This is also possible with certain other State verbs (e.g. *understand*):

(68) Thanks to his intensive training, he *was able* to run the marathon in record time.
Their Arabic had become a bit rusty, but they *managed to* get their point across.
There was fog that morning, but I *was able to/could* see the top of the mountain anyway.
We *were able to/could* understand everything they were saying.

Note that in negative sentences *couldn't* is used to refer to general inability or non-actualized ability. Negative sequences tell you that the Subject referent did not manage to do something. In other words, either he did not have the skills to do something (general inability (69a)) or, even though he tried to make use of his ability and skills to achieve something, the actualization failed (non-actualized ability (69b)):

(69) (a) The apprentice plumber *couldn't* fix sinks yet. He hadn't learned.
(b) The plumber *couldn't* fix the sink; he had to order a missing part.

5.2.2.4 Future (in)ability

As in the case of permission, a periphrastic form rather than a modal has to be used if the ability is located in the post-present time-sphere. Here, the periphrastic form is *will be able to*:

(70) Some claim that in the future, we*'ll be able to* spend our holidays in outer space.
Rogue governments *will be able to* build and use nuclear weapons if we do not intervene.

It is possible to use *can* to refer to present ability (71) or inability (72) with future actualization, but *can* is impossible if it involves a change in ability between the present and the post-present time-sphere:

(71) (a) Sarah *can* speak Italian with our clients from Milan at next week's meeting.
(b) *Sarah's just begun an Italian class. In two months' time, she *can* speak Italian fluently.
(cf. Two months from now, she *will be able to* speak Italian fluently.)

(72) (a) I *can't* walk with you to the city centre tomorrow. I have to take my car.
(b) *I *can't* walk tomorrow. I'm being operated on today and will be off my feet for a few days.
(cf. I *won't be able to* walk tomorrow as I'm being operated on today.)

The potential ability to 'speak Italian' (71a) and 'walk' (72a) exists both now and in the post-present time-sphere. However, the potential inability to speak Italian in (71b) will not exist until a future point in time, just as the potential ability to walk in (72b) will not end until a point posterior to the moment of speech.

5.2.3 Mere (im)possibility

Mere possibility is a convenient cover term for uses of non-epistemic possibility that do not express permission or ability. It is expressed by *can*. In more formal contexts, *may* is sometimes used as well:

> (73) Use of this medication *can* (or *may*) cause unpleasant side effects.
> The female of this rare species *can* (or *may*) grow up to 25 centimetres in length.

In such sentences, we simply state that a situation is theoretically possible: the state of the world or the circumstances are such that it is possible for a particular situation to actualize.[18] When in doubt use *can* rather than *may* to express mere possibility.

Be to can express mere possibility as well when followed by a passive infinitive:

> (74) Many species of bird *are to be seen* in the more remote areas of the county.
> Delightful nature walks *are to be discovered* throughout the area.

To refer to mere possibility in the past, we use *could*:

> (75) Ether, used as an anaesthetic in the nineteenth century, *could* be extremely dangerous.
> Scientists believe that the sauropod dinosaurs *could* live for up to 100 years.

To refer to mere possibility in the future, we use *will be possible*:

> (76) It *will be possible* to cross the river once the water level has gone down.

Having given an overview of the non-epistemic possibility meanings, we can turn to non-epistemic necessity. There is a whole set of verbs that can communicate non-epistemic necessity, and while the semantic core is that of 'necessity', there are some differences in the shades of meaning. We will address these in the next section.

---

[18]In examples like 'Children can be cruel' or 'Lighting can be dangerous', there is a touch of habitual meaning as well: children are sometimes cruel (or some children are cruel) and lightning is sometimes dangerous.

5.3 Non-epistemic necessity and non-epistemic prohibition

5.3.1 Modal verbs

There is an impressive range of verbs that express non-epistemic necessity in English, including *must, have to, need to, should, ought to, be to* and (auxiliary) *need*. Pinning down the exact difference in communicative effect between each of these modals is quite a challenge. While it is possible to find sentences illustrating varying shades of meaning, there are actually many contexts in which the same non-epistemic necessity modals seem to be interchangeable without any dramatic change in meaning. Consider the following examples:

> (77) If emergency access is required, then the entrant *must* only touch what they *have to* and *must* simply make the area safe. The person responsible for the area *must* be contacted as soon as possible. (www)

In all three instances of *must*, the person conveying this message directs (with a degree of speaker authority) what to do in a certain circumstance (here, an emergency). It is fairly clear here that the speaker of the utterance is the source of the necessity. This same speaker makes use of *have to* to refer to what ordinarily has to be done in these circumstances – the source of the necessity here is of the general type and is not perceived as stemming from the speaker. *Have to* cannot be replaced by *must* here. However, in the pairs in (78) and (79), where each sentence in the pair is both semantically and lexically similar to the other, they seem to be interchangeable. The modal verbs reflect a potential difference in strength rather than a fundamental difference in meaning to be captured in terms of the source of the necessity:

> (78) The problem of global warming is a real and dangerous one and *must* be tackled as soon as possible before it is too late. (www)
> Domestic violence *has to* be tackled as soon as possible so that those involved are not permanently damaged by their experiences. (www)

> (79) If the consumer has paid any money before exercising the right to cancel, a full refund *has to* be made as soon as possible and in any event within 30 days. (www)
> Section 3.46 states that a refund *must* be made as soon as possible after the cancellation but within 30 days at the latest. (www)

Some linguists have looked at the source of the necessity and have tried to associate particular sources with particular modals. The general argument is that *have to* communicates 'external obligation' whereas *must* communicates 'speaker ~ hearer obligation' (with the speaker as the source of necessity in affirmative statements (*I'm telling you to*) and the hearer as the source of necessity in questions (*Do you want me to?*)). As shown in (77), there is certainly evidence that this distinction can exist, but it is definitely not the whole story, as the examples in (78) to (79) illustrate.

There does not appear to be a limited set of criteria or features that is sufficient to define and contrast unambiguously the different shades of meaning of non-epistemic necessity. The following guidelines, however, can be useful in choosing a modal verb to express non-epistemic necessity:

5.3.1.1 Unmarked necessity with *have to*

The unmarked form to communicate non-epistemic necessity meaning is *have to*. If you use this form to say that a situation is necessary or that it is necessary for someone to do something, the sentence will nearly always be acceptable. The source of the necessity is often felt to lie outside the speaker:

(80) Sorry, but I *have to* go now. I have an appointment with my shrink.
You *have to* book your ticket in advance if you want to pay less.
My sister *has to* work two jobs. Otherwise, she just can't make ends meet.

5.3.1.2 *Must*

Must communicates a particularly pressing or strong obligation. It can be either an obligation that results from an inward urge (as in the first sentence in (81)) or an obligation stipulated in regulations. *Must* is used in public notices or rules, for instance, which communicate quite clearly that there are to be no exceptions:

(81) I simply *must* find the opportunity to invite him over.
All visitors *must* sign in before visiting the premises.
Hikers *must* stay off these trails in order to preserve the natural habitat.
Students *must* remain seated until the exam time has expired.
Your parking permit *must* be displayed at all times on your vehicle's windscreen.

As pointed out above, *must* has traditionally been associated with an obligation in which the speaker is identified as the source of the necessity. In affirmative sentences, it is the speaker who is the source of the modality (*She must = I (the speaker) am telling her to*); in interrogatives, it is the hearer (*Must we? = Do you (the hearer) want us to?*). Because of this feature, the modality is sometimes said to be **discourse-oriented** (or speaker ~ hearer oriented). Much like *may* when it is used to ask for or grant permission, *must* often reflects the difference in hierarchic status between the speaker and the hearer. In the final example in (82), we find a case of self-imposed obligation. This is also a case of speaker ~ hearer obligation, only here the speaker is directing the obligation to herself rather than to the hearer:

(82) You *must* give it back to me.
They *must* stop making so much noise. It's disturbing the neighbours.
She *must* finish her meal before she can have dessert.
I *must* be going now. I hope I haven't overstayed my welcome.

Orders given with *must* are not only rather pressing, but they can also serve to remind the hearer of his (lower) hierarchic position with respect to the speaker. As with *may*, such blunt indications of power relations do not often occur in real life and are perhaps overrepresented in pedagogical grammars. The principal characterizing feature of *must* seems to be the strength of the obligation rather than the source that the obligation originates in. As such, it can very often be (and often is) replaceable by *have to*.

This notion of strength is exploited to achieve certain rhetorical effects, as for instance when formulating an enthusiastic recommendation or invitation:

(83) You *must* go and see that exhibition. It's absolutely amazing.
You *must* come and visit us in our country home. We'd just love to have you.

The examples in (83) express non-epistemic necessity, but it is not necessity in the sense of imposing an obligation. It is simply a context in which the speaker is being particularly earnest.

5.3.1.3 *Need to*

Need to as in (84) is a quite neutral expression of necessity which, like *have to* and *must*, can be paraphrased as 'it is necessary to'. Like *have to*, it is very common, and in many instances there is no important difference between the two. *Need to*, though, is quite often used when the speaker has a clear purpose, outcome or goal in mind:

(84) You *need to* work hard if you want to succeed.
I want to buy a new computer, so I *need to* save money.

Another typical context is one in which there is reference to internal necessity:

(85) He *needs to* talk to his mother at least once a day.
(= He feels the need to, or feels compelled to.)
I *need to* feel valuable in the workplace. Otherwise, I lose my motivation.

Need to, like *have to,* is a lexical modal verb. Both require *do*-insertion in inverted interrogative clauses and negatives:

(86) We *need to/have to* remodel our kitchen sometime soon.
Do you need to/Do you have to have a shower before we leave?
Tell them they *don't need to/don't have to* bring anything.

Although it is subtle, there is one potential difference between *need to* and *have to.* Unlike *have to, need to* does not always express necessity in the strictest sense, that of giving an order or expressing an obligation. In many cases, *need* primarily points to an existing lack of something which can only be overcome by bringing about a situation. The idea of necessity is certainly not absent in the following examples, but it does seem to take second place to the expression of need:

(87) We *need to* understand more about this drug before we put it on the market.
(lack of understanding at the moment of speech: we do not yet understand)

To process the form, I *need to* know the last four digits of your social security number.
(lack of information at the moment of speech: I do not yet have these numbers)

Apart from the different syntactic contexts in which the auxiliary *need* (as in *you needn't do it*) and the full verb *need to* (*you (don't) need to do it*) occur (see Section 2.1), certain speakers recognize shades of meaning between the two. For them, auxiliary *need* is felt to be more speaker ~ hearer-oriented than *need to.* In negative declarative sentences, the speaker is felt to be the source expressing lack of necessity; in interrogative sentences, it is the hearer. Note that *need to* can be used in these contexts as well – many speakers use *need to* almost exclusively:

(88) You *needn't* do it. (I don't think it's necessary for you to do it.)
(*You don't need to do it* is also possible here with the same meaning.)

Need she stay at home? (Do you think it's necessary for her to stay at home?)
(*Does she need to stay at home?* is also possible here with the same meaning.)

On the other hand, *not need to* is the usual form used to refer to general lack of necessity, that is, necessity not stemming from the speaker – *needn't* is not ordinarily found in such contexts:

(89) He *doesn't need to* be told he's addicted to his mobile – he knows it.
(?He *needn't* be told this.)
You *don't need to* have exact change to get a soft drink from this machine.
(?You *needn't* have exact change.)

It is best to use lexical *(don't/doesn't) need to* if you are not sure which is more appropriate.

Another difference in meaning exists between *needn't have (done)* and *didn't need to (do)*. Like *should have (done)* and *ought to have (done)*, *needn't have (done)* refers to a counterfactual situation, that is, a past situation that was not necessary but that actualized nonetheless:

> (90) You *needn't have checked* the file for typos – I'd done it already.
> (The file was checked for typos twice.)
> Thanks so much, but really, you *needn't have brought* flowers!
> (This is a sort of politeness strategy – upon seeing the flowers, the speaker expresses appreciation by saying that the gesture was not necessary.)

Didn't need to also refers to a situation in the past that was not necessary. Here, though, the idea is that because it was not necessary, no action was taken:

> (91) I *didn't need to check* the file for typos. My colleague had already done it.
> (The file was checked for typos only once.)
> My sister had already bought flowers at the supermarket, so I *didn't need to buy* any.
> (I realized it was unnecessary to buy any, and therefore did not.)

Using *didn't need to (do)* instead of *needn't have (done)* is possible provided the context brings out the counterfactual meaning. This means that the sentences in (92) can have the same meaning as the sentences in (90):

> (92) You *didn't need to check* the file for typos – I'd done it already.
> Thanks so much, but really, you *didn't need to bring* flowers.

The opposite is not true: using *needn't have (done)* necessarily implies that some unnecessary action was taken. When the context makes it clear that no action was taken, only *didn't need to (do)* is possible:

> (93) He told me I *didn't need to check* the file for typos, and so I didn't.
> (*He told me I *needn't have checked* the file for typos, and so I didn't.)
> They knew they *didn't need to bring* flowers, and so they didn't.
> (*They knew they *needn't have brought* flowers, and so they didn't.)

5.3.1.4. *Should* and *ought to*

When used to express non-epistemic necessity, *should* and *ought to* both express the idea that the situation being referred to – based either on the speaker's subjective point of view or on some societal norm – is fitting, right or appropriate. Given that the meaning is often simply that the situation is 'a good idea', it is the form most often used to give advice. Negative forms express that it is necessary not to do something, or that doing it is not 'a good idea':

> (94) You're working too hard; you *should* (*ought to*) ask for some time off.
> (asking for some time off is a good idea)
> You *shouldn't* (*oughtn't to*) work such long hours; you'll exhaust yourself.
> (working such long hours is not a good idea)

It has been argued that *should* is more speaker-oriented than *ought to*, but in most cases, differences in meaning between *should* and *ought* are hard to pin down and are not very important. More helpful to the learner is the fact that *should* is considerably more common than *ought to*. Note, though, that *should* can be found as a weaker version of *must* (where it is not paraphrasable by any of the shades of meaning given above), in which case *ought to* is impossible:

> (95) (owners' manual) This laser printer *should* (*ought to) be kept out of direct sunlight.
> Interested applicants *should* (*ought to) turn in all relevant forms at the same time.

Should and *ought to* are clearly less forceful than *must* and *have to*. As a result, it is *should/ought to* that will be used in a context of 'escapable obligation':

> (96) He *should/ought to* (*must) tell her to stop, but he won't. He's too non-confrontational.
> I know I *should/ought to* (*must) keep my opinions to myself, but I don't like him.

5.3.1.5. *Be to*

Be to is used to refer to an obligation resulting from a formal order (97a) or is the formal order itself (97b):

> (97) (a) I *am to* prepare a brief presentation on Monday.
> (b) You *are to* apologize to your sister at once!

5.3.2 Past non-epistemic necessity

Have to, need to and *be to* can have past-time inflections. Accordingly, the use of past tense forms expresses necessity in the past:

(98) We all *had to* pitch in and help clean up the mess.

They *needed to* wait nearly a year before the adoption papers were approved.

My mother was categorical: I *was to* apologize to my sister immediately.[19]

The other modal verbs expressing non-epistemic necessity (*must, should, ought to, needn't*) do not have a form that unambiguously conveys past time. The base form can have past time reference only when it is used in reported speech and embedded in a main clause with a past tense:

(99) I insisted that he *must* finish painting the bathroom (and he did).

He told me I *should* leave (and so I left).

You suggested that I *ought to* get a new dictionary (so I bought a new one yesterday).

I insisted that he *needn't* bring anything (and this explains why he brought nothing).

In each of these cases, the modal situation of necessity lies in the past ('it was necessary to'). The bracketed additions show that P may actualize in the past sector. However, the actualization of P is not necessarily past when the forms are embedded in a main clause; P can also have present or future time reference:

(100) I insisted that he *must* finish painting the bathroom (and I hope he will).

He told me I *should* leave (but I'm not going anywhere).

You suggested that I *ought to* get a new dictionary (so I'm going to buy one tomorrow).

I insisted that he *needn't* bring anything (so I'm sure that he won't).

Should, ought to and *needn't* can have past time reference (i.e. M can be located in the past sector) when they are followed by a perfect infinitive (*have* + past participle). Note, though, that when followed by a perfect infinitive to establish past time reference, the necessary situations that the clause refers to (P) did not actualize (or, if the clause is negative, did actualize):

(101) You *should have tried* harder (but you didn't).

She really *ought to have told* him the truth (but she didn't).

You *needn't have brought* champagne (but you did).

---

[19]Incidentally, this is also a case of free indirect speech. See Section 3.7.1 in Chapter 4.

5.3.3 Future non-epistemic necessity

To situate necessity in the post-present time-sphere, *will* is combined with *have to* or *need to*:

> (102) Eventually, the government *will need to* make some unpopular decisions.
> In two years' time, everyone *will have to* file their taxes electronically.

6. *Shall* and *will*[20]

The verbs *shall* and *will* traditionally feature in the list of core modal auxiliaries. While they share the formal characteristics of the core modals, their meanings cannot always be captured in straightforward terms of possibility or necessity. The question as to whether their different uses are modal or temporal is one that we will not address in detail in this book. Some are clearly modal. These include the epistemic necessity use of *will* (103a) or the (less common) non-epistemic necessity use of *shall* (103b):

> (103) (a) That'*ll* be John. Could you let him in, please?
> (b) Don't argue with me, young man: you *shall* do as I say!

Other uses of *will* and *shall* are more difficult to understand as referring to a non-factual situation or as being crucially concerned with possibility or necessity. Furthermore, it is not always obvious what the relation is between modal meaning and temporal meaning. These are theoretical questions that go beyond the scope of this discussion. What we will look at here are the more practical aspects of using *will* and *shall*.

6.1 *Shall*

We saw in Chapter 4 that, in theory, *shall* is a formal alternative for *will* in the first person when it is a future tense marker. This particular use of *shall* is not common in North America:

---

[20]In Chapter 4, we presented a system of tenses and time-spheres that includes a future tense: *Tomorrow, he will turn fifty*. When dealing with forms that refer to future time, however, we pointed out that there is no unanimous view on whether or not a future tense actually exists in English. One of the reasons for rejecting the existence of a future tense is that we are no longer referring to facts in the same way as when we look at the past or the present: it is inherent in future time reference that, to a certain degree, we are making a prediction. Futurity, then, is closely related to the discussion of modality insofar as its reference to factual situations is necessarily different from straightforward reference to the past and present.

(104) I *will* (or *shall*) be away for some time.
We *will* (or *shall*) address these questions at a later time.

The speaker refers to a future situation and in doing so makes a prediction. From that point of view, one might argue that sentences of this type convey epistemic meaning, albeit of a different kind from that discussed earlier in this chapter. As pointed out in Chapter 4 (note 18), the use of the contracted form *'ll* is very common in spoken English, meaning that it is not always clear whether we are dealing with *will* or *shall*.

In the context of legal documents (especially contracts), *shall* can communicate obligation and *shall not* prohibition. This context might be useful to recognize but is not one that the ordinary user of the language is likely to make wide use of:

(105) Neither party *shall* be entitled to enter into agreements or other arrangements on behalf of the other and it is intended that both parties *shall* retain their independence. (www)
The parties *shall not* engage in any activity, practice or conduct which would constitute an offence under Bribery Act 2010. (www)

One common use of *shall*, however, is in questions communicating an offer of service or a suggestion; often, other modals can be used in this context as well:

(106) *Shall* I drop you off at the station? (*Can* I … ? *Would* you like me to … ?)
Shall we go now? (*Should* we … ?)

All and all, *shall* is on the decline everywhere in the English-speaking world. Simply put, it is often replaceable by another modal.

6.2 *Will*

Will can be used as a marker of strong epistemic necessity:

(107) That *will* be the postman.

The meaning here is very close to *That is the postman*; epistemic *will* is used in a context where certainty is high (for example if the deduction is based on the fact that the postman always arrives at the same time). *That must be the postman* is also very close in meaning. In any case, the use of *will* here is comparatively rare and subject to constraints, which is why we do not include it among the other modals in our general discussion of epistemic modality in Section 4.

As we mentioned in Chapter 4, *will* also communicates volition, which is often regarded as a major category of non-epistemic modality in classifications of modal meanings. Negative *will not* (or the short negative *won't*) is interpreted as refusal, that is, the opposite of volition:

(108) I *will* give you a hand if you like.
My car *won't* start (= 'refuses' to start).

When negative *won't* is used in a yes-no interrogative clause, the Subject referent is pushed into giving an affirmative answer:

(109) *Won't* you come with us tonight? We'd love it if you did.
Won't you stay for a while? It's been such a long time.

We also pointed out in Chapter 4 (Section 3.6.1) that the speaker may choose to use progressive aspect, which can serve to disambiguate between modal meaning (*will* + non-progressive) and temporal meaning (*will* + progressive):

(110) (a) *Will* you *stay* for dinner? (= invitation, willingness: do you want to stay?)
(b) *Will* you *be staying* for dinner? (= inquiry into the future: are you going to stay?)

(111) (a) I *won't* come to the meeting. (= present time refusal)
(b) I *won't* be coming to the meeting. (= the future non-actualization of the situation)

In (110b) and (111b), the progressive does not convey its unmarked meaning of ongoingness.

Finally, a use of *will* that is likely the most distantly related to modality as we have discussed it in this chapter is to refer to what some call characteristic behaviour:

(112) She loves reading. Sometimes she'*ll* read (or *she reads*) for hours alone in her room.
People *will* often complain (or *people often complain*) if you don't answer their e-mail right away.

The sentences in (112) show that, with this meaning, there is little difference between *will* + verb base and the (non-progressive) present tense.

It is interesting to observe what happens to the meanings when the past form *would* is used. As is clear from the examples below, in some cases, *would* communicates past time, as in (113). In other cases, *would* makes it clear that the situation referred to is posterior to the other situation referred to in the main clause, as in (114). It can result in a more tentative statement with the same meaning as *will*, as in (115). In still other cases, it establishes hypothetical meaning, as in (116):

> (113) My car *wouldn't* start. (cf. My car *won't* start.)
> As a child, she *would* read for hours at a time.[21] (cf. She *will* read for hours at a time.)

> (114) He asked me if I *would* help him. (cf. *Will* you help me?)
> I told him I *would* be coming. (cf. I *will* be coming.)
> I told him I *wouldn't* come. (cf. I *won't* come.)

> (115) *Would* you (or *will you*) give me a hand, please? I need your help.

> (116) If we lived closer to each other, we *would* see each other more often.

Will followed by a perfect infinitive (*will have done*) can be used to draw a conclusion about a situation located in the past time-sphere. It is more common than the epistemic *will* in (107) above. Its meaning is close to 'I conclude now (M) that something in the past happened/was the case (P)'. This use is illustrated in the following example:

> (117) Pro-whaling countries [...] failed to muster a majority today that would have allowed them to set the agenda at the International Whaling Commission's annual meeting. The failure *will have pleased* the British delegation, which is among those arguing against the return of commercial whaling after a ban of almost 20 years. (www)

The meaning of *will* in (117) is clearly modal: the speaker draws a conclusion on the basis of her knowledge. An unusual strategy is used in this sentence: it is as though the speaker shifts her perspective from the present to the future and chooses to draw a conclusion about a situation located in the past (the fact that the British delegation were pleased) at a future moment in time, even if we know that the conclusion is one that is drawn at present.

---

[21] *Would* communicates the idea of habit in the past in this example. *Used* to can do so as well:

   (i)   As a child, she *used to* read for hours at a time. (cf. (113))
   (ii) She *used to smoke* (= she's an ex-smoker)./She *didn't use to smoke* (= but now she does).
   (iii) There *used to be* (*would be) a church on that corner.

Used to conveys that idea the situation is no longer the case. The example in (iii) shows that *used to* can also refer to a past State rather than a past habit. This is not possible with *would*. Note that *to* is an infinitive marker: it is followed by the base form of the verb. In *She's used to reading for hours at a time*, *used* (= accustomed) is an adjective, and *to* is a preposition, followed by an *-ing* clause.

Recall that in our discussion of the future perfect in Chapter 4 (Section 3.6.6), we visualized the temporal structure of the future perfect as shown in Figure 5.1. This means that *will* followed by a perfect infinitive can also refer to a situation that is located in the post-present time-sphere, as in the following example:

> (118) For mainstream journalism, blogging is yesterday's news. Twitter is currently the focus of media ridicule, but next month the circus *will have moved* on to something else. (www)

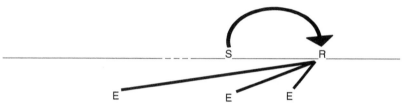

Figure 5.1 Representation of the future perfect in terms of E, R and S.

In (118), the P {*the circus – move on to something else*} is located in the post-present time-sphere, which is not the case for the P in example (117), above. Note that in this kind of example, it is more difficult to tease apart the modal shades of meaning (prediction) from the temporal meaning (future time reference): in (118) the idea of inference or logical conclusion comes less to the fore than in (117).

This completes our discussion of modal verbs and the meaning(s) they express. In the following sections, we address other verb forms that represent situations as less than factual.

7. The subjunctive

7.1 Form

We began this chapter by saying that modal sentences do not represent situations as facts and that this kind of meaning can be communicated by several forms. One of the forms we mentioned was the **subjunctive**. When it comes to the subjunctive, English differs from languages like Spanish and French in two respects. To begin with, the form is invariable. The form the subjunctive takes is always identical to the verb base[22]:

---

[22]Some grammars call the use of *were* in *if*-clauses (*If I/she were rich*) or in inverted structures (*Were she/I rich*) a **past subjunctive**. We analyse these as modal pasts, albeit with a form different from the indicative past form, where we find *was* (rather than *were*) with a first- and third-person Subject. *Were* (alongside *was*) is also found after *I wish: I wish I were (was) rich*.

(119) The board requires that two files *be* submitted for your application.
It is imperative that he *arrive* on time effective immediately.

A second difference is that the form is less commonly used than in many other languages that have a subjunctive. In English, the subjunctive is used in a limited number of rather formal contexts.

7.2 Contexts of use

The first context in which the subjunctive is used is in subordinate *that*-clauses after main clause verbs like *advise, ask, demand, insist, propose, recommend, request, require, suggest* and *urge*, or after nouns like *condition, demand, request, requirement, suggestion* and *wish*. It is also found after adjectives such as *crucial, desirable, essential, necessary* and *vital*. In other words, it is used in contexts in which volition is expressed, meaning that the speaker wants a certain situation to be brought about. This is often called the **mandative subjunctive**, and in British English, it is often replaced by *should* followed by the verb base. The subjunctive is more common in North American English, whereas *should* + verb base is often preferred in British English:

(120) They demanded that he *return* the library books immediately. (or 'that he *should return*')
I suggest that you *speak* to him directly. (or 'that you *should speak*')
My suggestion that he *find* a new job was unpopular. (or 'that he *should find*')
It is crucial that a teacher *remain* aware of her students' needs. (or 'that a teacher *should remain*')

The subjunctive is particularly common in (though certainly not restricted to) journalistic texts:

(121) [Zaha Hadid's] plane taxied from its stand, developed a minor fault, and stopped. She refused to believe the reassurances that the delay would be brief, and demanded that she *be* put on another flight. (*Guardian*, 8 September 2013)
The *New York Post* reported that Mr. Cosmo was released on the condition that he *remain* confined to his parents' home with electronic monitoring and private guards while awaiting trial. (*New York Times*, 27 July 2009)

The present subjunctive also features in idioms or set expressions. Some examples include the following:

(122) God *bless* America; God *save* the Queen; God *forbid*
     if need(s) *be*
     so *be* it
     suffice it to say
     far *be* it from me

Here are a few examples in context:

(123) If need *be*, I can type the letters myself.
     She's not coming? So *be* it! I didn't want her to come anyway.
     I can't go into detail, but *suffice* it to say that he's not doing well.

8. The modal past and the modal past perfect

Modal indicative forms are important markers of modal meaning. In their unmarked use, indicative forms refer to facts. However, they can be used in contexts in which they acquire modal meaning: part or all of their normal temporal meaning disappears. A very common use of modal indicative forms is in the *if*-clause of a conditional sentence:

(124) (a) I'd love it if you *came*. Please do try to make it.
     (b) If she/I *were* rich (*was* is also possible), she'd/I'd buy a yacht.
     (c) If you *had come*, you would have met my boyfriend.

It should be clear that the past form *came* in (124a) does not communicate past meaning: it refers to a future situation. Particularly important in the context of this chapter is the idea that such situations are not represented as facts but as possible situations or as counterfactual situations. This is the main reason we say that the past here is modal. One peculiarity concerns the verb *be*, as in (124b): when used as a modal past after *if*,[23] *be* usually has the form *were* with all Subjects, although *was* (with first- and third-person singular subjects, that is) is often found as well.[24]

---

[23]*If* does not necessarily introduce a conditional clause; it also functions as a subordinator in embedded questions as an alternative for *whether*, as in the following examples (see Chapter 1, Section 3.1.4):
    He asked me whether/if I *had had* a good time at the party last night.
The past perfect has its unmarked temporal meaning here (anteriority in the past) and does not communicate modal meaning.
[24]Although we can say both *If I was rich...* or *If I were rich*, the form **If I was you...* is considered incorrect by many speakers of English.

In a similar way, the past perfect becomes modal in *if*-clauses (124c): like the indicative (or non-modal) past perfect, it establishes past time reference, but here it is not used to represent one situation as anterior to another (recall E before R before S from Chapter 4). Rather, the past perfect here communicates counterfactual meaning in the past: there is reference to a situation which in theory could have actualized but did not.

Sentences with a modal past conditional clause (in conjunction with a main clause with *would* + verb base) are often called **hypothetical** conditionals (125a); sentences with a modal past perfect conditional clause (in conjunction with a main clause with *would* + perfect infinitive) are called **counterfactual** conditionals (125b):

> (125) (a) We *would be* greatly *honoured* if you *agreed* to speak at our conference.
> (hypothetical: perhaps you will, perhaps you will not)
> (b) What an honour it *would have been* if he *had agreed* to speak at our conference.
> (counterfactual: he did not agree to speak at the conference)

While these are the canonical sentence types associated with hypothetical and counterfactual meaning, other combinations of forms are possible as well. A modal past can also be used to refer to a counterfactual situation in an *if*-clause if it has present time reference, in which case *would* + verb base (with present time reference or future time reference) or *would* + perfect infinitive (with past time reference) can be used in the main clause:

> (126) If I *were* good at maths (NOW), I *wouldn't be struggling* to solve this equation (NOW).
> If I *were* good at maths (NOW), I *wouldn't have struggled* to solve this equation (PAST).
> If I *were* good at maths (NOW), I *would pass* tomorrow's test without any problems (FUTURE).

Similarly, while there is usually past time reference in the canonical counterfactual past perfect + *would have* construction (127a), other temporal constellations are possible as well ((127b) and (127c)):

> (127) (a) If I *had been* good at maths (PAST), I *would have passed* yesterday's test (PAST).
> (b) If Breughel *had been living* now (NOW), he *would have been making* films (NOW). (www)
> (c) If you *had phoned me* tomorrow (FUTURE) instead of today, you *wouldn't have reached* me (FUTURE).

The following are some more contexts in which modal indicative forms are used:

(128) I *wish* she *didn't complain* so much. It's really tiresome.
    (counterfactual: she does complain a lot)
I *wish* you *hadn't told* everyone I was pregnant.
    (counterfactual: you did tell everyone I was pregnant)
Even if he *had* enough money to invest, he wouldn't spend it on real estate.
    (counterfactual: he does not have enough money to invest)
She looked completely indifferent. It was *as if* she *hadn't heard* a word I said.
    (counterfactual: she did hear what I said)
It*'s (high) time* someone *told* him his behaviour is unacceptable.
    (hypothetical: I'm hoping someone will tell him)
He*'d sooner* we *talked* about the matter in private.
You can come tomorrow if you like, but I*'d rather* you *came* on Friday instead.

A modal past or a modal past perfect is used after a form of *wish*, after *(would/'d) rather* or *(would/'d) sooner*. It communicates counterfactuality in clauses introduced by *even if* and *as if*, and it refers to a hypothetical situation when it is used in a clause after *it is (high) time*. Note that when *wish* is followed by the past future (*would* + verb base), the meaning communicated is not counterfactuality. Rather, it has future time meaning:

(129) I wish you *didn't smoke*. (counterfactual: you do smoke)
I wish you *hadn't smoked*. (counterfactual: you did smoke)
I wish you *wouldn't smoke*. (said to discourage someone who is about to light up)

9. Conclusion

In this chapter, the focus was on verbal forms that do not represent situations as facts. Table 5.2 sums up the forms that establish modal meaning.

Table 5.2 Verbal forms that express modal and non-modal meaning

	Forms	
Modal meaning	Subjunctive	So *be* it!
	Modal past	I wish you *didn't drink* so much.
	Modal past perfect	If only you *had stayed* with her.
	Modal auxiliaries	You *may* be right.
		He *could* have forgotten.
		You *must* work harder.
Non-modal meaning	Indicative forms	He *is* tired.
		He *left* at 8 this morning.

Modal verbs either communicate epistemic meaning or non-epistemic meaning. Some contrastive examples are given of non-epistemic/epistemic necessity and non-epistemic/epistemic (im)possibility in Table 5.3.

Table 5.3 Epistemic versus non-epistemic meaning

	Epistemic	Non-epistemic
Possibility	The door *may* be locked.	The door *can* be locked from inside.
Necessity	You *must* be exhausted after such a long hike.	You *must* eat something before going on that long hike – I insist.
Impossibility	She *can't* be as young as she says she is.	She *can't* get into the club because she's too young.

We trust that the discussion of modality in this chapter – especially as concerns modal verbs – has given you a clear idea as to how the concept of modality fits into the grammar of English. It should also be clear at this point that aspectual distinctions are relevant when we add modal meaning to the equation. We have also shown that there is very delicate interaction between situation types, various facets of temporal reference and modal meaning. In this respect, it is useful to bear in mind the distinction between the modal meaning and the proposition expressed, as negation likewise interacts in different ways with these two components that make up a modal utterance. And once again, we have insisted on the importance of keeping distinct the very basic notions of form and function.

In the final chapter, we will focus on aspects of grammar that relate to the wider discourse: we will look at ways in which semantic links are established between clauses and between sentences and study the grammatical features that contribute to cohesion in a stretch of speech or written text.

Exercises

Exercise 1. Identify the kind of modality expressed in the following utterances. Is the modal meaning in each case epistemic or non-epistemic? Does it express necessity or possibility?

1. You must come and visit us sometime. The kids haven't seen you for ages.
2. His oldest son must be at university by now. He's at least twenty years old, isn't he?
3. The baby must be sleeping. I haven't heard any crying for some time now.
4. I may be back at work on Monday. It depends on what the doctor says.

5. You may go back to work on Monday, but do take it easy for another week or so.
6. You should be able to get a table for four at that restaurant if you get there before 8.
7. You should get to the restaurant before 8 if you want a table for four. It's a busy place.
8. Candidates for the job must have finished their degree at the time of application.
9. She must have finished the race well before me – she was waiting for me at the finish line.
10. Next time, look both ways before you cross the street – you might have been killed!
11. The soldier has not been seen for over a week. His unit thinks he might have been killed.
12. Daniel Radcliffe has become a contemporary art collector, despite the best efforts of a New York dealer who wanted a more high-profile client than the world's most famous teenager. The dealer must not have watched Radcliffe grow up year by year on camera. (www)
13. (amateur photography contest) The closing date for entries is Tuesday 23 June at midday. All entries must not have been previously published anywhere. (www)
14. He met all the requirements for the position. He could have applied for it, but in the end he didn't.

Exercise 2. Consider the forms in italics in the utterances below and determine whether or not they locate the modal meaning in the past time-sphere. In other words, is the verb paraphrased as 'it is possible' or 'it was possible'?

1. *Could* I borrow your pencil?
2. I *could* swim much faster before I started smoking.
3. *Could* you help me, please? I'm too short to reach that box.
4. He *might* be willing to do the job himself.
5. We'd been told that it *might* be hot in Madrid during the summer.

Exercise 3. Consider the forms in italics in the utterances below and determine whether or not they locate the situation in the past time-sphere.

1. I guess you're right, but if he *was* there, I didn't see him.
2. If he *were* here, he'd be able to tell us what to do.
3. It's high time you *took* a real holiday. Go to the seaside for a week.
4. They *took* a week-long holiday at the seaside last August.
5. They *weren't* surprised when they *heard* she had resigned.

Exercise 4. Determine in the following sentences whether the scope of the negation is over the proposition or over the modal verb. Provide a paraphrase demonstrating your understanding.

1. (a) On my way to the meeting, I suddenly said to myself, 'You know, you could not go to the meeting and just make up an excuse.' And then I went straight back home.
   (b) Unfortunately, I could not go to the meeting and had to ask a colleague to fill me in on what I'd missed.
2. (a) Sorry, but John may not accompany you on the camping trip. He's grounded for the next two weeks.
   (b) John may not accompany us on the camping trip after all. Things are a bit difficult at home, and he's not sure he'll be able to get away.
3. (a) He's a non-native speaker, but you needn't speak to him so slowly. He's lived here for years and understands our language perfectly.
   (b) He's a non-native speaker, but you mustn't speak to him so slowly. His English won't improve unless he hears it spoken at normal speed.

Exercise 5. Make the following utterances negative using *not*. Then determine whether the scope of the negation is over the proposition or over the modal verb. If two interpretations are possible, explain.

1. He may have another bowl of ice cream.
2. There might be enough time to change the document.
3. He has to work next weekend.
4. I can help you finish the project this afternoon.
5. You should tell her about it.
6. What he said about her might be true.

Exercise 6. Use the cues below to determine what you would say in the following situations; use modals to formulate your utterances. Some situations refer to granting or refusing permission, and some to asking for permission. Explain your choices when more than one form is possible.

1. You really want a puppy. Your father has already refused. Say please. Promise to take care of it by yourself.
2. You'd like to know if it's okay to park in front of your neighbour's house for a few minutes.
3. At the end of an interview, you'd like to ask a couple of questions about the job.
4. You tell your cousin that it's not a problem if his son plays in the garden.
5. You're speaking to a slightly hostile committee and tentatively want to make just one small suggestion.
6. You want to persuade your parents to let you watch, just this once, a television programme that's on late at night. (It's a school night. They're likely to refuse.)
7. You apologize to a library card holder but explain that borrowing encyclopedias is not allowed.

8. You've been told that people are not allowed to borrow encyclopedias from the library. You want to persuade the librarian to let you borrow a volume for just one hour.
9. You're a teacher. Tell your students that if they work silently for fifteen minutes, you'll let them leave ten minutes early.
10. You're a teacher. Tell your students that using a calculator during the maths test is not allowed.

Exercise 7. Which of the following situations refer to mere possibility, and which modals can you use here to express it? What sort of modality is expressed in the other sentences, and which modals can you use to complete them?

1. You _____ sleep in my bed. I'm happy to sleep on the couch for the night.
2. Sunbathing _____ permanently harm your skin. Use appropriate protection at the beach.
3. Potted orchids _____ grow heartily in almost any climate.
4. That _____ be poison ivy – I wouldn't go near it if I were you.
5. Tell Peter that he _____ stay for dinner if he likes. He should call home first, though.
6. Further information concerning our degree programme _____ be found on our website.
7. I _____ be 72 years old, but sometimes I feel as young as when I was 20.
8. Our vitamin supplements _____ cause slight allergic reactions in some people.
9. My sister lived in Europe for ten years. She _____ speak French, Italian and German.
10. It _____ take up to a week for a letter from the United States to arrive in France.

Exercise 8. Use *may, might, can* or *could* in the following sentences. There may be several possible answers. What generalizations can you make regarding which forms can and cannot be used? Some of the sentences express epistemic possibility whereas others do not. Comment on the kind of modality illustrated in each sentence.

1. He looks like a sweet child, but appearances _____ be deceptive. He's quite a trouble-maker.
2. Have you seen my briefcase? I can't find it. – I don't know. _____ it be next to the computer?
3. Whose glasses are these? – I don't know, but they _____ be Aaron's.
4. _____ there be another, more ecological solution to disposing all this waste?
5. Some people _____ come to the picnic with their children, so let's organize some activities.
6. My parents _____ not come for Christmas this year, depending on the price of tickets.

7. I'm taller than all my brothers and sisters. – That _____ be, but that doesn't mean you have any authority over them.
8. You've made strong claims about the results. But _____ you be wrong about some things?
9. It _____ rain this afternoon. You really should take your umbrella just in case.
10. I've taken a look at the financial report. The situation _____ not be as bad as we'd thought.
11. Check your policy closely. Your basic health insurance _____ not cover long stays in hospital.
12. You and your friends _____ organize the party in our basement if you want.

Exercise 9.

(i) First, decide whether *mustn't* or *needn't* best completes the sentences below. In some cases (but not all), both are possible. Explain your choices, paying particular attention to contexts where both *mustn't* and *needn't* are possible – what is it about the context of certain sentences that allows both to be used?

(ii) In those sentences where only *needn't* is possible, can you think of other forms that can complete the sentences without changing the basic meaning? What about the sentences where only *mustn't* is possible? Be able to explain your choices.

1. I _____ forget to ring up my mother tomorrow. She turns 50.
2. You can bring a bottle of wine if you'd like, but you _____ bring a thing. There'll be plenty.
3. Rebecca is flying into town this weekend. It's a big secret, so if you see Adam, you _____ let on that you know.
4. Thanks for putting me up for the night. You _____ make a fuss. I won't be any trouble.
5. Travelling through Europe _____ cost a fortune. Inexpensive accommodation is out there.
6. Children, you _____ speak so loudly. It's late, and you're liable to wake up the neighbours.
7. Doing the housework _____ be a chore – doing a bit every day makes it manageable.
8. The fact that you can't speak any foreign languages _____ stop you from travelling abroad.
9. You _____ worry about me, I've been camping hundreds of times.
10. You _____ book a room in advance; at that time of year there are not many tourists.
11. You _____ leave those tools outside overnight. If it rains, they'll rust.
12. If you need a little extra help from me, you _____ hesitate to ask. I'd be happy to help.

Exercise 10. Find a verb that can logically complete the sentences below. Use the same verb in (a) and (b). In one sentence, use *didn't need to* (+ verb base); in the other, use *needn't have* (+ past participle). Explain your choices. Can you think of any other modal forms that can be used with similar or different meaning?

1. (a) They insisted when they invited us that we _____ anything, so we arrived empty-handed.
   (b) We _____ our umbrellas after all. It's going to be sunny and warm all afternoon.
2. (a) The flat we rented was furnished. That's why we chose it. We _____ any new furniture.
   (b) We really _____ so much food. How are we ever going to eat all of it before it goes bad?
3. (a) We _____ here. It was a waste of petrol. We should have walked or taken our bikes.
   (b) Where's your car? – You know, our place is only a fifteen-minute walk from here, so we _____.
4. (a) I _____ to the doctor's. He said an over-the-counter cough suppressant was all I needed.
   (b) You _____ to so much trouble. It must have taken you weeks to organize. Thanks a lot!
5. (a) I'm going to be much too early for my appointment. I _____ so early. What was I thinking?
   (b) Since we _____ before that afternoon, we spent the entire morning lazing around.

Exercise 11. Choose the correct form or forms in the following sentences. There may be more than one correct answer, in which case you must choose all correct answers. Be able to justify your choices.

1. According to this book, goldfish [*might/can/could/may*] live for up to thirty or even forty years. So that fish of yours [*might/can/could/may*] even outlive you!
2. French citizens travelling to Italy [*don't need to/needn't/don't have to*] have a passport. Their national identity card is enough.
3. You [*had better/should/ought to*] take an umbrella with you. It [*could/may/ought to/might*] rain this afternoon.
4. In my opinion, young children [*should/had better/ought to*] spend more time with their grandparents.
5. When I was a child, my mother [*would sing/sang/will sing/used to sing*] to me every night at bedtime.
6. Peter called on his mobile to say he [*might/can/would*] be late. Traffic's bad again.
7. Ask your father before you call to book a room, just to be sure. He [*might/can/will*] have done it already.

8. They [*couldn't/weren't able to*] find the key I'd hidden. Still, in the end they [*were able to/could*] get inside since the next-door neighbour had a spare.

9. [*Can/Could/May*] I stay out until midnight? –Yes, you [*can/could/may*].

10. Years ago, people [*used to/would*] get dressed up when they went to a concert. Now, they [*will wear/wear/should wear*] just about anything, even torn jeans and ripped T-shirts.

11. She [*must/has to/can*] be Martha's daughter. I mean, she looks just like her! – No, she [*mustn't/doesn't have to/can't/couldn't*] be. She's much too old.

12. You [*don't need to/needn't/don't have to*] worry about me. I'll be just fine on my own.

13. Sorry, but I [*can't/couldn't/won't be able to*] stay too late. I [*must/have to/need to/should*] get at least eight hours of sleep every night.

14. She said she'd never set eyes on the criminals before, but she [*could/can/might*] have been lying.

15. You [*don't need to/needn't/don't have to*] be French to study at a French university.

16. Joanne [*might/can/would/will*] be bringing a friend with her.

17. [*Can/Could/May*] I park my car here? –Yes, you [*can/could/may*].

18. High-speed TGV trains in France [*could/can/might/may*] reach a speed of over 300 kilometres an hour.

19. Note that all students seeking on-campus lodging [*had better/should/ought to/need to*] turn in their applications at least two months before the university year.

20. Sorry, but I [*can't/couldn't/wasn't able to*] find any information on the subject on the internet.

21. They [*had better/should/ought to*] take plenty of water with them. It [*could/ would/will/might*] be very hot this afternoon. Are they even aware of how hot it [*can/might/may*] get in this part of the country?

22. There [*used to/would*] be a newsstand on this corner. My father [*would buy/bought/used to buy*] his paper there every morning.

23. In this country, you [*don't need to/needn't/don't have to*] have an international driving licence to hire a car.

24. Unfortunately, I [*wasn't able to/couldn't*] finish the job on time, but thankfully I [*was able to/could*] get a short extension.

25. Some people [*will/might/may*] do anything to be on television.

26. John [*must/has to/can*] have left already – his car is gone.

Exercise 12. Rewrite the following sentences, incorporating in each case the Adjunct provided in brackets. What generalizations do the new sentences bring to the fore? Indicate in each case whether the context conveys permission, ability or mere possibility.

1. I can use a French-English bilingual dictionary. (for last week's translation exam)

2. Students can bring a calculator. (to Mr Regan's maths class last year)

3. It can take up to two days to get there by train. (in the early twentieth century)
4. Sarah can tell me how to get to the station. (when I rang her up this morning)
5. Sarah can't tell me how to get to the airport. (because she'd never been there before)
6. The female of the species can lay up to 3 million eggs a season. (before it became extinct)
7. My mother can translate the diplomat's speech for us. (last night/because she speaks Russian)
8. My mother can understand the diplomat's speech. (yesterday/because she speaks Russian)
9. My grandmother can speak Russian. (when she was younger)
10. The stadium can hold only 20,000 spectators. (before the extension was built)
11. She can come home as late as she wants. (when she was a teenager)
12. She can't stay out past midnight. (in those days)
13. It's a special occasion, so she can stay out later than usual. (that night)
14. We can hear the waves crashing against the rocks. (from where we were standing)
15. I can tell he's lying. (last night)
16. I can figure out the answer to the problem. (in the end)

Exercise 13. The following sentences all convey mere possibility. In addition to the basic idea that the situation is possible, some of them (but not all) further suggest that the situation regularly actualizes, that it is 'sometimes the case'. Decide which sentences include this additional reading of habituality, and give an appropriate paraphrase.

1. It can get cold in San Francisco, so pack accordingly.
2. You can apply a second coat of paint once the first has dried.
3. We can grab a bite to eat in the museum cafeteria.
4. Susan can be a little picky when it comes to food.
5. Raising a teenager can be a real challenge.
6. Any remaining credit can be used at a later day.

Exercise 14. Examine the following pairs of sentences and determine in which sentence the modal meaning expressed is stronger.

1. (a) I should call my mother – it's her birthday.
   (b) I've got to call my mother – it's her birthday.
2. (a) I have to tell my parents if I'm going to be home late.
   (b) I'm supposed to tell my parents if I'm going to be home late.
3. (a) That must be Peter. Will you answer the phone, please?
   (b) That will be Peter. Will you answer the phone, please?
4. (a) I ought to be going now – it's getting late.
   (b) I have to be going now – it's getting late.

5. (a) You'd better not tell anyone what I told you.
   (b) You shouldn't tell anyone what I told you.
6. (a) Looks like it could rain. You'd better take an umbrella.
   (b) Looks like it could rain. You should take an umbrella.
7. (a) Members are not to leave the meeting without permission.
   (b) Members aren't supposed to leave the meeting without permission.
8. (a) She is to report directly to me in such circumstances.
   (b) She ought to report directly to me in such circumstances.

Exercise 15. Consider non-epistemic *must* versus *have to*: which do you think is more likely in the following sentences? Are there any sentences where, given the context, the choice is less constrained? Be aware that there is a certain amount of latitude for possible answers. Be able to justify your choice, however.

1. You've been ill for almost a week now. You _____ go and see a doctor.
2. On Fridays, she _____ leave the office before 4.30 to avoid rush hour traffic.
3. Sorry, but it's getting late. I _____ go now.
4. I _____ work until seven, but I can meet you for drinks as soon as I've finished.
5. Quick, has anyone got a tissue? I _____ sneeze!
6. The book is good, but you _____ admit that the style is somewhat pretentious.
7. I _____ do something about my hair before the interview. It looks just awful!
8. All mobile phones _____ be turned off during the performance.
9. You absolutely _____ try the great new Indian restaurant down the street.
10. Thanks for the invitation, but I _____ look after my parents' cat that weekend.

Exercise 16. Determine the source of necessity with *don't/doesn't need to* versus *needn't*: which do you think is more likely in the following sentences? In which cases are both possible, and in which cases can you also use *don't/doesn't have to*? What generalizations can be made?

1. He _____ put a stamp on the envelope. Postage has been prepaid.
2. She inherited so much money from her grandfather that she _____ work any more.
3. Please! You _____ shout. We can all hear you perfectly well.
4. You _____ have an advanced degree to apply for the job, but it is recommended.
5. Tell her she _____ come to the meeting if she has more important things to do.
6. You _____ pick me up at the airport. I can get to the hotel myself.
7. Children under ten years of age _____ pay to visit the museum.
8. You _____ bring anything to the party. We're having it catered.

Exercise 17. Consider the negation of epistemic and non-epistemic *must*, giving the negative counterpart – or counterparts, if two solutions are possible – to the following sentences using *mustn't*, *needn't* or *can't*. When given, the information in brackets should be incorporated into your sentences.

1. He really must work harder. (so hard)
2. She must have known what was going to happen.
3. He must be working at this hour.
4. She must speak to the manager directly.
5. You must know him.
6. You must meet him.
7. We must tell them what we've decided.
8. He must have e-mailed them back. (already)
9. You must read this book.
10. That watch must be expensive. (that expensive)

Exercise 18. Based on whether the deduction being made is a logical deduction or a deduction stating that something is probably the case based on the usual state of affairs, decide in the following whether *must* or *should/ought to* is used.

1. You've been working all day. You _____ be exhausted.
2. If you buy the tickets, I'll pay you back. They _____ cost about £100 each.
3. I've sent them an e-mail, so I _____ get an answer soon.
4. It didn't take them long to get here. They _____ live close by.
5. Sarah said they're on their way. They _____ be here shortly.
6. I don't have my umbrella. I _____ have left it on the bus.

Exercise 19. First determine whether *will* or *shall* best completes the sentences below and in which cases either is possible. Then decide if any other modal verbs can be used in place of *will* or *shall* with similar meaning.

1. Both parties _____ abide by the contract and refrain from revision thereof.
2. He _____ disappear for hours at a time and never say what he's been up to.
3. I hope the lecture _____ start on time this week.
4. Your explanation was very clear. Next time, I _____ know who to ask for help.
5. What would you like to do tomorrow night? _____ we go to the cinema?
6. If you've ever been seasick, you _____ have been told to look at a distant point on the horizon.
7. _____ I send it to you over e-mail, or would you prefer a hardcopy?
8. _____ someone please explain what's going on here? Why is this place such a mess?
9. By 2050, the number of people over 60 in this country _____ have reached over 15 million.
10. How much wine _____ I buy? – Two or three bottles _____ be enough.
11. What's the new deadline? – I don't know, but you can ask Thomas. He _____ know.
12. If you _____ just have a seat here, I _____ be with you in just a few minutes.

Exercise 20. Using the following cues, come up with utterances beginning with *I wish*. Use the italicized verb in the second part of your sentence. In which time-spheres are the different parts of your different sentences located? What does your choice of progressive or non-progressive aspect convey? Note that some utterances will be better formulated using *would*. Which ones, and why?

1. I didn't *take* my umbrella with me when I left this morning. Now it's going to rain.
2. We don't *live* close to each other. This makes me feel unhappy sometimes.
3. It's *rain*ing. This depresses me.
4. It's raining. I want it to *stop*.
5. You didn't *come* to my party. What a pity. We all had a wonderful time.
6. I *slept* for ten hours straight. Now I've got a bad headache.
7. He's *com*ing tomorrow, not today. I'm disappointed.
8. You're smoking. It's bothering me. Please *put* that cigarette out.
9. I don't *have* a house of my own. I'm envious of people who do.
10. *I voted* for the opposition candidate. This turned out to be a very bad idea.
11. A Christmas with snow is so beautiful. Christmas is in two days. It hasn't *snow*ed.
12. He doesn't seem to want to *help* me. But I really need his help.
13. My father *smokes* too much. I don't like it that he does.
14. You smoke too much. Why not *consider* quitting once and for all?
15. I *feel* so lonely. I would like this not to be the case.

Exercise 21. Rewrite the following sentences using the words provided in italics to begin each sentence. Determine in each case whether the subjunctive is appropriate. Your rewritten sentences should have the same basic meaning as the initial sentences.

1. She wants to continue in spite of so much opposition. This is interesting.
   It is interesting that ...
2. For her to continue in spite of so much opposition is important.
   It is important that ...
3. This must not happen again. I am determined for this to be the case.
   I am determined that ...
4. He wants the top-secret documents to be declassified so as to facilitate the trial.
   He asks that ...
5. The opposition very much wants the president to suspend the proposed change until a referendum can be held.
   The opposition is demanding that ...
6. Your father must come to the meeting today as well since both parents are supposed to be present. I insist on it.
   I insist that ...

7. Her psychoanalyst thinks it'd be a good idea for her to write down every dream she can remember ever having.
   Her psychoanalyst recommends that …

8. My son is having trouble reading at the same level as his classmates. Perhaps he is dyslexic. This is what I think.
   I think that …

9. Do you really think his behaviour is a genuine threat to his success?
   Are you honestly suggesting that … ?

10. Do you actually think that she should be allowed to attend courses whereas she has not paid the enrolment fees?
    Are you actually suggesting that … ?

Exercise 22. The following examples all contain a conditional clause. Choose the right set of verbs from the choices that are given. Specify whether the sentence refers to a possible situation or to a counterfactual situation.

1. I'm glad you came today. If you _____ tomorrow, you _____ the kids.
   a) had come/wouldn't have seen
   b) came/wouldn't see
   c) come/won't see

2. I'm glad you came today. If you _____ yesterday, you _____ the kids. They were still away.
   a) had come/wouldn't have seen
   b) came/wouldn't see
   c) come/won't see

3. Can't you change your plans? If you _____ tomorrow, you _____ the kids before they _____.
   a) had come/wouldn't have seen/leave
   b) came/would see/leave
   c) come/will see/left

4. Can't you change your plans? If you _____ tomorrow, you _____ the kids before they _____.
   a) had come/wouldn't have seen/leave
   b) came/would see/will leave
   c) come/will see/leave

5. If everyone _____ the book, the discussion we're having right now _____ much more engaging.
   a) has read/is
   b) had read/would be
   c) had read/was

6. If everyone _____ the book, we _____ the book club meeting sooner rather than later.

      a) has read/can hold
      b) has read/could have held
      c) had read/could hold

7. If you _____ me for just a minute, I'll ask my supervisor if there's anything we can do.
      a) excuse
      b) will excuse
      c) excuse **OR** will excuse (both are possible)

8. If you _____ her absence this time, all the other students will take advantage of the situation.
      a) excuse
      b) will excuse
      c) excuse **OR** will excuse (both are possible)

Exercise 23. What difference in meaning – if any – is there between the following pairs of sentences? If the difference is salient enough, provide a context to demonstrate how they are different.

1. (a) They must sleep.
   (b) They must be sleeping.
2. (a) Lions may be dangerous.
   (b) Lions can be dangerous.
3. (a) He may not be as experienced as he says.
   (b) He cannot be as experienced as he says.
4. (a) I shall call you first thing tomorrow morning.
   (b) I will call you first thing tomorrow morning.
5. (a) You needn't rewrite the report.
   (b) You don't need to rewrite the report.
6. (a) You mustn't rewrite the report.
   (b) You don't have to rewrite the report.
7. (a) You must stop criticizing your colleagues so overtly.
   (b) You need to stop criticizing your colleagues so overtly.
8. (a) She couldn't go to the meeting.
   (b) She could not go to the meeting.
9. (a) I must make a decision about this.
   (b) I have to make a decision about this.
10. (a) I may ask my boyfriend to come along.
   (b) I might ask my boyfriend to come alone.
11. (a) She ought to be more tactful.
   (b) She should be more tactful.
12. (a) She could get in since she had the key to the front door.
   (b) She was able to get in since she had the key to the front door.

Exercise 24. Explain the ambiguity in the following sentences and provide unambiguous paraphrases demonstrating you understand the different meaning each sentence can have.

1. He may collaborate with you on this project.
2. You must be extremely meticulous.
3. Sally can read this book.
4. He might have been killed.
5. He could spend the evening with his buddies.
6. He would spend more time working on that.
7. I should be happy to participate in this initiative.
8. My keys should be on the kitchen table.

Exercise 25. Rewrite the following sentences using a modal auxiliary.

1. Watch out for that bee. Bee stings are sometimes fatal!
2. My mobile phone is broken. I am politely requesting to use yours.
3. Calling your mother on her birthday is always a good idea.
4. I hereby give you permission to use my notes for your presentation.
5. Perhaps I'll go to London next week. I'm not sure yet.
6. Marion needs my help. I hereby agree to help her in any way I can.
7. It is a requirement for all swimmers to wear a swimming cap in this pool.
8. Suzie knows how to ride a bike without training wheels.
9. As a boy, he was allowed to eat whatever he wanted for breakfast.
10. Exercising on a full stomach is not advisable.
11. I'm not certain, but I think John is the one who ate your chocolate.
12. As a child, he sometimes pouted for hours if he didn't get his way.
13. Someone's at the door. John said he'd be coming. I'm convinced it is him.
14. Are you strong enough to lift that heavy box?
15. Before my operation, I was able to swim quite fast.
16. He says he's surprised, but he necessarily knew what was going to happen.
17. Simone is in Japan all week. It is not possible that you saw her.
18. It is of the utmost importance that you not be late.
19. The lights are out in Josephine's office. It is not possible that she is still there.
20. I'm not allowed to have people over when my parents are out.

Exercise 26. What temporal information is communicated in the utterances below? In what time sphere is M located? What is the temporal relation between P and M? Can you establish a relationship between the form used (present or past form of the modal, bare infinitive or perfect infinitive) and the temporal information communicated by the utterances? What modal meaning do the verbs communicate?

1. Our firm specializes in synthetic fibres. We could produce the fibre that you need.
2. Our firm specializes in synthetic fibres. We can produce fibres to customers' specifications.
3. It could be John who did it.
4. They could be hiding in the cellar.
5. We can go out whenever we like.
6. We can stay out till 10 tonight.
7. You can buy Beaujolais Nouveau at the shop round the corner.
8. We could go out until 1 am when we were teenagers.
9. He might have decided he wanted to stay home after all.
10. He may have decided he wanted to stay home after all.
11. It will be possible to buy Beaujolais Nouveau sometime soon.
12. John may be working in his office. I saw him just a few minutes ago.
13. John may be working in accounting next month. He's asked for a transfer.
14. How could such a brilliant book have been written in such difficult circumstances?

6

Discourse

1. Cohesion

In the preceding chapters, we have attempted to come to a more solid under-standing of how we can build meaningful, grammatical sentences in English. We have done this from a number of angles, focusing basically on the clause and the constituents within it. We have also shown that there is a great deal of interaction and interdependence among the different constituents within the clause. Getting a handle on how the different pieces fit together is no less impor-tant than understanding them individually. We have seen, for example, that

- the Subject, most regularly an NP, determines the number (singular or plural) of the verb (see p. 156): *the student has finished* versus *the students have finished*;
- the choice of tense co-functions crucially with the Adjuncts mentioned in the clause, especially with respect to the past tense and the present perfect tense (see p. 212): *I saw him yesterday*, but **I've seen him yesterday*;
- the use of progressive aspect may be constrained by the presence of numer-ical NPs in the sentence (see p. 185): *Yesterday he ate three donuts*, but **Yesterday he was eating three donuts*;

> – a past time Adjunct can only combine with a past tense modal like *could* or
> *might* when the modal has the potential to refer to a situation in the past
> time-sphere (see p. 277): *I could swim when I was younger* versus **He might
> go to the cinema last night.* (cf. *He might go to the cinema tonight.*)

In other words, the tacit assumption has been that constituents do not function as isolated units: the underlying principles of the grammar of English can only be fully understood if we recognize the interaction between phrases at the level of the clause.

We have occasionally looked beyond the clausal level and hinted at the fact that knowing how to build a grammatical sentence is only part of the story. Indeed, in the same way that constituents work together to form sentences, sentences work together to create larger pieces of language. We will refer to this level of language as **discourse**, which we define as 'grammar beyond the level of the sentence'. The speaker ~ writer has principled ways of presenting the links between sentences and implicitly takes for granted that the hearer ~ reader understands how these links are established as well.

An illustration of this feature was provided in our discussion of the passive in Chapter 2 (see p. 80). Here it was pointed out that the speaker can choose to put the theme (rather than the agent or experiencer) in Subject position in order to preserve topic continuity. This discursive principle is particularly salient in English: the issue or item that we are talking about (in more technical terms, the **discourse topic**) tends to be put in initial position in the clause. As long as the discourse stays focused on the same topic, speakers will make sure that it is mentioned in Subject position since this facilitates comprehension. The speaker more or less consciously ensures that the information is presented in such a way that it will be easy for the hearer to take in.

There are further generalizations that can be made concerning the organization of information in a sentence and how it relates to the broader context surrounding it. These strategies are sometimes referred to as **information packaging**. Take, for instance, the underlined segment of the following real example in (1a) from a disgruntled restaurant customer. It illustrates a way in which a specific chunk of information can be made more prominent in the discourse:

(1) (a) The food here at this restaurant is great. However, <u>it's the terrible service that has prompted me to leave this review</u>. After 30 minutes of being ignored, we just walked out. (www)

    (b) The food here at this restaurant is great. However, the terrible service has prompted me to leave this review. After 30 minutes of being ignored, we just walked out.

You will probably agree that the 'terrible service' in (1a) is much more in the foreground of the speaker's message than the same element in (1b). The construction in (1a) is commonly called an **it-cleft**. It has the following structure, where X can be any constituent in the sentence. In (1a), the constituent happens to be the Subject:

(2) it + BE + constituent X + *that-/who*-subclause

A similar construction to the *it*-cleft is the **wh-cleft**:

(3) *wh*-clause + BE + constituent X

Consider the following real internet forum exchange about a trip to Italy. The excerpt includes two participants, A and B:

(4) (a) A: I think that Turin is more interesting than Milan, though in Turin there isn't anything as outstanding as the Milan cathedral.

    B (*reacting to A*): I disagree that there's nothing to do in Milan besides the cathedral, but I agree that Turin is more beautiful.

    A (*rectifying B*): I didn't say there isn't anything to do besides the cathedral in Milan. <u>What I said is that there isn't anything in Turin as beautiful as the cathedral in Milan</u>. (www)

(b) A (*rectifying B*): I didn't say there isn't anything to do besides the cathedral in Milan. <u>I said that there isn't anything in Turin as beautiful as the cathedral in Milan</u>.

If you compare the structure underlined in (4a) to the more basic structure in (4b), you'll again agree that (4a) brings 'there isn't anything in Turin [...]' into greater focus than in (4b). The first two parts of the exchange in (4a) give us some insight as to why speaker A might opt to focus on a specific part of the message.

Note that in both the *it*-cleft and the *wh*-cleft, the information communicated by 'constituent X' is what the speaker wants to highlight. In other words, specific slots in the clause are reserved for specific types of information; the information is packaged in a way so as to bring out the most important parts of the message and how they relate to the larger communicative context in which the clause is used.

It-clefts and *wh*-clefts are just two examples of non-canonical sentence types (compare to the canonical versions in (1b) and (4b)) that, like the passive, speakers use to organize and present information in ways that are largely determined by context outside of the sentence itself. Clauses with **extraposition** illustrate another discourse organizing principle. We mentioned this type of sentence in our discussion of complementation and the passive in Chapter 2 (Section 5.5.1.2). If the Subject or (in certain cases) the Direct Object is clausal, it tends not to feature in its default position in the sentence. This is particularly common when the clause is 'heavy'. When we say that a constituent is heavy, this mostly means that it is long. As such, a heavy constituent (here, a clause) contains a lot of information. Take a look at the following examples, where the subclause Subject (5a) and subclause Direct Object (5b) are underlined:

(5) (a) <u>That she has enormous talent</u> is undeniable.
    (b) *I consider <u>that you're blaming me for the situation</u> unfair.

Intuitively, speakers often avoid sentences of the type found in (5a), and a sentence such as (5b) is patently ungrammatical for most of them. They feel that the organization of the information is cognitively too demanding and that a subclause Subject (or subclause Direct Object which requires another complement (here, the AdjP 'unfair')) is easier to process if it features in end position. The strategy used is that of shifting the clausal constituent to the end of the sentence and using 'empty *it*' in the default Subject or Object position as a kind of place-holder for the extraposed element:

(6) (a) *It* is undeniable <u>that she has enormous talent</u>.
    (b) I consider *it* unfair <u>that you're blaming me for situation</u>.

In this chapter, we will look at more features that make the discourse flow, thus helping the hearer or reader to process and understand the spoken or written text. Addressing the ways in which information is organized in discourse and the linguistic markers that help to structure it naturally requires us to look at larger stretches of text. Consider, as a starting point, the opening paragraphs from an article on the Cancún Climate agreement:

(7) Climate Talks End with Modest Deal on Emissions
CANCÚN, Mexico – The United Nations climate change conference began with modest aims and ended early Saturday with modest achievements. But while the measures adopted here may have scant near-term impact on the warming of the planet, the international process for dealing with the issue got a significant vote of confidence.
The agreement fell well short of the broad changes scientists say are needed to avoid dangerous climate change in coming decades. But it lays the groundwork

for stronger measures in the future, if nations are able to overcome the emotional arguments that have crippled climate change negotiations in recent years.
(www)

The following are among the elements that enable the reader to establish
links between the clauses:

- The absence of an overt Subject in ' ... *and Ø ended early Saturday* ... ' invites
  the reader to look for the Subject earlier in the sentence; the Subject of the
  second VP is the same as that of the first (*the United Nations climate change
  conference ended*).
- *Here* tells the reader that the location of the conference has already been mentioned; if the reader wants to retrieve this information, *here* tacitly informs him
  that he can go back to the beginning of the text to recover the place where the
  conference was held (*Cancún*).
- In a similar way, *it* in the second paragraph invites the reader to look for the
  appropriate referent (*the agreement*) in the previous sentence.
- *But* in *But while the measures adopted* ... tells the reader that he should interpret the entire sentence which follows as in some way contrasting with the
  sentence that precedes it. The contrast here is between the *moderate success*
  mentioned in the introductory sentence and the *important step forward* mentioned in the following sentence.
- *While* is also a signal to the reader that a contrast is being made; this time the
  contrast is between the information in the subclause (*the immediate impact of
  the measures taken is limited*) and the main clause (*from an attitudinal point
  of view, the measures constitute an important step ahead*).
- *If* in the second paragraph shows the reader that the information in the preceding clause is subject to a condition (*better agreements may be arrived at in the
  future provided the parties involved adopt the right attitude*).
- *The measures adopted here* is used as an alternative for *modest achievements*: both NPs have the same referent. The first implies that progress
  was made; the second indicates that the conference was not a complete
  success. In other words, the lexical material used to refer to the agreement
  pinpoints alternative ways of perceiving the same thing.

Simply put, the introductory paragraphs to the article can be easily processed
thanks to the cues used by the writer of the text to help the reader to process the information efficiently. It is not enough that the sentences taken
individually are grammatically correct. Rather, the discourse is constructed
in such a way that the reader can establish logical semantic links within
and among the clauses. In technical terms, the kind of going back and forth
between clauses referred to above to recover meaning results in **cohesion**. We

will now explain and illustrate some of the (lexical and grammatical) markers that establish inter-sentential and inter-clausal semantic relationships and in this way contribute towards establishing cohesion in principled ways.

2. Markers of cohesion

In this section, we will first give a brief survey of some **grammatical markers of cohesion**, categories that were already discussed (especially) in Chapter 3, although less from a discourse perspective. Now that the notions of discourse and cohesion have been defined, it is possible to capture the function of the grammatical markers in question in a more explicit way. We will then move on to **lexical markers of cohesion**, a variety of forms whose lexical semantics establish links in the discourse. In the case of the markers in Section 2.1, the functional meaning of the grammatical form (pronoun, definite article, demonstrative pronoun/determiner) contributes to cohesion. In Section 2.2, it will be shown that in other cases, it is the lexical meaning of grammatical forms (coordinating conjunctions, subordinating conjunctions, prepositions, adverbs) that captures the semantic relation between the clauses.

2.1 Grammatical markers of cohesion (or grammatical discourse markers)

Many of the grammatical features we have discussed so far in this book in one way or another make the spoken discourse or written text stick together. In Chapter 3, for example, we saw how an indefinite (non-generic) NP is used to introduce a person or a thing into the discourse. Once reference has been established, we use the definite article to continue talking about it:

> (8) (a) Medical Centre researchers have discovered *a new fast-acting antidote to cyanide poisoning. The antidote* has potential to save lives of those who are exposed to *the chemical.* (adapted from www)
> (b) Medical Centre researchers have discovered *a new fast-acting antidote to cyanide poisoning. An antidote* has potential to save lives of those who are exposed to *a chemical.*

The definite NPs in the second clause in (8a) assume that the reader can identify the referent. In this specific context, the reader will look for identifying information in the preceding clause and as a result of this, a cohesive link is established. While the alternative version of the example in (8b) with indefinite

NPs is grammatical, the cohesive link between the two NPs headed by *antidote* is not the same. There is no longer any co-reference with respect to the first clause; the second clause is a definition of an antidote.

The use of **anaphors** (see Chapter 3, Section 3.3) or **cataphors** – that is, constituents containing forms that invite the reader to look back or forward for a suitable referent in the discourse (sometimes within the sentence, but very often beyond the sentence boundary) – also serves the purpose of establishing a link between clauses. Demonstrative pronouns as well as personal pronouns illustrate this discursive strategy:

(9) Forensic analysts can determine how rare *a particular DNA pattern* is and then choose to use *this* to identify possible culprits. (www)
A few days after Christmas, *my sister* sold the present I had given to *her*.
Where are *my glasses?* I always forget where I put *them*.
When *they* saw the child in the water, *the bystanders* called for help.
Listen to *this*: *I'm getting married!*

The indefinite pronoun *one* serves a similar purpose – it forces the reader to look for the corresponding noun in the preceding context:

(10) The final *clip*, and the most recent *one*, was filmed in Denver, Colorado, in February. (www) (the most recent *one* = the most recent *clip*)

Like nominal anaphora (pro-NPs), verbal anaphora (pro-VPs) serve the purpose of avoiding repetition and establishing cohesion:

(11) It is the patient's responsibility to *organize appointments at their convenience* when requested to *do so* (= organize appointments at their convenience). (www)
He's decided to *give up his job*. – Why would he *do that* (= give up his job)?

In the examples above, the reader has to go back to the preceding clause in order to recover what *do so* and *do that* stand for: in both cases it is a complete VP. Another substitute that contributes to cohesion is *so* in *if so*:

(12) Is 'reneg' a word? And *if so* what does it mean? (www)

The *so* in *if so* stands for *reneg is a word*; in other words, *so* represents not a VP, as above, but an entire clause. *So* is also used after verbs like *hope* and *believe*. (*Is he coming? – I hope/believe so* (= I hope/believe he is coming)).

Another common cohesive device is to leave out a word or constituent. As we saw in Chapter 2, this phenomenon is called **ellipsis**: Section 2.2.3

of Chapter 2 dealt with the ellipsis of a VP following an auxiliary. Although ellipsis is sometimes required for the sentence to be grammatical (13a), it is perhaps more often used as a cohesive device to avoid repetition (13b). The gap left by ellipsis (indicated below by Ø) is filled by establishing a link with the previous context:

(13) (a) She's coming to the party, isn't she Ø?
  (cf. *She's coming to the party, isn't she coming to the party?)
  Peter can drive, and so can his sister Ø.
  (cf. *Peter can drive, and so can his sister drive.)
 (b) Can you speak Russian? – Yes, I can Ø. Can you Ø?
  (= Yes, I can speak Russian. Can you speak Russian?)
  Why don't you ask Mary to help you? – Brilliant idea. I will Ø.
  (= Brilliant idea. I will ask Mary to help me.)

Nouns can sometimes be subject to ellipsis as well, most commonly in NPs where the head noun is preceded by an ordinal number (*first, second, third*) or by a comparative or superlative form:

(14) They had only two children; *the first* Ø, a son named William, died as an infant as he was followed in 1834 by another son, another William, in January 1834. (www)

(15) But a combined kidney and pancreatic transplant creates problems. *The most difficult* Ø is that the transplanted pancreas performs its insulin-secreting role so well that before the patient is off the operating table, blood-sugar levels are being naturally controlled. (www)

The following example combines substitution and ellipsis:

(16) (headline) Jessica Ennis aiming to start next season as she *did* the last Ø with Glasgow win over Lolo Jones (www) (= ... as she *started* the last *season*)

The discourse markers listed so far all contribute towards cohesion: they all invite the hearer to look for links between clauses, on the presumption that the discourse hangs together. While awareness of the ways in which grammatical markers establish cohesive links will help you to produce more natural-sounding texts and to process written texts more fluently, we would like to focus in particular on lexical markers of cohesion in this chapter, that is, lexical items that bring out semantic relations between clauses.

2.2 Lexical markers of cohesion (or lexical discourse markers)

Lexical discourse markers basically serve the same purpose as **grammatical discourse markers**, yet here it is the lexical meaning of the markers that makes it clear what the logical link is between two main clauses or between an embedding clause and a subclause. In other words, we classify discourse markers in this section in terms of the semantic link they express. It will become clear that in some cases, up to four different forms can express a specific semantic relationship.

2.2.1 Connectors of contrast, time, cause, consequence and addition

To establish cohesion, languages other than English often have connectors similar to those we discuss below. At times, the connectors are very close both in form and in use. There can, however, be subtle differences in how related languages use connectors that seem comparable on the surface.

2.2.1.1 Connectors of contrast

Take a look at the beginning of a movie review published in the *New York Times*. For the purpose of this discussion, we have slightly modified the original version:

> (17) 'Night Catches Us' [...] is haunted by the threat and the memory of violence. Its tone is sober and calm, almost serene. (*New York Times*, 2 December 2010)

The two sentences are grammatical, but something might strike you as strange when you read them: if the threat of violence is so prevalent in the film, does it not seem a bit odd to describe the film immediately afterwards as 'sober and calm, almost serene'? The two ideas seem almost to contradict each other, and this leaves us somewhat uncomfortable as we attempt to process exactly what the writer is trying to convey to us. Now read the following slightly different versions below:

> (18) (a) *Although* 'Night Catches Us' [...] is haunted by the threat and the memory of violence, its tone is sober and calm, almost serene. (< the original sentence in the *New York Times*)
>   (b) 'Night Catches Us' [...] is haunted by the threat and the memory of violence, *but* its tone is sober and calm, almost serene.

(c) 'Night Catches Us' [...] is haunted by the threat and the memory of violence. *However*, its tone is sober and calm, almost serene.

Any hesitation we might have had with respect to the link between the two ideas in (17) above disappears in (18a) to (18c): the use of *although, but* and *however* makes the link between the two ideas clear. All three of these function words roughly convey concession or contrast here, but they do so in different ways:

- Sentence (18a) contains *although*, a subordinating conjunction. The sentence has two clauses, an embedding clause and a subclause, and the position of *although* is fixed. It can only be found at the beginning of the clause that it introduces:
  - *Although* it is haunted by the threat and the memory of violence, the film
    ...
  - *It is, *although*, haunted by the threat and the memory of violence, the film ...
  - *It is haunted by the threat and the memory of violence *although*, the film
    ...

- The version in (18b) is also a single sentence made up of two clauses; here, though, the two are linked with the coordinating conjunction *but*. Its position, like that of *although* is fixed. It can only be found between the two clauses (and is usually preceded by a comma):
  - ..., *but* its tone is sober and calm, almost serene.
  - * ... its tone, *but*, is sober and calm, almost serene.
  - * ... its tone is sober and calm, almost serene, *but*.

In contrast to (18a), there is no hierarchical relationship between the clauses here. Note that traditional grammar frowns on beginning a sentence with a coordinating conjunction like *but*. In reality, sentences beginning with a coordinating conjunction are common:

  - ... the memory of violence. *But* its tone is sober and calm, almost serene.

- The (18c) version, finally, makes use of an adverb, *however*. Here we find two separate sentences; unlike the conjunctions in (18a) and (18b), the adverb *however* in the second sentence is relatively mobile:
  - *However*, its tone is sober and calm, almost serene.
  - Its tone, *however*, is sober and calm, almost serene.
  - Its tone is sober and calm, almost serene, *however*.

Note that two main clauses can also be joined with a semi-colon when the writer wants to establish a closer link between the clauses than a full stop might otherwise allow. In this case, the second clause does not begin with a capital letter:

  - 'Night Catches Us' [...] is haunted by the threat and the memory of violence; *however*, its tone is sober and calm, almost serene.

Although, but and *however* make an explicit link between the two clauses, but note that the position the connector occupies, as well as the overall syntax of the utterance, is different: *although* is found in initial position in the subclause, which happens to be mentioned first in (18a)[1]; *but* in (18b) is located between two clauses; and the syntactically mobile *however* is found not in the first, but in the second of two sentences in (18c). Finally, *though* can be used either as a subordinator (like *although* (19)) or as an adverb (like *however* (20)); contrary to *however*, *though* as an adverb can only occur medially or clause-finally:

(19) *Though* it is haunted by the threat and the memory of violence …

(20) Its tone, *though*, is sober and calm, almost serene.
Its tone is sober and calm, almost serene, *though*.
*Though, its tone is sober and calm, almost serene.

One final option the journalist might have exploited is a PrepP Adjunct with *in spite of* or *despite*:

(21) *In spite of/Despite* the fact that the film […] is haunted by the threat and the memory of violence, its tone is sober and calm, almost serene.

With respect to meaning, the sentence in (21) is easy enough to relate to the variants in (18) although it is quite different from it syntactically, as one of the clauses is located within a PrepP.[2]

The set *although* (subordinator), *but* (coordinator), *however* (adverb) and *though* (subordinator or adverb), as well as *in spite of/despite* (preposition), used to express contrast or concession, shows how connectors can be used in different syntactic configurations. There is a wide variety of other connectors as well. We will examine a few of these below.

---

[1]Note that the order of the two clauses is not fixed (which is not to say that the point of view is exactly the same). The subclause precedes the embedding clause in (i) but follows it in (ii):

    (i) *Although* 'Night Catches Us' […] is haunted by the threat and the memory of violence, its tone is sober and calm, almost serene.

    (ii) The tone of 'Night Catches Us' is sober and calm, almost serene, *although* it […] is haunted by the threat and the memory of violence.

[2]We mention the prepositions *in spite of/despite* here because their meaning is closely related to the sentences illustrating *although* and *but*. Note that we can observe similar effects even when the PrepP does not include a clause. *In spite of the rain* (= in spite of the fact that it was raining), *we enjoyed our afternoon in the countryside*.

2.2.1.2 Temporal connectors

When, before and *after* are the most basic of the temporal subordinators; *as soon as, until* and *while* are common as well, as is *since* (see Section 2.2.1.3). As we saw in Chapter 4, the use of the different tenses in these cases interacts with these subordinators very closely:

> (22) I started reading the book yesterday.//I knew I would like it.
> > (Even) *before/after/as soon as* I had started reading the book yesterday, I knew I would like it. ('I started' is also possible – an example of tense simplification. See Chapter 4, Section 3.5.3)

> (23) We'll have a drink.//The others will arrive.
> We'll have a drink *before/after/as soon as* the others arrive (or 'have arrived').
> We won't have a drink until the others arrive (or 'have arrived').
> (but not . . . *before/after/as soon as/until* the others will arrive/will have arrived – no future (perfect) tense here – see Chapter 4, Section 3.6.1)

The temporal relation expressed by *while* is always one of simultaneity. In addition to its temporal meaning, *while* can also be used to express a contrast (but not a reason):

> (24) *While* I peeled (was peeling) the potatoes, she chopped the carrots and celery.
> *While* I do understand where you are coming from, I still have some serious reservations.

2.2.1.3 Causal connectors

Subordinators can also express the notion of what we might broadly characterize as cause: *because*[3] is the main subordinator used to express reason; *since* and *as* – and, in a more formal register, *for* – all express similar meaning. The four are not always interchangeable, however. This becomes clear when we consider that only *because* is possible to answer a question with *why*:

> (25) Why aren't you going to the party? – *Because* (*Since/*As*) I wasn't invited.

Because straightforwardly gives the reason why. *As* and *since*, though similar to *because*, are used more to provide a kind of backdrop against which something in the foreground is explained or justified. In a sense, this is similar to one of

---

[3] *Because* is often reduced in the spoken language, and this form is reflected in casual spelling as *'cos, 'cuz* or *'cause*. These forms should not be used in formal writing, however.

the uses of progressive aspect in the past that we saw in Chapter 4. Whereas the background in (26a) is temporal, the background in (26b) is causal:

(26) (a) When we arrived (< *foreground*), it was raining (< *background*) and no one even took our wet coats or showed us where to leave our soaking umbrella. (www)

(b) Checked in and were assigned room 320. We were told that it overlooked the pool, and *since* we like higher floors (< *background*), we were delighted (< *foreground*). *Since* we flew in for a two week trip to the New England area (< *background*), we had lots of luggage (< *foreground*). (www)

Seen from this angle, it becomes clearer that *since* and *as* are less closely associated with the reason for something than is *because*. The following sentence does not really give a reason why the speaker made the suggestion; rather, it claims that, taking the situation into account, the suggestion made sense:

(27) *Since/As* she didn't know what to order, I suggested the fettuccini Alfredo.
(?I suggested the fettuccini Alfredo *because* she didn't know what to order.)

For, finally, is a coordinator rather than a subordinator, and one that is rarely used in speaking. It cannot be used at the beginning of a sentence. In addition to having a formal or literary register, *for* signals to the hearer that the clause that follows is an explanation rather than a reason:

(28) When the king heard that the princess was still alive, he wept tears of joy, *for* he had believed her dead and was certain he would never see her again.

When looking at *because, since* and *as*, bear in mind that *as* can also express simultaneity: *He came up to me as* (= *while*) *I was leaving my office*. For this reason, some consider that it should not be used at all to express causal relations, because doing so can result in an ambiguous sentence. In their defence, it is true that the following sentence, strictly speaking, might be considered ambiguous:

(29) The pupils mustn't be bothered *as* they're working individually on their end-of-term projects.

Opponents to causal *as* will claim that it is unclear whether the pupils in (29) must not be bothered *because* they're working on their projects or *while* they are working on them. In reality, the context is usually sufficient to make it clear what the intended meaning is. To be on the safe side, a comma before causal *as* can be helpful. The following will usually be understood as expressing cause alone, and not simultaneity:

(30) The pupils mustn't be bothered, *as* they are working individually on their end-of-term projects.

Despite prescriptivists' objections, causal *as* is widely used in English, but it can nearly always be replaced by causal *since*.

Remember too that *since* can also express temporal relations. We discussed temporal *since*-clauses in Chapter 4 (Section 3.4.3): *Since I first arrived/Since I've lived here, I've never had any trouble with my neighbours*. Again, real ambiguity is more theoretical than actual:

(31) *Since* his wife left him, he hasn't been happy.

Is the sentence in (31) supposed to mean *ever since* his wife left him (temporal) or *because* his wife left him (causal)? The context in which a sentence like this is used is probably enough to make the intended meaning clear. Avoiding such potential ambiguities is often more a matter of style than grammar. But given that it is something that certain speakers of English are aware of, it can be useful for all users of the language to be aware of it too.

2.2.1.4 Connectors of consequence

English also has a set of connectors expressing the idea of consequence: *therefore, consequently, as a result* and *as a consequence* are common adverbial connectors. Syntactically, they behave in a similar way to *however*:

(32) You have returned your library books late six times this year. *Therefore/Consequently/As a result/As a consequence*, your borrowing privileges have been suspended.

The meaning here is clear: connectors like *therefore* basically say 'the situation described in this clause is a result of the situation described in the previous clause' or 'the situation described in the previous clause is the cause of the situation described in this clause'. *Therefore, consequently, as a result* and *as a consequence* are probably more common in written discourse than in spoken, where the same idea is more commonly expressed not by an adverbial connector but by the subordinator *so* (or by *and so*, which functions like a coordinator):

(33) You have returned your library books late six times this year, *so/and so* your borrowing privileges have been suspended.

2.2.1.5 Connectors expressing addition

There is a final set of lexical connectors that express the idea of providing additional supporting information to a preceding clause: these include adverbials such as *moreover, furthermore, what is more* (or *what's more*), *in addition* and *too; besides* has a similar function.

Although some have argued for a subtle difference between *furthermore* and *moreover*, they are more or less interchangeable, with *furthermore* being less formal (and so more common) than *moreover. In addition* is the most neutral in register:

> (34) With several luxury hotels and restaurants, the city of Bloomsdale offers tour-ists both comfort and style. *In addition/Furthermore/Moreover/What's more*, the city now has an ultra-modern international airport with flights to most major North American cities.

The connector *too* is very common in speech, but cannot occur at the begin-ning of a clause; with this meaning, it is most often found clause-finally:

> (35) Bloomsdale has a lot of great hotels and restaurants. They have a new inter-national airport, *too*.

Both *beside* and *besides* are prepositions, the former meaning 'next to' and the latter meaning 'in addition to' (36a). They are not to be confused with the adverb *besides*, which means 'in addition to that' and which is often under-stood as providing an addition that is even more important than something previously mentioned (36b):

> (36) (a) *Besides* John, who do you think is the most talented musician? John is the one sitting *beside* me in the photograph.
> (b) I don't want to go out tonight. It's pouring rain. *Besides*, I'm exhausted. (Often understood to mean 'even if it were not raining, I would not want to go out'.)

The connectors described so far make explicit the semantic relation between the information presented in neighbouring clauses in a stretch of discourse. As will be shown in the next section, lexical discourse markers may contribute to cohesion in still different ways.

2.2.2 Inter-sentential discourse-structuring devices

Speakers have other ways of indicating connections in discourse. These can come in the form of constituents (PrepPs, AdvPs, even short clauses) which might be informally described as linguistic signposts. These signposts point back to what has just been said or point forward to what is about to be said. One could also look upon them as kind of meta-comment on the general context of speaking. They serve to make explicit a link between sentences that might not be immediately obvious were the signpost not there. Take the following examples:

(37) (a) … to take place in conference room B. *By the way*, my name's Christopher.
  (b) … expects far too much. *I mean,* it's not our responsibility to solve the problem.
  (c) … hasn't paid me back yet. *Incidentally*, you haven't paid me back yet either.

In (37a), *by the way* means 'What I'm about to say now is unrelated or only indirectly related to what I've just said'. The speaker might consider that without the signpost in the discourse, the hearer would find the introduction abrupt or unexpected. In (37b), *I mean* essentially means 'What I'm about to say now is meant to make what I've just said even clearer'. Finally, *incidentally* in (37c) means, here, 'What I'm about to say now is less important than what I've just said before, but what I said before reminds me of it'. The following are examples of the ever-evolving class of markers used as signposts. We have classified them in terms of their meaning, but it will be clear that these categories should be approached in terms of fairly loose semantic fields rather than as a tight taxonomy. Certain items can belong to more than one class:

> Reformulation, change of perspective: *actually, after all, all in all* (or *all in all, though*), *anyway, by the way, come to think of it, what I mean is, in particular, mind you*
>
> **Epistemic stance** (doubt, certainty, hearsay): *actually, no doubt, of course, guess what, to tell you the truth, up to a point, as a matter of fact, at least, if you ask me, funnily enough*
>
> Repetition, enumeration, summary: *as I was saying, to start with, to sum up, in retrospect, so to speak, strictly speaking*

Using and understanding these discourse markers requires a sensitivity to the context in which they are used. Indeed, often a range of meanings can be communicated by a single discourse marker of this type. By way of an example, consider the context of use of *anyway* and *actually*:

(38) anyway
  (i) = I'm about to change the topic of the conversation
    …, so I told her we'd have to reschedule the meeting. Anyway, how was your weekend?
  (ii) = I'm about to go back to what we were discussing before
    … going to marry John. Not the John she works with, but another John. Anyway, they're getting married in August …

(iii) = what I'm about to say is more important than what I've just said
I'll be there between 7:30 and 8. Probably closer to 8, though. Anyway, I'll be there.

(39) actually
(i) = what has just been said is incorrect – I'm about to give you the correct information
You must be Julia's mother. – Actually, I'm her sister.
(ii) = you might find what I've said or am about to say unexpected
What did you think of the exhibition? – Actually, I was quite disappointed.
(iii) = this information is more specific than the previous information
Do you know Kim? – Yes, I do. Actually, we work in the same office.

2.2.3 Intra-sentential commenting devices

While most of the lexical discourse markers discussed so far make explicit the semantic link between the situations referred to in two or more clauses, it is also possible to use markers that comment upon the entire clause they accompany. The comment a speaker makes about it is more or less subjective since it reveals the speaker's opinion or point of view. Consider the following sentence:

(40) *Obviously*, my request is not a priority. But I hope you can help me anyway.

In (40), the speaker underlines how she feels about what she is saying. A paraphrase might be 'what I am saying is obvious'. A very common way of commenting is by using what are called sentence adverbs (see Chapter 1, Section 3.1.3). The sentence adverb *obviously* has scope over the entire sentence. Other sentence adverbs that work like this include *curiously, fortunately, interestingly, ironically, predictably, regrettably, surprisingly* and *wisely*. All of these are derived from adjectives (*curious, fortunate, interesting* etc.). A paraphrase of sentence adverbs used this way might look something like this:

(41) ADVERB$_1$ (in *-ly*) = 'it is ADJECTIVE$_1$ that … ' OR 'the fact that … is ADJECTIVE$_1$,'
(The restaurant has) an excellent selection of drink for great prices given the hike-up of so many bars in the area. *Surprisingly,* they have a great wine choice, and it's worth heading along on a Monday when all of their bottles cost just £10. (www)
It is surprising that they have such great choice of wines OR *The fact that* they have such great choice in wines *is surprising*. (We might infer from this that other bars of the same calibre do not offer wine of the same quality.)

Now take a look at *apparently*:

(42) Lola has been fired. *Apparently,* she was spending too much time on Facebook.

At first sight, it might be tempting to assign to it the paraphrase 'It is apparent that … ' (i.e. a paraphrase on a par with the one we used for *obviously* and *surprisingly*). However, when speakers use *apparently*, they mean more than what the adjective in the paraphrase conveys. In (42), the speaker is saying 'Though the information is apparent, I cannot be held personally responsible for it.' Although the adjective *apparent* can mean both 'clear, obvious' or 'seemingly clear or obvious, but not necessarily so', the sentence adverb *apparently* is usually associated with the second meaning only.

There are many other adverbs that have scope over the whole sentence. However, they do not always have as straightforward a paraphrase as with *obviously, surprisingly* and *apparently*. To illustrate this, we will take a brief look at two other sentence adverbs – *basically* and *honestly*. Unlike the sentence adverbs discussed above, these comment on the context of the utterance rather the content of the utterance. Consider first the meaning of *basically* in the following examples:

(43) He wants to have his cake and eat it too. *Basically* what he wants is to have the security of a girlfriend but not the strings attached to one. I think you should dump this kid and find yourself someone more mature. (www)

It sounds like he wants all the benefits of a relationship without the title. He is *basically* using you for that stuff without having to be your boyfriend. (www)

In (43), two people have answered an internet user's request for advice about her boyfriend. It is telling that both have chosen, in their short reply, to make use of *basically*. The sentence adverb does not mean '*it is basic that … ' (cf. (41), above). Rather, *basically* specifies the point of view from which they are approaching the subject matter. It means that the comments the internet users are making are basic, succinct versions of something that is more complex. They are essentially saying 'this is a simplified version of what I think – in reality, there is more to it than this'.

Although the paraphrase here is different from that in (41), there is a close link between the adjective *basic* and the sentence adverb *basically*. But with other sentence adverbs, the meaning is often only indirectly related to the adjective they are derived from. Take the example of *honestly*:

(44) (a) *Honestly,* I have a problem with that.
(b) *Honestly,* that dog seems dangerous.

It is sometimes claimed that *honestly* in such sentences is best paraphrased as 'I am being honest when I say that … '. In other words, the speaker is not saying 'it is honest that … ', but is characterizing the conditions under which she is speaking. The basic meaning of the adjective *honest* is 'truthful, sincere, free of deceit' – and the adverb of manner *honestly* corresponds to this (Chapter 1, Section 3.1.3): *She answered him honestly* (= in a manner that was truthful and sincere). But while the sentence adverb *honestly* in (44a) means 'I am being truthful and sincere when I say I have a problem with that', in (44b) it does not really mean 'I am being truthful and sincere when I say that that dog seems dangerous'. Rather, it is a way for the speaker to emphasize that the statement is true. A better paraphrase of sentence adverb *honestly* might be: 'I am really convinced that … '. It follows from the discussion that while adverbs like *obviously* and *surprisingly* reveal the speaker's attitude towards what she's saying, adverbs like *basically* and *honestly* specify the conditions under which she's speaking.

Linguists have come up with some incredibly fine-tuned taxonomies to account for the different ways sentence adverbs can be used. Most dictionaries for advanced learners give reliable paraphrases showing how each one of these is used to comment upon the approach to what is said (or, in certain cases, what is being asked). Other commonly used sentence adverbs include *admittedly, briefly, certainly, clearly, conceivably, confidentially, evidently, hopefully, ideally, indeed, naturally, presumably, seriously, strangely, surely, thankfully, theoretically* and *ultimately*.

We saw in Chapter 1 that, whereas linguists attempt to describe how a language is used, there is also a tradition of prescribing the rules of a language and rejecting certain constructions as incorrect. To wrap up this brief outline of sentence adverbs, it is interesting to note there is a long tradition of prescriptivists' frowning on the use of certain sentence adverbs. *Hopefully* and *thankfully* are two sentence adverbs which have been the object of vehement criticism. People have argued that these adverbs should only be used as adverbs of manner. The objection to using them as sentence adverbs presumably stems from the fact that paraphrases of them do not correspond to the paraphrases of other sentence adverbs. We have attempted to show, however, that the point of view encoded in sentence adverbs is variable. The following examples are indicative of now well-established usage. From the linguistic approach we have adopted throughout this book, there is nothing objectionable about this usage:

(45) We could see the brightly coloured tops of some of the rides (of Alton Towers theme park) just over two miles away. But this broad, green landscape is,

thankfully, large enough to swallow up the carbuncles of [the] garish theme park. (*Guardian*, 15 March 2011)

(46) Spector [...] has recently moved into central midfield [...]. 'I'm delighted to be playing and *hopefully* I'll be able to continue in there and learn the position more and more.' (*Guardian*, 19 January 2011)

3. Conclusion

Our goal in this final chapter was to draw your attention to features that, while definitely part of the grammar of English, are particularly relevant to wider discourse. Discourse markers are in essence instructions indicating how to process spoken or written text. The preceding discussion has shown that grammatical as well as lexical cues in the discourse serve this purpose and reveal semantic links between the clauses. Our discussion of discourse markers is not exhaustive, but we have mentioned some of the more crucial connecting devices and discursive strategies. We have also drawn into the discussion sentence adverbs, which structure the discourse by revealing the speaker's attitude towards the information her utterance conveys.

Exercises

Exercise 1. Consider what devices are used to give cohesion to the following texts. The italicized segments are a guide, but you can comment on other features as well.

In our criminal justice system, an accused person is considered innocent until proven guilty. *However*, after a conviction *he* is considered guilty in spite of an incompetent defense (often court-appointed), mishandling of evidence or withholding of information by the prosecution. In an appeal, *he* is not allowed to introduce any new evidence, and it is extremely difficult to prove that *such errors or omissions* were made. *Furthermore*, it will likely take several years before *his case* will even be reviewed. *This system*, in which truth is less important than the 'legal process,' seems to be just fine with our Supreme Court. Why? Jim Wakeman, Long Beach (www)

Eighty per cent of US children under five years old using the internet: new study (*Independent*, 16 March 2011)
The results of a study by nonprofit organizations Joan Ganz Cooney Center and Sesame Workshop, released March 14, found that 80 percent of under fives in the US use the internet on a regular basis. *The study* was based on seven other previous studies conducted before 2010 and does not include internet usage through mediums such as tablet computers or smartphones. *The report* found that 80 percent of children aged between

0–5 in the United States used the internet on at least a weekly basis. *Surprisingly*, the number of children aged 6–9 years old using the internet on a weekly basis dropped to around 70 percent. The study included all types of internet usage, including watching films or TV online, which is likely to account for a large percentage of online activity, especially among the younger age groups. *However*, despite the popularity of the internet, television is still the favorite medium for children, with around 90 per cent of children over five watching at least three hours of programming per day. *Though* the report does not address any potential negative effects of this behavior, concerns over internet safety have led companies such as software giant Microsoft to publish guides on children's internet usage.

What can we do to save our planet? (*Independent*, 2 January 2009)
The *Independent* asked the world's leading climate scientists whether we should prepare a 'Plan B' to curb the worst effects of global warming. *Their* responses are fascinating – and sobering.

Frank Zeman, Director, Centre for Metropolitan Sustainability, New York Institute of Technology
Geoengineering is not an option *because* it is a self perpetuating problem. *That is*, geoengineering cannot be done in lieu of driving CO_2 emissions to zero as *the result* is a perpetual cycle with ever higher atmospheric CO_2 levels.

Eric Wolff, British Antarctic Survey, Cambridge
The challenge of keeping greenhouse gas concentrations to reasonable levels is so big now (*because* we have left it so late to act) that we have to explore everything – including energy choices many of us find unpalatable, and the possibility of geoengineering solutions. *However*, many of the proposed geoengineering schemes are dangerous, either because we don't know what other effects they will have, or because *they* assume that we will be able to service the solution forever. *Furthermore* the potential of many of *them* has been greatly oversold. I don't think a geoengineering 'strategy' will help, *but* sensible, sceptical research on the saner ideas should be pursued.

Mat Collins, Met Office Hadley Centre, Exeter
Ideas *like* injecting large amounts of aerosol into the stratosphere and the like may have unforeseen circumstances – *this risk* is just too high. *While* we, as climate scientists, agree on the fundamentals of climate change (i.e. the world is warming and greenhouse gases are to blame) we are still working out the detail.

Exercise 2. Combine each set of sentences using the markers provided. Pay attention to clause structure and punctuation.

after/afterwards/before/before that
1. We had a big breakfast. We set out for the long five-hour hike.
2. We'll need to read through all the applications carefully. We'll decide on which candidates we'll interview.

while/meanwhile
3. You cut the chicken into small pieces. You allow the vegetables to simmer for 20–25 minutes.
4. We stood there waiting in the rain. They were already in the restaurant having cocktails.

therefore/because/as
5. You haven't had a check-up in over two years. You'll have to fill out these forms again.
6. She was fined 150 dollars. Her driving licence had been expired for over two years.

whereas/on the other hand
7. He considers the latest development to be disastrous. His wife sees it as an opportunity to start anew.
8. Some think the mayor should be re-elected. Others are ready for someone younger.

Exercise 3. Combine the two sentences in three different ways, using (i) *however*, (ii) *(al)though*, (iii) *but* and (iv) *in spite of* (or *despite*). Make any necessary changes. Be careful of how you punctuate each result. In two cases, linking the sentences with these connectors will not be possible.

1. The young girl could already read and write.
   The young girl was only three years old.
2. Most of the students had studied for the exam.
   Nearly all of the students got a very high mark.
3. I thought the novel was really good.
   I would not recommend the novel to everyone.
4. Your CV is impressive and your experience is, too.
   We are not hiring at this time.
5. The lead singer of the band had lost her voice.
   They had to cancel the concert at the last minute.
6. The weather was lousy, and the hotel was not up to standard.
   We had a lot of fun in Mexico.

Exercise 4. For the four pairs of sentences you chose above, which can be reformulated using the adverb *though* clause-finally? For the two sentences you did not choose, what discourse markers could be used to connect them?

Exercise 5. Rewrite the following sentences using the marker provided.

1. They've been to the sea every year since 1998, so they've decided to spend their holidays in the mountains instead. (*as*)

2. Since I think I might be interested in linguistics, I've signed up for a linguistics course. (*so*)
3. I made more money this year than last, and so I'm going to have to pay more income tax. (*because*)
4. You're hosting the party, so you don't have to prepare anything – we'll bring food and drink. (*since*)
5. The princess knew the frog was really a prince, so she smiled coyly before kissing it. (*for*)
6. They had a difficult time the first time round, so they decided not to try again. (*such ... that*)
7. She was very tired and could hardly keep her eyes open. (*so ... that*)
8. I decided that a cleaning lady was a worthwhile investment because I was spending my entire weekend doing the housework. (*and therefore*)

Exercise 6. Find the discourse marker that fits most appropriately in the contexts below, and then give a paraphrase showing you understand the underlying function of the marker. There may be more than one possible answer, but use each one only once.

luckily, though,	as a matter of fact	seriously, though,
even so	thankfully	all in all, though,

1. I agree that they had no other choice but to cancel. _____, they could have let us know a little earlier.
2. I'd left my wallet at home. _____, my friends had enough cash on them to pay for my meal.
3. So what did you think of their production of *Macbeth*? Impressive, wasn't it? – _____, I didn't like it at all. I thought it was very amateurish.
4. The introduction and the conclusion are weak, and there are some important references missing. _____, your hypotheses are convincing and well thought out.
5. So, you've been a billionaire all this time, and I never knew it! _____, do you think you can afford a new sports car right now?
6. The accident took place right after the fog descended and involved three cars and a biker. _____, no one was seriously hurt.

Exercise 7. Find the discourse marker that fits most appropriately in the contexts below, and then give a paraphrase showing you understand the underlying function of the marker. There may be more than one possible answer, but use each one only once.

up to a point	to start with	come to think of it
granted	if you ask me	so to speak

1. They finally wised up and fired Jake Peters in Accountancy. _____, they should have fired him long ago.
2. I agree with you _____. But I wouldn't go so far as to say that we should cut off all ties with them. That seems a bit extreme.
3. I think I'm going to love my new job. _____, the salary's not great. But it's exactly the sort of position I've been looking for.
4. After his most recent collection of poetry, he quickly became *persona non grata*, _____. Even his publisher has taken some distance from him due to the violent nature of his writing.
5. I really didn't like his latest film. _____, I don't really like any of his films.
6. The new law has raised a number of serious problems. _____, it's not even clear whether the law is constitutional.

Exercise 8. Find the discourse marker that fits most appropriately in the contexts below, and then give a paraphrase showing you understand the underlying function of the marker. There may be more than one possible answer, but use each one only once.

in retrospect	I mean	funnily enough
strictly speaking	to be honest	after all

1. _____, her application should not be accepted. The deadline was yesterday. But I'm willing to make an exception given her credentials.
2. We should really give them a second chance. They're only children _____. And anyone can make a mistake.
3. How about going out for Italian tonight? – _____, I'd rather have something else. I've had Italian twice already this week.
4. I really don't like this CD. _____, I'm sure the singing is very professional, but I just don't like countertenors.
5. After the audition, she asked if her accent was going to be a problem. _____, I hadn't even noticed her accent. She's Irish, it seems.
6. _____, I should have rejected their suggestion immediately. But in the heat of the moment, I didn't have the time to think clearly.

Exercise 9. The sentence adverbs in the following sentences can be put into three broad categories:

a) The adverb is used to indicate how likely the speaker considers the proposition to be the case
The adverb is related to the adjective it is derived from, such that
ADVERB < *it is ADJECTIVE that* …
b) The adverb is used to qualify the Subject referent

The adverb is related to the adjective it is derived from, such that ADVERB < [Subject] *is ADJECTIVE*

c) The adverb is used to specify the point of view from which the proposition is considered by the speaker
The adverb is related to the adjective it is derived from, such that
ADVERB < from an ADJECTIVE point of view

Decide in each case to which category each sentence adverb belongs, and provide a straightforward paraphrase. Then come up with a context of your own showing you know how the adverb is used.

1. They were planning to take out a huge loan to buy that house. *Wisely*, though, they decided to buy something more in their price range.
2. How was the opera? – *Visually*, it was outstanding – great costumes, great scenery. But the singing was not good at all.
3. I thought she was happy in her new job. *Apparently*, she's already looking for something else.
4. How are things with your new business? – *Financially*, everything is going very well. But the amount of work required is more than I'd ever imagined.
5. He's *undoubtedly* one of the brightest students I've ever seen. I'm sure he'll go far.
6. *Generously*, the alumni club has donated 1 million dollars to start a scholarship fund for underprivileged students.
7. I'm not arguing with the legality of the ruling. *Morally*, I'm not sure I approve, however.
8. When will the director announce his decision? – Sometime next week, *presumably*. No one knows for sure.
9. He asked her if she'd be interested in a promotion. It caught her unawares and, *stupidly*, she told him that she was very happy with her current position.
10. Science never ceases to amaze me. We're able to do things today that only three or four years ago were unthinkable, *technically*.

List of sources of examples

Chapter 1

(17) http://www.dailymail.co.uk/tvshowbiz/article-1310557/Kelsey-Grammer-gushes-Kayte-Walsh-pair-make-official-appearance.html

http://news.bbc.co.uk/2/hi/uk_news/england/cornwall/8665998.stm

(18) https://www.theguardian.com/artanddesign/booksblog/2010/nov/13/writers-photographs-decade-philip-pullman-hilary-mantel

Exercise 13. http://www.bbc.co.uk/news

Exercise 14.
1. https://www.theguardian.com/books/2005/dec/03/featuresreviews.guardianreview16
2. https://www.theguardian.com/uk/2010/oct/28/terrorism-police-stop-search-arrests
4. https://www.ibtimes.com/federer-sinks-nadal-take-london-title-248656
6. http://www.bbc.co.uk/tyne/content/articles/2008/11/18/gnr09_trace_allen_feature.shtml
7. https://www.independent.co.uk/news/business/news/starbucks-to-more-than-double-store-opening-rate-2132888.html
9. https://metro.co.uk/author/keith-watson-ukmetro/page/54/
10. https://www.theguardian.com/environment/2008/may/29/food.householdbills
12. http://www-groups.dcs.st-and.ac.uk/history/Biographies/Boyle.html
13. https://www.nytimes.com/2011/01/07/books/07huck.html
14. https://www.theguardian.com/music/2011/feb/12/warpaint-interview

Chapter 2

(6) http://www.yourlocalguardian.co.uk/news/8945305.UPDATE__13-year-old_may_have_been_bullied_before_death/

(21) https://www.theguardian.com/technology/2017/jul/09/everybody-lies-how-google-reveals-darkest-secrets-seth-stephens-davidowitz

http://news.bbc.co.uk/2/hi/special_report/1998/04/98/microsoft/284219.stm

(22) http://www.bbc.co.uk/blogs/theeditors/2009/05/whos_watching_you_1.html

(44) https://www.chroniclelive.co.uk/news/north-east-news/who-shoot-doorman-mystery-surrounds-1505383

https://www.chroniclelive.co.uk/news/north-east-news/week-politics-new-north-mps-1414952

(133) adapted from http://universitybenchmarks.com/schools/college_of_william_and_mary.html

(135) https://globenewswire.com/news-release/2009/01/16/20015/0/en/Fraud-detected-by-the-Spanish-subsidiary-Vestas-E%C3%B3lica-S-A-U-has-been-reported-to-the-authorities-in-Barcelona-Spain.html

adapted from http://news.bbc.co.uk/2/hi/uk_news/england/devon/7285944.stm

(136) adapted from http://en.wikipedia.org/wiki/EBay

Exercise 17
3 (b) adapted from
https://healthcareitstrategy.com/2011/04/15/ehr-strategy-its-all-about-thawing-chicken/

Exercise 19
Adapted from www.wikipedia.org

Exercise 20
http://news.bbc.co.uk/2/ hi/africa/6510675.stm

Exercise 24
1. http://home.att.net/~jdhodge/Yogurt.htm
4. http://www.europeanenergyreview.eu/site/pagina.php?id=478
5. http://news.bbc.co.uk/sport2/hi/football/world_cup_2006/teams/ france/5164094.stm
6. https://www.scribd.com/document/197524878/Rethinking-Interdisciplinar-iry-Ian-Hacking-Steven-Fuller-Et-Al

Chapter 3

(10) http://www.shareeducation.com.ar/pastissues3/184.htm

(11) https://www.exportersindia.com/samudragarh-modern-rice/black-rice-india-498631.htm

(14) http://onlinerecnik.com/recnik/srpski/engleski/šaran

Footnote 12
https://www.womanmagazine.co.uk/fashion-beauty/fashion/slimming-fashion/slim-ming-trousers-this-party-season-40803
https://www.bestore.fr/en/shorts/394-trinity.html

(43) https://en.wikipedia.org/wiki/List_of_bottle_types,_brands_and_companies

(95) Barack Obama … http://news.bbc.co.uk/2/hi/americas/7586375.stm

(98) https://www.thetimes.co.uk/article/shannon-matthews-kidnap-police-arrest-mother-8ksr7bj706f
http://news.bbc.co.uk/2/hi/asia-pacific/8162433.stm
https://www.oldbaileyonline.org/static/Population-history-of-london.jsp
http://www.londononline.co.uk/factfile/population/

(135) It's hard to see … https://www.theguardian.com/commentisfree/2009/dec/21/british-foreign-policy-democratic-deficit

(143) https://www.telegraph.co.uk/news/earth/environment/globalwarming/6300329/Sceptics-welcome-BBC-report-on-global-cooling.html

Chapter 4

(27) (a) https://www.ableskills.co.uk/blog/diy-hacks-of-the-week-portable-swings-magnetic-bbqs/
(b) https://en.tripadvisor.com.hk/ShowUserReviews-g48894-d3580935-r374209384-Marco_s_Italian_Deli-Williamsville_New_York.html
(c) https://www.dorsetecho.co.uk/leisure/stage/15280064.Community_play_about_an_exotic__ukulele-hating__ringmistress_is_leaping_into_action/

(38) https://www.pcreview.co.uk/threads/excel-2002-save-reminder.1792061/

(39) https://www.independent.co.uk/sport/football/premier-league/vassell-gets-brotherly-advice-from-villa-veteran-129434.html

(54) www.independent.co.uk/arts-entertainment/music/features/how-we-met-john-the-white-rapper-amy-winehouse-828125.html
https://www.theguardian.com/culture/2005/oct/30/art

(128) http://www.haydonabbeyschoolandpreschool.co.uk/ks1-letters-1/

(139) http://news.bbc.co.uk/2/hi/south_asia/3607323.stm

Exercise 3
https://www.theguardian.com/world/2008/oct/01/australia

Exercise 31
7. https://www.nytimes.com/2003/09/17/arts/bolshoi-decides-it-s-over-before-fat-lady-dances.html

Chapter 5

(36) [S]ome people – who *must not* realise … https://www.huffingtonpost.co.uk/2014/03/07/project-breastfeeding-campaign-men-stigmatisation_n_4917754.

html?guccounter=1&guce_referrer_us=aHR0cHM6Ly93d3cuZ29vZ2xlLmJlLw&-
guce_referrer_cs=ELfSCgsXXyLx5dPzsRjTeQ

(37) https://www.streetdirectory.com/travel_guide/34748/handbags/purses_and_hand-
bags_as_accessories.html

(77) https://zapdoc.tips/code-of-practice-controlling-access-to-hazardous-or-sensitiv.html

(79) If the consumer … https://www.digitrains.co.uk/terms-and-conditions/

(105) https://www.candidatesource.uk.com/terms-and-conditions/
https://www.ideal.co.uk/terms-and-conditions

(117) https://www.theguardian.com/environment/2005/jun/20/whaling.japan

(118) https://www.theguardian.com/technology/2009/sep/13/tenth-birthday-blogger

(127) https://www.telegraph.co.uk/culture/film/starsandstories/6280878/Terry-Gilliam-in-
terview-for-The-Imaginarium-of-Doctor-Parnassus.html

Exercise 1
12. https://www.theguardian.com/uk/2009/jul/03/daniel-radcliffe-harry-potter-art

Chapter 6

(4) A: I think that Turin is more … adapted from https://www.tripadvisor.com/Show-
Topic-g187849-i143-k9442438-How_long_to_stay_in_Milan-Milan_Lombardy.html

(7) https://www.nytimes.com/2010/12/12/science/earth/12climate.html

(8) (a) adapted from https://www.sciencedaily.com/releases/2007/12/071227183912.htm

(10) https://www.telegraph.co.uk/news/newstopics/howaboutthat/ufo/8357258/UFO-
sightings-caught-on-film.html

(11) http://www.dalblairmedicalpractice.co.uk/info.aspx?p=10

(15) https://www.thetimes.co.uk/article/transplants-that-could-hold-key-to-diabetes-
5lh3m6259ff

(16) https://www.dailymail.co.uk/sport/othersports/article-1340896/Jessica-Ennis-aiming-
start-season-did-Glasgow-win-Lolo-Jones.html

(26) (a) https://www.tripadvisor.com/ShowUserReviews-g187457-d805520-r103236653-
Arzak-San_Sebastian_Donostia_Province_of_Guipuzcoa_Basque_Country.html
(b) https://www.tripadvisor.com/ShowUserReviews-g41521-d300479-r75413127-
Fairfield_Inn_Boston_Dedham-Dedham_Massachusetts.html

Appendix: Irregular verbs

No two lists of English irregular verbs are exactly the same. The criterion we have used in drawing up this particular list was usefulness to the student rather than exhaustiveness. Irregular forms of rare verbs such as *abide, bereave, beseech* and *cleave* have been eliminated entirely, and verbs with competing regular forms (such as *learn* and *spell*) are given in a separate list.

List 1 is a traditional alphabetized list of 145 irregular verbs and can be used for quick consultation. Sixty high-frequency verbs are in **boldface**. The choice here is based on the corpora used for the *Longman Dictionary of Contemporary English*: these sixty verbs are among the 1000 most common words in both spoken and written contemporary English. Students wishing to consolidate their mastery of irregular forms should naturally prioritize these.

List 2 presents the same verbs organized based on their form so as to facilitate the study of verbs in clumps of verbs that have similar irregular forms. The characterizing features are not meant to reflect anything about the history of the forms. The sixty high-frequency verbs are in **boldface** here as well.

List 3 brings together those verbs which, although they have irregular forms, also have regular forms, many of which are quite frequent.

The *verb base* has several functions: the (non-progressive) present tense (except for the third-person singular: *he eats*), the imperative, the infinitive (with or without *to*) and the subjunctive.

The *past tense* locates a situation in the past time-sphere.

In spite of its name, the *past participle* has little to do with the past. Its two primary functions are the formation of the perfect tenses in conjunction with the auxiliary *have* (*he has/had/will have seen*) and the formation of the passive voice, in conjunction with the auxiliary *be* (*The house was built in the 18th century*). It can also be used as an adjective (*Broken glass is dangerous.*)

List 1: Alphabetized list

Verb base	Past tense	Past participle
arise	arose	arisen
awake	awoke	awoken
be	**was/were**[1]	**been**
bear	bore	borne[2]
beat	beat	beaten
become	**became**	**become**
begin	**began**	**begun**
bend	bent	bent
bet	bet	bet
bid	bid	bid
bind	bound	bound
bite	bit	bitten
bleed	bled	bled
blow	blew	blown
break	**broke**	**broken**
breed	bred	bred
bring	**brought**	**brought**
broadcast	broadcast	broadcast
build	**built**	**built**
burst	burst	burst
buy	**bought**	**bought**
cast	cast	cast
catch	**caught**	**caught**
choose	**chose**	**chosen**
cling	clung	clung
come	**came**	**come**
cost[3]	**cost**	**cost**
creep	crept	crept

[1]*Be* is the only verb in English that has two past tense forms: *was* is used with the first-person singular (*I was*) and the third-person singular (*he/she was*); otherwise, *were* is used (*you were, those people were, we all were*).

[2]*Borne* is spelled *born* when it is part of the expression 'be born' that refers to the birth of the Subject referent. Contrast *That woman has borne many children* (= given birth to) and *I was born on March the 7th* (= came into the world).

[3]*Cost* is irregular with its ordinary meanings 'require money in exchange for' (*The trip cost us a lot of money*) or 'cause to lose something' (*The incident cost him his job*). More rarely, *cost* means 'determine the cost of', in which case it is regular (*They have not yet costed the proposal* = determined the cost of).

Verb base	Past tense	Past participle
cut	**cut**	**cut**
deal	**dealt**	**dealt**
dig	dug	dug
do	**did**	**done**
draw	**drew**	**drawn**
drink	drank	drunk
drive	**drove**	**driven**
eat	**ate**	**eaten**
fall	**fell**	**fallen**
feed	fed	fed
feel	**felt**	**felt**
fight	**fought**	**fought**
find	**found**	**found**
fit[4]	fit	fit
flee	fled	fled
fling	flung	flung
fly	flew	flown
forbid	forbade	forbidden
forecast	forecast	forecast
forget	**forgot**	**forgotten**
forgive	forgave	forgiven
freeze	froze	frozen
get	**got**	**got (gotten US)**
give	**gave**	**given**
go	**went**	**gone**
grind	ground	ground
grow	**grew**	**grown**
hang[5]	hung	hung
have	**had**	**had**
hear	**heard**	**heard**
hide	hid	hidden
hit	hit	hit
hold	**held**	**held**
hurt	hurt	hurt
keep	**kept**	**kept**

[4]*Fit* is usually irregular with its ordinary meanings 'be the right size' (*The dress fit her perfectly*) or 'be appropriate with respect to' (*The punishment fit the crime*). It is usually regular when it means 'equip' or 'put something into place': *The doctor fitted her for the new brace.*
[5]Prescriptive tradition and most dictionaries state that *hang* is regular when it refers to execution, and many people do make a distinction between *They hung the picture on the wall* and *They hanged the criminal.*

Verb base	Past tense	Past participle
know	**knew**	**known**
lay[6]	laid	laid
lead	**led**	**led**
leave	**left**	**left**
lend	lent	lent
let	**let**	**let**
lie[7]	lay	lain
lose	**lost**	**lost**
make	**made**	**made**
mean	**meant**	**meant**
meet	**met**	**met**
mislay	mislaid	mislaid
mistake	mistook	mistaken
pay[8]	**paid**	**paid**
put	**put**	**put**
quit	quit	quit
read[9]	**read**	**read**
rid	rid	rid
ride	rode	ridden
ring	rang	rung
rise	rose	risen
run	**ran**	**run**
say	**said**[10]	**said**
see	**saw**	**seen**
seek	sought	sought
sell	**sold**	**sold**
send	**sent**	**sent**
set	**set**	**set**
shake	shook	shaken
shed	shed	shed

[6]*Lay* is only irregular with respect to spelling: we write *laid* and not *layed*. Otherwise the verb can be considered regular. For the confusion between *lay* and *lie*, see note 7.

[7]Native speakers confuse the past and participial forms of *lay* and *lie*. *Lay* is a transitive verb, meaning 'put something down': *he (has) laid the hammer on the table*. *Lie* is an intransitive verb meaning 'be in or assume a horizontal position': *he lay (has lain) in the sun for too long*. Note finally that the verb *lie* meaning 'not tell the truth' is always regular: *He (has) lied about his age on the application form*.

[8]*Pay* is only irregular with respect to spelling: we write *paid* and not *payed*. Otherwise the verb can be considered regular.

[9]All three forms are spelled the same way, but pronunciation differs: the verb base *read* is pronounced /riːd/, rhyming with the word 'seed'; the past and participial forms *read* are pronounced /red/ and are pronounced the same as the word 'red'.

[10]The past and participial forms *said* are pronounced /sed/, rhyming with the word 'red'.

Verb base	Past tense	Past participle
shine[11]	shone	shone
shoot	shot	shot
show	**showed**	**shown**
shrink	shrank	shrunk
shut	shut	shut
sing	sang	sung
sink	sank	sunk
sit	**sat**	**sat**
sleep	slept	slept
slide	slid	slid
sling	slung	slung
slit	slit	slit
speak	**spoke**	**spoken**
spend	**spent**	**spent**
spin	span/spun	spun
spit	spat/spit	spat/spit
split	split	split
spread	spread	spread
spring	sprang	sprung
stand	**stood**	**stood**
steal	stole	stolen
stick	stuck	stuck
sting	stung	stung
stink	stank	stunk
strike	struck	struck
strive	strove	striven
string	strung	strung
swear	swore	sworn
sweep	swept	swept
swim	swam	swum
swing	swung	swung
take	**took**	**taken**
teach	taught	taught
tear	tore	torn
tell	**told**	**told**
think	**thought**	**thought**
throw	**threw**	**thrown**

[11]*Shine* is almost always regular when it means 'polish (ones shoes)': *I shined my shoes before the wedding.* The form *shone* is pronounced /ʃɒn/ (rhyming with 'on') in Britain and /ʃəʊn/ (rhyming with 'bone') in North America.

Verb base	Past tense	Past participle
thrust	thrust	thrust
tread	trod	trodden
understand	**understood**	**understood**
undertake	undertook	undertaken
upset	upset	upset
wake	woke	woken
wear	**wore**	**worn**
weave	wove	woven
weep	wept	wept
wet	wet	wet
win	**won**	**won**
wind	wound	wound
withdraw	withdrew	withdrawn
wring	wrung	wrung
write	**wrote**	**written**

List 2: Verbs organized based on their forms

Set 1

These verbs have a single form for the verb base, the past tense and the past participle.

Verb base	Past tense	Past participle
bet	bet	bet
bid	bid	bid
broadcast	broadcast	broadcast
burst	burst	burst
cast	cast	cast
cost	**cost**	**cost**
cut	**cut**	**cut**
fit	fit	fit
forecast	forecast	forecast
hit	hit	hit
hurt	hurt	hurt
let	**let**	**let**
put	**put**	**put**
quit	quit	quit
rid	rid	rid
set	**set**	**set**

Verb base	Past tense	Past participle
shed	shed	shed
shut	shut	shut
slit	slit	slit
spit	spit (also spat)	spit (also spat)
split	split	split
spread	spread	spread
thrust	thrust	thrust
upset	upset	upset
wet	wet	wet

Set 2A

These verbs have the same form for the past tense and the past participle.

Verb base	Past tense	Past participle
cling	clung	clung
dig	dug	dug
fling	flung	flung
hang	hung	hung
sling	slung	slung
stick	stuck	stuck
sting	stung	stung
strike	struck	struck
string	strung	strung
swing	swung	swung
wring	wrung	wrung
bring	**brought**	**brought**
buy	**bought**	**bought**
catch	**caught**	**caught**
fight	**fought**	**fought**
seek	sought	sought
teach	taught	taught
think	**thought**	**thought**
creep	crept	crept
keep	**kept**	**kept**
sleep	slept	slept
sweep	swept	swept
weep	wept	wept

Verb base	Past tense	Past participle
bleed	bled	bled
breed	bred	bred
feed	fed	fed
flee	fled	fled
bend	bent	bent
lend	lent	lent
send	**sent**	**sent**
spend	**spent**	**spent**
bind	bound	bound
find	**found**	**found**
grind	ground	ground
wind	wound	wound

Set 2B

The past tense and past participle of the following verbs both end in -*d* and often have a vowel sound that is different from the vowel sound in the verb base. Otherwise, they have nothing in common with each other or with the groups above.

Verb base	Past tense	Past participle
have	**had**	**had**
hear	**heard**	**heard**
hold	**held**	**held**
lay	laid	laid
lead	**led**	**led**
make	**made**	**made**
mislay	mislaid	mislaid
pay	**paid**	**paid**
read	**read**	**read**
say	said	said
sell	**sold**	**sold**
slide	slid	slid
stand	**stood**	**stood**
tell	**told**	**told**
understand	**understood**	**understood**

Set 2C

The past tense and past participle of the following verbs both end in -*t* and often have a vowel sound that is different from the vowel sound in the verb base. Otherwise, they have nothing in common with each other or with the groups above.

Verb base	Past tense	Past participle
build	built	built
deal	dealt	dealt
feel	felt	felt
get	got	got (gotten US)
leave	left	left
lose	lost	lost
mean	meant	meant
meet	met	met
shoot	shot	shot
sit	sat	sat
spit	spat (also spit)	spat (also spit)

Set 2D

The past tense and past participle of these two verbs have a vowel sound different from the verb base and both end in -*n*.

Verb base	Past tense	Past participle
shine	shone	shone
win	won	won

Set 3A

The following verbs have three distinct forms for the verb base, the past tense and the past participle.

Verb base	Past tense	Past participle
begin	began	begun
drink	drank	drunk
ring	rang	rung
shrink	shrank	shrunk

sing	sang	sung
sink	sank	sunk
spin	span	spun
spring	sprang	sprung
stink	stank	stunk
swim	swam	swum
arise	arose	arisen
awake	awoke	awoken
drive	**drove**	**driven**
ride	rode	ridden
rise	rose	risen
strive	strove	striven
write	**wrote**	**written**
blow	blew	blown
fly	flew	flown
grow	**grew**	**grown**
know	**knew**	**known**
throw	**threw**	**thrown**
bear	bore	borne
swear	swore	sworn
tear	tore	torn
wear	**wore**	**worn**
break	**broke**	**broken**
choose	**chose**	**chosen**
speak	**spoke**	**spoken**
freeze	froze	frozen
steal	stole	stolen
wake	woke	woken
mistake	mistook	mistaken
take	**took**	**taken**
undertake	undertook	undertaken

forgive	forgave	forgiven
give	**gave**	**given**
draw	**drew**	**drawn**
withdraw	withdrew	withdrawn

Set 3B

The following verbs also have three distinct forms but do not pattern like any of the groups in Set 3A.

Verb base	Past tense	Past participle
be	**was/were**	**been**
bite	bit	bitten
do	**did**	**done**
eat	**ate**	**eaten**
fall	**fell**	**fallen**
forbid	forbade	forbidden
forget	**forgot**	**forgotten**
go	**went**	**gone**
hide	hid	hidden
lie	lay	lain
see	**saw**	**seen**
shake	shook	shaken
show	**showed**	**shown**
tread	trod	trodden
weave	wove	woven

Set 4

The three verbs in this list have a past participle that is identical to the verb base. The past tense form is distinct.

Verb base	Past tense	Past participle
become	**became**	**become**
come	**came**	**come**
run	**ran**	**run**

The verb *beat* is highly unusual in that the verb base and past tense are identical whereas the past participle has a different form.

beat	beat	beaten

List 3: irregular verbs with a common regular variant

Verb base	Past tense	Past participle
burn	burnt (burned)	burnt (burned)
dream	dreamt (dreamed)	dreamt (dreamed)
dwell	dwelt (dwelled)	dwelt (dwelled)
kneel	knelt (kneeled)	knelt (kneeled)
knit	knit (knitted)	knit (knitted)
lean	leant (leaned)	leant (leaned)
leap	leapt (leaped)	leapt (leaped)
learn	learnt (learned)	learnt (learned)
light	lit (lighted)	lit (lighted)
prove	proved	proven (proved)
smell	smelt (smelled)	smelt (smelled)
speed	sped (speeded)	sped (speeded)
spell	spelt (spelled)	spelt (spelled)
spill	spilt (spilled)	spilt (spilled)
spoil	spoilt (spoiled)	spoilt (spoiled)

Bibliography

Aarts, B. (2011), *Oxford Modern English Grammar*. Oxford: Oxford University Press.

Aarts, B. (2018), *English Syntax and Argumentation* (5th edn). Basingstoke: Palgrave Macmillan.

Algeo, J. (2006), *British or American English*. Cambridge: Cambridge University Press.

Biber, D., Johansson, S., Leech, G., Conrad, S. and Finegan, E. (1999), *Longman Grammar of Spoken and Written English*. London/New York: Longman.

Brinton, L. and Brinton, D. M. (2010), *The Linguistic Structure of Modern English: A Linguistic Introduction* (2nd edn). Amsterdam/Philadelphia: John Benjamins.

Cappelle, B. (2005), *Particle Patterns in English. A Comprehensive Coverage*. KULeuven. Unpublished PhD Dissertation.

Celce-Murcia, M. and Larsen-Freeman, D. (2009), *The Grammar Book: an ESL/EFL Teacher's Course* (2nd edn). Boston, MA: Heinle & Heinle.

Coates, J. (1983), *The Semantics of the Modal Auxiliaries*. London/Canberra: Croom Helm.

Collins, P. (2009), *Modals and Quasi-modals in English*. Amsterdam/New York: Rodopi.

Comrie, B. (1976), *Aspect*. Cambridge: Cambridge University Press.

Comrie, B. (1985), *Tense*. Cambridge: Cambridge University Press.

Declerck, R. (1991a), *Tense in English. Its Structure and Use in Discourse*. London: Routledge.

Declerck, R. (1991b), *A Comprehensive Descriptive Grammar of English*. Tokyo: Kaitakusho.

Dekeyser, X., Devriendt, B., Tops, G. A. J. and Geukens, S. (1993), *Foundations of English Grammar* (2nd edn). Antwerpen: Quickprinter.

Depraetere, I. (1995), 'On the necessity of distinguishing between (un)boundedness and (a)telicity'. *Linguistics and Philosophy*, 18(1), 1–19.

Depraetere, I. (1998), 'On the resultative character of present perfect sentences'. *Journal of Pragmatics*, 29(5), 597–613.

Depraetere, I. (1999), 'Resultativeness and the indefinite progressive perfect', in G. Tops, B. Devriendt and S. Geukens (eds), *Thinking English Grammar. To honour of X. Dekeyser, Professor Emeritus*. Leuven: Peeters, pp. 227–38.

Depraetere, I. (2003), 'Verbal concord with collective nouns in British English'. *English Language and Linguistics*, 7(1), 85–127.

Depraetere, I. (2007), '(A)telicity and intentionality'. *Linguistics*, 45(2), 243–69.

Depraetere, I. (2012), 'Time in sentences with modal auxiliaries', in Robert I. Binnick (ed.), *The Oxford Handbook of Tense and Aspect*. New York: Oxford University Press, pp. 989–1019.

Depraetere, I. (2014), 'Modal meaning and lexically-regulated saturation'. *Journal of Pragmatics*, 71: 160–77.

Depraetere, I. (2015), 'Categorization principles of modal meaning categories: A critical assessment'. *Anglophonia*, http://anglophonia.revues.org/453. doi: 10.4000/anglophonia.476.

Depraetere, I. and Langford, C. (2011), 'On the meaning(s) of need to'. Paper presented at ISLE 2, Boston.

Depraetere, I. and Reed, S. (2000), 'The present perfect progressive: constraints on its use with numerical object NPs'. *English Language and Linguistics*, 4(1), 97–114.

Depraetere, I. and Reed, S. (2006), 'Mood and modality in English', in B. Aarts and A. McMahon (eds), *An Introduction to English Linguistics*. Malden, MA: Blackwell Publishers, pp. 269–90.

Depraetere, I. and Tsangalidis, T. (2019), 'Tense and aspect', in B. Aarts, J. Bowie and G. Popova (eds), *The Oxford Handbook of English Grammar*. Oxford: Oxford University Press. 396–417.

Depraetere, I. and Verhulst, A. (2008), 'Source of modality: a reassessment'. *English Language and Linguistics*, 12(1), 1–25.

Donnellan, K. (1966), 'Reference and definite descriptions'. *The Philosophical Review*, 75, 281–304.

Fenn, P. (1987), *A Semantic and Pragmatic Examination of the English Perfect*. Tübingen: Gunther Narr Verlag.

Greenbaum, S. (1995), *The Oxford English Grammar*. Oxford: Oxford University Press.

Grice, H. P. (1975), 'Logic and Conversation', in P. Cole and J. Morgan (eds), *Syntax and Semantics 3: Speech Acts*. New York: Academic Press, pp. 41–58.

Hewings, M. (1999), *Advanced English Grammar* (1st edn). Cambridge: Cambridge University Press.

Hewings, M. (2005), *Advanced English Grammar* (2nd edn). Cambridge: Cambridge University Press.

Huddleston, R. (1984), *Introduction to the Grammar of English*. Cambridge: Cambridge University Press.

Huddleston, R. and Pullum, G., in collaboration with Bauer, L., Birner, B., Briscoe, T., Collins, P., Denison, D., Lee, D., Mittwoch, A., Nunberg, G., Palmer, F., Payne, J., Peterson, P., Stirling L. and Ward, G. (2002), *The Cambridge Grammar of the English Language*. Cambridge: Cambridge University Press.

Langford, C. (2017), 'Grammar issues 2: Noun combinations'. *Teaching Times*, 79: 7–9.

Larreya, P. and Rivière, C. (2014), *Grammaire Explicative de l'Anglais* (4th edn). Montreuil: Pearson France.

Leech, G. (2004), *Meaning and the English Verb* (3rd edn). London/New York: Longman.

Leech, G. and Svartvik, J. (1994), *A Communicative Grammar of English*. London/New York: Longman.

Murphy, R. (2012), *English Grammar in Use* (4th edn). Cambridge: Cambridge University Press.

Myhill, J. (1996), 'The development of the strong obligation system in American English'. *American Speech*, 4, 339–88.

Palmer, F. R. (1990), *Modality and the English Modals* (2nd edn). London/New York: Longman.

Putseys, Y. (1996), *A Modular Approach to the Grammar of English*. Herent: Devano.

Quirk, R., Greenbaum S., Leech, G. and Svartvik, J. (1985), *A Comprehensive Grammar of the English Language*. London: Longman.

Reichenbach, H. (1941), *Elements of Symbolic Logic*. New York: Collier-Macmillan, pp. 287–98.

Salkie, R. (1995), *Text and Discourse Analysis*. London: Routledge.

Salkie, R. (2010), 'Will: tense or modal or both?' *English Language and Linguistics*, 4(2), 187–215.

Schopf, A. (1984), *Das Verzeitungssystem im Englischen une seine Textfunktion*. Tübingen: Niemeyer.

Sinclair, J. (ed.) (1990), *Collins Cobuild English Grammar*. London: HarperCollins Publishers.

Smith, C. S. (1997), *The Parameter of Aspect* (2nd edn). Dordrecht: Kluwer Academic Press.

Swan, M. (2017), *Practical English Usage* (4th edn). Oxford: Oxford University Press.

Thomson, A. J. and Martinet, A. V. (1991), *A Practical English Grammar* (4th edn). Oxford: Oxford University Press.

Valdman, A. (1988), 'Classroom foreign language learning and language variation: The notion of pedagogical norms'. *World Englishes*, 7(2), 221–36.

Van der Auwera, J. and Plungian, V. (1998), 'Modality's semantic map'. *Linguistic Typology*, 2, 79–124.

Van Valin, Jr. R. D. and Wilkins, D. P. (1999), 'The case for "effector": case roles, agents, and agency revisited', in S. Masayoshi and S. A. Thompson (eds), *Grammatical Constructions*. Oxford: Clarendon Press, pp. 189–232.

Vendler, Z. (1967), 'Verbs and times', in Z. Vendler (ed.), *Linguistics in Philosophy*. Ithaca, NY: Cornell University Press, pp. 97–121.

Lexical index

Subject index